JEWISH TRAVEL GUIDE 1998

International Edition

Published in association with
the *Jewish Chronicle*, London

VALLENTINE MITCHELL

First published in 1998 in Great Britain by
VALLENTINE MITCHELL & CO. LTD.
Newbury House, 900 Eastern Avenue
London IG2 7HH

and in the United States of America by
VALLENTINE MITCHELL
c/o ISBS, Inc.
5804 N.E. Hassalo Street
Portland, Oregon 97213-3644

Copyright © 1998 Vallentine Mitchell and the Jewish Chronicle

ISBN 0 85303 338 2
ISSN 0075 3750

Printed in Great Britain by
Creative Print and Design (Wales), Ebbw Vale

Contents

Abridged Jewish Calendar

1998 (5758–5759)

Fast of Esther	Wednesday	March 11th
Purim	Thursday	March 12th
First Day Pesach	Saturday	April 11th
Second Day Pesach	Sunday	April 12th
Seventh Day Pesach	Friday	April 17th
Eighth Day Pesach	Saturday	April 18th
Holocaust Memorial Day	Thursday	April 23rd
Israel Independence Day	Thursday	April 30th
Jerusalem Day	Sunday	May 24th
First Day Shavuot	Sunday	May 31st
Second Day Shavuot	Monday	June 1st
Fast of Tammuz	Sunday	July 12th
Fast of Av	Sunday	August 2nd
First Day Rosh Hashanah	Monday	September 21st
Second Day Rosh Hashanah	Tuesday	September 22nd
Fast of Gedaliah	Wednesday	September 23rd
Yom Kippur	Wednesday	September 30th
First Day Succot	Monday	October 5th
Second Day Succot	Tuesday	October 6th
Shemini Atseret	Monday	October 12th
Simchat Torah	Tuesday	October 13th
First Day Chanucah	Monday	December 14th

Yizkor in 1998

Yizkor is recited in synagogues on the following days: Eighth day Pesach, Saturday, April 18th; Second day Shavuot, Monday, June 1st; Yom Kippur, Wednesday, September 30th; Shemini Atseret, Monday, October 12th.

Some Notable Days in 1999 (5759–5760)

First Day Pesach	Thursday	April 1st
Eighth Day Pesach (Yizkor)	Thursday	April 8th
First Day Shavuot	Friday	May 21st
Second Day Shavuot (Yizkor)	Saturday	May 22nd
First Day Rosh Hashanah (5759)	Saturday	September 11th
Second Day Rosh Hashanah	Sunday	September 12th
Yom Kippur (Yizkor)	Monday	September 20th
First Day Succot	Saturday	September 25th
Shemini Atseret (Yizkor)	Saturday	October 2nd

Publisher's Note

The format of this year's *Jewish Travel Guide*, for those of you who have been using the book regularly over the years, has been redesigned for greater clarity and for more consistent categorisation of information.

The more extensive change, however, is hidden a little deeper than typefaces and columns. A concerted effort has been made not just to indicate the kashrut of a venue, but to provide the traveller with details of who provides the *hashgacha*. While all restaurants listed in this guide *claim* to be either kosher or vegetarian, only those for which supervision details are included are known to have had *hashgacha* at the time we went to press. Particular attention must also be drawn to the fact that establishments change hands from time to time, in some instances ceasing to be kosher. It is therefore in the interest of travellers to consider obtaining confirmation of kashrut claims prior to visiting an establishment.

Another area of revision has been the synagogue listings. While we have continued for the most part to provide complete listings for smaller areas that have a limited number of synagogues, for major Jewish centres, instead of presenting a mass listing, we have recommended that travellers contact relevant organisations whose details are included to ascertain the location of the synagogue nearest them along with minyan times.

The revision has been a monumental task and the Publisher would like to thank Rachel Joseph, Daphne Money and Michael Zaidner for their contribution to this endeavor. It is our hope, as time goes by, that those who wish to be listed in our pages will become more responsive to our requests for information, that supervising bodies will take the initiative and inform us of those places which lose or gain their *hashgacha*, and that conscientious travellers will continue to provide us with as much new and relevant information as possible.

Extensive research is undertaken for each annual revision of the *Jewish Travel Guide* and every effort is made to ensure accuracy. Nevertheless, no responsibility can be accepted for any errors or omissions, or for kashrut and other claims by establishments listed in the guide.

Many thanks to the following people for their specific contributions: Michael Anisfeld for Chicago; Nechama Goldman for Israel; Toni L. Kamins for New York; Esther Schenker for New York; and David Wiseman and Reid Heller for Dallas, Texas. Thanks also to world travellers Jack Goldfarb, Barry Graham, Judith Keshet, Nachum Pessin, Harvey M. Ross and Susan Zoladz for keeping their eyes open at all times and in all places. Contributions of this type are always welcome for consideration.

Readers are asked to advise us of any errors or omissions they discover on their travels. Forms and contact information are provided for this purpose at the end of the book.

London
November 1997

Afghanistan

From a peak of some 40,000 a century ago, Afghanistan's Jewish population has dwindled to about 120 today. Most are of Persian origin. There are some 12 families in Kabul, the capital, and five or six in Heart. All of them, in both cities, are strictly Orthodox. There is one rabbi/shochet in the country. Jewish settlement in Afghanistan goes back much further than the last century. There were Jews in the country 800 years ago, although little is known of their history until about 120 years ago. In recent years, many have emigrated to Israel.

GMT + 4 ½ hours
Country calling code (93)

Kabul

Synagogues
2nd Floor, Charshi Torabazein Street

Albania

Jews have lived in Albania since Roman times. Remnants of an ancient synagogue have been found in Dardania, northern Albania. Sephardic Jews came during the Inquistion. Shabbetai Zevi, the false messiah, died in exile near the town of Berat in 1676, and an annual fair is held on his assumed burial site. Most of the modern Jews of Albania, numbering about 350, emigrated to Israel in Spring 1991, arriving on the last day of the Gulf War. Their World War II history then became known: 99 per cent of the Albanian Jews survived the Nazi Occupation by being protected and hidden by Muslims and Christians. Today only a handful of Jews are left in the country, but there are active branches of the Albanian-Israel Friendship Society in Tirana and other cities, who are glad to provide information.

GMT + 1 hour
Country calling code (355)

Tirana
Area telephone code (42)

Contact Information
Albanian-Israel Friendship Society
Rruga 'Barrikatave' 226   22611

Algeria

There are approximately 200–300 Jews in Algeria today. Most live in Algiers, and there are a few families in Blida, Constantine and Oran. Algiers is the headquarters of the Algerian Consistoire. In 1962, when Algeria became independent, the community numbered 130,000. Of this total almost a quarter – 30,000 – lived in Algiers. By 1968, only some 2,000 Jews remained in the country, and their number has continued to dwindle over the years.

GMT + 1 hour
Country calling code (213)

Algiers
Area telephone code (2)

Representative Organisations
Association Consistoriale Israélite d'Alger
6 rue Hassena Ahmed, formerly rue de Suffren
62-85-72

Federation des Communautes Israelites d'Algerie
6 rue Hassena Ahmed   62-85-72

Synagogues
6 rue Hassena Ahmed   62-85-72

Blida
Area telephone code (3)

Representative Organisations
Consistoire d'Algerie
29 rue des Martyrs   49-26-57

Argentina

The Argentine community, which includes about 50,000 Sephardim, is estimated to total about 250,000. About a fifth live in rural areas. It is by far the largest Jewish community in Latin America. The Ashkenazi majority come from eastern European stock. Immigration from Russia and other eastern European countries began in 1889.

Greater Buenos Aires, the capital, is home to some 160,000 Jews. There are important communities in 11 provincial centres: Rosario (15,000), Cordoba (10,000), Santa Fé (5,000), La Plata (4,000), Bahia Blanca (4,000), Mendoza (4,000), Mar del Plata (4,000), Parana (3,000), Resistencia (2,000), Corrientes (1,500) and Salta (1,500). Altogether there are about 90 Jewish communities in Argentina, including a number of families in the former colonies set up by the Jewish Colonization Association (JCA), who live on the land or from economic activities linked with agriculture. Several of these colonies were in the provinces of Buenos Aires, Santa Fé, La Pampa and Entre Rios.

The three most important Jewish colonies are Moiseville (where 20 per cent of the total population of 3,000 are Jews) in the province of Santa Fé, Rivera (with a Jewish population of 1,000 – half the total) in La Pampa, and General Roca (1,000 Jews) in Rio Negro, in the south.

GMT – 3 hours
Country calling code (54)

Bahia Blanca
Area telephone code (91)

Contact Information
Beit Jabad Bahia Blanca
C.C. 405, 8000   36582

Buenos Aires
Area telephone code (1)

Representative Organisations
AMIA (Central Ashkenazi community)
Pasteur 633   953-9777; 953-2862
Asociacion Israelita Sefaradi Argentina
(AISA)
Paso 493   952-4707

DAIA (Political representative body of Argentine Jewry)
Pasteur 633, Fifth floor   953-5380; 953-5394
ECSA (Central Sephardi body)
Larrea 674, Fourth floor   953-9777; 953-2862
Vaad Hakehillot
Pasteur 633, Second floor   953-9777;
                                        953-2862

Synagogues
All Conservative synagogues are affiliated to the World Council of Synagogues; all Reform and Liberal synagogues to the World Council for Progressive Judaism.

Ashkenazi Orthodox
Baron Hirsh
Billinghurst 664   862-2624
Bet Rajel, Ecuador 522   862-2701

Brit Abraham
Antezana 145 — 855-6567

Etz Jaim, Julian Alvarez 745 — 772-5324

Sinagoga Israelita Lituana
Jose Evaristo Uriburu 348 — 952-7968

Torah Vaaboda
Julian Alvarez 667 — 854-0462

Zijron le David
Azcuenaga 736 — 953-0200

German Orthodox
Ajdut Yisroel
Moldes 2449 — 783-2831

Sephardi Orthodox
Aderet Eliahu
Ruy Diaz de Guzman 647 — 302-9306

Agudat Dodim
Avellaneda 2874 — 611-0056

Bajurim Tiferet Israeil
Helguera 611 — 611-3376

Comunidad Israelita
Camargo 870 — 854-1952; 854-0287

Etz Jaim, Carlos Calvo 1164 — 302-6290

Jaike Grimberg
Campana 460 — 672-2347

Kehal Jaredim
Helguera 270, Once — 612-0410

Od Yosef Jai
Tucuman 3326 — 963-2349

Or Misraj, Ciudad de la Paz 2555 — 784-5945

Shaare Tefila
Paso 733 — 962-2865

Shaare Tzion
Helguera 453 — 612-9484

Shalom, Olleros 2876 — 552-2720

Shuba Israel
Ecuador 627 — 862-0562

Sinagoga Rabino Zeev Gringberg
Canalejas 3047 — 611-3366

Sucath David
Paso 724 — 962-1091

Yeshurun
Republica de la India 3035 — 802-9310

Yesod Hadat
Lavalle 2449 — 961-1615

Conservative
Beit Hilel, Araoz 2854, Palermo — 804-2286

Colegio Wolfson, Comunidad Or-El
Amenabar 2972 — 544-5461

Comunidad Bet El
Sucre 3338 — 552-2365

Dor Jadash, Murillo 649, Villa Crespo — 854-4467

Nueva Comunidad Israelita
Arcos 2319 — 781-0281

Or Jadash, Varela 850, Flores — 612-1171

Templo la Paz (Chalom)
Olleros 2876 — 552-6730

Reform
Templo Emanu-El
Tronador 1455 — 552-4343

Progressive
Benei Tikva
Vidal 2049 — 795-0380

Mikvaot
José Hernandez 1750, Belgrano
Moldes 2449, Belgrano — 783-2831
Larrea 734, Once
Helguera 270, Once — 612-0410
Ecuador 731, Once
Bogota 3015, Flores

Kashrut Information
The Central Rabbinate of the Vaad Hakehillot
Ecuador 1110, Once — 961-2944
The Orthodox Ashkenazi Chief Rabbi of Argentina is Rabbi Shlomo Benhamu Anidjar.

Contact Information
Asociacion Shuva Israel
Paso 557, Once — 962-6255

Beit Jabad Belgrano
O'Higgins 2358, 1428, Belgrano — 781-3848

Beit Jabad Villa Crespo
Serrano 69 — 855-9822

Chabad Lubavitch Argentina
Agüero 1164, 1425, Flores — 963-1221

Congregacion Israelita de la Republica Argentina
Libertad 785, Centro — 476-2474/371-8929

Oldest Argentine Synagogue. The total number of synagogues in Buenos Aires where there is a minyan at least Friday night and Shabbat morning exceeds fifty. Call either of the above numbers to locate the synagogue nearest you.

Jabad Lubavitch La Plata
Calle 50 No. 463, 1900 — 25-8304
Kehot Lubavitch
S. Luis 3281, 1186 — 865-0629

Embassy
Embassy of Israel
Av. de Mayo 701 — 342-1465

Media

Newspapers
Comunidades
Die Presse
Kesher Kehilari
La Voz Judia
Mundo Israelita
Nueva Sion

Restaurants
Burguer Cash'r
Viamonte 2613, Once — 961-2440
Delicias Kasher
Argerich 404, Flores — 637-1465
Dell Gorro Blanco
Av. Pueyrredón 900, Once — 963-8030
Parrilla al Galope
Tucumán 2637, Once — 963-6888
Restaurant Kasher
Av. Nazca 544, Flores — 611-9686
Sucath David
Tucumán 2449, Once — 952-8878
Summer only.

Pizzerias
Gueulah, San Luis 2537, Once — 962-5249
Roberto Helueni
Pinzón 1235, Barracas — 302-4341
Soultani, San Luis 2528, Once — 961-3913

Bakeries
Confitería Aielet
Aranguren 2911, Flores — 637-5419
Confitería Ganz
Paso 752, Once — 961-6918
Confitería Helueni
Tucumán 2620, Once — 961-0541
Confitería Mari Jalabe
Bogota 3228, Flores — 612-6991

Panadería Malena
Av. Pueyrredón 880, Once — 962-6290

Groceries
Almacén Behar
Campana 347, Flores — 613-2033
Almacén Shalom
San Luis 2513, Once — 962-3685
Autoservicio Ezra
Ecuador 619, Once — 963-7062
Autoservicio Siman Tov
Helguera 474, Flores — 611-4746
Azulay, Helguera 507, Flores
Battías, Paso 706, Once
Kahal Jaredim, Argerich 386, Flores — 612-4590
Kaler, San Luis 2810, Once
Kol Bo Brandsen, Brandsen 1389, Barracas
Kol Bo I, Ecuador 855, Once — 961-3838
Kol Bo II, Viamonte 2537, Once — 961-2012
Kosher Delights
La Pampa 2547, Belgrano — 788-3150
La Esquina Casher
Aranguren 2999, Flores — 637-3706
La Quesería
Viamonte 2438, Once — 961-3171
La Tzorja, Ecuador 673, Once — 961-1096
Yehuda Kosher Foods
Moldes 2452, Belgrano — 637-1465

Museums
Museo Judio de Buenos Aires
Libertad 769 — 45-2474

Libraries
Sociedad Hebraica Argentino
Sarmiento 2233 — 952-5570
Also has art gallery.
YIVO Library
Pasteur 633, Third floor — 45-2474

Booksellers
Agudat Dodim
Bogota 2973, Flores — 613-7900
E. Milberg, Lavalle 2223 — 951-1979
Ediciones del Seminaro Rabínico Latinoamericano
José Hernandez 1750, Belgrano — 783-2009
Editorial Yehuda
Lavalle 2168, Oficina 37

Kehot Lubavitch Sudamerica
San Luis 3281
Librería Editorial Sigal
Av. Corrientes 2854, 1193   861-9501;
                                          865-7208
          Fax: 962-7931; 865-7208
          Email: sigal@einstein.com.ar
Otzar Hatora
Viamonte 2712   865-7208
                                   Fax: 962-7931

Concordia
Area telephone code (45)

Contact Information
Beit Jabad Concordia
Entre Rios 212, 3200   21-1934

Cordoba
Area telephone code (51)

Contact Information
Jabad Lubavitch Cordoba
Sucre 1380, Barrio Cofico, 5000   71-0223

Groceries
Sucre 1378, Barrio Cofico, 5000   71-0223

Rosario
Area telephone code (41)

Contact Information
Beit Jabad Rosario
S. Lorenzo 1882 P.A., 2000   25-2899

Groceries
La Granja Kasher
Montevideo 1833   49-6210

San Luis
Area telephone code (783)

Restaurants
Gueulah, 1056 Bs. As.   962-5249; 951-2330

Tucuman
Area telephone code (81)

Contact Information
Beit Jabad Tucuman
Lamadrid 752, 4000   31-1257

Groceries
Almacén
Lamadrid 752, 4000   31-1257
Almacén y Carnicería
9 de Julio 625   31-0227

Australia

Jews have lived in Australia since 1788. Sixteen known Jews, and possibly others, arrived on the first fleet of convict ships in 1788, although it was not until the 1820s that the first regular, organised worship began. In 1832, the government recognised the establishment of the congregation in Sydney. It was also in Sydney that the first synagogue in Australia was built – in 1844. Jews rose to prominence in political, commercial and cultural life in nineteenth-century Australia. In more recent times, there have been two Jewish Governors-General, as well as a Jewish Chief Justice and Commander-in-Chief of the armed forces (in the First World War).

However, the country's Jewish population has always been small, never reaching 0.6 per cent of its total population. Only because of waves of immigration at crucial periods has Jewish life remained viable. Today, Australian Jewry exceeds 100,000, one of the few Diaspora societies whose Jewish population is rising. There are about 40,000 in Melbourne, 35,000 in Sydney, with smaller communities in the federal capital, Canberra, as well as Perth, Brisbane and Adelaide.

GMT + 7 to 10 hours
Country calling code (61)

Australian Capital Territory

Canberra

Area telephone code (6)

Synagogues

The A.C.T. Jewish Community Synagogue
National Jewish Memorial Centre, cnr
Canberra Ave & National Circuit, 2603, Forrest
295-1052
Fax: 295-8608
Postal address: POB 3105, Manuka 2603

Embassy

Embassy of Israel
6 Turrana Street, 2600, Yarralumla   73-1309

New South Wales

Newcastle

Area telephone code (49)

Synagogues

122 Tyrell Street, 2302   26-2820

Sydney

Area telephone code (2)

Representative Organisations

**Executive Council of Australian Jewry
(National Roof Body)**
146 Darlinghurst Road, Second floor, 2010,
Darlinghurst   9360-5415
Fax: 9360-5416

Australia

Religious Organisations
Beth Din, 166 Castlereagh Street   9267-2477
Fax: 9264-8871

Synagogues
Adath Yisroel
243 Old South Head Road, Bondi   9300-9447

Central Synagogue
15 Bon-Accord Avenue, Bondi Junction
9389-5622

Coogee Synagogue
121 Brook Street, Coogee   9315-8291

Cremorne & District
12a Yeo Street, Neutral Bay   9908-1853

Great Synagogue
166 Castlereagh Street   9267-2477
Fax: 9264-8871
Houses the Rabbi L.A. Falk Memorial Library
and the A.M. Rosenblum Jewish Museum.

Illawarra Synagogue
502 Railway Parade, Allawah   9587-5643

Kehillat Masada
9-15 Links Road, St Ives   9988-4417

Machzike Hatorah
54 Roscoe Street, Bondi   9365-1812

Maroubra Synagogue (K.M.H.C.)
635 Anzac Parade, Maroubra   9344-6095

Mizrachi, 339 Old South Head Road, Bondi
9130-2031

North Shore Synagogue
15a Treatts Road, Lindfield   9416-3710

Paramatta Synagogue
116 Victoria Road, Paramatta   9683-5381

Sephardi Synagogue
40-42 Fletcher Street, Bondi Junction
9389-3355
Fax: 9369-2143

Shearit Yisrael
146 Darlinghurst Road, 2010, Darlinghurst
9365-8770

South Head & District Synagogue
666 Old South Head Road, Rose Bay
9371-7300

Strathfield & District Synagogue
19 Florence Street, Strathfield   9642-3550

Western Suburbs Synagogue
20 George Street, Newtown   9349-3319
Yeshiva, 36 Flood Street, Bondi   9387-3822

Liberal
North Shore Temple Emanuel
28 Chatswood Avenue, Chatswood
9419-7011

Temple Emanuel
7 Ocean Street, 2025, Woollahra   9328-7833

Mikvaot
117 Glenayr Avenue, Bondi   9130-2509

Kashrut Information
NSW Kashrut Authority
PO Box 206, 2026, Bondi   9369-4286
Fax: 9369-4329

Embassy
Consulate General
31 York Street, 2000

Media

Newspapers
Australian Jewish Times
146 Darlinghurst Road, 2010, Darlinghurst
9360-5100
Fax: 9332-4207

Restaurants

Meat
Aviv, 49 Hall Street, Bondi   9130-5921
Supervision: NSW Kashrut Authority.
Glatt kosher.

Front Page at Jaffa's Hakoah Club
61 Hall Street, Bondi   9389-8256
Supervision: NSW Kashrut Authority.
Glatt kosher. Open Tuesdays and Wednesdays
only.

Lewis Continental Kitchen
2 Curlewis Street, Bondi   9365-5421
Supervision: NSW Kashrut Authority.
Glatt kosher.

Savion
1/38 Wairoa Avenue, Bondi   9130-6357
Supervision: NSW Kashrut Authority.
Glatt kosher.

Tibby's Kosher Restaurant
2d Campbell Parade, Bondi Beach   9130-5051
Fax: 9365-6608
Supervision: NSW Kashrut Authority.
Open Saturday and Sunday for dinner and
Sunday lunch. Continental and Chinese food,
Sephardi and Israeli. Glatt kosher.

Pizzerias

Toovya the Milkman
379 Old South Head Road, 2026,
North Bondi   9130-4016
Supervision: NSW Kashrut Authority.
Vegetarian and vegan food. Eat in or take
away. Hours: Sunday to Thursday, 5 pm to
10 pm; Saturday, after Shabbat to midnight.

Bakeries

Carmel Cake Shop, 14 O'Brien Street, Bondi
Supervision: NSW Kashrut Authority.

Grandma Moses
511 Old South Head Road, Rose Bay
                               9371-0874
Supervision: NSW Kashrut Authority.

Butchers

Eilat, 173 Bondi Road, Bondi   9387-8881
Supervision: NSW Kashrut Authority.

Hadassa, 17 O'Brien Street, Bondi   9365-4904
Supervision: NSW Kashrut Authority.

Self-catering

Shalom College, University of
New South Wales, 2052   9663-1366
This is a Jewish residential college and the
central address of the Jewish student
movement in New South Wales.
Accommodation for travellers available on
occasion. Kitchen and dining facilities.
Inquiries to Dr Hilton Immerman.

Museums

Sydney Jewish Museum
148 Darlinghurst Road, 2010, Darlinghurst
                               9360-7999
                          Fax: 9331-4245
                Email: cohenj@tmx.com.au
    Mobile tel: (612) 416-041-950 (International)

Hospitals

Wolper Jewish Hospital
8 Trelawney Street, Woollahra   9328-6077

Sydney Jewish Museum

Location	148 Darlinghurst Road, Darlinghurst	
	1.5km from centre of Sydney	
Hours of Opening	Sunday	11 am–5 pm
	Monday-Thursday	10 am–4 pm
	Friday	10 am–2 pm
Admission	Adults $6, Family $15, Child $3, Concession $4	
Phone	(02) 9360 7999	

Tour information 9328-7604
For information about tours of Jewish Sydney, contact the Great Synagogue at the number listed above or Karl Maehrischel at this number.

Booksellers

Geniza Book Shop
4/38 Waiora Avenue, 2026, Bondi   365-5783

Gold's Book & Gift Company
166 O'Brien Street, 2026, Bondi   300-0495

Shalom Gifts
323 Pacific Highway, Lindfield   416-7076

Queensland

Brisbane

Area telephone code (7)

Community Organisations

Jewish Communal Centre
2 Moxom Road, 4156, Burbank   3349-9749

Religious Organisations

Brisbane Chevra Kadisha, 242 Kingsford Smith Drive, 4007, Hamilton   3262-6564
The number listed is Mr Philips' home number.

Chabad House of Queensland
43 Cedar Street, 4120, Greenslopes 3848-5886

Synagogues

Brisbane Hebrew Congregation
98 Margaret Street, 4000   3229-3412

Givat Zion, 43 Bunya Street, 4000, Greenslopes   3848-5886

Temple Shalom, 13 Koolatah Street, 4152, Camp Hill   3398-8843

Mikvaot

Queensland Mikvah, 46 Bunya Street, 4120, Greenslopes   3848-5886

Bakeries

Brumby's Bakery
408 Milton Road, 4066, Auchenflower
3371-8744

Gold Coast

Area telephone code (75)

Community Organisations

Association of Jewish Organisations
31 Ranock Avenue, 4217, Benown Water
5597-2222

Religious Organisations

Chevra Kadisha   5597-2239

Synagogues

Gold Coast Hebrew Congregation
34 Hamilton Avenue, 4215, Surfers Paradise
5570-1851

Temple Shalom
25 Via Roma Drive, 4217, Isle of Capri
5570-1716

Bakeries

Goldstein's Bakery
509 Olsen Avenue, 4214, Ashmore City
5539-3133
Fax: 5597-1064
Supervision: Rabbi Gurevitch, Gold Coast Hebrew Congregation.
Under the umbrella of the NSW Kashrut Authority. Challah and kosher breads available at 14 stores along the Gold Coast, including Surfers Paradise shop. (Tel) 5531-5808.

South Australia

Adelaide

Area telephone code (8)

Synagogues

Orthodox

Adelaide Hebrew Congregation
13 Flemington Street, 5065, Glenside
8338-2922
Fax: 8379-0142
Mikva on premises. Mailing address: PO Box 320, Glenside 5065.

Progressive
Beit Shalom
41 Hackney Road, 5069, Hackney   8362-8281
Mikva on premises.

Bakeries
Bagel Boys
134 Goodwood Road, 5034   8271-0818
Open 7 days.
Bakers Delight, Frewville Shopping Centre,
Green Osmond Road

Groceries
Kosher Imports
c/o Hebrew Congregation, 13 Flemington
Street, 5065, Glenside   8338-2922
Judaica and Kosher products available.

Tasmania

Hobart

Area telephone code (3)

Synagogues
Hobart Synagogue
PO Box 128B, 7001   6228-4097
The synagogue is the oldest in Australia,
having been consecrated in July 1845. Open
Saturday 10 am and every second Friday in the
month at 6:15 pm. Other days by
arrangement.

Contact Information
Chabad House
93 Lord Street, 7005, Sandy Bay   6223-7116
Contact in advance for Shabbat meals.

Launceston

Synagogues
PO Box 66, St John Street, 7250   6343-1143
The synagogue in St John Street is the second
oldest in Australia, founded in 1846.

Contact Information
Chabad House   6334-0705

Victoria

Melbourne

Area telephone code (3)

Representative Organisations
Jewish Community Council of Victoria
306 Hawthorn Road, 3161, South Caulfield
9272-5566
Fax: 9272-5560
Email: jccv@netspace.net.au
Roof body of Melbourne Jewish community.

Religious Organisations
Orthodox
**Association of Rabbis and Ministers of
Australia and New Zealand**, c/o 12
Charnwood Grove, 3182, St Kilda   9537-1433
Fax: 9525-3759

Council of Orthodox Synagogues of Victoria
c/o Jetset House, 5 Queens Road, 3000
828-8000

Melbourne Beth Din
Synagogue Chambers, 572 Inkerman Road,
3161, North Caulfield   9527-8337

Rabbinical Council of Victoria
c/o Rabbi Mordechai Gutnick, Mizrachi
Organisation, POB 164, 3162, South Caulfield
9525-9833
Fax: 9527-5665

Progressive
Victorian Union for Progressive Judaism
78 Alma Road, 3182, St Kilda   9510-1488
Fax: 9521-1229

Synagogues
Orthodox
Adass Israel
16-24 Glen Eira Avenue, 3182, Ripponlea
9568-3344
Also provide kashrut services.

Brighton Synagogue, 134 Marriage Road,
3186, East Brighton   9592-9179

Burwood Hebrew Congregation
38 Harrison Avenue, 3125   9808-3120

Caulfield Hebrew Congregation
9572 Inkerman Road, 3161, Caulfield
9525-9492

Elwood Talmud Torah Congregation
39 Dickens Street, 3184, Elwood   9531-1547

Kew Synagogue
53 Walpole Street, 33101, Kew   9853-9243

Melbourne Hebrew Congregation
Cnr. Toorak & St Kilda Roads, 3141, South
Yarra   9866-2255

Mizrachi
81 Balaclava Road, 3161, Caulfield 9527-5680

Moorabbin & District Synagogue
960 Nepean Highway, 3189, Moorabbin
    9553-3845

Sephardic Synagogue Congregation
Rambam, 90 Hotham Street, 3183, East St
Kilda   9527-3285

South Caulfield Synagogue, 47 Leopold
Street, 3162, South Caulfield   9578-5922

St Kilda Synagogue, 12 Charnwood Grove,
3182, St Kilda   9537-1433

Yeshiva Shule, 92 Hotham Street, 3183, East
St Kilda   9525-3759

Liberal

Bentleigh Progressive Synagogue
549 Centre Road, 3204   9563-9208

Leo Baeck Centre
33 Harp Road, 3102, East Kew   9819-7160

Temple Beth Israel
76 Alma Road, 3182, St Kilda   9510-1488

Independent

Bet Hatikva Synagogue, 233 Nepean
Highway, 3185, Gardenvale   9576-9755

Mikvaot

Adass Israel, 16-24 Glen Eira Avenue, 3182,
Ripponlea   9568-3344

Contact Information

Mizrachi Hospitality Committee
81 Balaclava Road, 3161, Caulfield 9525-9166
    Fax: 9527-5665

Media

Newspapers

Jewish News, PO Box 1000, South Caulfield
Publish weekly newspaper.

Restaurants

Lamzinis, 219 Carlisle Street, Balaclava
    9527-1283
Supervision: Melbourne Kashrut.

Dairy

Café 296, 296 Carlisle Street, Balaclava
    9525-8099
Supervision: Melbourne Kashrut. Chalav
Yisrael.

Sheli's Coffee Shop, 306 Hawthorn Road,
3162, South Caulfield   9272-5607
Supervision: Melbourne Kashrut.
Chalav Yisrael. Catering also undertaken.

Pizzerias

Rutti's Place, 223 Carlisle Street, 3183,
Balaclava   9525-9939
Supervision: Melbourne Kashrut.
Catering also undertaken.

Bakeries

Atlantic Bakeries, 62 Sheehan Road,
Heidelberg West   9548-2244
Supervision: Melbourne Kashrut. Pat Yisrael.

Big K Kosher Bakery, 316 Carlisle Street,
3183, Balaclava   9527-4582
Supervision: Rabbi A.Z. Beck, Adass Israel.

Glicks Cakes and Bagels, 330a Carlisle Street,
3183, Balaclava   9527-2198
Supervision: Melbourne Kashrut. Pat Yisrael.

Greenfield Cakes, 7 Willow Street, Elsternwick
Supervision: Rabbi A.Z. Beck, Adass Israel.
At same location is King David Kosher Meals
on Wheels (Refuah), hospital meals, airline and
TV dinners.

Haymishe Bakery, 320 Carlisle Street, Shop 4,
3183, Balaclava   9527-7116
Supervision: Rabbi A.Z. Beck, Adass Israel.

Kosher Delight Bakery
75 Glen Eira Road, Ripponlea
Supervision: Rabbi A.Z. Beck, Adass Israel.

Lowy's Cakes & Catering
59 Gordon Street, Elsternwick
Supervision: Rabbi A.Z. Beck, Adass Israel.

Butchers

Continental Kosher Butchers, 155 Glenferrie
Road, 3144, Malvern   9509-9822
    Fax: 9509-9099
Supervision: Rabbi J.S. Cohen, Melbourne
Kashrut. Kosher meats and small goods.
Distributor to other Australian states.

Melbourne Kosher Butchers, 251 Inkerman
Street, 3182, East St Kilda   9525-4230
Supervision: Rabbi A.Z. Beck, Adass Israel.
Sell kosher products as well.

Solomon Kosher Butchers, 140-144 Glen Eira Road, 3185, Elsternwick   9532-8855
Fax: 9532-8896
Supervision: Rabbi Y.D. Groner, Agudas Chabad Kashrut Committee.

Yumi's Kosher Seafoods, 29 Glen Eira Road, 3183, Ripponlea   9523-6444
Fax: 9532-8189
Supervision: Rabbi A.Z. Beck, Adass Israel. Suppliers of fresh fish, wholesale and retail. Processors, manufacturers and distributors of a range of kosher dips, mousses, pates, smoked salmon, herrings, salads, mayonnaise, gefilte fish and other smoked fishes to all major kosher groceries around Australia.

Delicatessens

E.S. Delicatessen, 74 Kooyong Road, 3161, Caulfield   9576-0804
Supervision: Melbourne Kashrut.
Catering also undertaken.

Eshel Take-Away Foods & Catering
59 Glen Eira Road, Ripponlea
Supervision: Rabbi A.Z. Beck, Adass Israel.

Masada Hospital
26 Balaclava Road, East St Kilda
Supervision: Rabbi A.Z. Beck, Adass Israel. Kosher kitchen only.

Caterers

Rishon Foods Party Ltd., 23 Williams Street, 3183, Balaclava   9527-5142

Groceries

Bessa Foods, 57 Kooyong Road, 3162, Caulfield   9509-2387
Fax: 9509-2387

Blusztein's Corner Store, 636 Inkerman Street, 3162, Caulfield North   9527-5349

Dairy Bell Ice Cream, 60 Belgrave Road, 3145, Malvern East   9571-9211
Fax: 9572-2865

Gefen Liquor Store, 144 Chapel Street, 3183, Balaclava   9531-5032
Fax: 9525-7388
Australia's largest selection of kosher wines and spirits.

Milecki's Balaclava Health Food, 277 Carlisle Street, 3183, Balaclava   9527-3350
Open every day except Shabbat and all Jewish holidays.

Tempo Kosher Supermarket, 391 Inkerman Street, 3183, St Kilda   9527-5021
Supervision: Rabbi A.Z. Beck, Adass Israel.

Hotels

Kimberley Gardens, 441 Inkerman Street, 3183, Balaclava   9526-3888
Fax: 9525-9691

Strictly Glatt kosher.

Museums

Jewish Holocaust Centre
29 Mackinnon Road   9578-7148

Jewish Museum of Australia
26 Alma Road, 3182, St Kilda   9543-0083
Fax: 9543-0844

North Eastern Jewish War Memorial Centre
6 High Street, 3108, Doncaster   9857-4430
Fax: 9816-3516

Libraries

Kadimah Jewish Cultural Centre & National Library
7 Selwyn Street, 3185, Elsternwick 9523-9817

Makor Library
306 Hawthorn Road, 3162, South Caulfield
9272-5611
Fax: 9272-5540

Booksellers

Chevrat Serarim Chabad Book Co-op
92 Hotham Street, 3183, East St Kilda
9527-4177

Gold's Book & Gift Company
36 William Street, 3183, Balaclava 9527-8775

M. & L. Balberyszki
98 Acland Street, 3183, St Kilda   9534-6003

Mazeltov Bookshop
275 Cantalo Street, 3183, East St Kilda
9527-3462

Western Australia

Perth

Area telephone code (8)

Representative Organisations

Council of Western Australian Jewry
J.P. PO Box 763, 6062, Morley

Synagogues

Jewish Centre, Woodrow Avenue, 6060, Mt
Yokine   9276-8572

Northern Suburbs Congregation
4 Vernon Street, 6062, Noranda   9275-5932

Perth Hebrew Congregation
Freedman Road, 6050, Menora   9271-0539

Lubavitch

Chabad House, 396 Alexander Drive, 6062,
Dianella   9275-4912

Liberal

Temple David, 34 Clifton Crescent, 6050, Mt
Lawley   9271-1485

Austria

Nazi Germany's annexation and occupation of Austria in 1938 marked the beginning of the end for an ancient and numerous community. There were some 200,000 Jews in Austria at that time – 180,000 of them in Vienna – with a documented history going back to 906 C.E., although there were Jewish settlers in the area several hundred years earlier.

As the centuries passed, Austrian Jewry's fortunes waxed and waned, protection alternating with persecution, which reached a peak in 1420, after a charge of ritual murder had been levelled against the Jews. Almost the entire Jewish population of Austria was burnt to death, forcibly baptised or expelled.

Those who remained were harried and hounded until at the beginning of the 17th century, Jews were allowed to settle in an area outside the walls, only to be driven away from this second ghetto by Leopold I in 1670. Rich Jews were subsequently granted permission to return to the city in order to better the financial situation of the Empire. They were to live under considerable disabilities until 1867, when they were accorded full rights.

From then onwards, until 1938, the Austrian Jewish community flourished, despite the endemic antisemitism which, as in so many other European countries, was a feature of life in Austria. Between 1938 and 1940 about 120,000 Jews managed to leave. Some 60,000 men, women and children were killed in Nazi death camps. Today, there are about 12,000 Jews in Austria, 10,000 of them in Vienna.

GMT + 1 hour
Country calling code (43)

Baden
Area telephone code (2236)

Synagogues

Grabengasse 14   26383
Services are held Shabbat mornings from May to September.

Cemeteries

Jewish Cemetery
Halsriegelstrasse 30   85405
Contains some 3,000 graves.

Edlach

Monument

A memorial to Dr Theodor Herzl, erected by the Viennese Jewish community, can be seen in the garden of the local sanatorium, where the founder of the Zionist movement died in 1904.

Eisenstadt

Area telephone code (26)

Museums

Austrian Jewish Museum
Unterbergstrasse 6   821-5145
The museum now also comprises the restored
private synagogue of Samson Wertheimer,
Habsburg court Jew and Chief Rabbi of
Hungary (1658–1724). The museum is open
daily except Monday from 10 am to 5 pm. The
Eruv Arch, spanning Unterbergstrasse, is at the
end near the Esterhazy Palace. The road chain
was used in former times to prevent vehicular
traffic on Shabbat and Yom Tov.

Cemeteries

Old Cemetery
The old cemetery, closed around 1875,
contains the grave of Rav Meir ben Isak (Mram
Asch), who died in 1744. To this day it is the
scene of pilgrimages, particularly on the
anniversary of his death. Keys to the cemetery
are with the porter of the local hospital, which
adjoins the old cemetery.

Graz

Area telephone code (316)

Community Organisations

Community Centre
Synagogenplatz 1   912-468

Innsbruck

Area telephone code (512)

Community Organisations

Community Centre
Zollerstrasse 1   586-892

Kobersdorf

Area telephone code (2618)

Cemeteries

Jewish Cemetery, Waldgasse

The keys of the cemetery on the Lampelberg
are with Mr Piniel, Waldgasse 25 (one of the
two houses to the left of the cemetery) and
Mr Grässing, Haydngasse 4. The synagogue is
currently being rebuilt.

Linz

Area telephone code (70)

Community Organisations

Community Centre
Bethlehemstrasse 26   779-805

Salzburg

Area telephone code (662)

Community Organisations

Community Centre
Lasserstrasse 8, 5020   875-665
Community synagogue and mikva are to be
found at the same address.

Semmering

Area telephone code (663)

Hotels

Hotel Alpenhof
Spital   808-439
Open July through August.

Vienna

Area telephone code (1)

Synagogues

Orthodox

Agudas Yeshurun
Riemergasse 9, 1010

Agudas Yisroel
Grünangergasse 1, 1010   512-8331

Agudas Yisroel
Tempelgasse 3, 1020   24-92-62

Machsike Haddas
Desider Friedmann-Platz, 1010   214-1347

Misrachi
Judenplatz 8, 1010   535-4153
Ohel Moshe
Lilienbrunngasse 19, 1020   216-8864
Sephardi Centre
Tempelgasse 7, 1020
Shomre Haddas
Glasergasse 17, 1090
Thora Etz Chayim
Grosse Schiffgasse 8, 1020   214-5206

Mikvaot

Agudas Yisroel
Tempelgasse 3, 1020   214-9262
Machsike Haddas
Fleischmarkt 22, 1010   512-5262

Kashrut Information
Vaad Hakashrut
Karmelitergasse 13, 1020   33-73-64

Contact Information
Jewish Community Centre
Seitenstettengasse 2   53104
Jewish Welcome Service
Stephansplatz 10, 1010   533-8891
Fax: 533-4098
Rabbi Paul Chaim Eisenberg
Chief Rabbi of Vienna   531-0417

Embassy
Embassy of Israel
Anton-Frankgasse 20, 1180   470-4741

Media
Maps and Guides
Jewish Vienna: Heritage and Mission
513-8892
Fax: 513-4015

Restaurants
Arche Noah
Seitenstettengasse 2, Judengasse, 1010
533-1374
Supervision: Rabbi Grünfeld, Agudas Yisroel.

Vegetarian
Wrenkh, 1 Bauermarket, 1010   533-1526
Hours: 11:30 am to 2:30 pm and 6 pm to
midnight.

Bakeries
Engländer
Hollandstrasse 10, 1020   214-5617
Supervision: Rabbi Abraham Yonah Schwartz.

Butchers
B. Ainhorn
Stadtgutgasse 7, Grosse Pfarrgasse 6, 1020
214-5621
Supervision: Rabbi Abraham Yonah Schwartz.
Rebenwurzel
Grose Mohrengasse 19, 1010   216-6640
Supervision: Rabbi Abraham Yonah Schwartz.
Sephardi Butcher
Volkertmarkt, 1020   214-9650

Groceries
Kosher Supermarket & Shutnes Laboratory
Hollandstrasse 7, 1020   26-96-75
Supervision: Rabbi Abraham Yonah Schwartz.
Raffi's
Ferdinandstrasse, 1020   214-3394
Food imported from Belgium.
Vinothek Gross
Liechtensteinstrasse 32, 1090   317-5277
Fax: 317-5277
Vinothek Gross
Taborstrasse 15, 1020   212-6299

Hotels
Stefanie
12 Tabor Strasse, 1020   211-500
Four star hotel with kosher breakfast on
request.

Bed & Breakfasts
Pension Lichtenstein
Grosse Schifgasse 19, 1020   216-8498
Fax: 214-790
Supervision: Rabbi Abraham Yonah Schwartz.
The pension consists of 'suites' (sleeping area,
living area, kitchenette and bathroom). The
stove can be used as a hot plate for Shabbat.
It is within walking distance of the old Jewish
quarter of Vienna in one direction, and 5-20
minutes from some small synagogues, kosher
bakery in the other direction. Should be
coordinated in advance as there is no front
desk reception; the key is kept in the owner's
office around the block. Recommended for
families and couples interested in self-catering.

Museums

Jewish Museum of the City of Vienna
Dorotheergasse 11, A-1010   535-0431
                                  Fax: 535-0424
Hours: Sunday to Friday, 10 am to 6 pm;
Thursday, 10 am to 9 pm. Cafeteria and
bookshop on site.

Sigmund Freud Museum
Berggasse 19, 1090   319-1596

Sites

Mauthausen Memorial Site   072-38/24-39
Those wishing to visit the site should contact
the Jewish Welcome Service.

Seitenstettengasse Synagogue
Seitenstettengasse 4, 1010
Built in 1824-26 and partly destroyed during
the Nazi period, this beautiful synagogue was
restored by the community in 1988. Guides to
the synagogue are available from the Jewish
Community Centre. For information about
guided tours, contact the Community Centre
offices.

Cemeteries

Floridsdorfer Cemetery
Ruthnergasse 28, 1210
Those wishing to visit must first obtain a
permit from the community centre.

Rossauer Cemetery
Seegasse 9, 1090
This is the oldest Jewish cemetery in Vienna,
dating from the sixteenth century. It has now
been restored after being devastated by the
Nazis and is open daily from 8 am to 3 pm.
Access is via the front entrance of the
municipal home for the aged at Seegasse
9-11, but a permit must first be obtained from
the community centre.

Vienna Central Cemetery
Simmering district, 1110   76-6252
There is a Jewish section at Gate 4 and an
older Jewish part at Gate 1.

Währinger Cemetery
Semperstrasse 64a, 1180
Those wishing to visit must first obtain a
permit from the community centre.

Documentation Centres

**Documentation Centre of Austrian
Resistance Movement**
Old City Hall, Wipplingerstrasse 8, 1010
                                  534-36-332
**Documentation Centre of Union of Jewish
Victims of the Nazis**
Salztorgasse 6, 1010   533-9131

Tour Information

The Vienna Tourist Board   513-8892
                                  Fax: 513-4015

Tourist Information Centre
Kärntnerstrasse 38   313-8892
Open daily, 9 am to 7 pm.

Booksellers

Chabad-Simcha-Center
Hollandstrasse 10, 1020   216-2924
Chai Vienna
Lessinggasse 5, 1020   216-4621
Jewish Museum
Dorotheergasse 11, A-1010   512-5361

Azerbaijan

GMT + 5 hours
Country calling code (994)

Baku
Area telephone code (12)

Synagogues
Mountain Jews
Dmitrova Street 39, 370014   892-232-8867

Ashkenazi
Pervomoskaya Street 271   892-294-1571

Embassy
Embassy of Israel
Stroiteley Prospect 1

Kuba

Synagogues
46 Kolkhoznaya Street

Bahamas

The Jewish population of these islands, formerly a British colony, is put at round around 100. However, it is estimated that at least 350,000 of the 3 million tourists who visit the Bahamas every year are Jewish. In Nassau, the capital, on New Providence Island, there are a number of Jewish residents. The Jewish cemetery is a walled-off section of the public cemetery. Most major hotels can make special arrangements for kosher food.

GMT – 5 hours
Country calling code (1242)

Synagogues
Luis de Torres Synagogue
East Sunrise Highway, PO Box F41761,
Freeport, Grand Bahama Island   373-2008
Services are held fairly regularly. The president of the congregation, Jack Turner, can be reached at 373-1041.

Embassy
Consul General of Israel   362-4421

Tours
Geoff Hurst   373-4025
          Fax: 373-4025
          Email: hurst-gr@gbonline.win.net
He is happy to make arrangements for tourists.

Barbados

A Jewish community was formed on the island of Barbados by refugees
from Brazil after its reconquest by the Portuguese in about 1650. In 1802
all political disabilities of the Jews were removed, although this was not
confirmed by Parliament until 1820.

Nevertheless, Barbados was the first British possession to grant full
political emancipation to its Jews. The island gained its independence in
1966, remaining a member of the British Commonwealth. A synagogue
building in Bridgetown, dating from 1833 (although parts are much older,
going back to 1654), remains from the days of the original Jewish
population. In 1929, the synagogue building was sold, because only one
Jew still remained on the island, and turned into offices. The synagogue
and the cemetery in Synagogue Lane which surrounds it and is still in use,
are in the process of restoration and repair after years of neglect. The
restoration of the synagogue is now 95 per cent completed and the original
clock and chanuka lamp among other items have been returned from the
museum. What is most urgently needed now is the restoration of the
tombstones in the adjoining cemetery whose condition has deteriorated. In
the 1930s and 1940s Jews returned to Barbados. There were more than 30
European Jewish families on the island in the 1940s, but only about 20
remain today.

GMT – 4 hours
Country calling code (1246)

Community Organisations

Barbados Jewish Community
PO Box 651, Bridgetown   427-0703
                           Fax: 436-8807

Caribbean Jewish Congress
PO Box 1331, Bridgetown   436-8163

Synagogue Restoration Project
PO Box 256, Bridgetown   432-0840
Local inquiries to Henry Altman, 'Sea Shell',
Gibbes Beach, St Peter. Tel: 422-2664.

Synagogues

Barbados Synagogue
Synagogue Lane
Services are held Friday evenings at 7 pm at
'True Blue', Rockley New Road, Christ Church,
during the summer, and at the synagogue in
winter.

Belarus

GMT +2 hours
Country calling code (375

Baranovichi

Synagogues
39 Svobodnaya St.

Bobruisk

Synagogues
Engels St.

Borisov

Synagogues
Trud St.

Brest

Synagogues
Narodnaya St.

Gomel

Synagogues
13 Sennaya St.

Minsk

Synagogues
Kommunisticheskaya St.
22 Kropotkin St.   558-270

Embassy
Embassy of Israel
Partizanski Prospekt 6A, 220002

Moghilev

Synagogues
1 2nd Krutoy La.

Orsha

Synagogues
Nogrin St.

Rechitsa

Synagogues
120 Lunacharsky St.

Belgium

Belgian Jewry, like the communities of other European countries, achieved religious equality nearly 160 years ago — in 1831, when Belgium became a kingdom and religious equality was made part of the fundamental law of the State.

By the late 1930s, there were 100,000 Jews in Belgium, including refugees from Nazi Germany, but their respite from persecution was a short one. When Hitler's armies invaded Belgium in 1940 and swept on to occupy the whole of Western Europe as far as the Spanish border, few Belgian Jews managed to escape to safety. After introducing their racialist legislation, the Nazis began rounding up the Jews and deported 25,000 of them to concentration camps.

The names of the 23,838 who did not return after the end of the Second World War are engraved on the national monument to the Jewish Martyrs of Belgium. This stands in the Anderlecht district of Brussels.

There are about 40,000 Jews in Belgium today, most of them in Antwerp and Brussels.

GMT + 1 hour
Country calling code (32)

Antwerp
Area telephone code (3)

Synagogues

Orthodox
Machsike Hadass
Oostenstrasse 43
Machsike Hadass
Jacob Jacobsstrasse 22

Mikvaot
Machsike Hadass
Steenbokstrasse 22   239-7588
Shomre Hadass
Van Diepenbeeckstrasse 42   239-0965

Contact Information
Machsike Hadass (Israelitische Orthodoxe Gemeente)
Jacob Jacobsstrasse 22   233-5567

Machsike Hadass Rabbinate
Jacob Jacobsstrasse 22   232-0021
Rabbi Ch. Kreiswirth, Quinten Matsijslei 35, 234-3148; Dayan E. Sternbuch, 233-7194; Dayan T. Weiss, 230-2163.

Shomre Hadass (Israelitische Gemeente)
Terliststrasse 35   232-0187
Shomre Hadass Rabbinate
Terliststrasse 35   226-0554
Dayan J. Kohen, 230-3581; Rabbi D. Lieberman, Belgiëlei 194, 239-1883.

Embassy
Consulate General
Postbus 126, B- 2018 14

Media

Newspapers
Belgisch Israelitisch Weekblad
Pelikaanstrasse 106-108   233-7043

Belgium

Restaurants

Blue Lagoon
Lange Herentalsestrasse 70   226-0114
          Fax: 281-1702
Supervision: Machsike Hadass.
Also sell chocolates. Five minutes from Central station.

Dresdner, Simonstrasse 10   232-5455
Jacob, Lange Kievitstrasse 49   233-1124
Sam (Diamantbeurs)
Pelikaanstrasse 28   233-9289
Snack Bar, Romi Goldmuntz Centre,
Nerviersstrasse 12   239-3911
Snack Bar Hoffy's
Lange Kievitstrasse 52   234-3535

Bakeries

Gottesfeld, Mercatorstrasse. 20   230-0003
Grosz, Pelikaanstrasse 130   233-9110
Kleinblatt, Provinciestrasse 206   233-7513; 226-0018
Steinmetz, Lange Kievitstrasse 64   234-0947

Butchers

Berkowitz, Isabellalei 9   218-5111
Farkas, Lange Kievitstrasse 66   232-1385
Fruchter, Simonstrasse 22   233-1811
Kosher King
Lange Kievitstrasse 40   233-6749
Kosher King
Isabellalei 7   239-4189
Mandelovics
Isabellalei 96   218-4779
Moszkowitz, Lange Kievitstrasse 47   232-1485
Weingarten
Lange Kievitstrasse 124   233-2828

Groceries

Col-Bo, Jacob Jacobsstrasse 40   234-1212
Grosz-Modern
Terliststrasse 28   232-4626
Herzl & Gold
Korte Kievitstrasse 38   232-2365
Stark, Mercatorstrasse 24   230-2520
Super Discount
Belgielei 104-108   239-0666

Museums

Plantin-Moretus Museum
Vrijdagmarkt (nr Groenplaats)   233-0688
Open daily (except Monday). Contains examples of early Jewish printing, such as the famous Polyglot Bible.

Tour Information

Antwerp Tourist & Inquiries Office
Suikerrui 19   232-0103

Booksellers

Epstein, Van den Nestlei 7   232-7562
I. Menczer, Simonstrasse 40   232-3026
N. Seletsky
Lange Kievitstrasse 70   232-6966
Stauber, Van Leriusstrasse 3   231-8031

Arlon

Area telephone code (63)

Synagogues

Rue St Jean   217-985
Established 1863. The secretary, J.C. Jacob, can be reached at 11 rue des Martyrs, 6700. A monument has been erected in the new Jewish cemetery to the memory of the Jews of Arlon deported and massacred by the Nazis.

Brussels

Area telephone code (2)

Community Organisations

Centre Communautaire Laic Juif
52 rue Hotel des Monnaies   537-8216

Religious Organisations

Communaute Israelite de Bruxelles
2 Rue Joseph Dupont, 1000
          512-4334; 512-9237
Consistoire Central Israelite de Belgique
2 Rue Joseph Dupont, 1000   512-2190
          Fax: 512-3578
Machsike Hadass (Communauté Israélite Orthodoxe de Bruxelles)
67a rue de la Clinique   524-1486; 521-1289

Machsike Hadass Beth Din
67a rue de la Clinique   522-0717

Synagogues

Orthodox

Adath Israel, 126 rue Rogier, Schaerbeek
241-1664

Ahavat Reim, 73 rue de Thy, St Gilles
648-3837

Beth Hamidrash, rue du Chapeau, Anderlecht
524-1486

Beth Itshak
115 Ave du Roi, 1060   538-3374; 520-1359

Maale, 11 Ave de Messidor   344-6094

Machsike Hadass
67a rue de la Clinique   522-0717

Or Hahayim
77 rue P. Decoster, 1190   344-2342

Sephardi

Communauté Sepharadite de Bruxelles
47 rue du Pavaillon, 1030   215-0525

Liberal

Member of World Union for Progressive Judaism, 96 Ave Kersbeek   332-2528

Mikvaot

Machsike Hadass
67a rue de la Clinique   537-1439

Contact Information

Beth Chabad, 87 Ave du Roi   537-1158

Embassy

Embassy of Israel
40 Avenue de l'Observatoire, 1180   373-5500

Media

Newspapers

Centrale, 91 Av. Henri Jaspar   538-8036
Monthly

Kehilatenou, 2 rue Joseph Dupont   512-4334
Monthly

La Tribune Sioniste, 68 Ave Ducpétiaux
Fortnightly

Regards
52 rue Hotel des Monnaies   538-4908
Fax: 537-5565
Fortnightly

Restaurants

Centre Ben Gurion
89 Chaussee de Vleurgat   648-1859
Hours: daily, noon to 2:30 pm and 6 pm to 9 pm except Friday evenings and Shabbat afternoons.

Bakeries

Bornstein, 62 rue de Suéde, St Gilles 537-1679

Butchers

Lanxner, 37 Ave Jean Volders   537-0608
Lanxner, 121 rue de Brabant   217-2620

Museums

Jewish Museum
74 Ave de Stalengrad, 1000   512-1963

Sites

National Monument to the Jewish Martyrs of Belgium
corner rue Emile Carpentier and rue Goujons, Square of the Jewish Martyrs, Anderlecht
This monument commemorates the Jews of Belgium who were deported to concentration camps and killed by the Nazis during the Second World War. The names of all 23,838 are engraved on the monument, which has been erected in the Brussels district of Anderlecht.

Booksellers

Colbo, 121 rue du Brabant   217-2620
Menorah
12 Ave. J. Voldens, 1060   537-5073

Charleroi
Area telephone code (71)

Community Organisations
Community Centre
56 rue Pige-au-Croly

Ghent
Area telephone code (9)

Contact Information
Jacques Bloch
Veldstrasse 60 225-7085
The treasurer of the community, he will be
happy to meet Anglo-Jewish visitors. As the
community is a very small one, there is no
permanent synagogue. Services are held on
the High Holy Days.

Knokke
Area telephone code (50)

Synagogues
30 Van Bunnenlaan 611-0372

Restaurants
Maison Steinmetz
Piers de Raveschootlaan 129, 8300 61-0265
Open July-August.

Liège
Area telephone code (41)

Community Organisations
Community Centre
12 Quai Marcellis, 4020

Synagogues
19 rue L. Frédéricq, 4020 436-106

Museums
Musee Serge Kruglanski
19 rue L. Fredericq, 4020 438-043

Mons
Area telephone code (65)

Contact Information
SHAPE, 7010 445-808; 444-809
Nearby, at Casteau, the International Chapel
of NATO's Supreme Headquarters Allied
Powers Europe, includes a small Jewish
community, established 1951, that holds
regular services. Call for further information.

Ostend
Area telephone code (59)

Synagogues
Van Maastrichtplein 3
Services during July and August. Inquiries to
Mrs Liliane Wulfowicz, Parklaan 21, B-8400.
Tel: 802-405.

Hotels
Hotel Royal Astor
Hertsstraat 15 803-773
Open for Sukkot.

Bermuda

There is a small but active Jewish community in Bermuda. High Holy-day services are normally held at the US Naval Air Station chapel.

GMT – 4 hours
Country calling code (1 441)

Ferry Reach

Contact Information

Diana Lynn
17 Biological Lane, GE01   297-2267
Fax: 297-8143
Email: dlynn@bbst.edu

Hamilton

Community Organisations

Jewish Community of Bermuda
PO Box HM 1793, HM HX   291-1785

Bolivia

Although there have been Jews in Latin America for many centuries, they are comparative newcomers to Bolivia, which received its first Jewish immigrants only in 1905. They remained a mere handful until the 1920s, when some Russian Jews made their way to the country. After 1935, German Jewish refugees began to arrive in Bolivia. They came from Rumania and mostly from Poland. Today some 640 Jews live there, mostly in the capital of La Paz, Cochabamba and Santa Cruz.

GMT – 4 hours
Country calling code (591)

Cochabamba
Area telephone code (42)

Representative Organisations
Asociacion Israelita de Cochabamba
PO Box 349, Calle Valdivieso

Synagogues
Calle Junin y Calle Colombia, Casilla, 349

La Paz
Area telephone code (2)

Synagogues
Circulo Israelita de Bolivia
Casilla 1545, Calle Landaeta 346,
PO Box 1545   32-5925
                            Fax: 34-2738
Representative body of Bolivian Jewry. All La Paz organisations are affiliated to it. Service Shabbat morning only.

Comunidad Israelita Synagogue
Calle Canada Stronguest 1846, PO Box 2198
Affiliated to the Circulo. Friday evening services are held here. There is a Jewish school at this address.

Tour information
Centro Shalom
Calle Canada Stronguest 1846

Santa Cruz
Area telephone code (3)

Representative Organisations
WIZO, Castilla, 3409

Community Organisations
Centro Cruceño
PO Box 469

Bosnia Hercegovina

The Jewish community, some 600-strong, is struggling to secure continuity shattered by the recent civil war. Jews – mostly Sephardic – settled here in the beginning of the sixteenth century after expulsion from Spain in 1492. Jewish life is organised by the Jewish community in Sarajevo. Other small Jewish communities are in Mostar, Doboj, Tuzla and Zenica. The non-sectarian humanitarian activities in the civil war, by the community and especially by its Humanitarian and Cultural Society 'La Benevolencija', have brought fame to the small community.

GMT + 1 hour
Country calling code (387)

Sarajevo
Area telephone code (71)

Synagogues
Synagogue and Community Centre
Hamdije Kresevljakovica 59   663-472
Fax: 663-473
Email: labelova@utic.net.ba

Museums
Jewish Museum
Mulamustafe Baseskije Street
This historic museum, placed in the oldest synagogue in Sarajevo, with priceless relics dating back to the expulsion from Spain, is temporarily closed to the public.

Novi Hram
This gallery is also located in a former synagogue. The president of the community will gladly show you around.

Cemeteries
Kovacici
This historic Jewish cemetery is in town. Not far from the centre of town, on a hill called Vraca, there is a monument with the names of the 7,000 Jews from the area who fell victim to the Nazis.

Brazil

Marranos from Portugal and, later, Sephardim from Holland were the first Jews to settle in Brazil about 400 years ago. Their early history was bedevilled by the struggle for power in this vast country between the Portuguese and Dutch, as well as by the Inquisition, which the Portuguese revived when they were on top, and which was abolished when the Dutch gained the upper hand.

Finally, in 1822, Brazil declared her independence of Portugal. Some Marranos reverted to open Judaism when liberty of worship was proclaimed, and in the years that followed, European Jews, mainly Ashkenazim, began to immigrate. Communities grew up in Rio de Janeiro, Recife, Bahia, Sao Paulo and elsewhere and continued to grow, especially after the First World War, in the 1930s and again after the Second World War.

Today, Brazil's Jewish population numbers about 175,000. All save about 25,000 live in Rio and Sao Paulo. The overwhelming majority, some 140,000, are Ashkenazim.

GMT – 3 to 4 hours
Country calling code (55)

Amazonas

Manaus

Community Organisations
Grupo Kadima, Rua Ramos Ferreira 596

Bahia

Salvador
Area telephone code (71)

Synagogues
Rua Alvaro Tiberio 60   3-4283
Community centre and Zionist organisation
are at the same address.

Brasilia
Area telephone code (61)

Synagogues
ACIB, Entrequadras Norte 305-306, Lote A
23-2984
Community centre is at the same address.

Embassy
Embassy of Israel, Av. das Nacoes Sul, Lote
38   244-7675; 7875;
5886; 4886

Minas Gerais

Belo Horizonte
Area telephone code (91)

Representative Organisations
Associacao Israelita Brasileira
Rua Rio Grande do Norte 477   221-0690

Comunidade Religiosa Israelita Mineira
Rua Rio Grande do Norte 477
Uniao Israelita de Belo Horizonte
Rua Pernambuco 326   224-6013

Synagogues
Av. Leonardo Malchez 630, Centro

Mikvaot
Rua Rio Grande do Norte 477   221-0690

Contact Information
Lojinha do Beit Chabad
Av. Serzedelo Corrêa 276   241-2250

Para

Belém
Area telephone code (91)

Community Organisations
Community Centre, Travessa Dr. Moraes 37

Synagogues
Eshel Avraham, Travessa Campos Sales 733
Shaar Hashamaim
Rua Alcipreste Manoel Theodoro 842

Contact Information
Lojinha do Beit Chabad
Av. Serzedelo Corrêa 276   241-2250

Parana

Curitiba
Area telephone code (41)

Community Organisations
Community Centre and S. Guelman School
Rua Nilo Pecanha 664   233-734

Synagogues
Orthodox
Francisco Frischman, Rua Cruz Machado 126

Pernambuco

Recife
Area telephone code (81)

Community Organisations
Community Centre, Rua da Gloria 215

Synagogues
Rua Martins Junior 29

Rio de Janeiro

Campos
Community Organisations
Community Centre
Rua 13 de Maio 52

Greater Rio de Janeiro
Area telephone code (21)

Representative Organisations
Organição Israelita do Estado do Rio de Janeiro
Rua Mexico 90/5   532-0925
Rabinado do Rio de Janeiro
Rua Pompeu Loureiro 40
                             Fax: 236-0249

Religious Organisations
Chevre Kedishe
Rua Barao de Iguatemi 306   248-8716

Synagogues
Grande Templo Israelita
Rua Tenente Possolo 8, 20230, Centro
                                     232-3656

Orthodox
Agudat Israel
Rua Nascimento Silva 109, 22421, Ipanema

Kehilat Yaakov, Rua Capelao Alvares da Silva, 22041, Copacabana

Liberal
Associacao Religiosa Israelita, Rua General Severiano 170, 22290, Botafogo   226-9666; 237-9283

Mikvaot
Kehilat Yaakov, Rua Capelao Alvares da Silva 15, 22041, Copacabana

Embassy
Consulate General
Av. Copacabana 680   255-5432

Restaurants
Shalom, Rua Pompeu Loureiro 40, Copacabana   236-0249

Groceries
Kosher House
Rua Anita Garibaldi 37 lj. A, Copacabana   255-3891

Museums
Jewish Museum, Rua Mexico 90-1, Andar

Libraries
Biblioteca Bialik, Rua Fernando Osorio 16, 22230, Flamengo   205-1946
Biblioteca Sholem Aleichem, Rua Sao Clemente 155, 22260, Botafogo   226-7740

Niteroi

Community Organisations
Centro Israelita
Rua Visconde do Uruguai 255, 24030
Sociedade Hebraica
Rua Alvares de Azevedo 185, Icarai, 24220

Petropolis
Area telephone code (242)

Religious Organisations
Machane Israel Yeshiva
Rua Duarte de Silveira 1246, 25600   45-4952

Synagogues
Sinagoga Israelita Brasileira
Rua Aureliano Coutinho 48, 25600

Rio Grande do Sul

Erechim

Synagogues
Av. Pedro Pinto de Souza 131

Passo Fundo

Synagogues
Rua General Osório 1049

Pelotas

Synagogues
Rua Santos Dumont 303

Porto Alegre
Area telephone code (51)

Cultural Organisations
Instituto Cultural Judaico Marc Chagall - Projeto Memoria
Rua Dom Pedro II, 1220/sala 216   343-5748

Religious Organisations
City Rabbinate
Rua Henrique Dias 73   219-649

Synagogues
Orthodox
Beit Chabad
Rua Felipe Camarão 748   330-7078
Daily services.
Centro Israelita Porto Alegrense
Rua Henrique Dias 73   228-1935
Daily services.

Linath Ha-Tzedek
Rua Bento Figueredo 55   332-1065
Daily services.

Poilisher Farband
Rua João Telles 329   226-0379
Daily services.

União Israelita Porto Algrense
Rua Barros Cassal 750   224-6515
Daily services.

Sephardi

Centro Hebraico Riograndense
Rua Cel. Machado 1008
Services on Shabbat only.

Liberal

SIBRA, Mariante 772   331-8133
Services on Shabbat only.

Mikvaot

Rua Francisco Ferrer 170

Butchers

Kosher Butcher
Rua Fernandes Vieira 518   250-441

Museums

Museu Judaico
Rua João Telles 329   226-0379

Santa Maria

Location of first Jewish settlement in Brazil, established by the Jewish Colonization Association.

São Paulo

Campinas

Area telephone code (19)

Synagogues

Beth Yacob, Rua Barreto Leme 1203   314-908
Fax: 442-171

Guaruja

Area telephone code (013)

Synagogues

Beit Yaacov, Av. Leomil 628   387-2033
Neve Itzhak, Av. Leomil 950   386-3167

Mogi Das Cruzes

Community Organisations

Jewish Society
Rua Dep. Deodato Wertheimer 421   469-2505

S. Jose dos Campos

Area telephone code (11)

Synagogues

Beit Chabad
Rua Republica do Ira 91   3064-6322

Santo Andre

Synagogues

Beit Chabad
Rua 11 de Junho 172   449-1568

Santos

Area telephone code (132)

Community Organisations

Club, Rua Cons. Neblas 254   32-9016

Synagogues

Beit Sion, Rua Borges 264
Sinagoga Beit Jacob, Rua Campos Sales 137

São Caetano do Sul

Synagogues

Sociedade Religiosa S. Caetano do Sul
Rua Para 67   442-3514

São Paulo

Area telephone code (11)

Religious Organisations

Centro Judaico Religioso de Sao Paulo
220-5642
Office hours: 9 am to 1 pm weekdays.

Comunidade Israelita Ortodoxa de Sao Paulo, Hitachdut Kehilot Hacharedim, Rua Haddock Lobo 1279, 1091   282-1562;
852-9710
This Community centre has two synagogues.

Synagogues

Hungarian

Adas Yereim
Rua Talmud Tora 86   282-1562; 852-9710

Orthodox

Beit Chabad Central
Rua Chabad 60   282-8711
Fax: 280-2380

Beit Itzchak
Rua Haddock Lobo 1279, 1091   881-3804

Kehal Machzikei Hadat
Rua Padre Joao Manuel 727   280-5111

Sinagoga Israelita Paulista – Beit Chabad
Rua Augusta 259, 01305-000   258-7173

Hasidic

Kehal Chassidim, Rua Mamore 597 224-0278

Sephardi

Templo Israelita Brasileiro Ohel Yaacov
Rua Abolicao 457   606-9982
Fax: 227-6793

Liberal

Congregaco Israelita Paulista
Rua Antonio Carlos 653   256-7811
Fax: 257-1446

Mikvaot

Rua Haddock Lobo 1279   881-3804

Associacão Mekor Haim
Rua S. Vicente de Paulo 254   826-7699

Beit Chabad Central
Rua Chabad 60   282-8711
Fax: 280-2380

By appointment only.

Beit Chabad Perdizes
Rua Manoel Maria Tourinho 261   65-0615
By appointment only.

Bom Retiro, Rua Bandeirantes 465   228-9845

Sinagoga Monte Sinai
Rua Piaui 624   66-5303

Embassy

Consulate General
Rua Luis Coelho 308, 7th Floor   257-2111;
257-2814

Media

Newspapers

O Hebreu, Rua Cunha Gago 158   870-1616
Fax: 816-1324
Monthly.

Resenha Judaica
Rua Antonio Carlos 582/5   255-8794
Weekly.

Tribuna Judaica
Rua Tanabi 299   871-3234
Fax: 3675-0072
Weekly.

Restaurants

Buffet Mosaico
Rua Hungria 1000
815-6788; 815-6980; 818-8831
Supervision: Rabbi Eliahu B. Valt. Inside the Hebraica São Paulo club. Closed Mondays, open Saturday night 1½ hours after Shabbat.

Kosher Center
Rua Corrèa de Melo 68   223-1175

Kosher Deli
Rua Consolação 3679   852-6473; 853-1250

Kosher Pizza
Rua P. João Manoel 881   0800-114-666

Restaurant Beit Chinuch
Rua P. João Manoel 727   280-5111

Bakeries

Buffet Mazal Tov
Rua Peixoto Gomide 1724   883-7614
Fax: 3064-5208
Supervision: Rabbi Iliowitz.

Matok Bakery, Al. Barros 921   66-7514
Supervision: Rabbi I. Dichi.

Matok Bakery
Rua P. João Manoel 709   3064-6668
Supervision: Rabbi I. Dichi.

Butchers

Casa de Carnes Casher
Rua Fortunato 241   221-2240
Under supervision of Rabbi Elyahu B. Valt.

Mehadrin, Rua S. Vicente de Paulo   67-9090
Under supervision of Rabbi M.A. Iliovitz.

Mehadrin, Rua Prates 689   228-1771
Under supervision of Rabbi M.A. Iliovitz.

Groceries

All Kosher, Rua Albuquerque Lins 1170
                                      825-1131

Amazonas, Rua Amazonas 91   229-1336

Chazak, Rua Afonsa Pena 348a   229-5607

Chazak, Rua Haddock Lobo 1002   3068-9093

Dom Bosco, Rua Guarani 114   228-6105

Mazal Tov, Rua Peixoto Gomide 1724
                                      883-7614
                            Fax: 3064-5208

Sta. Luzia, Al. Lorena 1471   883-5844
Look for kosher section.

Zilanna, Rua Itambé 506   257-8671

Travel Agencies

Carmel Tur, Rua Xavier de Toledo 121/10
                                      257-2244

Sharontur, Rua de Graca 235   223-8388

Vertice, Rua Sao Bento 545/10   3115-1960
                            Fax: 3068-0325

Booksellers

Livraria Sêfer, Rua Conselheiro Brotero 986,
01232-010   826-1366
                            Fax: 826-4508

Oitzer Haseforim
Rua Augusta 2299/3   881-3255

Sorocaba

Synagogues

Community Centre
Rua Dom Pedro II 56   31-3168

Bulgaria

Bulgarian Jewry dates from the second century CE when, after the Byzantine conquest, Greek Jews established a congregation in Serdica (now Sofia). After the establishment of the Bulgarian State in 681, Jewish settlement in the country increased, and during the reign of King Ivan Alexander (1331–71) the Jewish community flourished. His Queen was Theodora, a former Jewess whose original name was Sarah.

Rabbi Shalom of Nitra founded the first rabbinical school in Vidin, in 1370. His successor, Rabbi Dosa Ajevani, became famous for his commentary on Rashi. In the middle of the fifteenth century, Ashkenazi Jews driven out of Bavaria settled in Bulgaria and built a synagogue in Sofia. More than 30,000 Jews, expelled from Spain, arrived at the end of the fifteenth century, among them Joseph Caro, the codifier of the Shulchan Aruch. By the end of the 16th century Bulgaria's Sephardi Jews had assimilated the Ashkenazi and other groups.

By the beginning of the Second World War in 1939, there were about 50,000 Jews in Bulgaria. Since 1948, about 45,000 have emigrated to Israel; and today's Jewish population is about 5,000, of whom 3,200 live in Sofia. The others are scattered throughout the rest of the country. It is worth noting that few Jews became victims of the Nazis during the German occupation of Bulgaria in the Second World War, even though the Bulgarian Government was allied to Nazi Germany, thanks to the support of the Bulgarian population.

In the town museum of Nikopol there is a room dedicated to Joseph Caro.

GMT + 2 hours
Country calling code (359)

Pazardjik
Area telephone code (34)

Community Organisations
Community Centre
Asson Zlatarov St. 26   28-364

Plovdiv
Area telephone code (32)

Synagogues
Tsar Kalojan St. 15
In the courtyard of a large apartment complex.

Libraries
Library and House of Culture
Vladimir Zaimov St. 20   761-376

Russe

Area telephone code (82)

Synagogues

Community Centre
Ivan Vazov Sq. 4   270-540

Sofia

Area telephone code (2)

Community Organisations

Social & Cultural Organisation of Bulgarian Jews, Shalom, Alexander Stambolisky St. 50
          870-163

Publishes a periodical 'Evreiski Vesti' and a yearbook. It also maintains a museum devoted to 'The Rescue of Bulgarian Jews, 1941–1944'. At the same address are the offices of El Al, the Joint and the Jewish Agency.

Religious Organisations

Synagogue & Central Jewish Religious Council
Ekzarh Josef St. 16
Above the synagogue is a museum dedicated to the history of Bulgarian Jewry.

Embassy

Embassy of Israel
Seventh floor, NDK Administrative Building, 1 Bulgaria Square

Cemeteries

Jewish Cemetery
Orlandovtzi suburb
Take a tram (Nos. 2, 10 or 14) to the last stop for this large Jewish cemetery.

Canada

Jews played some part in the British military occupation of Canada and a number settled in Montreal at an early date. But in the ten years following the conquest of Quebec in 1759, there were only ten Jews in Canada. A century later, this figure had grown to 1,250. At the end of the nineteenth century, large-scale emigration began from eastern Europe, and many emigrants chose to settle in Canada. Today, the Jewish population is about 356,500. Chief centres are Montreal, Toronto and Vancouver.

GMT – 3 to 8 hours
Country calling code (1)

Alberta

Calgary
Area telephone code (403)

Representative Organisations
B'nai Brith Canada
Western Region, 10655 Southport Rd S.W.,
Suite 1400, T2W 4Y1   225-5256
                              Fax: 278-0176
Calgary Jewish Community Council
1607 90TH Av. S.W.   253-8600
                              Fax: 253-7915
The Council issues a booklet 'Keeping Kosher in Calgary'.

Religious Organisations
Calgary Rabbinical Council   253-8600
                                   Fax: 253-7915

Synagogues

Orthodox
House of Jacob
1613 92nd Av. S.W., T2V 5C9   259-3230

Conservative
Beth Tzedec
1325 Glenmore Trail S.W., T2Y 4Y8   255-8688

Reform
Temple B'nai Tikvah
Calgary Jewish Centre, 1607 90th Av. S.W.,
T2V 4V7   252-1654

Media

Newspapers
Jewish Free Press
Box 72113, 16900 90th Av. S.W., T2V 5H9
                              252-9423
                              Fax: 255-5640

Restaurants
Karen's Cafe
Calgary Jewish Centre, 1607 90th Av. S.W.
                              255-5311
Hours: Sunday to Thursday, 10 am to 7 pm;
Friday, 10 am to 1 pm.

Bakeries
Susan's Kosher Bakery   238-5300

Delicatessens
Schaier's Meat & Kosher Deli
2515 90th Av. S.W.   251-2552
Wolf's Kosher World & Deli
42 180-94 Av. S.E   253-3354
Hours: Sunday to Thursday, 10 am to 8 pm;
Friday, 10 am to 2 pm.

Edmonton
Area telephone code (403)

Representative Organisations
Edmonton Jewish Federation
7200 156th St., T5R 1X3   487-0585
                                  Fax: 481-1854
Contact for additional information.

Synagogues

Beth Israel
10205 119th St., T5K 1Z3   482-2840

Beth Shalom
11916 Jasper Av., T5K 0N9   488-6333

Reform

Temple Beth Ora
7200 156th St., T5R 1X3   487-4817

Media

Newspapers

Edmonton Jewish Life
10342-47 St., T5J 2W2   488-7276
                                      Fax: 487-4342

Edmonton Jewish News
#330, 10036 Jasper Ave, T5J 2W2   421-7966
                                      Fax: 424-3951

Restaurants

Andy's Valleyview IGA
9106 142 St   483 1525

King David Pizza
1195 8770-170 St, West Edmonton Mall
                                      486-9020

Kosher Restaurant at Jewish community centre
7200-156 St, T5R 1X3   444-4460

Butchers

Kosher Mart
14804 Stony Plain Rd, T5N 3S5   453-3988

Delicatessens

Hello Deli, 10725-124 St   454-8527

Lethbridge

Synagogues *(Orthodox)*

Beth Israel
914 15th St. S., T1J 3A5   (403) 327-8621

Medicine Hat

Synagogues *(Orthodox)*

Sons of Abraham
540 5th St. S.E., T1A 1S6   (403) 526-3880

British Columbia

Kelowna

Area telephone code (604)

Synagogues

Traditional

Beth Shalom Sanctuary
OJCC, 108 North Glenmore Road   862-2305
Shabbat services last Saturday of the month, 9:30 am.

Richmond

Synagogues

Orthodox

Eitz Chaim
8080 Frances Road, V6Y 1A4   275-0007
Daily, 7 am; Friday, sunset; Shabbat, 9 am and sunset; Sunday, 9 am. Wheelchair access.

Young Israel Congregation Schaare Tzion
8360 St Albans Road   272-2113
Monday and Thursday, 7 am; Sunday, 9 am; Shabbat, 9:30 am. Wheelchair access.

Conservative

Beth Tikvah
9711 Geal Road, V7E 1R4   271-6262
Friday, 8 pm; Shabbat, 9:30 am. Wheelchair access.

Kashrut Information

Orthodox Rabbinical Council of British Columbia
8080 Francis Road, V6Y 1A4   275-0042
                                      Fax: 277-2225
Kashrut Director, Rabbi A. Feigelstock; Kashrut Administrator: Rabbi Levy Teitlebaum.

Bakeries

Garden City Bakery
#360-9100 Blundell Road   244-7888
Supervision: Orthodox Rabbinical Council of British Columbia.

Surrey – White Rock

Community Organisations

White Rock/South Surrey Jewish Community Centre, PO Box 75186, V4A   541-9995
Monthly Shabbat services. Wheelchair access.

Synagogues

Hasidic

The Centre for Judaism of the Lower Fraser Valley, 2351 128th Street   541-4111
First Friday of each month, kabbalat Shabbat and kiddush, 7 pm; Shabbat, 10 am. Wheelchair access.

Vancouver

Area telephone code (604)

Community Organisations

Jewish Community Centre of Greater Vancouver
950 West 41st Avenue, V5Z 2N7   257-5111

Synagogues

Orthodox

Louis Brier Home
1055 West 41st Avenue, V6M 1W9   261-9376
Daily mincha, 4:30 pm; Friday, 4:15 pm; Shabbat, 9 am. Wheelchair access.

Schara Tzedeck
3476 Oak Street, V6H 2L8   736-7607
Monday and Thursday, 7 am; Tuesday, Wednesday and Friday, 7:15 am; weekdays, sunset; Friday, 7:30 pm; Shabbat, 9 am and half hour before sunset; Sunday, 8:30 am.

Sephardic Orthodox

Beth Hamidrash
3231 Heather Street, V5Z 3K4
                        872-4222; 873-2371
Daily, 7 am; Shabbat, 9 am; Sunday and public holidays, 8:30 am; Friday, 5 pm; Shabbat, sunset.

Hasidic

Chabad-Lubavitch
5750 Oak Street, V6M 2V9   266-1313
Daily, 7 am and sunset; Shabbat, 10 am; Sunday, 9 am. Wheelchair access.

Conservative

Beth Israel
4350 Oak Street, V6H 2N4   731-4161
Daily, 8 am (public holidays, 9 am) and 6 pm; Friday, 8:15 pm; Shabbat, 9:15 am and 6 pm; Sunday, 9 am and 6 pm. Wheelchair access.

Har El
North Shore, JCC, 1305 Taylor Way, V7V 1Y8, West Vancouver   922-8245
Friday, 7 pm; Shabbat, 10 am.

Traditional

Burquest Jewish Community
                        526-7235
Oneg Shabbat services second Friday of each month, 8 pm. Wheelchair access.

Shaarey Tefilah
785 West 16th Avenue   873-2700
Friday evening, call for time; Shabbat and Sunday, 9 am. Wheelchair access.

Reform

Temple Sholom
7190 Oak Street, V6P 3Z9   266-7190
Monday and Wednesday, 7:15 am; Friday, 8:15 pm; Shabbat, 10 am.

Jewish Renewal

Or Shalom
710 East 10th Avenue, V5T 2A7   872-1614
Wednesday, 7 am; family kabbalat Shabbat and potluck dinner once a month, 6 pm; Shabbat, 10 am. Wheelchair access.

Contact Information

Jewish Federation of Greater Vancouver
950 West 41st Avenue, V5Z 2N7   257-5100
Executive Director Drew Staffenberg

Shalom Vancouver
950 West 41st Avenue, V5Z 2N7   257-5111
                        Fax: 257-5121
Jewish Information Referral & Welcome Service for newcomers and visitors. Publishes a 'Guide to Jewish life in British Columbia'. Co-ordinator Janet Kolof.

Media

Newspapers

Jewish Bulletin
#203-873 Beatty Street, V6B 2M6   689-1520
                        Fax: 689-1525

Restaurants

Aviv Kosher Meats
1011 West 49th Avenue   261-2727
Supervision: Orthodox Rabbinical Council of
British Columbia.
Fresh meats, poultry, sandwiches, pastries,
cakes and breads. Eat in, take out and
catering. Hours: Monday to Thursday, 8 am to
8 pm; Friday, 7 am to 3 pm; Sunday, 8 am to
3 pm.

Cohen's Gourmet
4054 Cambie Street   879-9044
Fresh kosher, vegetarian, dairy dishes and
gourmet pizza. Dine in or take out. Hours:
Monday to Thursday, 8 am to 8 pm; Friday, 8
am to 5 pm; Shabbat closed; Sunday, 11 am
to 8 pm.

Omnitsky Kosher B.C.
5866 Cambie Street   321-1818
Supervision: Orthodox Rabbinical Council of
British Columbia.
Fresh meats, poultry. Manufacturers of all beef
delicatessen products under B.C.K.

Bakeries

Sabra
3844 Oak Street, V6H 2M5   733-4912
Fax: 733-4911
Supervision: Orthodox Rabbinical Council of
British Columbia.
Fresh kosher cookies, muffins, falafel, salads
and more items. Take-out, eat-in and catering.
Dairy, pareve (meat is take-out only). Hours:
Monday to Thursday, 8:30 am to 8 pm; Friday,
8:30 am to 2 pm; Sunday, 10 am to 6:30 pm.

Cafeterias

Cafe Sabra Too (Jewish Community Centre)
950 West 41st Avenue, V5Z 2N7   257-5111
Supervision: Orthodox Rabbinical Council of
British Columbia.
Fresh kosher cookies, muffins, falafel, salads
and more items. Take-out, eat-in and catering.
Dairy, pareve (meat is take-out only). Hours:
Monday to Thursday, 8:30 am to 8 pm; Friday,
8:30 am to 2 pm; Sunday, 10 am to 6:30 pm.

Victoria
Area telephone code (250)

Synagogues (Conservative)

Emanu-El
1461 Blanshard, V8W 2J3   382-0615
Thursday, 7 am; Shabbat, 9 am. Wheelchair
access.

Manitoba

Winnipeg
Area telephone code (204)

Community Organisations

Winnipeg Jewish Community Council
200-370 Hargrave Street, R3B 2K1   943-0406
Fax: 956-0609

Cultural Organisations

Jewish Historical Society of Western Canada
404-365 Hargrave Street, R3B 2K3   942-4822
Fax: 942-9299

Mikvaot

Mikva Chabad-Lubavitch
455 Hartford Avenue, R2V 0W9   339-4761

Kashrut Information

Vaad Ha'Ir
370 Hargrave Street, R3B 2K1   949-9180
Fax: 956-0609
The Vaad Ha'Ir will be pleased to give
information about kashrut.

Media

Newspapers

Jewish Post & News
117 Hutchings Street, R2X 2V4   694-3332
Fax: 694-3916
Jewish Radio Hour Weekly – Sundays, at
1:30pm. Yiddish TV, Channel 11.

Restaurants

Y.M.H.A. Jewish Community Centre
370 Hargrave Street, R3B 2K1   946-5257
Kosher café.

Bakeries

City Bread
238 Dufferin Avenue, R2W 2X6   586-8409

Goodies' Bake Shop
2 Donald Street, R3L 0K5   489-5526

Gunn's
247 Selkirk Avenue, R2W 2L5   582-2364

Miracle Bakery
1385 Main Street, R2W 3T9   586-6140

Butchers

Omnitsky's
1428 Main Street, R2W 3V4   586-8271

Tuxedo Quality Foods
1853 Grant Avenue, R3N 1Z2   987-3830

Groceries

Bathurst Street Market
1570 Main Street, R2W 5J8   338-4911

Libraries

Jewish Public Library
1725 Main Street, R2V 1Z4   338-4048

Theatre

Winnipeg Jewish Theatre
504-365 Hargrave Street, R3B 2K3   943-3222
Fax: 949-1739

New Brunswick

Fredericton

Area telephone code (506)

Synagogues

Orthodox

Sgoolai Israel
Westmoreland Street, E3B 3L7   454-9698
Mikva on premises.

Moncton

Area telephone code (506)

Synagogues

Tiferes Israel
56 Steadman Street, E1C 4P4   858-0258
Mikva on premises.

Saint John

Area telephone code (506)

Synagogues

Conservative

Shaarei Zedek
76 Carleton Street, E2L 2Z4   657-4790
Community centre on premises as well.

Museums

Jewish Historical Museum
29 Wellington Row, E2L 3H4   633-1833

Newfoundland

St John's

Area telephone code (709)

Synagogues

Conservative

Hebrew Congregation of Newfoundland & Labrador (Beth El)
122-126 Elizabeth Avenue,
PO Box 724, A1C 5L4   737-6548
Fax: 737-6995

Nova Scotia

Glace Bay

Area telephone code (902)

Synagogues (Orthodox)

1 Prince Street, B1A 3C8   849-8605

Halifax

Area telephone code (902)

Community Organisations

Atlantic Jewish Council
1515 S. Park Street, Suite 304, B3J 2L2
      422-7491
Also at this address: Canadian Jewish
Congress, Canadian Zionist Federation, United
Israel Appeal, ORT, Young Judea, B'nai B'rith,
Hadassah, Jewish National Fund, Atlantic
Provinces Jewish Student Federation and
Chabad Lubavitch.

Synagogues

Orthodox

Beth Israel
1480 Oxford Street, B3H 3Y8   422-1301
Mikva on premises.

Conservative

Shaar Shalom
1981 Oxford Street, B3H 4A4   423-5848

Media

Newspapers

Shalom Magazine, 1515 S. Park Street, Suite
305, B3J 2L2   422-7491
      Fax: 425-3722

Sydney

Area telephone code (902)

Synagogues

Conservative

Temple Sons of Israel, P.O. Box 311, Whitney
Avenue, B1P 6H2   564-4650

Yarmouth

Contact Information

R & V Indiq
13 Parade Street, B5A 3A5
Will be happy to provide details of the local
Jewish Community.

Ontario

Belleville

Area telephone code (613)

Synagogues

Conservative

Sons of Jacob
211 Victoria Avenue, K8N 2C2   962-1433

Brantford

Area telephone code (519)

Synagogues

Orthodox

Beth David
50 Waterloo Street, N3T 3R8   752-8950

Chatham

Synagogues

Conservative

Children of Jacob
29 Water Street, N7M 3H4   352-3544

Cornwall

Area telephone code (613)

Synagogues

Beth-El, 321 Amelia Street, K6H 3P4 932-6373

Guelph
Area telephone code (519)

Synagogues
Traditional
Beth Isaiah
47 Surrey Street W., N1H 3R5   836-4338

Hamilton
Area telephone code (905)

Representative Organisations
Hamilton Jewish Federation
1030 Lower Lions Club Road, P.O. Box 7258,
L9G 3N6, Ancaster   648-0605
                    Fax: 648-8350

Synagogues
Orthodox
Adas Israel
125 Cline Avenue S., L8S 1X1   528-0039

Conservative
Beth Jacob
375 Aberdeen Avenue, L8P 2R7   522-1351

Reform
Anshe Sholom
215 Cline Avenue N., L8S 4A1   528-0121

Media
Newspapers
Hamilton Jewish News
P.O. Box 7528, L9G 3N6, Ancaster   648-0605
                    Fax: 648-8388

Butchers
Hamilton Kosher Meats
889 King Street West, L8S 1K5

Delicatessens
Westdale Deli
893 King Street West, L8S 1K5   529-2605

Kingston
Area telephone code (613)

Community Organisations
B'nai B'rith Hillel Foundation
26 Barrie Street   542-1120

Synagogues
Orthodox
Beth Israel
116 Centre Street, K7L 4E6   542-5012

Reform
Temple Iyr Hamelech
331 Union Street West, K7L 2R3   789-7022

Kitchener
Area telephone code (519)

Synagogues
Traditional
Beth Jacob
161 Stirling Avenue S., N2G 3N8   743-8422

Reform
Temple Shalom
116 Queen Street North, N2H 2H7   743-0401

London
Area telephone code (519)

Community Organisations
Jewish Community Council
536 Huron Street, N5Y 4J5   673-3310
          Email: ljf@icis.on.ca
Communal inquiries to Executive Director at
the above number.

Synagogues
Orthodox
Beth Tefilah, 1210 Adelaide Street North, N5Y
4T6   433-7081
Mikva on premises.

Conservative
Congregation Or Shalom
534 Huron Street, N5Y 4J5   438-3081
                    Fax: 439-2994

Reform
Temple Israel
651 Windermere Road, N5X 2P1   858-4400

Media
Newspapers
London Jewish Community News
536 Huron Street, N5Y 4J5   673-3310
Fax: 673-1161
There are no kosher establishments, but kosher frozen meat, prepared foods and select groceries are available at local A&P and IGA Loeb Stores.

Mississauga
Area telephone code (905)

Synagogues
Reform
Solel Congregation
2399 Folkway Drive, L5L 2M6   820-5915

Niagara Falls
Area telephone code (416)

Synagogues *(Conservative)*
B'nai Jacob
5328 Ferry Street, L2G 1R7   354-3934

North Bay
Area telephone code (705)

Synagogues *(Orthodox)*
Sons of Jacob
302 McIntyre Street West, P1B 2Z1   474-2170

Oakville
Area telephone code (905)

Synagogues
Reform
Shaarei-Beth El
186 Morrison Road, L6L 4J4   845-0837

Oshawa

Synagogues
Orthodox
Beth Zion
144 King Street East, L1H 1B6   723-2353

Ottawa
Area telephone code (613)

Religious Organisations
Vaad Ha'ir (Jewish Community Council)
151 Chapel Street, K1N 7Y2   232-7306
Fax: 563-4593
Vaad Hakashruth located here for all kashrut information.

Embassy
Embassy of Israel
Suite 1005, 50 O'Connor Street, K1P 6L2

Restaurants
JCC Drop in Diner
151 Chapel Street, K1N 7Y2   789-1818
Tuesdays, 12 pm to 1:30 pm.

Bakeries
Rideau Bakery
1666 Bank St   737-3355
Rideau Bakery
384 Rideau St   234-1019
Kosher bread and other products are available in both branches.

Butchers
United Kosher Meat & Deli Ltd
378 Richmond Road   722-6556
Kosher meals and sandwiches available on weekdays.

Owen Sound
Area telephone code (519)

Synagogues *(Conservative)*
Beth Ezekiel
3531 Bay Shore Road, N4K 5N3   376-8774

Pembroke

Area telephone code (613)

Synagogues

Beth Israel
322 William Street, K8A 1P3   732-7811

Peterborough

Area telephone code (705)

Synagogues

Conservative
Beth Israel
Waller Street   745-8398

Richmond Hill

Area telephone code (905)

Synagogues

Beth Rayim
9711 Bayview Avenue, L4C 9X7   770-7639
The Country Shul
Carville Road and Bathurst Street   770-4191

St Catharine's

Area telephone code (416)

Community Organisations

Community Centre
Newman Memorial Building   685-6767

Synagogues

Traditional
B'nai Israel
190 Church Street, L2R 4C4   685-6767
Fax: 685-3100

Reform
Temple Tikvah
83 Church Street, PO Box 484, L2R 3C7
682-4191

Sudbury

Area telephone code (705)

Synagogues

Orthodox
Shaar Hashomayim
158 John Street, P3E 1P4   673-0831

Thornhill

Area telephone code (905)

Restaurants

Dairy
Cafe Sheli
441 Clark Avenue West, L4J 6W7   886-7450
King David Pizza North
7000 Bathurst Street, L4J 7L1   669-0660
My Zaidy's Cafe
7241 Bathurst Street, L4J 6J8   731-3831
My Zaidy's Pizza North
441 Clark Avenue, L4J 6W8   731-3029
Not Just Yoghurt
800 Steeles Avenue West, L4J 7L2   738-1322

Delicatessens
Marky's Delicatessen North
7330 Yonge Street, L4J 1V8   731-4800
Wok'n'Deli
441 Clarke Avenue West, L4J 6W7   882-0809

Booksellers
Israel's Judaica Centre
441 Clark Avenue West, L4J 6W7   881-1010
Matana Judaica, 248 Steeles Avenue West,
#6, L4J 1A1   731-6543
Fax: 882-6196

Thunder Bay

Area telephone code (807)

Synagogues

Orthodox
Shaarey Shomayim
627 Gray Street, P7E 2E4   622-4867

Toronto

Area telephone code (416/905)

Community Organisations

Bernard Betal Centre
1003 Steeles Avenue W., M2R 3T6   225-2112
Has two separate minyanim: Beth Joseph and
Tehilla Yerushalayim.

Jewish Federation of Greater Toronto
4600 Bathurst Street, M2R 3V2, North York
635-2883

Religious Organisations

JEP/Ohr Somayach Centre
2939 Bathurst Street, M6B 2B2   785-5899
Has a minyan.

Rabbinical Vaad Hakashrut
4600 Bathurst Street, M2R 3V2   635-9550
All enquiries about kashrut here.

Contact Information

Jewish Information Services
4600 Bathurst Street, Suite 345, M2R 3V2,
Willowdale   635-5600
    Fax: 631-5715
Publishes a Jewish Community of Services
Directory for Greater Toronto.

Embassy

Consulate General
180 Bloor Street West, Suite 700, M5S 2V6
961-1126
Israel Government Tourist Office   964-3784.

Media

Newspapers

Canadian Jewish News, 10 Gateway Blvd,
Suite 420, M3C 3A1, Don Mills   422-2331
    Fax: 422-3790
Jewish Tribune, 15 Hove Street, M3H 4Y8,
Downsview   633-6227
    Fax: 630-2159

Restaurants

Chicken Nest
3038 Bathurst Street, M6B 4K2   787-6378
Hakerem, 1045 Steeles Avenue West, M2R
2S9, Willowdale   736-7227

King Solomon's Table, 3710 Chesswood
Drive, M3J 2W4, Downsview   630-0666
Kosher Facilities, York University, 4700 Keele
Street, M3Y 1P3, Downsview   736-5965
Kosher Hut
3428 Bathurst Street, M6A 2C2   787-7999

Dairy

Brooklyn Pizza
3028 Bathurst Street, M6B 3B6   256-1477
Dairy Treats Cafe
3522 Bathurst Street, M6A 2C6   787-0309
King David Pizza
3020 Bathurst Street, M6B 2B6   781-1326
Milk'n Honey, 3457 Bathurst Street, M6A 2C5,
Downsview   789-7651
My Zaidy's Pizza
3456 Bathurst Street, Willowdale   789-0785
Tovli Pizza, 5792 Bathurst Street, M2R 1Z1,
Willowdale   650-9800

Bakeries

Bagels Galore
First Canadian Place, M5X 1E1   363-4233

Delicatessens

Marky's Delicatessen
280 Wilson Avenue, Downsview   638-1081
Mati's Fallafel House
3430 Bathurst Street, M6A 1C2   783-9505
Sells dairy products only.

Memorials

Holocaust Education & Memorial Centre
4600 Bathurst Street, M2R 3V2, Willowdale
635-2883

Booksellers

Israel's Judaica Centre, 897 Eglinton Avenue
West, M6C 2C1   256-2858
Miriam's, 3007 Bathurst Street   781-8261
Negev Importing Co Ltd
3509 Bathurst Street, M6A 2C5   781-9356
Pardes Hebrew Book Shop
4119 Bathurst Street   633-7113
Zucker's Books & Art, 3453 Bathurst Street

Windsor

Area telephone code (519)

Community Organisations

Jewish Community Council
1641 Ouellette Avenue, N8X 1K9   973-1772

Synagogues

Orthodox

Shaar Hashomayim
115 Giles Blvd East, N9A 4C1   256-3123

Shaarey Zedek
610 Giles Blvd East, N9A 4E2   252-1594

Reform

Congregation Beth-El
2525 Mark Avenue, N9E 2W2   969-2422

Media

Periodicals

Windsor Jewish Community Bulletin
Fax: 973-1774

Quebec

Montreal

Area telephone code (514)

Representative Organisations

Canadian Jewish Congress National Headquarters
Samuel Bronfman House, 1590 Docteur
Penfield Avenue, H3G 1C5   931-7531
Fax: 931-3281
Publishes the National Synagogue Directory.
Contact to find out which of the many
synagogues in Montreal is nearest you.

Community Organisations

Federation CJA
5151 ch. de la Côte Ste-Catherine, H3W 1M6
735-3541
Operates the Jewish Information and Referral
Service (JIRS), Tel: 737-2221.

Jewish Community Council, 5491 Victoria
Avenue, Suite 117, H3W 2P9   739-6363

Fax: 739-7024
Visitors requiring additional information about
kosher establishments should contact the
Vaad Ha'ir at the above numbers. Also apply
to them for a list of kosher butchers, bakeries
and caterers.

Embassy

Consulate General
1155 Boulevard Rene Levesque Ouest, Suite
2620, H3B 4S5

Media

Newspapers

Canadian Jewish News
6900 Decarie Blvd, #341, H3X 2T8   735-2612

Restaurants

**B'nai B'rith Hillel Foundation/Yossi's
Dizengoff Café,** 3460 Stanley St   845-9171
Fax: 842-6405
Email: hillel@vir.com
Supervision: Vaad Hair.
Hours: Daily, 11 am to 6 pm.

Chabad House, 3429 Peel Street   842-6616
Supervision: Vaad Hair.

Ernie's & Elie's Place
6900 Decarie Blvd, H3X 2T8   842-6616
Supervision: Vaad Hair.

Foxy's, 5987A Victoria Avenue   739-8777
Supervision: Vaad Hair.

Golden Age Cafeteria
5700 Westbury Avenue, H3W 3E8   739-4731
Supervision: Vaad Hair.

Golden Spoon (Cuiller d'or)
5217 Decarie Blvd   481-3431
Supervision: Vaad Hair.

Kotel
1422 Stanley Street, H3W 3E8   739-4731
Supervision: Vaad Hair.

Kotel Restaurant
3429 Peel Street   987-9875
Supervision: Vaad Hair.

L'Elysee Dame, 70 Notre Dame   842-6016
Supervision: Vaad Hair.

Odelia Snack Bar
5897A Victoria Avenue   733-0984
Supervision: Vaad Hair.

Y.M.H.A. Cafeteria
5500 Westbury Avenue   737-8704
Supervision: Vaad Hair.

Meat

El Morocco II
3450 Drummond Street   844-6888; 844-0203
Supervision: Vaad Hair.
Open for lunch and dinner until 10 pm.
Located downtown near hotels and boutiques.

Le Passeport
5071 Queen Mary, H3W 1X4   733-4768
Supervision: Vaad Hair.

Dairy

La Casa Linga
5095 Queen Mary, H3W 1X4   737-2272
Supervision: Vaad Hair.

Pizza Pita, 5710 Victoria Avenue   731-7482
Supervision: Vaad Hair.
Also at 2145 St Louis Ville St Laurent

Libraries

Jewish Public Library
5151 Côte Ste-Catherine Road, H3W 1M6
                                                345-2627
There are also branches in other parts of
Montreal.

Booksellers

Kotel
6414 Victoria Avenue, H3W 2S6   739-4142

**Rabbi J. Rodal's Hebrew Book Store
& Gift Shop**
5689 Van Horne Avenue, H3W 1H8   733-1876

Victoria Gift Shop
5875 Victoria Avenue, H3W 2R6   738-1414

Quebec City

Area telephone code (418)

Synagogues

Beth Israel Ohev Sholom
20 Cremazie Street East, G1R 1Y2   523-7346

Ste. Agathe-des-Monts

Area telephone code (819)

Synagogues

House of Israel Congregation
31 Albert Street, J8C 1Z6   326-4320

Saskatchewan

Moose Jaw

Area telephone code (306)

Synagogues

Conservative

Moose Jaw Hebrew Congregation
937 Henry Street, S6H 3H1   692-1644

Regina

Area telephone code (306)

Synagogues

Orthodox

Beth Jacob
4715 McTavish Street, S4S 6H2   757-8643
                                  Fax: 352-3499

Reform

Temple Beth Tikvah, Box 33048, Cathedral
Post Office, S4T 7X2   761-2218

Saskatoon

Area telephone code (306)

Synagogues

Conservative

Agudas Israel
715 McKinnon Avenue, S7H 6H2   343-7023
                                  Fax: 343-1244
Rabbi R. Pavey, 343-6960, will be pleased to
welcome visitors.

Cayman Islands

GMT – 5 hours

Country calling code (1345)

Grand Cayman

Contact Information

Harvey DeSouza
P.O. Box 72, Grand Cayman, Cayman Islands,
British West Indies

Chile

The Jewish population is 22,000, of whom the great majority live in Santiago, the capital, and its environs.

GMT – 4 hours
Country calling code (56)

Arica
Area telephone code (80)

Community Organisations
Sociedad Israelita Dr Herzl, Casilla 501

Concepción
Area telephone code (41)

Community Organisations
Communidad Israelita, 111

Iquique
Area telephone code (81)

Community Organisations
Comunidad Israelita
Playa Ligade 3263, Playa Brava

La Serena
Area telephone code (51)

Community Organisations
Community Centre
Cordovez 652

Rancagua

Community Organisations
Comunidad Israelita, Casilla 890

Santiago
Area telephone code (2)

Representative Organisations
Communal Headquarters (Comite Representativo de las Entidades Judias de Chile)
Miguel Claro 196   235-8669

Synagogues

Orthodox
Bicur Joilim
Av. Matte 624

Jabad Lubavitch
Gloria 62, Las Condes   228-2240

Jafets Jayim
Miguel Claro 196

Ashkenazi
Comunidad Israelita de Santiago
Serrano 214-218   639-387

German
Sociedad Cultural Israelita B'ne Jisroel
Portugal 810   221-993

Hungarian
Maze, Pedro Bannen 0166   274-2536

Sephardi
Maguen David
Av. R. Lyon 812

Embassy
Embassy of Israel
San Sebastian 2812, Casilla 1224   246-1570

Restaurants
La Idishe Mama
M. montt 1273, Esquina Bilbao   209-8131
Kosher style.

Temuco
Area telephone code (45)

Community Organisations
Comunidad Israelita
General Cruz 355

Valparaiso
Area telephone code (32)

Community Organisations
Comunidad Israelita
Alvarez 490, Vina del Mar   680-373

Valdivia

Community Organisations
Community Centre
Arauco 136 E.

Colombia

GMT – 5 hours
Country calling code (57)

Baranquilla
Area telephone code (53)

Community Organisations
Centro Israelita Filantropico
Carrera 43, No 85-95, Apartado Aereo 2537
342-310; 351-197
Comunidad Hebrea Sefaradita
Carrera 55, No 74-71, Apartado Aereo 51351
340-054; 340-050

Bogota
Area telephone code (1)

Religious Organisations
Union Rabinica Colombiana
Tranversal 29, No 126-31 274-9069; 218-2500

Synagogues
Congregacion Adath Israel
Carrera 7a, No 94-20   257-1660; 257-1680
Mikva on premises.

Orthodox
Comunidad Hebrea Sefaradi
Calle 79, No 9-66   256-2629; 249-0372
Mikva on premises.

Jabad House
Calle 92, No 10, Apt. 405   36408
Rabbi's Tel: 257-4920

Ashkenazi
Centro Israelita de Bogota
Transversal 29, No 126-31   274-9069
Kosher meals available by prior arrangement
with Rabbi Goldschmidt, 218-2500.

German
Asociacion Israelita Montefiore
Carrera 20, No 37-54   245-5264

Embassy
Embassy of Israel
Calle 35, No 7-25, Edificio Caxdax
245-6603; 245-6712

Media
Monthly
Menorah, Apartado Aereo 9081

Cali
Area telephone code (2)

Representative Organisations
Union Federal Hebrea
Apartado Aereo 8918   443-1814
Fax: 444-5544
An umbrella organisation co-ordinating all
Jewish activities in Cali.

Synagogues
Ashkenazi
Sociedad Hebrea de Socoros
Av. 9a Norte # 10-15, Apartado Aereo 011652
668-8518
Fax: 668-8521

German
Union Cultural Israelita
Apartado Aereo 5552   668-9830
Fax: 661-6857

Sephardi
Centro Israelita de Beneficiencia
Calle 44a, Av. 5a Norte Esquina, Apartado
Aereo 77   664-1379
Fax: 665-5419

Medellin
Area telephone code (4)

Community Organisations
Union Israelita de Beneficencia
Carrera 43B, No 15-150, Apartado Aereo 4702
668-560

Costa Rica

GMT – 6 hours
Country calling code (506)

San Jose

Contact Information

Centro Israelita Sionista de Costa Rica
Calle 22 y 22, Apdo 1473-1000   233-9222
Fax: 233-9321

Embassy

Embassy of Israel
Calle 2, Avenidas 2 y 4, 5147
216-011; 216-444

Groceries

Little Israel Pita Rica
Frente a Shell, Pavas   290-2083
Fax: 296-4802
The only mini-market in Costa Rica.

Hotels

Barcelo San Jose Palacio
Apdo 458-1150   220-2034; 220-2035
Fax: 220-2036
Email: Palacio@sol.racsa.co.cr
Hotel has separated kosher kitchen and its key
in the mashgiach's (Rabbi Levkovitz) hands.
The hotel is about a half hour walk to the
synagogue.

Camino Real
Autopista Prospero Fernandez y Blvd, Apdo
11856-1000   289-7000
Fax: 289-8930
Email: caminoreal@ticonet.co.cr
Hotel has new separated kosher kitchen, with
the key in the mashgiach's (Rabbi Levkovitz)
hands.

Melia Confort Corobici
PO Box 2443-1000   232-8122
Fax: 231-5834
Email: corobici@sol.racsa.co.cr
There is no separate kosher kitchen, but it is
fairly close to the Orthodox synagogue.

Croatia

GMT + 1 hour
Country calling code (385)

Dubrovnik
Area telephone code (20)

Synagogues

Zudioska Street 3
Zudioska means 'Street of the Jews'. This is the second oldest synagogue in Europe and is located in a very narrow street off the main street – the Stradun or Placa. The Jewish community office is in the same building. Zudiosla Street is the third turning on the right from the town clock tower. There are about 30 Jews in the city. Tourists help to make up a minyan in the synagogue on Friday night and High Holy Days.

Osijek
Area telephone code (31)

Community Organisations

Brace Radica Street 13   24-926
The community building contains objects from the synagogue that was destroyed during the Second World War. The community numbers about 150 members and has two cemeteries. No regular services are held. A former building of the second pre-war synagogue in Cvjetkova Street is a Pentecostal church today. There is a plaque at the site of the destroyed synagogue in Zupanijska Street.

Rijeka
Area telephone code (51)

Synagogues

Filipovica Street 9, PO Box 65   425-156
The community numbers about 150. Services are held in the well maintained synagogue on Jewish holidays.

Split
Area telephone code (21)

Community Organisations

Zidovski Prolaz 1   45-672
The synagogue at Split is one of the few in Yugoslavia to have survived the wartime occupation. The Jewish community numbers about 200. There is a Jewish cemetery, established in 1578. More information from the community offices at the above number.

Zagreb
Area telephone code (1)

Community Organisations

Federation of the Jewish Community
Palmoticeva Street 16, PO Box 986   434-619
                                   Fax: 434-638
Before the war Zagreb had 11,000 Jews. There are now only about 1,500, but they remain very active in Jewish communal life. Services are held in the community building on Friday evenings and holidays.

Media

Books
Voice of the Jewish Communities of Croatia
                    Email: JCZ@OLEH.SRCE.HR

Monuments
Central Synagogue
Praska Street 7
There is a plaque on the spot of this pre-war synagogue.
Mirogoj Cemetery
There is an impressive monument in this cemetery to the Jewish victims of the Second World War.

Cuba

GMT – 5 hours
Country calling code (53)

Havana
Area telephone code (7)

Synagogues

Orthodox
Hadath Israel
Calle Picota 52, Habana Vieja   61-3495

Conservative
Patronado de la Casa de la Comunidad Hebrea de Cuba
Calle 13 e I, Vedado   32-8953
Modern community centre as well.

Reform
The United Hebrew Congregation
Av. de los Presidentes 502
The Jewish cemetery is at Guanabacoa.

Santiago de Cuba
Area telephone code (22/226)

Synagogues

The synagogue in Santiago de Cuba was recently re-dedicated and the community numbers 85.

Cyprus

GMT + 2 hours
Country calling code (357)

Nicosia
Area telephone code (2)

Community Organisations
Committee of the Jewish Community of Cyprus
PO Box 4784   427-982
Contact Mrs Z. Yeshurun for information.

Embassy
Embassy of Israel
4 Grypari Street

Czech Republic

The beautiful buildings of the ancient Jewish quarter of Old Prague are a monument to what was once a great and flourishing Jewish community. The Jews of Prague have been in the Czech capital for close on 1,000 years and elsewhere in Bohemia almost as long. Between the 16th and 18th centuries, Prague Jewry enjoyed its 'golden age.' One of the largest and most important communities in Europe, the Prague community lived in an extensive and self-contained Jewish quarter (Judenstadt).

Its ancient synagogues, two with regular religious services, two belonging to the Jewish community in Prague, the others forming part of the Jewish Museum, its scholars, its Hebrew printing press, its Jewish craft guilds, its communal institutions, lent added lustre to an already illustrious part of the Jewish people.

In 1745, however, the Jews were exiled from Prague and allowed to return only three years later, on payment of exorbitant taxes. Full equality was granted to Prague Jews in 1848, and the ghetto later abolished.

When the Republic of Czechoslovakia was formed in 1918, after the First World War, it became the first country in the world to recognise Jewish nationality. By 1935, there were an estimated 150,000 Jews in Slovakia, 120,000 (including 40,000 refugees from Nazi Germany) in Bohemia and Moravia, and 105,000 in Ruthenia (now part of the Ukraine). The German occupation in 1939 spelt the end for the 375,000 Jews of Czechoslovakia. Some managed to emigrate, but many were rounded up by the Nazis and killed in concentration camps. The names of all 77,297 Bohemian and Moravian Jews who died in the camps were engraved on the inside walls of the famous old Pinkas Synagogue in Prague's Jewish quarter. (The synagogue, now part of the Jewish Museum, is being rebuilt.) By 1968, the 25,000 Jews still in Czechoslovakia in 1945, the end of the Second World War, had dwindled to 18,000 or so. According to the Federation of Jewish Communities in the Czech Republic, there are some 10,000 Jews in Czechoslovakia today, of whom 6,000 live in the Czech Republic.

There are ten communities in Bohemia and Moravia in the regional cities of Prague, Plzen, Karlovy Vary, Dêcin, Ústinad Labem, Teplice, Liberec, Brno, Olomouc and Ostrava. There is a kosher kitchen in Prague supervised by the Chief Rabbi and there are plans to open kosher restaurants in Karlovy Vary and Brno.

GMT + 1 hour
Country calling code (420)

Tour Operators

ITS, 546-550 Royal Exchange, Old Bank Street,
Manchester, M2 7EN   (0161) 839-1111
                    Fax: (0161) 839-0000
          Group Hotline: (0161) 839-2222
          Email: all@its-travel.u-net.com
Have put together a tour including Vienna,
Prague, Brno, Cracow, Budapest, Bratislava,
Sopron and Eisenstadt.

LestAir Services, 1 The Grove, Edgware,
Middlesex, HA8 9QA   (0181) 958-9340
                    Fax: (0181) 958-1212
Run Jewish Heritage Tours for Belarus, Czech
Republic, Germany, Hungary, Lithuania,
Poland and the Ukraine.

Boskovice

Sites

Medieval Ghetto
17th century synagogue and Jewish cemetery.

Brno

Area telephone code (5)

Community Organisations

Community Centre
Kpt. Jarose 3   21-5710
The community president can be reached at
77-3233.

Synagogues

Skorepka 13

Holesov

Museums

Schach Synagogue
Dating from 1650, this synagogue is now a
museum. Open in the mornings. At other
times the curator will show visitors around, if
contacted. The old cemetery is close by.

Karlovy Vary
(Karlsbad)

Area telephone code (17)

Synagogues

Community Centre
Masaryka 39
Services, Friday evening and Shabbat morning.

Liberec (Reichenberg)

Area telephone code (48)

Synagogues

Community Centre
Slavickova 5   24341; 24470

Mikulov (Nikolsburg)

Sites

Only one synagogue, still being restored,
remains of the many which flourished here
when the town was the spiritual capital of
Moravian Jewry and the seat of the Chief
Rabbis of Moravia. The cemetery contains the
graves of famous rabbis.

Olomouc

Area telephone code (68)

Synagogues

Community Centre
Komenskeho 7   522-3119

Ostrava

Area telephone code (69)

Synagogues

Community Centre
Ceskobratrska 17   611-2389

Plzen *(Pilsen)*
Area telephone code (19)

Synagogues
Community Centre
Smetanovy Sady 5   723-5749
Services Friday evenings. The Great Synagogue is now closed.

Prague
Area telephone code (2)

Contact Information
Jewish Town Hall
Maislova 18, 1
Houses the Federation of Jewish Communities in the Czech Republic as well as the Shalom restaurant.

Embassy
Embassy of Israel
Badeniho Street 2, 7

Restaurants
Metzada, Michalska 16, 1   2421-3418
                  Fax: 2421-3418
Supervision: Chief Rabbi of Prague.
Hours: 8:30 am to midnight. Upmarket restaurant, meat served upstairs, dairy downstairs.
Shalom, Maislova 18, 1   2481-0929
Supervision: Chief Rabbi of Prague.
Hours: 11:30 am to 8 pm; January to March, 12 pm to 2 pm. Serves dinner Friday night. Meals for Shabbat have to be ordered and paid for in advance at the community's official travel agency.

Groceries
Kosher Shop
Brehova 5, 1   232-4729
Osem products are available at K-mart at Ovecnytrh.

Hotels
Hotel Intercontinental
Extremely close to the Jewish Quarter (for visitors who do not want to do too much walking on Shabbat).

Museums
Jewish Museum
Jachymova 3

Tours
Heritage Tours   472-1068

Wittmann Tours
Uruguayská 7, 2

Travel Agencies
Matana Travel Agency
Maiselova 15, 1   232-1049

Teplice *(Teplitz-Schönau)*
Area telephone code (417)

Synagogues
Community Centre
Lipova 25   26-580

Terezin *(Theresienstadt)*

Museums
There is a new museum in the town dedicated to the Jews who were deported from Theresienstadt to Auschwitz. There is also a cemetery in which 11,250 individual and 217 mass graves and the crematorium are placed: 34,000 people died in Terezin.

Usti Nad Labem *(Aussig)*
Area telephone code (47)

Synagogues
Community Centre
Moskevska 26   520-8082

Denmark

There are 8,000 Jews in Denmark today, nearly all of whom live in Copenhagen. A small community of Israelis, Poles and others has been formed in Aarhus.

The Royal Library (Amiliegaden 38, Copenhagen) houses a Jewish collection including the famous 'Bibliotheca Simonseniana' and part of the library of the late Professor Lazarus Goldschmidt. The library has a Jewish Department under the direction of Ulf Haxen. In the Liberty Museum there is a special division devoted to the Resistance Movement, and also a section dealing with 'The Persecution of the Jews'.

GMT + 1 hour
Country calling code (45)

Copenhagen

Community Organisations

Jewish Community Centre
Ny Kongensgade 6, 1472   3312-8868
                                Fax: 3312-3357

Synagogues

12 Krystalgade, 1172
Daily and Shabbat services.
9 Oestbaneg, 2100   3526-3540
                                Fax: 3929-2517

Orthodox

Machsike Hadass
Ole suhrsgade 12, 1354   3315-3117
Holds regular daily and Shabbat services.

Mikvaot

12 Krystalgade, 1172   3393-7662; 3332-9443
Jewish Community Centre
Ny Kongensgade 6, 1472   3312-8868
                                Fax: 3312-3357

Embassy

Embassy of Israel
Lundevangsvej 4, Hellerup, 2900   3962-6288

Bakeries

Mrs Heimann   3332-9443

Butchers

I. A. Samson
Rorholmsgade 3   3313-0077
                                Fax: 3314-8277

Kosher Delikatesse
87 Lyngbyvej, 2100   3118-5777

Hornbaek

Synagogues

Granavenget 8   4220-0731
Open from Shavuot to Succot.

Hotels

Hotel Villa Strand
Kystvej 12, 3000   4396-9400
                                Fax: 4396-9137

Dominican Republic

GMT – 4 hours
Country calling code (1 809)

Santo Domingo
Area telephone code (809)

Representative Organisations
Consejo Dominicano de Mujeres Hebreas
PO Box 2189
Fax: 688-2058

Synagogues
Centro Israelita de la Republica Dominicana
Av. Ciudad de Sarasota 21   535-6042

Embassy
Embassy of Israel
Av. Pedro Henriquez Urena 80, 1404
542-1635; 542-1548

Sosua
Area telephone code (809)

Contact Information
Felix G. Koch   571-2284
Welcomes all Jewish visitors.

Ecuador

GMT – 5 hours
Country calling code (593)

Guayaquil
Area telephone code (1)

Synagogues
Community Centre
cnr. Calle Paradiso & El Bosque

Quito
Area telephone code (2)

Community Organisations
18 de Septiembre 954, Casilla 17-03-800
502-734
Fax: 502-733

Embassy
Embassy of Israel
Av. Eloy Alfaro 969, Casilla 2463   547-322;
548-431

Egypt

GMT + 2 hours
Country calling code (20)

Alexandria
Area telephone code (3)

Synagogues
Eliahu Hanavi
69 Nebi Daniel Street, Ramla Station
492-3974; 597-4438

Cairo
Area telephone code (2)

Community Organisations
13 Sebil el-Khazendar St., Midan el-Geish,
Abassiya   824-613; 824-885

Synagogues
Ben-Ezra, 6 Harett il-Sitt Barbara, Mari Girges,
Old Cairo   847-695

Meir Enaim, 55 No.13 Street, Maadi
This is a small American-Israeli congregation,
which holds occasional services.
Shaarei Hashamayim
17 Adli Pasha Street, Downtown Cairo
749-025
Services are held on holidays. There is an
interesting library across from the temple,
which is only accessible with a key. Ask the
guards.

Tourist information
Israel Government Tourist Office
6 Ibn Malek St., 4th Floor   729-734; 730-997

Embassy
Israel Embassy
6 Ibn Malek St., Gizeh   845-260; 845-205;
28862

El Salvador

GMT – 6 hours
Country calling code (503)

San Salvador

Community Organisations

Comunidad Israelita de El Salvador
Aptdo. Postal 06-182   981-388

Synagogues

Conservative

23 Blvd. del Hipodromo 626,
Colonia San Benito   237-366
Friday evening services only.

Embassy

Colonia Escalon
85 Av. Norte, No 619   238-770; 239-221

Estonia

GMT + 2 hours
Country calling code (372)

Tallinn

Area telephone code (2)

Community Organisations

Jewish Community of Estonia
Karu Street 16, PO Box 3576, EE0090
                                        43-8566
Publishes a monthly, called 'Hashaher', in
Russian and operates a radio programme on
Radio 4 (Thurs., 22:15-23:00). Information on
vegetarian eateries available.

Synagogues

9 Magdalena Street, PO Box 3576, EE0090
                                        55-7154

Ethiopia

The Jews of Ethiopia, who sometimes call themselves Beta Israel, and are known as Falashas, represent one of the oldest Jewish communities in the world. As a result of Operation Moses and extensive emigration to Israel in the past few years and now following a further mass exodus to Israel, the community probably numbers fewer than 1,500, when account is taken of casualties from the famine and the hazards of reaching the refugee camps in the Sudan, estimated at between 3,000 and 4,000. This is about a third of the number in 1981, when the World Ort Union was forced to suspend its aid programme. The Falashas' origin is uncertain, but it is believed that Judaism first reached Ethiopia during the first or second centuries C.E., probably from Egypt, where flourishing Jewish communities existed.

GMT + 3 hours
Country calling code (251)

Addis Ababa
Area telephone code (1)

Community Organisations
PO Box 50   111-725; 446-471

Asmara

Synagogues
Via Hailemariam Mammo 34

Fiji

GMT + 12 hours
Country calling code (679)

Community Organisations
Fiji Jewish Association, P.O. Box 882, Suva

Finland

The settlement of Jews in Finland dates from about 1850. The original community consisted mostly of Jewish soldiers in the Russian Army in Finland, so-called Cantonists who decided, after 25 years of military service, to settle there with their families. There are about 1,500 Jews in Finland today, about 1,200 of whom live in Helsinki.

GMT + 2 hours
Country calling code (358)

Helsinki

Area telephone code (9)

Community Organisations

Community Centre
Malminkatu 26   6921297; 6941302
Fax: 6948916

Synagogues

Malminkatu 26
Services: Monday to Friday, 7.45am; Friday evening, 7.45pm (summer), 5pm (winter); Shabbat and Sunday, 9am.

Embassy

Israel Embassy, Vironkatu 5a   1356177
Fax: 1356959

Restaurants

Kosher Deli, Malminkatu 24   6854584
Hours: Tuesday to Wednesday, 1pm to 5pm; Thursday, 9am to 5pm; Friday, 9am to 2pm.

Community Centre, Malminkatu 26
Kosher meals available. Telephone 6941296 or 877967 to arrange.

Turku

Synagogue

Brahenkatu, 17   2312557
Fax: 2334689

France

The first Jewish settlers in France arrived with the Greek founders of Marseilles about 500 B.C.E. After the destruction of the Second Temple, Jewish exiles established new communities, or reinforced old ones, in the South of France, where they lived on equal terms with their Gentile neighbours. Rabbis who become known for their oratory attracted Christians to the synagogues. But gradually the priesthood inculcated in the masses a hatred of the Jews which, with the coming of the Crusades, vented itself in pogroms. Yet it was during this period that French Jewry achieved its noblest spiritual flowering.

Rashi and Rabenu Tam are the best known of hundreds of brilliant medieval French rabbis and scholars. In 1394 the Jews were banished from the whole of France, save the small area under the jurisdiction of the Popes of Avignon. When Alsace-Lorraine became part of France early in the 17th century, the Jews there were unmolested, and small numbers trickled into the rest of France. Ten years before the French Revolution, the 500 Jews of Paris built their first ritual bath. In 1791 the emancipation of French Jewry was the signal for the ghetto walls to crumble throughout Europe. During the Second World War, under German occupation, 120,000 Jews were deported or massacred; but the post-war influx from Central and Eastern Europe and North Africa has increased the Jewish population to some 700,000.

There are about 380,000 in the Paris area; 85,000 in Marseille; between 30,000 and 35,000 in Lyon; between 25,000 and 30,000 in Nice; between 20,000 and 23,000 in Toulouse; 18,000 in Strasbourg: and about 8,000 each in Bordeaux and Grenoble.

The Consistoire Central Israélite de France et d'Algérie (17, rue Saint Georges, 75009 Paris) publishes its 'Annuaire', listing all the communal organisations of France.

GMT + 1 hour
Country calling code (33)

Agen

Synagogue
52 rue Montesquieu, 47000   05.53.66.24.20

Aix-en-Provence

Synagogue
3 bis rue de Jérusalem, 13100   04.42.26.69.39

Butchers
C.C.V.A. Zouaghi
7 rue Sevigné, 13100   04.42.59.93.94
Supervision: Grand Rabbinate of Marseille.

Aix-les-Bains

Synagogue
Rue Paul Bonna, 73100   04.79.35.28.08
Mikva on premises

Mikvaot

Pavillon Salvador
rue du Président Roosevelt, 73100
04.79.35.38.08

Butchers

Berdah
29 Av. de Tresserve, 73100   04.79.61.44.11
Eurocach
Av. d'Italie

Hotels

Kosher

Auberge de La Baye
Chemin du Tir-Aux-Pigeons   04.79.35.69.42

Amiens

Synagogue

38 rue du Port d'Amont, 8000

Angers

Synagogue

12 rue Valdemaine, 49100

Annency

Synagogue

18 rue de Narvik, 74000.   04.50.45.82.22

Annemasse

Butchers

Yarden
59 rue de la Libération, 74240 Gaillard
04.50.92.64.05

Antibes

Synagogue

Villa La Monada, Chemin des Sables, 06600
04.93.61.59.34

Restaurants

Bamboo Grill
5 rue Alexandre III

Chez Andre
Chaim's Marchés, 13 Av. Louis Gallet, Juan les
Pins   04.93.61.44.72
Mid-March to Mid-September

Pizza Beverley
Blvd. Charles Guillaument
Also holds Sephardi services on Shabbat.

Butchers

André Sebbah
28 Av. Maiziers, 06600   04.93.34.60.11
Krief
3 rue Louis-Gallet, 06160   04.93.74.73.30
Ohayon
28 Av. Admiral Courbet   04.93.67.25.08
Fax: 04.92.93.05.72

Arcachon

Synagogue

Cours Desbey
Open July & August only.

Avignon

Synagogue

2 Place de Jérusalem, 84000   04.90.85.21.24

Mikvaot

7 rue des Sept-Baisers, 84140 Montfavet
04.90.86.30.30

Butchers

Bensoussan
25 rue Ninon Vallin, 84000   04.90.29.56.95
Supervision: Grand Rabbinate of Marseille.
Chelly
1-5 rue Chapeau Rouge, 84000
04.90.82.47.50
Supervision: Grand Rabbinate of Marseille.

Sites
The Conseil Géneral de Vaucluse, Place Campana, B.P.147, 84008 Avignon publishes a guide to the Jewish sites of the Vaucluse.
04.90.86.43.42

Bar-le-Duc

Synagogue
7 Quai Carnot

Bayonne

Synagogue
35 rue Maubec, 64100   05.59.55.03.95

Beauvais

Synagogue
Rue Jules Isaac, 60000

Belfort

Community Organisations
27 rue Strolz, 90000   03.84.28.55.41
Publishes 'Notre Communauté' (quarterly).

Synagogue
6 rue de l'As-de-Carreau, 90000
03.84.28.55.41
Fax: 03.84.28.55.41

Benfeld

Community Organsations
6 rue du Grand Rempart, 67230

Synagogue
7a rue de la Dome, 67230

Besançon

Community Organisations
10 rue Grosjean, 25000   03.81.80.82.82

Synagogue
23c Quai de Strasbourg, 25000

Restaurants
M.Croppet
18 rue des Granges   03.81.83.35.93
Thursday only.

Beziers

Synagogue
19 Place Pierre-Sémard, 34500
04.67.28.75.98
Operates a kosher food store.

Biarritz

Synagogue
rue de Russie (cnr. rue Pellot), 64200
Services Yom Kippur only.

Bischheim-Schiltigheim

Synagogue
9 Place de la Synagogue, 67800
02.38.33.02.87

Bitche

Synagogue
28 rue de Sarreguemines, 57230
Services, Rosh Hashana & Yom Kippur.

Bordeaux

Community Organisations
15 Pl. Charles-Gruet, 33000   05.56.52.62.69

Synagogue
8 rue du Grand-Rabbin-Joseph-Cohen, 33000
05.56.91.79.39

Mikvaot
213 rue Ste. Catherine, 33000 05.56.91.79.39

Restaurants
Mazal Tov
137 Crs Victor Hugo   05.56.52.37.03
Sabra
144 Crs Victor Hugo   05.56.92.83.38

Boulay

Synagogue
Rue du Pressoir, 57220   03.87.79.28.34

Boulogne-sur-Mer

Synagogue
63 rue Charles Butor

Bouzonville

Synagogue
Rue des Bénédictins, 57320

Brest

Synagogue
40 rue de la Républic, 29200
Services, Friday, 7.30 pm.

Caen

Synagogue
46 Av. de la Libération, 14000 02.31.43.60.54

Butchers
M. Lasry, 26 rue de l'Engannerie, 14000
02.31.86.16.25
Open Thursday.

Cagnes-sur-Mer

Synagogue
5 rue des Capucines, 06800

Caluire et Cuire

Synagogue
107 Av. Fleming, 69300
Pres.: J. Wolff.   04.78.23.12.37

Cannes

Synagogues
Habad Lubavitch
22 rue Cdt Vidal (crn. Bd. de Lorraine), 06400
04.92.98.67.51
20 Blvd. D'Alsace, 06400   04.93.38.16.54

Restaurants
Le Tovel
3 rue Gerard Monod, 06400   04.93.39.36.25

Butchers
Marcel Benguigui, 17 rue Maréchal-Joffre,
06400   04.93.39.57.92
J.-Y. Zana
44 rue Jean-Jaurés, 06400   04.93.38.46.59

Accommodation
Hotel King David
16 Blvd. d'Alsace, 06400   04.93.99.16.16
Under the supervision of Rabbi Mordechai
Bensoussan, Regional Rabbi of Nice, Côte
d'Azur & Corsica

Carpentras

Services are held on festivals in the ancient synagogue in the Place de la Mairie, 84200, classed as a national monument. Built in 1367 and rebuilt in 1741, it is worth a visit. Hours 10-12; 3-5. Inquiries to 04.90.63.39.97.

Cavaillon

The remains of the old synagogue, built in 1774, are regarded as a French historical monument. The Musées et Patrimoine de Cavaillon organise tours. Contact 52 Place de Castil-Blaze, 84300.   04.90.76.00.34
Fax: 04.90.71.47.06

Chalons-sur-Marne

Synagogue
21 rue Lochet, 51000

Chalon-sur-Saône

Synagogue
10 rue Germiny, 71100

Chambéry

Synagogue
44 rue St.-Réal
Services, Friday, 7 pm and festivals.

Chateauroux

Contact Information
Michel Touati
3 Allée Emile Zola, Montierchaume, 36130
Déols   02.54.26.05.47

Clermont-Ferrand

Synagogue
6 rue Blatin   04.73.93.36.59

Colmar

Synagogue
3 rue de la Cigogne, 68000   03.89.41.38.29
Fax: 03.89.41.12.96
The Chief Rabbi of the Haut-Rhin region is Rabbi Jacky Dreyfus, 1 rue des Jonquillles, 68000   03.89.23.13.11

Compiègne

Synagogue
4 rue du Dr.-Charles-Nicolle, 60200

Creil

Synagogue
1 Place de la Synagogue, 60100
     03.44.25.16.37
Fax: 03.44.25.48.41

Deauville

Synagogue
14 rue Castor, 14800   02.31.81.27.06

Dieuze

Synagogue
Av. Foch, 57260

Dijon

Synagogue
5 rue de la Synagogue   03.80.66.46.47
Mikva on premises.

Butchers
Albert Lévy
25 rue de la Manutention   03.80.30.14.42
Albert Sultan
4 petit rue Pouffier   03.80.73.31.38

Dunkerque

Synagogue
19 rue Jean-Bart, 59140

Elbeuf

Synagogue
29 rue Grémont, 76500   02.35.77.09.11

Epernay

Synagogue
2 rue Placet, 51200   03.26.55.24.44
Services, Yom Kippur only.

Epinal

Synagogue
Rue Charlet, 88000   03.29.82.25.23

Erstein

Synagogue
Rue du Vieux-Marché, 67150
Services, Rosh Hashana & Yom Kippur only.

Evian-les-Bains

Synagogue
Adjacent to 1 av. des Grottes, 74500
          04.50.75.15.63

Faulquemont-Crehange

Synagogue
Place de l'Hotel de Ville, 57380
Services, festivals & High Holydays only.

Forbach

Synagogue
98 Av. St.-Rémy, 57600   03.87.85.25.57

Fréjus

Synagogue
98 Villa Ariane, rue du Progrés, Fréjus-Plage,
83600   04.94.52.06.87

Grasse

Synagogue
82 Route de Nice, 06130   04.93.36.05.33

Grenoble

Religious Organisations
Rabbinate
4 rue des Bains, 38000   04.76.47.63.72

Synagogues
11 rue André Maginot, 38000 04.76.87.02.80
Mikva on premises.
Beit Habad
10 rue Lazare Carnot, 38000   04.76.43.38.58
Synagogue and Community Centre
4 rue des Bains, 38000   04.76.46.15.14

Media

Radio
Radion Kol Hashalom
4 rue des Bains, 38000   04.76.87.21.22

Restaurants
Pizzeria Pinocchio
1 rue des bons Enfants, 38000 04.76.46.88.66

Butchers
C. Cohen
19 rue Turenne, 38000   04.76.46.48.14
Sebbag
6 rue Aubert-Dugayet, 38000   04.76.46.40.78

Groceries
David France
75 ave de Vizille   04.76.70.49.15
La Rose de Sables
15 place Gustave Rivet   04.76.87.80.94
Aux Délices du Soleil
49 rue Thiers   04.76.46.19.60

Grosbliederstroff

Synagogue
6 rue des Fermes, 57520

Hagondange

Synagogue
Rue Henri-Hoffmann, 57300

Haguenau

Synagogue
3 rue du Grand-Rabbin-Joseph-Bloch, 67500
03.88.73.38.30

Mikvaot
7 rue Neuve

Restaurant
Maison les Cigognes   03.88.93.21.58

Hyères

Synagogue
Chemin de la Ritorte, 83400   04.94.65.31.97

Ingwiller

Synagogue
Cours du Château, 67340

Insming

Synagogue
Rue de la Synagogue, 57670

Izieu

Museums
The Izieu Children's Home
recording 04.79.87.20.00;
booking 04.79.87.20.08
Through photographs and audio-visual
displays, visitors can gain an understanding of
the horror of the fate of the 44 children who
lived here in 1944, and also of the 11,000
Jewish children who were sent from France to
death camps. This commemorative museum
was pivotal evidence in the Klaus Barbie trial
(the 'butcher of Lyons'). A guide is available in
English although the captions and videos are
all in French.

Juan-les-Pins

See Antibes

La Ciotat

Synagogue
1 Square de Verdun, 13600.   04.42.71.92.56
President: C. Michel. Services, Friday 7 pm
(Winter), 7.30 pm (Summer). Saturday 9 am.

La Rochelle

Contact Information
Pierre Guedj, 19 rue Bastion d'Evangile, 17000
05.46.67.38.91

La Seyne-sur-Mer

Synagogue
5 rue Chevalier-de-la-Barre, 83500
04.94.94.40.28

Butcher
Elie Benhamou
17 rue Baptistin-Paul, 83500   04.94.94.38.60

Le Havre

Synagogue
38 rue Victor-Hugo, 76600   02.35.21.14.59

Le Mans

Synagogue
4-6 Blvd. Paixhans, 72000   02.43.86.00.96

Libourne

Synagogue
33 rue Lamothe, 33500

Lille

Synagogue
5 rue Auguste-Angellier, 59000
03.20.30.69.86;
03.20.85.27.37
Mikva on premises.

Groceries
Kosher department at Monoprix, rue du
Molinel, at Shopping Centre Euralille, 59000.

Limoges

Synagogue
25-27 rue Pierre-Leroux, 87000 05.55.77.47.26

Lixheim

Synagogue
Rue de la Synagogue, 57110

Lorient

Synagogue
c/o Mme. Frandji, 18 rue de la Patrie, 56100
Services, festivals & Holy-days only.

Luneville

Synagogue
5 rue Castara, 54300

Lyon

Religious Organisations

Regional Chief Rabbi
Rabbi Richard Wertenschlag, 13 Quai Tilsitt,
69002   04.78.37.13.43

Consistoire Israélite de Lyon
Address as above   04.78.37.13.43
Fax: 04.78.38.26.57

Beth Din
34 rue d'Armenie, 3e   04.78.62.97.63
Fax: 04.78.95.09.47

Consistoire Israélite Sepharade de Lyon
Yaacov Molho Com. Centre, 317 rue
Duguesclin, 69007   04.78.58.18.74
Fax: 04.78.58.17.49

Mikvaot

Chaare Tsedek (N. African), 18 rue St.-
Mathieu, 69008   04.78.00.72.50
Jewish Day School, 40 rue Alexandre Boutin,
Villeurbanne, 69100   04.78.24.38.91

Neveh Chalom (Sephardi), 317 rue
Duguesclin, 69007   04.78.58.18.54

Orah Haim, 17 rue Albert-Thomas, St.-Fons,
69190   04.78.67.39.78

Rav Hida (N. African), La Sauvegarde, La
Duchére, 69009   04.78.35.14.44

Synagogue de la Fraternité (Sephardi), 4 rue
Malherbe, Villeurbanne, 69100 04.78.84.04.32

Yeshiva Pinto, 20 bis rue des Mûriers,
Villeurbanne, 69100   04.78.03.89.14

1 rue de Dublin, Rillieux, 69140 04.78.88.50.89

Media

CIV News, 4 rue Malherbe, Villeurbanne,
69100   04.78.84.04.32

Hachaar
18 rue St. Mathieu, 69008   04.78.00.72.50

La Voix Sépharade
317 rue Duguesclin, 69007   04.78.58.18.74

Le Bulletin
13 Quai Tilsitt, 69002   04.78.37.13.43

Radio Judaïca Lyon (R.J.L.), P.O.B. 7063,
69341 (FM 94.5)   04.78.03.99.20

Restaurants

Le Grillon d'Or
20 rue Terme, 69001   04.78.27.33.09
Happy to prepare a meal to go.

Booksellers

Decitre, Place Bellecour, 69002

F.N.A.C., rue de la République, 69002

Levi-Its'hak
3 Passage Cazenove   04.78.93.16.17

Mazal
46 rue Jean-Claude-Vivant, Villeurbanne,
69100   04.78.52.85.94

Menorah
(Ouaknine), 52 rue Montesquieu, 69007
          04.78.69.09.35

Mâcon

Synagogue
32 rue des Minimes, 71000

Marignane

Synagogue
9 rue Pilote-Larbonne, 13700

Marseille

Religious Organisations

Consistoire de Marseille
117 rue de Breteuil, 13006   04.91.37.49.64;
          04.91.81.13.57
          Fax: 04.91.53.98.72

Embassy

Consulate General
146 rue Paradis, 13006

Restaurants

Meat

Prince David
67 rue de la Palud, 13001   04.91.54.37.98
Supervision: Grand Rabbinate of Marseille.

Sunset Plaza
24 rue Pavillon, 13001   04.91.33.27.77
Supervision: Grand Rabbinate of Marseille.

Avyel Cash
28 rue St Suffren, 13006   04.91.37.95.27
Supervision: Grand Rabbinate of Marseille.

Eden Place
64 rue du Rouet, 13006   04.91.79.49.94
Supervision: Grand Rabbinate of Marseille.

Natanya
17 rue du Village, 13006   04.91.42.05.31
Supervision: Grand Rabbinate of Marseille.

David'son
Parade G. Pompidou, 13007   04.91.77.90.91
Supervision: Grand Rabbinate of Marseille.

Byblos
38 blvd Barral, 13008   04.91.22.87.87
Supervision: Grand Rabbinate of Marseille.

China Tov
63 rue Negresco, 13008   04.91.22.16.02
Supervision: Grand Rabbinate of Marseille.

Le Liandier
58 rue Liandier, 13008   04.91.80.53.37
Supervision: Grand Rabbinate of Marseille.

ORT, 3-9 rue des Forges, 13010
          04.91.79.61.65
Supervision: Grand Rabbinate of Marseille.

Dairy

Pizza Atikva
43 avenue des Chartreux, 13004
04.91.50.40.30
Supervision: Grand Rabbinate of Marseille.

Venice Beach
341 C. Kennedy, 13007   04.91.22.15.75
Supervision: Grand Rabbinate of Marseille.

Piz Mazal
8 blvd Gustave Ganay, 13008   04.91.26.28.90
Supervision: Grand Rabbinate of Marseille.

Pizza Tova
Vert Bocage, 13009   04.91.75.70.92
Supervision: Grand Rabbinate of Marseille.

Les Délices d'Eden
Avenue Paul Claudel, 13010   04.91.74.20.18
Supervision: Grand Rabbinate of Marseille.

Presto Pizza Cash
1 Cial résidence Bellevue, 13010
04.91.75.19.00
Supervision: Grand Rabbinate of Marseille.

Cacher Food
31 blvd Barry, 13013   04.91.70.13.43
Supervision: Grand Rabbinate of Marseille.

Pizza Menorah
86 rue A. Daudet, 13013   04.91.66.68.75
Supervision: Grand Rabbinate of Marseille.

Bakeries

Avyel Cash
28 rue St Suffren, 13006   04.91.37.95.25
Supervision: Grand Rabbinate of Marseille.

Atteia et Fils
19 place Gaillardet, 13013   04.91.66.33.28
Supervision: Grand Rabbinate of Marseille.

Cacher Food
31 blvd Barry, 13013   04.91.70.13.43
Supervision: Grand Rabbinate of Marseille.

L'Entremets
206 avenue de la Rose, 13013   04.91.70.72.19
Supervision: Grand Rabbinate of Marseille.

Patisserie Atteia
Le Parvé-72, Avenue A. Daudet, 13013
04.91.66.95.16
Supervision: Grand Rabbinate of Marseille.

Butchers

Attias
3 rue Halles Delacroix, 13001   04.91.54.02.96
Supervision: Grand Rabbinate of Marseille.

Ayad
8 cours Belsunce, 13001   04.91.90.73.40
Supervision: Grand Rabbinate of Marseille.

Dav Cacher
3-5 rue du Musée, 13001   04.91.55.09.21
Supervision: Grand Rabbinate of Marseille.

Dayan, 4 rue de la Glace, 13001
04.91.54.03.70
Supervision: Grand Rabbinate of Marseille.

Léon et Marco
61 rue d'Aubagne, 13001   04.91.54.11.95
Supervision: Grand Rabbinate of Marseille.

Zennou Raphael
20 marché Capucins, 13001   04.91.54.02.54
Supervision: Grand Rabbinate of Marseille.

Emouna
20 rue Max Dormoy, 13004   04.91.34.98.84
Supervision: Grand Rabbinate of Marseille.

Guedj, 6 cours Julien, 13006   04.91.48.44.24
Supervision: Grand Rabbinate of Marseille.

Zouaghi
2 blvd Latil, 13008   04.91.80.01.20
Supervision: Grand Rabbinate of Marseille.

Garabli
11 avenue Mistral-Ste Marguerite, 13009
04.91.75.27.73
Supervision: Grand Rabbinate of Marseille.

Haddad Raphael
9 blvd G. Ganay, 13009   04.91.75.04.56
Supervision: Grand Rabbinate of Marseille.

Raphael Cash, 299 avenue de Mazargues,
13009   04.91.76.44.13
Supervision: Grand Rabbinate of Marseille.

Ste Jamap
13 place Mignard, 13009   04.91.71.11.70
Supervision: Grand Rabbinate of Marseille.

Zouaghi
206 blvd Paul Claudel, 13009   04.91.74.30.01
Supervision: Grand Rabbinate of Marseille.

Eric Hadjedj
2 place Migranier, 13010   04.91.35.10.27
Supervision: Grand Rabbinate of Marseille.

King Cacher
25 rue F. Mauriac, 13010   04.91.80.00.01
Supervision: Grand Rabbinate of Marseille.

Yad Kel
143 blvd Paul Claudel, 13010   04.91.75.03.57
Supervision: Grand Rabbinate of Marseille.

Sebanne
59 rue Alphonse Daudet, 13013
04.91.66.98.76
Supervision: Grand Rabbinate of Marseille.

Groceries

Avyel Cash
28 rue St Suffren, 13006 — 04.91.37.95.25

Emmanuel
93 avenue Clot Bey, 13008 — 04.91.77.46.08

Raphael Cash
299 avenue de Mazargues, 13009
04.91.76.44.13

King Cacher
25 rue François Mauriac, 13010
04.91.80.00.01

Les Délices d'Eden
Ctre Cial residénce Bellevue, 13010
04.91.75.03.57

Taim Venaim
Montée de St Menet, 13011 — 04.91.44.11.21

Delicash
94 blvd Barry, 13013 — 04.91.06.39.04

Melun

Synagogue
Cnr. rues Branly & Michelet, 770000
01.64.52.00.05

Menton

Synagogue
Centre Altyner, 106 Cours du Centenaire
04.93.35.28.29

Merlebach

Synagogue
19 rue St.-Nicolas 57800

Metz

Religious Organisations

Rabbi Bruno Fiszon
Chief Rabbi of Moselle, 57000 03.87.75.04.44

Synagogues
2 rue Paul Michaux, 57000

Adass Yechouroun
41 rue de Rabbin Elie-Bloch, 57000

Main Synagogue and Community Centre
39 rue du Rabbin Elie-Bloch, 57000
03.87.75.04.44
This street was renamed from rue de l'Arsenal, in memory of a youth movement rabbi deported and killed by the Nazis during the Second World War.

Oratoire Sepharade
39 rue du Rabbin Elie-Bloch, 57000

Mikvaot
Contact Madame Elalouf — 03.87.32.38.04

Restaurants
Galil, 39 rue du Rabbin Elie-Bloch, 57000
03.87.75.04.44
Supervision: Chief Rabbi of Moselle.
Open until noon every weekday.

Butchers
Claude Sebbag
22 rue Mangin, 57000 — 03.87.63.33.50
Supervision: Chief Rabbi of Moselle.

Groceries
Atac, 23 rue de 20e Corps Américain, 57000
Galaries Lafayette, 4 rue Winston Churchill, 57000 — 03.87.38.60.60

Montauban

Synagogue
14 rue Ste.-Claire, 82000 — 05.63.03.01.37

Montbéliard

Synagogue
Rue de la Synagogue, 25200

Montpellier

Community Organisations
Centre Communautaire et Cultural Juif
560 blvd. d'Antigone, 3400   04.67.15.08.76

Synagogues
Ben-Zakai
7 rue Géneral-Laffon, 34000   04.67.92.92.07

Mazal Tov, 18 rue Ferdinand-Fabre, 34000
04.67.79.09.82

Butchers
Camille Bensoussan, Place Millenaire-
Antigone, 34000   04.67.66.03.22

Gilbert Bensoussan
41 rue de Lunaret, 340000   04.67.72.67.94

Cooperative casher, 18 rue Ferdinand Fabre,
3400.

Mulhouse

Synagogue
2 rue des Rabbins, 68100   03.89.66.21.22
Fax: 03.89.56.63.49
Mikva on premises. The old cemetery is also
worth a visit – enquire at centre.

Butchers
Chez Nessim
Passage des Halles, 68100   03.89.66.55.65

Nancy

Community Organisations
19 Blvd. Joffre, 54000   03.83.32.10.67

Synagogue
17 Blvd. Joffre, 54000   03.83.32.10.67

Restaurant
Restaurant Universitaire
19 Blvd. Joffre, 54000   03.83.32.10.67
Open weekdays until noon.

The Musée Historique Lorrain, 64 Grand Rue,
has an important collection of sifrei Torah,
prayer books and other ritual objects.

Nantes

Synagogues
5 Impasse Copernic, 44000   02.40.73.48.92
Mikva on premises.

Nice

Religious Organisations
Centre Consistorial and Synagogue
22 rue Michelet, 06100   04.93.51.89.80
Publishes an annual calendar and guide to
Nice and district.

Main Synagogue
7 rue Gustave-Deloye, 06000   04.93.92.11.38

Rabbinate
Regional Chief Rabbinate of Nice, Côte d'Azur
and Corsica: 1 rue Voltaire 06000
04.93.85.82.06

Mikvaot
22 rue Michelet, 06100   04.93.51.89.80

A list of kosher butchers and bakers can be
obtained from Chief Rabbi Mordehai
Bensoussan   04.93.85.82.06

Restaurants
Le cheme Chamayime
22 rue Rossini   04.93.88.47.01

Le Leviathan
1 ave Georges Clemenceau   04.93.87.22.64

Restaurant Mazal
11 rue Paganini, 06000   04.93.87.93.50

Roi David Ten Li Hai
9 rue Clément-Roassal, 06000   04.93.87.65.25

Booksellers
Librairie Tanya
25 rue Pertinax, 06000   04.93.80.21.74

Nîmes

Community Organisations
5 rue d'Angoulème, 30000   04.66.26.19.51

Synagogue
40 rue Roussy, 30000   04.66.29.51.81
Mikva on premises.

Obernai
Synagogue
Rue de Sélestat, 67210

Orléans
Synagogue
14 rue Robert-de-Courtenay (to the left of the cathedral), 45000. Kosher meat available every Wednesday, 4.30 pm to 7.30 pm. At Pithiviers, near Orléans, there is a monument to the Jewish victims of Nazi persecution.

Paris
The city of Paris is divided into districts (arrondissements) designated by the last two digits of the postcode. In the categories below, establishments are listed in numerical order according to the postcode (that is, -01, -02, -03 and so on).
The historic centre of Paris Jewish life is found in the Marais area (4th arrondissement). Another more central area is that around rue Richer (9th arrondissement) which although not historic as such has many kosher restaurants of varying styles and price range.

Religious Organisations
Communauté Israélite Orthodoxe de Paris
10 rue Pavée, 75004   01.42.77.81.51
                            Fax: 01.48.87.26.29

Synagogues
Orthodox
15 rue Notre-Dame de Nazareth, 75003
                            01.42.78.00.30

Groupe Rabbi Yehiel de Paris
25 rue Michel-Leconte, 75003 01.42.78.89.17
Netzach Israël Ohel Mordehai
5 rue Sainte-Anastase, 75003

21 bis rue des Tournelles, 75004
          01.42.74.32.65; 01.42.74.32.80
                            Fax: 01.40.29.90.27
The secretary can be reached at 01.40.27.96.74.
14 place des Vosges, 75004   01.48.87.79.45
                            Fax: 01.48.87.57.58

Adath Yechouroun
25 rue des Rosiers, 75004   01.44.59.82.36
Agoudas Hakehilos Instit Yad Mordekhai
10 rue Pavée, 75004   01.48.87.21.54
Fondation Roger Fleishmann
18 rue des Ecouffes, 75004   01.48.87.97.86
Oratoire Mahziké Adath Mouvement Loubavitch, 17 rue des Rosiers, 75004
Synagogue Tephilat Israël Frank-Forter
24 rue du Bourg-Tibourg, 75004
                            01.46.24.48.94

Centre Rachi
30 boulevard du Port-Royal, 75005
                            01.43.31.98.20
Séminaire Israélite de France
9 rue Vauquelin, 75005   01.47.07.21.22
                            Fax: 01.43.37.75.92
Centre Edmond Fleg
8 bis rue de l'Epéron, 75006 01.46.33.43.31
Houses the Union des Centres Communautaires (UCC), which can be contacted via the same telephone number. Their fax number is 01.43.25.86.19.
Tikvaténou, the Jewish youth movement of the Consistoire, is also located here. Tel: 01.46.33.43.24; Fax: 01.43.25.20.59.
E.E.I.F.
27 avenue de Ségur, 75007   01.47.83.60.33
Hékhal Moché, 218-220 rue du Faubourg St-Honoré, 75008   01.45.61.20.25
28 rue Buffault, 75009   01.45.26.80.87
                            Fax: 01.48.78.44.02
5 rue Rochechouart, 75009   01.49.95.95.92
                            Fax: 01.42.80.10.66
44 rue de la Victoire, 75009 01.40.82.26.26
                            Fax: 01.42.81.92.46
Beth-El, 3 rue Saulnier, 75009 01.45.23.34.89
Beth-Israël
4 rue Saulnier, 75009   01.45.23.34.89

France

(Paris cont.)

Kahal Adath Yéreim
10 rue Cadet, 75009   01.42.46.36.47
                             Fax: 01.42.47.04.95

Kollel Rav Lévy
37 boulevard de Strasbourg, 75009
Rachi Chull, 6 rue Ambroise-Thomas,
75009   01.48.24.86.95
Siège du Beth Loubavitch
8 rue Lamartine, 75009   01.45.26.87.60
                             Fax: 01.45.26.24.37
Synagogue Berit Chalom
18 rue Saint-Lazare, 75009   01.48.78.45.32;
                             01.48.78.38.80
Tiferet Yaacob
71 rue de Dunkerque, 75009   01.42.81.32.17;
                             01.42.49.65.12
4 rue Martel, 75010
9 rue Guy-Patin, 75010   01.42.85.12.74
A.U.J., 130 rue du Faubourg Saint-Martin,
75010   01.40.05.98.34
Beth-Eliaou
192 rue Saint-Martin, 75010 01.40.38.47.53
                             Fax: 01.40.36.41.95
Rav Pealim (Braslav), 49 boulevard de la
Villette, 75010   01.42.41.55.44
UNAT La Fraternelle, 13-15 rue des Petites-
Ecuries, 75010   01.42.46.65.02
Adath Israël
36 rue Basfroi, 75011   01.43.67.89.20
Ets Haim
18 rue Basfroi, 75011   01.43.48.82.42
Ora Vesimha
37 rue des Trois-Bornes, 75011 01.43.57.49.84
Ozar Hatorath Shoul
40 rue de l'Orillon, 75011   01.43.38.73.40
                             Fax: 01.43.38.36.45
Synagogue Don Isaac Abravanel
84-86 rue de la Roquette, 75011
                             01.47.00.75.95
Chivtei Israel
12-14 Cité Moynet, 75012   01.43.43.50.12
                             Fax: 01.43.47.36.78
Provisional entrance: 1 rue Montgallet.
Névé Chalom
29 rue Sibué, 75012   01.43.42.07.70
                             Fax: 01.43.48.44.50
Oratoire de la Fondation Rothschild
76 rue de Picpus, 75012   01.43.44.78.10

61-65 rue Vergniaud, 75013   01.45.88.93.84
19 rue Domrémy, 75013
Avoth Ouvanim
59 avenue d'Ivry, 75013   01.45.82.80.73;
                             01.45.85.94.39
6 bis villa d'Alésia, 75014 01.45.40.82.35
                             Fax: 01.45.40.72.89

223 rue Vercingétorix, 75014 01.45.45.50.51
Beith Chalom
25 villa d'Alésia, 75014   01.45.45.38.71
                             Fax: 01.43.37.58.49
14 rue Chasseloup-Laubat, 75015
                             01.42.73.36.29
Ohel Mordekhai
13 rue Fondary, 75015   01.40.59.96.56
6 bis rue Michel-Ange, 75016 01.44.14.71.23
                             Fax: 01.42.24.08.58
5 bis rue Montevideo, 75016 01.45.03.42.93
                             Fax: 01.40.72.83.76
23 bis rue Dufrénoy, 75016   01.45.04.94.00;
                             01.45.04.66.73
Ohel Avraham
31 rue Montevideo, 75016   01.45.05.66.73
                             Fax: 01.40.72.83.76

10 rue Barye, 75017   01.48.88.90.87;
                             01.40.53.91.57
Beth Hamidrach Lamed
67 rue Bayen, 75017   01.45.74.52.80
Centre Rambam
19-21 rue Galvani, 75017   01.45.74.52.80
42 rue des Saules, 75018   01.42.64.65.00
80 rue Doudeauville, 75018   01.42.62.77.63
Synagogue de Montmartre
13 rue Sainte-Isaure, 75018 01.42.64.48.34
54 avenue Secrétan, 75019   01.42.08.57.26
Beth Chalom
11-13 rue Curial, 75019   01.40.37.65.16;
                             01.40.37.12.54
Beth Loubavitch
25 rue Riquet, 75019   01.40.36.93.90
Beth Loubavitch
53 rue Compans, 75019   01.42.02.20.35
Chaare Tora
1 rue Henri-Turot, 75019   01.42.06.41.12
                             Fax: 01.42.06.95.47
Collel Hamabit
7 rue Rouvet, 75019   01.40.38.13.59

(Paris cont.)

Heder Loubavitch
25 rue des Solitaires, 75019   01.42.02.98.95
Fax: 01.42.02.04.62

Kollel Ysmah Moché
36 rue des Annelets, 75019   01.43.63.73.94

Ohaley Yaacov
11 rue Henri-Murger, 75019   01.42.49.25.00

Ohr Tora
15 rue Riquet, 75019   01.40.38.23.36;
01.40.36.42.23

Ohr Yossef
44-48 Quai de la Marne, 75019
01.42.45.74.20
Fax: 01.40.18.10.74

Pah'ad David
11 rue du Plateau, 75019   01.42.46.47.03
Fax: 01.42.46.47.56

Rabbi David ou Moché
45 rue de Belleville, 75019   01.40.18.30.63
Fax: 01.40.18.30.62

Synagogue Michkenot Israel
6 rue Jean-Nohain, 75019   01.48.03.25.59
Fax: 01.42.00.26.87

120 boulevard de Belleville, 75020
01.43.66.66.93

17 rue de la Cour-des-Noues, 75020
01.43.58.14.70

50 bis rue des Prairies, 75020   01.43.66.35.27
Fax: 01.43.66.97.18

Beth Loubavitch
93 rue des Orteaux, 75020   01.40.24.10.60

Beth Loubavitch
47 rue Ramponeau, 75020   01.43.66.93.00

Maor Athora
16 rue Ramponeau, 75020   01.47.97.69.42

Ohr Chimchon Raphaël
5 passage Dagorno, 75020   01.46.59.39.02
Fax: 01.46.59.14.99

Synagogue Achkenaze & Sephardi
49 rue Pali Kao, 75020   01.46.36.30.10

Synagogue Bet Yaacov Yossef
5 square des Cardeurs, 43 rue Saint-Blaise,
75020   01.43.56.03.11

Synagogue Michkan-Yaacov
118 boulevard de Belleville, 75020
01.43.49.39.59

Mikvaot

176 rue du Temple, 75003   01.42.71.89.28
The mikvah is located in the centre of Paris,
near Place de la République, at the rear of the
building. English-speaking staff.

6 rue Ambroise Thomas, 75009
01.48.24.86.94

10 rue Cadet, 75009   01.42.46.36.47;
01.42.47.01.95
For men.

19-21 rue Galvani, 75017   01.45.74.52.80

Mayan Hai Source de Vie Haya Mouchka
2-4 rue Tristan Tzara, 75018   01.40.38.18.29;
01.46.36.11.09

25 rue Riquet, 75019   01.40.36.40.92;
01.48.03.28.01; 01.40.38.01.94
For men and women.

1 rue des Annelets, 75019   01.42.45.57.87
For men and women.

31 rue de Thionville, 75019   01.42.45.74.20

Ohr Haim ve Moche
11 rue du Plateau, 75019   01.42.08.25.40

93 rue des Orteaux, 75020   01.40.24.10.60
For men.

75 rue Julien-Lacroix, 75020   01.46.36.39.20;
01.46.36.30.10

For men and women.

Embassy

Embassy of Israel
3 rue Rabelais, 75008

Restaurants

Juliette
12/14 rue Duphot dans la cour, 75001
01.42.60.18.10
Fax: 01.42.60.18.98
Supervision: Beth Din of Paris.

Natania
27 rue Poissonnière, 75002   01.42.33.58.36
Supervision: Beth Din of Paris.

Ninou, 20/30 rue Léopold Bellon, 75002
01.45.08.05.44
Supervision: Beth Din of Paris.

Restaurant Henri
13/15 Passage du Ponceau, 75002
01.40.13.91.72
Supervision: Beth Din of Paris.

Yung Pana
41 rue d'Aboukir, 75002   01.42.21.46.25
Supervision: Beth Din of Paris.

France

(Paris cont.)

Café Ninette
24 rue Notre-Dame de Nazareth, 75003
01.42.72.08.56
Supervision: Beth Din of Paris.

Chez Sarah
21 boulevard Saint-Martin, 75003
01.42.78.08.88
Supervision: Beth Din of Paris.

La Petite Famille
32 rue des Rosiers, 75003   01.42.77.00.50
Supervision: Beth Din of Paris.

Les Tables de la Loi
15 rue Saint-Gilles, 75003   01.48.04.38.02
Supervision: Beth Din of Paris.

Contini
42 rue des Rosiers, 75004   01.48.04.78.32
Supervision: Beth Din of Paris.

Korcarz
29 rue des Rosiers, 75004   01.42.77.39.47
Supervision: Chief Rabbi Mordechai
Rottenberg.

Koscher Pizza
1 rue des Rosiers, 75004   01.48.87.17.83
Supervision: Chief Rabbi Mordechai
Rottenberg.

La Pita
26 rue des Rosiers, 75004   01.42.77.93.13
Supervision: Beth Din of Paris.

Micky's Deli
23 bis rue des Rosiers, 75004   01.48.04.79.31
Supervision: Chief Rabbi Mordechai
Rottenberg.

Tel Aviv Haketana
9 rue des Rosiers, 75004   01.44.61.07.53
Supervision: Chief Rabbi Mordechai
Rottenberg.

Tutti Frutti
38 rue des Rosiers, 75004   01.42.76.04.75
Supervision: Chief Rabbi Mordechai
Rottenberg.

Yahalom
22 rue des Rosiers, 75004   01.42.77.12.35
Supervision: Chief Rabbi Mordechai
Rottenberg.

Adolphe / Centre Rachi
39 rue Broca, 75005   01.47.70.91.25
Supervision: Beth Din of Paris.

Chez Gaby
50 rue Broca, 75005   01.43.31.04.14
Supervision: Beth Din of Paris.

Centre Edmond Fleg
8 bis rue de l'Eperon, 75006   01.46.33.43.31
Supervision: Beth Din of Paris.

La Table de David
64 avenue Marceau, 75008   01.40.73.06.86
Supervision: Beth Din of Paris.

Le Sabra
64 avenue Marceau, 75008   01.40.70.03.23
Supervision: Beth Din of Paris.

Sivane
36 rue de Berry, 75008   01.49.53.01.21
Supervision: Beth Din of Paris.

Adolphe
14 rue Richer, 75009   01.47.70.91.25
Supervision: Beth Din of Paris.

Azar & Fils
6 rue Geoffroy-Marie, 75009   01.47.70.08.38
Supervision: Beth Din of Paris.

Berberche Burger
47 rue Richer, 75009   01.47.70.81.22
Supervision: Beth Din of Paris.

Casa Rina
18 rue du Fbg Montmartre, 75009
01.45.23.02.22
Supervision: Beth Din of Paris.

Centre Communautaire
5 rue Rochechouard, 75009   01.49.95.95.92
Supervision: Beth Din of Paris.

Chez David
11 rue Montyon, 75009   01.44.83.01.24
Supervision: Beth Din of Paris.

Douieb
11 bis rue Geoffroy-Marie, 75009
01.47.70.86.09
Supervision: Beth Din of Paris.

Falafel Meny
8 rue Geoffroy-Marie, 75009   01.42.46.76.46
Supervision: Beth Din of Paris.

Funny King
17 rue Montyon, 75009   01.47.70.24.64
Supervision: Beth Din of Paris.

Georges de Tunis
40 rue Richer, 75009   01.47.70.24.64
Supervision: Beth Din of Paris.

Hotel Alpha
11 rue Geoffroy Marie, 75009   01.45.23.10.59
Supervision: Beth Din of Paris.

Hotel Lebron
4 rue Lamartine, 75009   01.48.78.75.52
Supervision: Beth Din of Paris.

La Grillade
42 rue Richer, 75009   01.47.70.24.64
Supervision: Beth Din of Paris.

(Paris cont.)

Le Gros Ventre
7/9 rue Montyon, 75009   01.48.24.25.34
Supervision: Beth Din of Paris.

Les Ailes
34 rue Richer, 75009   01.47.70.62.53
Supervision: Beth Din of Paris.

Panino Café
31 rue St Georges, 75009   01.48.78.78.78
Supervision: Beth Din of Paris.

Snack Quick Delight
34 rue Richer, 75009   01.45.23.05.12
Supervision: Beth Din of Paris.

Synagogue Beth El
10 rue Saulnier, 75009   01.45.23.34.89
Supervision: Beth Din of Paris.

Yankees Cafe, 31 rue du Fbg Montmartre,
75009   01.42.46.52.46
Supervision: Beth Din of Paris.

Zazou Burger
19 rue du Fbg Montmartre, 75009
                               01.40.22.08.33
Supervision: Beth Din of Paris.

Cash Food
63 rue des Vinaigriers, 75010   01.42.03.95.75
Supervision: Beth Din of Paris.

Dolly's Food
9 rue Cité Riverain, 75010   01.48.03.08.40
Supervision: Beth Din of Paris.

Les Cantiques
16 rue Beaurepaire, 75010   01.42.40.64.21
Supervision: Beth Din of Paris.
Deliver.

Resto Flash
10 rue Lucien-Sampaix, 75010   01.42.45.03.30
Supervision: Beth Din of Paris.

La Fourchette d'Or
42 rue de l'orillon, 75011   01.42.01.29.45
Supervision: Beth Din of Paris.

Le Cabourg
102 boulevard Voltaire, 75011 01.47.00.71.43
Supervision: Beth Din of Paris.

Le Lotus de Nissan
39 rue Amelot, 75011   01.43.55.80.42
Supervision: Beth Din of Paris.

Le Manahattan
231 boulevard Voltaire, 75011 01.43.56.03.30
Supervision: Beth Din of Paris.

Yung Pana
115 boulevard Voltaire, 75011 01.43.79.20.48
Supervision: Beth Din of Paris.

Le Haim
6 rue Paulin Enfert, 75013   01.44.24.53.34
Supervision: Beth Din of Paris.

La Libanaise
13 rue des Sablons, 75016   01.45.05.10.35
Supervision: Beth Din of Paris.

Brasserie du Belvedere
109 avenue de Villiers, 75017 01.47.64.96.55
Supervision: Beth Din of Paris.

Eugenie
103 rue Jouffroy d'Abbans, 75017
                               01.47.64.33.11
Supervision: Beth Din of Paris.

Fradji
42 rue Poncelet, 75017   01.47.54.91.40
Supervision: Beth Din of Paris.

Jardins du Belvedere
111 avenue de Villiers, 75017 01.42.27.16.91
Supervision: Beth Din of Paris.

Les Ailes
15 rue des Fermiers, 75017   01.44.15.93.93
Supervision: Beth Din of Paris.

Mazel Tov
96 rue Nollet, 75017   01.42.28.52.59
Supervision: Beth Din of Paris.

Nini, 24 rue Saussier-Leroy, 75017
                               01.46.22.28.93
Supervision: Beth Din of Paris.

Alelouya
9 rue Charbonnière, 75018   01.42.52.52.92
Supervision: Beth Din of Paris.

Tib's Café
128 boulevard de Clichy, 75018
                               01.45.22.80.26
Supervision: Beth Din of Paris.

Allo Sarina
38 rue Curial, 75019   01.40.35.08.98
Supervision: Beth Din of Paris.

Apropo
81 rue de Crimée, 75019   01.42.03.10.10
Supervision: Beth Din of Paris.

Chez Marco
34 rue Curial, 75019   01.40.05.05.99
Supervision: Beth Din of Paris.

Chochana
54 avenue Secrétan, 75019   01.42.41.01.16
Supervision: Beth Din of Paris.

(Paris cont.)

Cotel Maaravi
69 avenue Armand-Carel, 75019
01.42.06.13.00
Supervision: Beth Din of Paris.

Mille Delices
52 avenue Secrétan, 75019   01.40.18.32.32
Supervision: Beth Din of Paris.

Tib's Manin
161 rue Manin, 75019   01.42.45.00.45
Supervision: Beth Din of Paris.

Auberge de Belleville
110 boulevard de Belleville, 75020
01.47.97.95.06
Supervision: Beth Din of Paris.

Chez François
5 rue Ramponeau, 75020   01.47.97.40.06
Supervision: Beth Din of Paris.

Chez Jeannot
112 boulevard de Belleville, 75020
01.47.97.35.06
Supervision: Beth Din of Paris.

Chez Rene et Gabin
92 boulevard de Belleville, 75020
01.43.58.78.14
Supervision: Beth Din of Paris.

Elygel
116 boulevard de Belleville, 75020
01.47.97.09.73
Supervision: Beth Din of Paris.

Le Petit Pelleport
135 rue Pelleport, 75020   01.40.33.13.17
Supervision: Beth Din of Paris.

Le Relais
69 boulevard de Belleville, 75020
01.43.57.83.91
Supervision: Beth Din of Paris.

Lumieres de Belleville
102 boulevard de Belleville, 75020
01.47.97.51.83
Supervision: Beth Din of Paris.

Dairy

Panini Folie
11 rue du Ponceau, 75002   01.42.33.14.55
Supervision: Beth Din of Paris.

Hamman Café
4 rue des Rosiers, 75004   01.42.78.04.46
Supervision: Beth Din of Paris.

Cine Citta Café
7 rue d'Aguesseau, 75008   01.42.68.05.03
Supervision: Beth Din of Paris.

Maestro Pizza
19 rue d'Anjou, 75008   01.47.42.15.60
Supervision: Beth Din of Paris.

Cine Citta Café
58 rue Richer, 75009   01.42.46.09.65
Supervision: Beth Din of Paris.

Dizengoff Café
27 rue Richer, 75009   01.47.70.81.97
Supervision: Beth Din of Paris.

King Salomon
46 rue Richer, 75009   01.42.46.31.22
Supervision: Beth Din of Paris.

Coktail Café
82 avenue Parmentier, 75011   01.43.57.19.94
Supervision: Beth Din of Paris.

Le New's
56 avenue de la République, 75011
01.43.38.63.18
Supervision: Beth Din of Paris.

Paradiso
126 boulevard Voltaire, 75011   01.48.06.79.33
Supervision: Beth Din of Paris.

Ranch Pizza
2 passage du Jeu de Boules, 75011
01.43.38.27.17
Supervision: Beth Din of Paris.

Panino Café
121 rue du Château des Rentiers, 75013
01.45.82.82.82
Supervision: Beth Din of Paris.

La Tour de Pizz
51 rue Bayen, 75017   01.45.72.07.06
Supervision: Beth Din of Paris.

Dolphino Café
26 allée Darius Milhaud, 75019
01.42.01.20.30
Supervision: Beth Din of Paris.

Gin Fizz
157 boulevard Serrurier, 75019
01.42.01.41.66
Supervision: Beth Din of Paris.

Pizza Curial
44 rue Curial, 75019   01.40.37.15.00
Supervision: Beth Din of Paris.

Bakeries

Contini
42 rue des Rosiers, 75004   01.48.04.78.32
Supervision: Beth Din of Paris.

Korcarz
29 rue des Rosiers, 75004   01.42.77.39.47
Supervision: Beth Din of Paris/Chief Rabbi
Mordechai Rottenberg.

France

(Paris cont.)

Marciano
14 rue des Rosiers, 75004   01.48.87.48.88
Supervision: Chief Rabbi Mordechai
Rottenberg.
Mezel, 1 rue Ferdinand Duval, 75004
                                                 01.42.78.25.01
Supervision: Beth Din of Paris.
Barbotte
229 rue du Fg St-Honoré, 75008
Supervision: Beth Din of Paris.
Douieb
11 bis rue Geoffroy Marie, 75009
                                                 01.47.70.86.09
Supervision: Beth Din of Paris.
Golan, 10 rue Geoffroy Marie, 75009
                                                 01.48.00.94.71
Supervision: Beth Din of Paris.
Korcarz
25 rue de Trévise, 75009   01.42.46.83.33
Supervision: Beth Din of Paris/Chief Rabbi
Mordechai Rottenberg.
Les Ailes
34 rue Richer, 75009   01.47.70.62.53
Supervision: Beth Din of Paris.
Zazou, 20 rue du Fbg Montmartre, 75009
                                                 01.47.70.81.32
Supervision: Beth Din of Paris.
Dahan, 7 rue Maillard, 75011 01.43.79.43.55
Supervision: Beth Din of Paris.
Mendez
3 Ter rue de la Présent, 75011 01.43.57.02.03
Supervision: Beth Din of Paris.
Nathan de Belleville
67 blvd de Belleville, 75011   01.43.57.24.60
Supervision: Beth Din of Paris.
Aux Delices de Maxime
69 rue de Crimée, 75019   01.40.36.44.76
Supervision: Beth Din of Paris.
Charles Tr. Patissier
10 rue Corentin Cariou, 75019 01.47.97.51.83
Supervision: Beth Din of Paris.
Contini
116 avenue Simon Bolivar, 75019
                                                 01.42.00.70.80
Supervision: Beth Din of Paris.
Jaffa Pita
5 rue Dampierre, 75019   01.46.07.27.77
Supervision: Chief Rabbi Mordechai
Rottenberg.

Kadoche
2 avenue Corentin Cariou, 75019
                                                 01.40.37.00.14
Supervision: Beth Din of Paris.
Le Relais Sucre
135 rue Manin, 75019   01.42.41.20.98
Supervision: Beth Din of Paris.
Mat'amim
17 rue de Crimée, 75019   01.42.40.89.11;
                                                 01.42.40.89.23
Supervision: Beth Din of Paris.
Medayo
71 rue de Meaux, 75019   01.40.03.04.20
Supervision: Beth Din of Paris.
Eliyor
21 rue du Bisson, 75020   01.43.49.12.66
Supervision: Beth Din of Paris.
Lilo, 20 rue Desnoyer, 75020 01.47.97.63.20
Supervision: Beth Din of Paris.
Nani, 104 blvd de Belleville, 75020
                                                 01.47.97.38.05
Supervision: Beth Din of Paris.
Zazou, 8 rue Rouvet, 75020 01.40.36.67.61
Supervision: Beth Din of Paris.

Butchers

Bensimon
40 rue des Rosiers, 75004   01.42.77.38.28
Boucherie Goldstein
13 rue Ferdinand Duval, 75004
                                                 01.42.77.00.82
Supervision: Chief Rabbi Mordechai
Rottenberg.
Lewkowicz
12 rue Des Rosiers, 75004   01.48.87.63.17.
Saada, 17 rue des Rosiers, 75004
                                                 01.42.77.76.22
Tordjemann
40 rue St Paul, 75004   01.42.72.93.22
Adolphe
14 rue Richer, 75009   01.48.24.86.33
Berbeche
46 Rue Richer, 75009   01.47.70.50.58
Boucherie Goldstein
9 rue Rodier, 75009   01.42.80.92.76
Supervision: Chief Rabbi Mordechai
Rottenberg.
Charlot
33 Rue Richer, 75009   01.45.23.10.34
Chez Andre
7 Rue Geoffroy Marie, 75009 01.47.70.49.03

(Paris cont.)

Chez Claude
1 rue Saulnier, 75009   01.48.24.71.22

La Charolaise R
51 rue Richer, 75009   01.47.70.01.57

La Rose Blanche
43 rue Richer, 75009   01.48.24.84.65

Chez Jacques
19 rue Bouchardon, 75010   01.42.06.76.13

Chez Andre
69 bld de Belleville, 75011   01.43.57.80.38

Chez Halak B. Y.
51 rue Richard Lenoir, 75011   01.43.48.62.26

Chez Jojo
20 rue Louis Bonnet, 75011   01.43.55.10.29

Chez Lucien
180 rue de Charonne, 75011   01.43.70.59.29

Maurice Zirah
91 rue de la Roquette, 75011   01.43.79.62.53

Boucherie Guy
266 rue de Charenton, 75012   01.43.44.60.90

J V Temim
2 rue de Dr Goujon, 75012   01.43.45.78.77

B Berbeche
6 rue du Moulinet, 75013   01.45.80.89.10

B Berbeche
5 rue Vandrezanne, 75013   01.45.88.86.50

Chez Alain
8 rue Fagon, 75013   01.42.16.80.25

La Goulette
90 rue Didot, 75014   01.43.95.01.48

B Claude
174 rue Lecourbe, 75015   01.48.28.02.00

Kassab
88 bd Murat, 75016   01.40.71.07.34

Sarl Gm Levy
83 rue de Lonchamp, 75016   01.45.53.04.24

Ste Delicatess
209 av de Versailles, 75016   01.46.51.00.55

Berbeche
39 rue Jouffroy, 75017   01.44.40.07.59

E Courses Elles
117 rue de Courcelles, 75017   01.47.63.36.26

Krief, 104 rue Legendre, 75017
    01.46.27.15.57

Berbeche
48 av de Clichy, 75018   01.45.22.39.04

A Viandes Cacheres
6 av Corentin Cariou, 75019   01.40.36.02.41

Andre-Manin
135 rue Manin, 75019   01.42.38.00.43

Berbeche
15/17 rue Henri Ribiere, 75019   01.42.08.06.06

Chez Meyer
16 rue Menadier, 75019   01.42.45.22.09

Emsalem
18 rue Corentin Cariou, 75019   01.40.36.56.64

Emsalem
17 Quai de la Gironde, 75019   01.40.36.56.64

Even Shapir
15 rue de Crimee, 75019   01.42.02.43.00

Hayot, 1 rue Edouard Pailleron, 75019
    01.42.45.72.22

Maguen David
11/13 rue Curial, 75019   01.40.37.46.00

Boucherie Smadja
90 bd de Belleville, 75020   01.46.36.25.36

Henrino
122 bd de Belleville, 75020   01.47.97.24.52

Groceries

Doueib
11 bis rue Geoffroy Marie, 75009
    01.47.70.86.09

Francois
45 rue Richer, 75009   01.47.70.17.43

Le Haim
6 rue Paulin Enfert, 75013

Chekel
14 av de Villiers, 75017   01.48.88.94.97
Supervision: Beth Din of Paris.
Also sell delicatessen and French sandwiches.

Compt Pdts Aliment
111 av de Villiers, 75017   01.42.27.16.91

Les Ailes Boutiques
15 rue des Fermiers, 75017   01.44.15.93.93

Chochana
54 Av Secretan, 75019

Elygel
116 Bld de Belleville, 75020   01.47.97.09.73

Hotels

Hôtel Aïda Opéra Comotel
17 rue du Conservatoire, 75009
    01.45.23.11.11
Fax: 01.47.70.38.73
Email: comotel@easynet.fr
Supply kosher breakfast.
Supervised by the Beth Din of Paris.

(Paris cont.)

Hôtel Alpha
11 rue Geoffroy Marie, 75009   01.45.23.10.59
Fax: 01.44.79.06.90
Supply kosher meals on Shabbat.
Hôtel Touring
21 rue Buffault, 75009   01.48.78.09.16
Fax: 01.48.78.27.74

L'Hotel de Mericourt
50 rue Folie Mericourt, 75011 01.43.38.73.63
Fax: 01.43.38.66.13
Ten kosher restaurants in vicinity.

Paris Suburbs

Alfortville

Butchers
Tiness
12 rue Etienne Dollet, 94140   01.49.77.95.79

Antony

Synagogues

Orthodox
Community Centre and Synagogue
1 rue Sdérot, Angle 1, Rue Barthélémy, 92160
01.46.66.19.17

Butchers
A.B.C.
96 av de la D Leclerc, 92160   01.46.66.13.43

Asnières

Synagogues
Orthodox
73 bis rue des Bas, 92600   01.47.99.32.55

Mikvaot
82 rue du R.P. Christian-Gilbert, 92600
01.47.99.26.59

Athis-Mons

Synagogues

Orthodox
55 rue des Coquelicots, 92100 01.69.38.14.29

Aulnay-sous-Bois

Synagogues
80 rue Maximilien Robespierre, 93600
01.48.69.66.93

Bagneux

Bakeries
Princiane, 1 rue de l'Egalité, Parc de Garlande,
92200   01.47.35.90.77
Supervision: Beth Din of Paris.

Butchers
Isaac, 188 av Aristide Briand, 92220
01.45.47.00.21

Bagnolet

Bakeries
Sonesta, 27 rue Adélaide Lahaye, 93000
01.43.64.92.93
Fax: 01.43.60.51.26
Supervision: Beth Din of Paris.

Bobigny

Restaurants
Chez Charly et Cecile, 2-24 rue Henri
Barbusse, 93000   01.48.43.79.00
Supervision: Beth Din of Paris.

Bondy

Synagogues *(Orthodox)*
Maison Communautaire
28 avenue de la Villageoise, 93140
01.48.47.50.79

(Paris suburbs cont.)

Boulogne

Synagogues
43 rue des Abondances, 92100
01.46.03.90.63

Bakeries
Ariel, 143 avenue J.B. Clément, 92100
01.46.04.24.42
Supervision: Beth Din of Paris.

Groceries
Ednale
28 rue Georges Sorel, 92100   01.46.03.83.37

Bussière

Mikvaot
Domaines de Melicourt, 77750
01.60.22.54.85; 01.60.22.53.01

Champigny-sur-Marne

Synagogues
Orthodox
Synagogue Beth-David, 25 avenue du
général-de Gaulle, 94500   01.48.85.72.29

Charenton

Butchers
Mazel Tov
14 rue Victor Hugo, 94220   01.43.68.41.23

Chelles

Synagogues
Orthodox
14 rue des Anémones, 77500   01.60.20.92.93

Choisy-le-Roi

Synagogues
28 avenue de Newburn, 94600
01.48.53.48.27

Mikvaot
28 avenue de Newbum, 94600
01.48.53.43.70; 01.48.92.68.68

Butchers
Chez Ilane, 131 Marechal de Lattre de
Tassigny, 94600   01.48.52.27.74

Clichy-sous-Bois

Restaurants
Nathaneli
1 rue Poyer, 92110   01.42.70.97.06
Supervision: Beth Din of Paris.

Clichy-sur-Seine

Synagogues
Orthodox
26 rue de Mozart (Espace Clichy), 92210
01.47.39.02.43

Créteil

Synagogues
Community Centre
rue du 8 Mai 1945, 94051   01.43.77.01.70;
01.43.39.05.20
Fax: 01.43.99.03.60

Mikvaot
Rue du 8 Mai 1945, 94000   01.43.77.01.70;
01.43.77.19.68

Restaurants
Daidou, 9 Esplanade des Abîmes, 94000
01.43.99.44.39
Supervision: Beth Din of Paris.
Fast Food Boucherie Chalom
41 allée Parmentier, 94000   01.48.99.15.45
Supervision: Beth Din of Paris.

(Paris suburbs cont.)

L'Aile et la Cuisse
C.C. Kennedy, 94000   01.49.80.04.25
Supervision: Beth Din of Paris.

Promo Cacher
17 allée du Commerce, 94000   01.49.80.04.25
Supervision: Beth Din of Paris.

Dairy
Le Laguna, 8 rue d'Estienne-d'Orves, 94000
                              01.42.07.10.38
Supervision: Beth Din of Paris.

Bakeries
Caprices et Delices
5 rue Edouard Manet, 94000   01.43.39.20.20
Supervision: Beth Din of Paris.

La Nougatine, 20 Esplanade des Abîmes,
94000   01.49.56.98.56
Supervision: Beth Din of Paris.

Les Jasmins de Tunis
C.C. Kennedy, 94000   01.43.77.50.66
Supervision: Beth Din of Paris.

Quick Chaud
26 allée Parmentier, 94000   01.48.99.08.30
Supervision: Beth Din of Paris.

Tov 'Mie, 25 rue du Dr Paul Casalis, 94000
                              01.42.07.94.81
Supervision: Beth Din of Paris.

Butchers
Boucherie Chalom
41 allee Parmentier, 94000   01.48.99.15.45
Boucherie Patrick
2 rue Edouard Manet, 94000   01.43.39.29.64
La Charolaise Julien
Cte Commercial Kennedy, Loge 13 rue Gabriel
Peri, 94000   01.43.39.20.43

Enghien

Synagogues
Orthodox
47 rue de Malleville, 95880   01.34.12.42.34

Mikvaot
47 rue de Malleville, 95880   01.34.17.37.11

Épinay

Butchers
Chalom
90 av Joffre, 93800   01.48.41.50.64

Fontainebleau

Synagogues
Orthodox
38 rue Paul Seramy, 77300   01.64.22.68.48

Fontenay-aux-Roses

Synagogues
Centre Moise Meniane, 17 avenue Paul-
Langevin, 92660   01.46.60.75.94

Fontenay-sous-Bois

Mikvaot
Haya Mossia
177 rue des Moulins, 94120   01.48.77.53.90;
                              01.48.76.83.84

Garges-lès-Gonesse

Synagogues
Orthodox
Maison Communautaire Chaare Ra'hamim
14 rue Corot, 95140   01.39.86.75.64

Mikvaot
15 rue Corot, 95140   01.39.86.75.64

Butchers
Abner, C C P de la Dame Blanche, 95140
                              01.39.86.43.63
Boucherie Berbeche
C C P de la Dame Blanche, 95140
                              01.39.86.53.81
Chez Harry
1 rue J B Corot, 95140   01.39.86.53.81

(Paris suburbs cont.)

Issy-les-Moulineaux

Synagogues

Orthodox
72 boulevard Gallieni, 92130   01.46.48.34.49

Butchers

Cash Elysees, 40 bis rue Ernest Renan, 92130
01.46.62.67.67

La Courneuve

Synagogues

Orthodox
13 rue Saint-Just, 93120   01.48.36.75.59

La Garenne-Colombes

Synagogues

**Synagogue and Community Centre of
Courbevoie / La Garenne-Colombes**
13 rue L.M. Nordmann, 92250 01.47.69.92.17

La Varenne-St-Hilaire

Synagogues

10 bis avenue du chateau, 94210
01.42.83.28.75

Centre Hillel
30 rue St-Hilaire, 94210   01.48.86.52.09

Le Blanc-Mesnil

Synagogues

65 rue Maxime-Gorki, 93150   01.48.65.58.98

Le Chesnay

Mikvaot

39 rue de Versailles, 78150   01.39.54.05.65;
01.39.07.19.19

Le Kremlin-Bicêtre

Synagogues

Orthodox
41-45 rue J.F. Kennedy, 94270 01.46.72.73.64

Le Perreux-sur-Marne

Synagogues

**Synagogue-Nogent/Le Perreux/Bry-sur-
Marne**, 165 bis avenue du Gal-de Gaulle,
94170   01.48.72.88.65

Le Raincy

Synagogues

Maison Communautaire
19 allée Chatrian, 93340   01.43.02.06.11

Mikvaot

67 boulevard du Midi, 93340 01.43.81.06.61

Le Vésinet

Synagogues

Orthodox
Maison Communautaire
29 rue Henri-Cloppet, 78110   01.30.53.10.45

Mikvaot

29 rue Henri Cloppet, 78110   01.30.53.10.45;
01.30.71.12.26

Les Lilas

Butchers

B Des Lilas
6 rue de la Republique, 93260 01.43.63.89.15

Levallois

Restaurants

Delicates Eden
102 rue Rivay, 92300   01.42.70.97.06
Supervision: Beth Din of Paris.

(Paris suburbs cont.)

Maisons-Alfort

Mikvaot
92-94 rue Victor-Hugo, 94700   01.43.78.95.69

Massy

Synagogues

Orthodox
Allée Marcel-Cerdan, 91300   01.69.20.94.21

Mikvaot
Allée Marcel-Cerdan, 91300   01.42.37.48.24

Meaux

Synagogues
Orthodox
11 rue P. Barennes, 77100   01.64.34.76.58

Meudon-la-Forêt

Synagogues
Maison Communautaire
rue de la Synagogue, 92360   01.48.53.48.27

Mikvaot
Rue de la Synagogue, 92360   01.46.32.64.82;
01.46.01.01.32

Montreuil

Restaurants

Dairy
Pizza Monte Carlo
129 rue Marceau, 93100   01.48.59.55.15;
01.48.59.01.34

Supervision: Beth Din of Paris.

Bakeries
Gad Cachere
21 rue Gabriel Péri, 93100   01.48.59.28.98
Supervision: Beth Din of Paris.
Korcarz
134 bis rue de Stalingrad, 93100
01.48.58.33.45
Supervision: Beth Din of Paris/Chief Rabbi
Mordechai Rottenberg.
Le Relais Sucre
62 rue des Roches, 93100   01.48.70.22.60
Supervision: Beth Din of Paris.

Butchers
Andre Volailles
62 rue des Roches, 93100   01.48.57.57.17

Montrouge

Synagogues

Orthodox
Centre Communautaire Regional Malakoff-Montrouge
90 rue Gabriel-Péri, 92120   01.46.32.64.82
Fax: 01.46.56.20.49

Mikvaot
Ismah-Israel
90 rue Gabriel-Péri, 92120   01.42.53.08.54

Butchers
Boucherie Vivo
2 rue Camille Pelletan, 92120   01.47.35.23.06

Neuilly

Synagogues
Orthodox
12 rue Ancelle, 92200   01.46.24.49.15
Secretary: 01.47.47.78.76

Restaurants
King David
14 rue Paul-Chatrousse, 92200   01.47.45.18.19
Supervision: Beth Din of Paris.
Hours: 8am-10pm.

(Paris suburbs cont.)

Butchers

Neuilly Cacher
2/6 rue de Chartres, 92200   01.47.45.06.06

Groceries

King David
14 rue Paul Chatrousse, 92200 01.47.45.18.19

Nogent-sur-Marne

Restaurants

Dairy
Beteavone
24 rue Paul Bert, 94130   01.48.73.48.48
Supervision: Beth Din of Paris.

Noisy-le-Sec

Synagogues

Orthodox
Beth Gabriel, 2 rue de la Pierre Feuillère,
93130   01.48.46.71.79

Pantin

Restaurants

Chez Jacquy, 24 rue du Pré-Saint-Gervais,
93500   01.48.10.94.24
Supervision: Beth Din of Paris.

Bakeries

Crousty Cash, 27 avenue Anatole France,
93100   01.48.40.89.74
Supervision: Beth Din of Paris.

Butchers

Chel Hida, 177 avenue Jean Lolive, 93500
                               01.48.40.08.29
Supervision: Chief Rabbi Mordechai
Rottenberg.
Levy Baroukh
5/7 rue Anatole France, 93500 01.48.91.02.14

Pavillons

Butchers

Societe Brami
36 av Victor Hugo, 93320   01.48.47.15.76

Ris-Orangis

Synagogues

Orthodox
1 rue Jean-Moulin, 91130   01.69.43.07.83

Roissy-en-Brie

Synagogues

Maison Communautaire
1 rue Paul-Cézanne, Centre Commercial Bois
Montmartre, 77680   01.60.28.36.38

Mikvaot

Rue Paul-Cézanne, C.Cial Bois Montmartre,
77680   01.60.28.34.65; 01.60.29.09.44

Rosny-sous-Bois

Synagogues

Orthodox
62-64 rue Lavoisier, 93110   01.48.54.04.11
                          Fax: 01.69.43.07.83

Rueil-Malmaison

Synagogues

6 rue René-Cassin, 92500   01.47.08.32.62

St-Brice-sous-Forêt

Synagogues

Orthodox
Centre Communautaire Ohel Avraham
10 rue Pasteur, 95350   01.39.94.96.10

(Paris suburbs cont.)

Restaurants

Changat Palace
40 boulevard Albert-Camus, 95350
01.39.92.29.73
Supervision: Beth Din of Paris.

Saint-Denis

Synagogues

51 boulevard Marcel-Sembat, next to the
Gendarmerie), 93200   01.48.20.30.87

St Germain

Butchers

Cash'Ruth, 155 bis rue du P Roosevelt, 78100
01.34.51.51.62

Saint-Leu-La-Forêt

Mikvaot

2 rue Jules Vernes, 95320   01.39.95.96.90;
01.34.14.24.15

St Ouen

Butchers

Chez Paul
37 rue Charles Schmidt, 93400 01.40.11.37.52

Saint-Ouen-L'Aumône

Synagogue *(Orthodox)*

Maison Communautaire
9 rue de Chennevières, 95310 01.30.37.71.41

Sarcelles

Synagogues

Maison Communautaire
74 avenue Paul-Valéry, 95200 01.39.90.59.59
Mikva on premises.

Mikvaot

74 avenue Paul-Valéry, 95200 01.39.90.20.51
Mayanot Rachel
14 avenue Ch.-Péguy, 95200   01.39.90.40.17

Restaurants

Berbeche Burger
13 avenue Edouard-Branly, 95200
01.34.19.12.02
Supervision: Beth Din of Paris.

Dairy

Marina
103 avenue Paul-Valéry, 95200 01.34.19.23.51
Supervision: Beth Din of Paris.

Bakeries

Louis D'or
90 avenue Paul Valéry, 95200 01.39.90.25.45
Supervision: Beth Din of Paris.
Natania
34 blvd Albert Camus, 95200   01.39.90.11.78
Supervision: Beth Din of Paris.
Oh Delices
71 avenue Paul Valéry, 95200 01.39.92.41.12
Supervision: Beth Din of Paris.
Zazou, C.C. les Flanades, 95200
01.34.19.08.11
Supervision: Beth Din of Paris.

Butchers

Boucherie Du Coin
60 bd Albert Camus, 95200   01.39.90.53.02
Hazeout
5 Av Paul Valery, 95200   01.39.90.72.95
Menorah
20 avenue Paul Valéry, 95200 01.34.19.37.64
Supervision: Chief Rabbi Mordechai
Rottenberg.

Sartrouville

Synagogues

Orthodox
**Synagogue Rabbi Shimon bar Yohai et
Rabbi Meir Baal Hannes**
1 rue de Stalingrad, 78500   01.39.15.22.57

France

(Paris suburbs cont.)

Savigny-sur-Orge

Mikvaot

1 avenue de L'Armée-Leclerc, 91600
01.69.24.48.25; 01.69.96.30.90

Sevran

Synagogues

Orthodox
Synagogue Mayan-Thora
25 bis rue du Dr Roux, BP. 111, 93270
01.43.84.25.40

Mikvaot

25 bis rue du Dr Roux, 93270 01.43.84.25.40
Mikva Kelim.

Stains

Synagogues

Orthodox
8 rue Lamartine (face n°2), Clos St-Lazare,
93240   01.48.21.04.12
Provisional address: 8 avenue Louis Bordes
(Ancien Conservatoire Municipal).

Thiais

Community Organisations

Community Centre Choisy-Orly-Thiais
Voie du Four, 128 avenue du Marechal de
Lattre de Tassigny, 94320   01.48.92.68.68
Fax: 01.48.92.72.82

Trappes

Synagogues

Orthodox
7 rue du Port-Royal, 78190   01.30.62.40.43

Velliers-sur-Marne

Synagogue

30 rue Léon-Douer, B.P. 15, 94350
01.49.30.01.47
Fax: 01.49.30.85.40

Versailles

Synagogue

10 rue Albert-Joly, 78000   02.39.07.19.19
Fax: 02.39.50.96.34
Mikva on premises.

Butchers

La Versaillaise
112 rue de la Paroisse, 78000 01.39.25.00.66

Villejuif

Bakeries

Eden Eclair, 30 rue Marcel Grosmenil, 94800
01.47.26.42.96
Supervision: Beth Din of Paris.

Villeneuve-la-Garenne

Synagogues

Orthodox
Maison Communautaire, 44 rue du Fond-de-
la-Noue, 92390   01.47.94.89.98

Mikvaot

42-44 rue du Fond-de-la Noue, 92390
01.47.94.89.98

Butchers

Chez Armand
6 rue Gaston Appert, 92390   01.47.98.52.00

(Paris suburbs cont.)

Villiers-Le-Bel

Synagogues

Orthodox
1 rue Léon-Blum, (Les Carreaux), 95400
01.39.94.30.49; 01.39.94.94.89

Mikvaot

1 rue Léon Blum, 95400   01.39.94.45.51;
01.34.19.64.48

Vincennes

Synagogues

Orthodox
Synagogue Achkenaze
30 rue Céline-Robert, 94300   01.43.28.82.83
Synagogue Sepharade
30 rue Céline-Robert, 94300   01.47.55.65.07

Butchers

Boucherie Des Levy
32 rue Raymond du Temple, 94300
01.43.74.94.18
Hayache
146 Av de Paris, 94300   01.43.28.16.04

Vitry

Synagogues

Orthodox
133-135 avenue Rouget-de-l'Isle, 94400
01.46.80.76.54; 01.45.73.06.58
Fax: 01.45.73.94.01

Yerres

Mikvaot

43/49 rue R. Poincaré, 91330   01.69.48.46.01;
01.69.48.44.67

(France cont.)

Pau

Synagogue

8 rue des Trois-Frère-Bernadac, 64000
05.59.62.37.85

Périgueux

Synagogue

13 rue Paul-Louis-Courrier, 24000
05.53.53.22.52

Perpignan

Synagogue

54 rue Arago, 66000

Butchers

Gilbert Sabbah
3 rue P.-Rameil, 66000   04.68.35.41.23

Cemeteries

There are two monuments of importance; the cemetery of Haut Vernet at Perpignan and the cemetery of Rivesaltes, near the camp from which thousands of Jews were deported to Auschwitz.

Phalsbourg

Synagogue
16 rue Alexandre-Weill, 57370

Poitiers

Synagogue
1 rue Guynemer, 86000

Reims

Synagogue
49 rue Clovis, 51100   03.26.47.68.47

Memorials
There is a war memorial in the Blvd. Général Leclerc with an urn containing ashes from a number of Nazi death camps.

Rennes

Synagogue
23 rue de la Marbaudais, 35000

Roanne

Synagogue
9 rue Beaulieu, 42300   04.77.71.51.56

Rouen

Synagogue
55 rue des Bons-Enfants, 76100
                              02.35.71.01.44
The Jewsh Youth Club can provide board residence for student travellers and holiday-makers

Saint-Avold

Synagogue
Pl. du Marché, 57500   03.87.91.16.16

Cemeteries
The American military cemetery here contains the graves of many Jewish soldiers who fell in the Second World War.

Saint-Die

Synagogue
Rue de l'Evêché, 88100
Services, festivals and Holy-days only.

Saint-Etienne

Synagogue
34 rue d'Arcole, 42000   04.77.33.56.31

Saint-Fons

Synagogue
17 Av. Albert-Thomas, 69190   04.78.67.39.78
Mikva on premises.

Saint-Laurent-du-Var

Synagogue
Villa 'Le Petit Clos', 35 Av. des Oliviers, 06700

Saint-Louis

Community Organisations
Community Centre
19 rue du Temple, 68300   03.89.70.00.48
Kosher products available.

Synagogues
Rue de la Synagogue, 68300
3 rue de Général Cassagnou, 68300

Cemeteries

The Hegenheim cemetery dates from 1673.

Saint-Quentin

Synagogue
11 ter Blvd. Henri-Martin   03.23.08.30.72

Sarrebourg

Synagogue
12 rue du Sauvage

Sarreguemines

Synagogue
Rue Georges-V, 57200   03.87.98.81.40
Mikva on premises.

Saverne

Synagogue
Rue du 19 Novembre, 67700

Sedan-Charleville

Synagogue
6 Av. de Verdun, 08200

Selestat

Synagogue
4 rue Ste.-Barbe, 67600

Sens

Synagogue
14 rue de la Grande-Juiverie, 89100
    03.86.95.16.65

Strasbourg

Religious Organisations
Consistoire Israélite du Bas-Rhin
23 rue Sellénick, 67000   03.88.25.05.75
    Fax: 03.88.25.12.75

Regional Chief Rabbi
Rabbi René Gutman, 5 rue du Général-de-
Castelnau, 67000   03.88.32.38.97

Synagogues
There are in all more than 15 synagogues in
Strasbourg; the following are among the
largest and oldest.

Adath Israël
2 rue St. Pierre-le-Jeune, 67000

Ets Haïm, 28a rue Kageneck, 67000
Mikva on premises.

Synagogue de la Paix
1a rue du Grand-Rabbin-René-Hirschler,
67000   03.88.14.46.50

Mikvaot
1a rue du Grand-Rabbin-René-Hirschler,
67000   03.88.14.46.50

Media
Echos-Unir (monthly newspaper), 1a rue du
Grand-Rabbin-René-Hirschler, 6700

Restaurants
Le King
28 rue Sellénick, 67000   03.88.52.17.71
Le Wilson
25 Blvd. Wilson, 67000   03.88.52.06.66
Restaurant Universitaire
11 rue Sellénick, 67000   03.88.25.67.97

Bakeries
Crousty Cash
4 rue Sellénick, 67000   03.88.35.71.79
Levy
4 rue Strauss, Durkheim   03.88.35.68.21
Meyer
9 rue de la Nuée-Bleue   03.88.32.73.79

Butchers
Buchinger
63 Faubourg de Pièrre, 67000 03.88.32.85.03
and 13 rue Wimpheling   03.88.61.06.98

David
20 rue Sellénick, 67000   03.88.36.75.01

Groceries
Franc Prix
31 Faubourg de Saverne, 67000
                               03.88.32.04.40
and 13 rue du Général-Rapp   03.88.36.16.51

Yarden
3 rue Finkmatt   03.88.22.49.76
and 13 Blvd. de la Marne   03.88.60.10.10

Vineyards
Kosher vineyard nearby at Goxwiller, R.
Koenig, 35 rue Principale   03.88.95.51.93

Booksellers
Librairie Du Cedrat
19 rue du Maréchal-Foch, 67000
Librairie Schné-Or
15 rue de Bitche, 67000   03.88.37.32.37

Tarbes
Synagogue
Cité Rothschild, 6 rue du Pradeau, 65000

Thionville
Synagogue
31 Av. Clémenceau, 57100   03.82.54.47.89

Toul
Synagogue
Rue de la Halle, 54200

Toulon
Synagogue
Av. Lazare Carnot, 83050   04.94.92.61.05
Mikva on premises.

Butchers
Abecassis, 8 rue Vincent Courdouant,
83000   04.94.94.39.86
Supervision: Grand Rabbinate of Marseille.
Fenech
15 avenue Colbert, 83000   04.94.92.70.39
Supervision: Grand Rabbinate of Marseille.

Toulouse
Religious Organisations
Regional Chief Rabbi
Rabbi Georges Haik, 17 rue Calvert, 31500
                               05.61.21.51.14
Grand Rabbinet du Toulouse et des Pays de la Garonne
17 rue Alsace-Lorraine, 31000 05.61.21.51.14

Community Organisations
Community Centre
14 rue du Rempart-St.-Etienne, 31000
                               05.61.23.36.54

Synagogues
Adat Yechouroun (Ashkenazi)
3 rue Jules-Chalande, 31000
(Sephardi), 2 rue Palaprat, 31000
                               05.61.62.90.41
14 rue du Rempart-St.-Etienne, 31000
                               05.61.21.69.56
Chaaré Emeth
35 rue Rembrandt, 31000   05.61.40.03.88

Mikvaot
15 rue Francisque Sarcey, 31000
                               05.61.48.89.84

Restaurants
Community Centre, 14 rue du Rempart-St.-Etienne, 31000   05.61.23.36.54
Students only.
Le Kotel
9 rue Clemence Isaaure   05.61.29.03.04

Butchers
Amsellem
6 rue de la Colombette, 31000 05.61.62.97.55
Bénichou
7 rue des Châlets, 31000   05.61.63.77.39

Cacherout Diffusion
37 Blvd. Carnot, 31000   05.61.23.07.59

Carmel, 1 rue Denfert-Rochereau, 31000
05.61.62.32.74

Ghnassia, 397 Route de St.-Simon, 31000
05.61.42.05.81

Lasry
8 rue Matabiau, 31000   05.61.62.65.28

Groceries
Novogel
14 rue E. Guyiaux, 31300   05.61.57.03.19

Otguergoust
21 pl. V. Hugo, 31000   05.61.21.95.36

Super Cach
Rondpoint de la Plaine Balma   05.61.24.66.75

Tours

Community Organisations
Community Centre
6 rue Chalmel, 37000

Synagogue
37 rue Parmentier, 37000   02.47.05.56.95

Troyes

Synagogue
5 rue Brunneval

Mikvaot
1 rue Brunneval   03.25.73.34.44

Memorials
A statue of Rashi was unveiled at the Troyes
cemetery in 1990.

Valence

Synagogue
1 Place du Colombier, 26000   04.75.43.34.43

Valenciennes

Synagogue
36 rue de l'Intendance, 59300   03.27.29.11.07

Venissieux

Synagogue
12 Av. de la Division-Leclerc, 69200
04.78.70.69.85

Verdun

Synagogue
Impasse des Jacobins, 55100

Vichy

Synagogue
2 bis rue du Maréchal Foch, 03200

Vitry-le-François

Synagogue
Rue du Mouton, 51300
Services Yom Kippur only.

Vittel

Synagogue
Rue Croix-Pierrot, 88800

Wasselonne

Synagogue
Rue des Bains, 67310

Other Départements

Corsica

Ajaccio

Contact Information
Jo Michel Reis
La Grande Corniche, Routes des Sanguinaires
9521-5752
There are between ten and fifteen families in
the town.

Bastia

Synagogues
3 rue du Castagno, 20200
Services Shabbat morning and festivals. This
port town has a Jewish population of 25–35
families.

Guadeloupe

Community Organisations
Bas du Fort, Gosier, Point-à-Pitre   909908
The synagogue, community centre and
restaurant/kosher store are all located here.

Martinique

Fort-de-France

Synagogues
Maison Grambin, Plateau Fofo, Voie 1, 97233
603-727
A community centre is also located here.

Réunion

Synagogues
Communauté Juive de la Réunion
8 rue de l'Est, St Denis, 97400   237-833
High Holy Day services and communal seder
held here.

Contact Information
Leon Benamou   290-545

Hotel
Hotel Astoria
Paul Dijan, 16 rue Juliette Dodu, St Denis,
97400   200-558
Fax: 412-630
Kosher.

Tahiti
(French Polynesia)

Papeete

Religious Organisations
ACISPO, BP rue Morenhout-Pirac, 4821
410-392
Fax: 420-909

Georgia

GMT + 4 hours
Country calling code (995)

Akhaltsikhe
Synagogues
109 Guramishvili Street

Batumi
Synagogues
6 9th March Street

Gori
Synagogues
Chelyuskin Street

Kulashi
Synagogues
170 Stalin Street

Onni
Synagogues
Baazova Street

Poti
Synagogues
Tskhakaya Street
23 Ninoshivili

Sukhumi
Synagogues
56 Karl Marx Street

Surami
Synagogues
Internatsionalaya Street

Tbilisi
Area telephone code (32)
Synagogues
45-47 Leselidze Street

Representative Organisations
Jews of Georgia Association
Tsarity Tamari Street 8, 380012   234-1057

Synagogues
Ashkenazi
65 Kozhevenny Lane
Sephardi
45–47 Leselidze Street

Tshkinvali
Synagogues
Isapov Street

Tskhakaya
Synagogues
Mir Street

Vani
Synagogues
4 Kaikavadze Street

Germany

Even the Nazis, with their extermination policy, failed to sever completely Jewish connections with Germany, which go back uninterruptedly to Roman times, although official Jewish communities are of more recent date. In West Berlin, for instance, the community celebrated its 300th anniversary in 1971.

Hitler was the latest and most virulent persecutor of German Jewry, but though he came nearest of all to wiping out the country's Jews, he did not succeed in obliterating their incalculable contribution over the centuries to German and world culture, the sciences, the economy and other fields of human endeavour.

When the Nazis gained power in 1933, more than half a million Jews lived in Germany, 160,000 in Berlin. Today there are only some 50,000 registered members of the German community, including some 9,400 in Berlin, 5,300 in Frankfurt and 4,100 in Munich and recent immigrants from Russia.

Buildings, monuments and relics of all kinds abound in Germany today, perpetuating the memory of a great and numerous community reduced to a pale shadow of its former self.

GMT + 1 hour
Country calling code (49)

Aachen
Area telephone code (241)

Representative Organisations
Bundesverband Jüdischer Studenten in Deutschland
Oppenhoffallee 50   75998

Alsenz

Sites
Synagogue, Kirchberg 1
Restored 18th century synagogue.

Amberg
Area telephone code (962)

Community Organisations
Community Centre
Salzgasse 5   113140

Andernach

Tourist sites
This Rhine Valley town contains an early 14th century mikva. Key obtainable from tourist office.

Annweiler
Area telephone code (623)

Cemeteries   53333
The oldest cemetery in the Palatinate dating
from 16th century.

Augsburg
Area telephone code (821)

Community Organisations
Community Centre
Halderstr. 8   517985
There is a Jewish museum in the restored
Liberal synagogue. See also Ichenhausen.

Bad Kissingen
Area telephone code (971)

Hotels
Eden-Park
Rosenstrasse 5-7, D-97688   717-200
                            Fax: 717-272
There is a restaurant on the premises that
serves kosher food and traditional meals.

Bad Kreuznach
Area telephone code (671)

Community Organisations
Community Centre
Gymnasialstr. 11   26991

Bad Nauheim
Area telephone code (603)

Synagogues
Community Centre
Karlstr. 34   25605

Restaurants
Club Shalom
Karlstr. 34   231157
Entrance from Friedensstr. Under the
supervision of Rabbi Wald.

Hotels
Accadia, Lindenstr. 15/Frankfurterstr. 22
                                 239068

Baden-Baden
Area telephone code (722)

Synagogues
Werder Str. 2   139-1021

Bamberg
Area telephone code (951)

Community Organisations
Community Centre
Willy-Lessing-Str. 7   23267

Bayreuth
Area telephone code (921)

Community Organisations
Community Centre
Munzgasse 2   65407

Berlin
Area telephone code (30)

Community Organisations
Community Centre
Rykestr. 53, 1055   448-5298
Community Centre
Fasanenstr. 79-80, off the Kurfurstendamm
                                 884-2030
This has been built on the site of a famous
synagogue, destroyed by the Nazi's.

Religious Organisations
Zentralrat der Juden in Deutschland
Oranienburger Str. 31, 10117   282-8714
Berlin Office.

Synagogues
Neue Synagogue Berlin
Centrum Judaicum, Oranienburger-Str. 28,
1040   280-1250

Request for Information

The Publishers welcome updated and new information to incorporate into subsequent editions of the *Jewish Travel Guide*. If you have suggestions for new places to be included or new categories to be incorporated, we would be pleased to hear about them.

Forms for new and updated information can be found at the end of the book.

Advertising Opportunities

Take this opportunity to advertise your goods and services to the greater travelling public.

Advertising details are available at the end of the book (p.423).

Address all inquiries to:

Jewish Travel Guide
Vallentine Mitchell & Co. Ltd.
Newbury House
890–900 Eastern Avenue,
Newbury Park, Ilford, Essex IG2 7HH
Tel: + 44(0)181-599 8866
Fax: + 44(0)181-599 0984
E-mail: jtg@vmbooks.com

Orthodox

Adass Jisroel
Tucholskystrasse 40, D-10117, Mitte 281-3135
Fax: 281-3122
Established 1869. Rabbinate, Kashrut
supervision and mohel can all be reached at
this number. Near its community centre, there
is a guest house, a kosher restaurant and a
shop which sells kosher products.

Liberal

Pestalozzistr. 14, 1000, 12   313-8411

Kashrut Information

Rabbinate of Adass Jisroel
Tucholskystrasse 40, D-10117, Mitte 281-3135
Fax: 281-3122

Tourist Information

Staatliches Israelisches Verkehrsbureau
Stollbergstrasse 6, 15   883-6759
Fax: 882-4093

Embassy

Consulate General
Schinkel Street 10, PO Box 330531, 14193

Media

Magazines

Judische Korrespondez
Judischer Kulturverein
Monthly. Published in German and Russian.

Newspapers

Allgemeine judische Wochenzeitung
Oranienburger Str. 31, 1040
238-6606; 282-8742
Weekly.

Nachrichten/Hadshot Adass Jisroel
Published by Adass Jisroel and obtainable
through their offices (see above for number).

Restaurants

Arche Noah Restaurant
Community Centre, Fasanenstr. 79-80, 12
884-2033/9

Beth Café
Tucholskystrasse 40, D-10117, Mitte 281-3135
Fax: 281-3122
Supervision: Rabbinate of Adass Jisroel.
Open daily, except Shabbat, from 11 am to 10
pm. Closes Friday two hours before Shabbat.

Café Oren
Oranienburger Str. 28, 10117 D   282-8228;
280-1201

Schalom Snack Bar
Wielandstr. 43   312-1131

Groceries

Kachol Lavan
4 Passaner Str.   217-7506
Kolbo
Auguststrasse 77-78, D-10117, Mitte
281-3135
In addition to kosher food and wines, sifrei
kodesh as well as general literature about
Jewish subjects and klei kodesh can be
obtained here.

Bed & Breakfasts

Guestrooms, Tucholskystrasse 40, D-10117
281-3135, Mitte   Fax: 281-3122
Prepaid meals for Oneg Shabbat and Shabbat
lunch after the religious service in the Adass
Jisroel Synagogue.

Cemeteries

Adass Jisroel
Wittlicherstrasse 2, D-13088, Weissensee
Established in in 1880, this historic cemetery is
used to this very day. Rabbi Esriel
Hildesheimer, Rabbi Prof. David Zvi Hoffmann,
Rabbi Eliahu Kaplan and many other wise and
pious Jews are buried here.

Libraries

Jewish Library
Oranienburger Str. 28   280-1229

Booksellers

Literaturhandlung
Joachimstaler-Str. 13, D-10719   882-4250
Fax: 885-4713

Bochum
Area telephone code (234)

Synagogues

Alte Wittener Str. 18, 44803   361563
Fax: 360187

Bonn/Bad Godesberg
Area telephone code (228)

Religious Organisations
Zentralrat der Juden
Rungsdorfer Str. 6, 53173   357023
    Fax: 361148

Synagogues
Templestr. 2-4, cnr. Adenauer Allee, 53113
    213560
    Fax: 213560

Embassy
Embassy of Israel
Simrock Allee 2, Postfach 200230, 53173
    934-6545

Media

Newspapers
Allgemeine judische Wochenzeitung
Rungsdorfer Str. 6, 53173   351021
    Fax: 355469
Fortnightly.

Braunschweig
Area telephone code (531)

Community Organisations
Community Centre
Steinstr. 4   45536

Museums
The Jewish Museum
Hinter Aegidien, 3300   484-2602
Founded in 1746, this museum was formerly
the oldest Jewish museum in the world. It was
reopened in 1987 under the auspices of the
Braunschweigisches Landesmuseum. Hours
Tues.-Sun: 10am to 5pm; Thurs. 10am to 8pm.

Bremen
Area telephone code (421)

Synagogues
Schwachauser Heerstr. 117   498-5104
    Fax: 498-4944

Chemnitz
Area telephone code (371)

Community Organisations
Community Centre
Stollberger Str. 28   32862

Coblenz
Area telephone code (261)

Community Organisations
Community Centre
Schlachthof Str. 5   42223

Cologne
Area telephone code (221)

Synagogues
Roonstr. 50, 50674   921-5600
    Fax: 921-5609
Daily services. There are a youth centre, Jewish
museum and library at the same address.

Restaurants
Community Centre
Roonstr. 50, 50674   240-4440
    Fax: 240-4440
Kosher meals available.

Hotels
Leonet (80)
Rubensstr. 33   236016

Darmstadt
Area telephone code (615)

Community Organisations
Community Centre
Wilhelm-Glassing-Str. 26   128897

Dortmund
Area telephone code (231)

Representative Organisations
Landesverband der Judischen Kultusgemeinden von Westfalen
Prinz-Friedrich-Karl-Str. 12, 44135   528495
                 Fax: 5860372

Synagogues
Prinz-Friedrich-Karl-Str. 9, 44135   528497

Dresden
Area telephone code (351)

Representative Organisations
Landesverband der Judischen Gemeinden von Sachsen
Thuringen, Bautzner Str. 20, 8060   578691
A memorial to the six million Jews killed in the holocaust stands on the site of the Dresden Synagogue, burnt down by the Nazis in November 1938.

Synagogues
Fiedlerstr. 3   693317

Dusseldorf
Area telephone code (211)

Synagogues
Zietenstr. 50   461-9120
              Fax: 485156

Hotels
Gildors Hotel
Collenbachstr. 51   488005
Israeli owned.

Emmendingen

Synagogues
Lenzhausle am Schlossplatz   (764) 157-1989

Erfurt

Community Organisations
Community Centre
Juri-Gagarin-Ring 16   (361) 24964

Essen

Community Organisations
Community Centre
Sedanstr. 46   (201) 273413

Essingen

Cemetery
Largest cemetery in the Palatinate, where Anne Frank's ancestors are buried, 16th-century. Key at the Mayor's office.

Frankfurt-Am-Main
Area telephone code (69)

Representative Organisations
Zentralwohlfahrtsstelle der Juden in Deutschland
Hebelstrasses 6, 60318   94 43 7115
             Fax: 49 48 17

Community Organisations
Community Centre
Westendstr. 43   74 07 21
This community produces a monthly magazine, "Judische Gemeinde-Zeitung Frankfurt".

Synagogues
Baumweg 5-7   439381 & 499-0758
Beth Hamidrash West End
Altkanigstr. 27   723805
Westend Synagogue
Freiherr-vom-Stein-Str. 30   726263
This is the city's main synagogue.

Sohar's
KOSHER RESTAURANT GMBH

Im Jüdischen Gerneindezenfrum
Savignystraße 66,
D-60325 Frankfurt am Main
Tel: 069-752341 Fax 069-7410116

- RESTAURANT
- ROOMS FOR PARTIES
- CATERING
- DELIVERY TO HOTELS
- AIRLINE CATERING
- GLATT KOSHER UNDER THE SUPERVISION OF OUR **RABBI MENACHEM HALEVI KLEIN**

Mikvaot

Westend Synagogue
Freiherr-vom-Stein-Str. 30   726263

Restaurants

Sohar's
Savignystrasse 66, D-60325   75 23 41
                                    Fax: 741 0116
Supervision: Rabbi Menachem Halevi Klein,
Frankfurt Rabbinate.
Hours: Tuesday to Thursday and Sunday,
12 pm to 8 pm; Friday, 12 pm to Shabbat;
Shabbat, 1:30 pm to 4 pm; Monday, closed.
Special arrangements can be made by phone.
Friday and Shabbat meals must be ordered in
advance. Provide party service, airline catering
and delivery to hotels. Fifteen minute walk
from synagogue, fair centre and main train
station.

Bakeries

Donath Werner
Raimundstr. 21   526202

Butchers

Aviv Butchery & Deli
Hanauer Landstr. 50   431539

Hotels

Hotel Excelsior & Monopol (200)
Mannheimer Str. 7-13, 6000, 1   256080

Luxor Hotel
Am Allerheiligentor 2-4   293067 / 69
This hotel, which is under Jewish
management, is within walking distance of
the Freiherr-vom-Stein-Str. synagogue.

Museums

Jewish Museum
Untermainkai 14-15   212-35000
Sun, Tues. & Thurs. 10am to 5pm; Wed 10am
to 8pm; Fri 10am to 3pm; Mon. closed.

Freiburg
Area telephone code (761)

Community Organisations

Community Centre
Nussmannstr. 14   383096

Friedberg/Hessen

Tourist Sites

Judengasse 20
The ancient mikva, built in 1260, is located
here. The town council has issued a special
explanatory leaflet about it, and it is now
scheduled as a historical monument of
medieval architecture.

Fulda
Area telephone code (66)

Community Organisations

Community Centre
von Schildeckstr. 13   170252
Services first Friday of each month, half an
hour before dusk.

Fürth

Area telephone code (91)

Community Organisations

Community Centre
Blumenstr. 31   177-0879

Tourist Sites

Julienstr. 2
There is a beautifully restored synagogue as
well as a historic mikva.

Gelsenkirchen

Area telephone code (20)

Community Organisations

Community Centre
Von-der-Recke-Str. 9   923143 & 206628

Hagen

Area telephone code (2331)

Community Organisations

Community Centre
Potthofstr. 16   711-3289

Halle/Saale

Area telephone code (345)

Community Organisations

Community Centre
Grosse Markerstr. 13   26963

Hamburg

Area telephone code (40)

Community Organisations

Community Centre
Schaferkampsallee 27, 20357   440-9440
                                     Fax: 410-8430

Synagogues

Hohe Weide 34, 20253   440-9440
Mikvah on premises.

Kosher food is available upon reservation.
                                        440-9441
                                    Fax: 410-8430

Hanover

Area telephone code (511)

Community Organisations

Community Centre
Haeckelstr. 10   810472

Synagogues

Haeckelstr. 10

Heidelberg

Area telephone code (6221)

Restaurants

College Restaurant
Theaterstr.
Kosher meals available (by arrangement & in
advance) Mon.-Fri at college restaurant, 100
yards from college.

Herford

Area telephone code (52)

Community Organisations

Community Centre
Keplerweg 11   212039

Hof/Saale

Area telephone code (92)

Community Organisations

Community Centre
An Wiesengrund 20   815-3249

Ichenhausen

Museums

Museum of Jewish History
Located in the fine baroque synagogue, not far from Ulm.

Ingenheim

Tourist Sites

Klingenerstr. 20
16th century cemetery can be visited. Key obtained from Klingenerstr. 20

Kaiserslautern

Area telephone code (63)

Community Organisations

Community Centre
Basteigasse 4   169720

Karlsruhe

Area telephone code (72)

Community Organisations

Community Centre
Knielinger Allee 11   172035

Kassel

Area telephone code (56)

Community Organisations

Community Centre
Bremer Str. 9   112960

Konstanz

Area telephone code (75)

Community Organisations

Community Centre
Sigismundstr. 19   312-3077

Krefeld

Area telephone code (21)

Community Organisations

Community Centre
Wiedstr. 17b   512-0648

Landau

Synagogues

Frank-Loebsche Haus, Kaufhausgasse 9

Leipzig

Area telephone code (341)

Community Organisations

Community Centre
Lahrstr. 10   291028

Lübeck

Area telephone code (451)

Synagogues

Synagogue & Community Centre
St Annen Str. 11, 23552   798-2182
                             Fax: 798-2182
Supervised through the Hamburg community.

Magdeburg

Area telephone code (391)

Community Organisations

Community Centre
Graperstr. 1a   52665

Mainz

Area telephone code (6131)

Community Organisations

Community Centre
Forsterstr. 2   613990

Tourist Sites

Untere Zahlbacherstr. 11
The key to the 12th century Jewish cemetery can be obtained at the 'new' Jewish cemetery.

Mannheim

Area telephone code (621)

Community Organisations

Community Centre
F 3-4   153974

Marburg/Lahn

Area telephone code (642)

Community Organisations

Community Centre
Unterer Eichweg 17   132881

Minden

Area telephone code (57)

Community Organisations

Community Centre
Kampstr. 6   123437

Mönchengladbach

Area telephone code (216)

Synagogues

Community Centre
Albertusstr. 54, 41363   123879
Fax: 114639

Mülheim/Ruhr-Oberhausen

Area telephone code (20)

Community Organisations

Community Centre
Kampstr. 7   835191

Munich

Area telephone code (89)

Community Organisations

Community Centre
Reichenbachstr. 27   271-2774; 271-8298

Synagogues

Possartstr. 15
Mikva on premises.
Reichenbachstr. 27
Mikva on premises.
Schulstrasse 30
Fri. evenings and Sabbath mornings only.
Reichenbachstr. 27
Schwabing Synagogue
Georgenstr. 71
Fri. evenings and Sabbath mornings only.

Restaurants

Reichenbachstr. 27   201-4565
Run by the community centre.
Hours: 12pm - 2.30pm; 6pm - 9pm. Shabbat meals must be ordered by Friday noon. Closed Sunday; August.

Museums

Judisches Museum Munchen
Maximilian Str. 36

Münster

Area telephone code (25)

Community Organisations

Community Centre
Klosterstr. 8-9   144909

Neustadt/Rheinpfalz

Area telephone code (63)

Community Organisations

Community Centre
Ludwigstr. 20   212652

Nuremberg
Area telephone code (91)

Community Organisations
Community Centre
Johann-Priem-Str. 20   156250
For the Jewish Aged.

Odenbach
Area telephone code (62)

Tourist Sites
There is a historic synagogue with baroque
paintings in this small village near Bad
Kreuznach.   353332; 532745

Offenbach
Area telephone code (69)

Community Organisations
Community Centre
Kaiserstr. 109   814874

Kashrut Information
Seligenstadter Strasse 153a   892198
                               Fax: 898396

Osnabrück
Area telephone code (54)

Community Organisations
Community Centre
In der Barlage 41, 49078   148420
                             Fax: 143-4701

Paderborn
Area telephone code (52)

Community Organisations
Community Centre
Pipinstr. 32   512-2596

Potsdam
Area telephone code (331)

Community Organisations
Potsdam Community Centre
Heinrich-Mann-Allee 103, Haus 16   872018

Regensberg
Area telephone code (94)

Community Organisations
Community Centre
Am Brixener Hof 2   157093; 21819

Rülzheim

Tourist Sites
The key to the early 19th century synagogue
in this village near Karlsruhe is obtainable
from the town hall.

Saarbrücken
Area telephone code (68)

Community Organisations
Community Centre
Lortzing Str. 8, 66111   135152

Synagogues
Synagogengemeinde Saar
Postfach 102838, 66028

Schwerin/
Mecklenburg
Area telephone code (38)

Community Organisations
Judische Gemeinde zu Schwerin
Schlachterstr. 3-5   555-07345

Speyer
Area telephone code (62)

Tourist Sites
This town contains the oldest (11th c.) mikva in Western Germany, Judenbadgasse. To visit it, obtain the key from the desk at the Hotel Trutzpfuff, in Webergasse, just around the corner, or contact Prof. Stein at the Historical Museum. There are some early 19th c. village synagogues in the wine-growing region of the Palatinate. For information tel: 353332.

Straubing
Area telephone code (94)

Community Organisations
Community Centre
Wittelsbacherstr. 2, 94315   211387

Stuttgart
Area telephone code (711)

Religious Organisations
Israelitische Religionsgemeinschaft Wurttembergs
Hospitalstr. 36, D 70174   228360
Fax: 2283618

Restaurants
Community Centre
Rabbiner Konferenz of German Rabbis at same address.

Sulzburg

Tourist Sites
There is a beautifully restored early 19th c. synagogue here, some 20 miles from Freiburg. Keys obtainable from Mayor's office.

Trier
Area telephone code (65)

Community Organisations
Community Centre
Kaiserstr. 25   140530; 33295

Wachenheim

Tourist Sites
A large 16th c. cemetery. Key available from the Town Hall. First records of registration of Jews in the year 831.

Wiesbaden
Area telephone code (6121)

Synagogues
Friedrichstr. 33   301870; 301282

Restaurants
Communal Offices
Friedrichstr. 33   301870
Inquiries regarding kosher meals.

Worms

Tourist Sites
The original Rashi Synagogue here, built in the eleventh century and the oldest Jewish place of worship in Europe, was destroyed by the Nazis in 1938. After the Second World War it was reconstructed and was reconsecrated in 1961. The building also contains a twelfth-century mikva and a Jewish museum. There is also an ancient Jewish cemetery.

Wuppertal
Area telephone code (202)

Community Organisations
Community Centre
Friedrich-Ebert-Str. 73   300233

Würzburg
Area telephone code (93)

Synagogues
Community Centre
Valentin-Becker-Str. 11, 97072   151190
                                   Fax: 118184

Mikvaot
Valentin-Becker-Str.11, 97072   151190
Appointments to be made.

Restaurants
Community Centre   151190
Also guest rooms for tourists available.

Museums
The Synagogue and Museum of Jewish Culture
6 Muhlgasse, Veilschochheim
Recently restored.

Tourist Sites
There are old Jewish cemeteries in Würzburg, Heidingsfeld and Höchberg.

Gibraltar

Gibraltar Jewry numbers about 600 Sephardi Jews, who settled there soon after the British occupation in 1704, coming from Italy, North Africa and, later, from England. The Shaar Hashamayim Synagogue was built in the middle of the eighteenth century. Gibraltar Jews are known for their hospitality.

The old Jewish cemetery is well worth a visit. It contains the graves of many saintly men, including that of the revered Rev. R. H. M. Benaim.

GMT + 1 hour
Country calling code (350)

Community Organisations
Managing Board of Jewish Community
10 Bomb House Lane   72606
                                 Fax: 40487

Cultural Organisations
Jewish Social & Cultural Club
7 Bomb House Lane   72606

Synagogues
Abudarham
20 Parliament Lane, 78506

Etz Hayim
Irish Town, 75955

Nefusot Yehuda
65 Line Wall Road, 73037

Shaar Hashamayim
19 Engineer Lane, 78069

Mikvaot
12 Bomb House Lane   77658
                                 Fax: 72359

Kashrut Information
There are no kosher hotels in Gibraltar, but the White's Hotel and Rock Hotel will provide vegetarian or fish diets. The Rock Hotel will provide kosher food if the parties consist of more than ten people.

Contact Information
Solomon Levi
3 Convent Place, PO Box 190   77789; 42818

The president of the Jewish community, he is happy to provide information for Jewish travellers.

Embassy
Israel Consulate
Marina View, Glacis Road, PO Box 141   77244

Restaurants
Jewish Club
Open daily from 10 am to 11 pm, except Shabbat, but arrangements can be made with this restaurant owner for Shabbat meals.
Leanse Restaurant   41751
Kosher.

Bakeries
J. Amar, 47 Line Wall Road   73516

Butchers
A. Edery, 26 John Mackintosh Sqaure

Delicatessens
Uncle Sam Garbass
82 Irish Town   79020
Provides kosher groceries and wine.

Groceries
M. I. Abudarham
32 Cornwall's Lane   78506

Greece

There have been Jewish communities in Greece since the days of antiquity. Before the Second World War, 76,500 Jews lived in Greece (56,000 in Salonika). Today there are barely 5,000, of whom 2,900 live in Athens, 1,200 in Salonika, 375 in Larissa, 166 in Volos, and the remainder in a number of other towns throughout Greece.

GMT + 2 hours
Country calling code (30)

Athens
Area telephone code (1)

Representative Organisations
Central Board of the Jewish Communities of Greece
2 Sourmeli Street   883-9951
                                       Fax: 823-4488

Synagogues
Sephardi
Beth Shalom
5 Odos Melidoni   325-2773

Embassy
Embassy of Israel
Marathonodromou Street 1, Paleo Psychico,
POB 65140, 15452   671-9530

Restaurants
Jewish Community Centre
8 Melidoni Street, 10553   32-52875
                                       Fax: 32-20761
Kosher meals for groups can be organised via the Jewish Community Centre. The only 'kosher' restaurant in Athens.

Museums
36 Amalias Avenue   323-1577
Open 9am to 1pm Sun to Fri.

Chalkis (Halkis)
Area telephone code (221)

Community Organisations
Community Centre
46 Kriezotou Street, 34100   27297
                                        Fax: 76700

Synagogues
Kotsou Street
This synagogue has been rebuilt and renewed many times on its original foundations. tombstone inscriptions in the cemetery go back more than fifteen centuries.

Kashrut Information
Community Centre   27297
                                        Fax: 76700

Corfu
Area telephone code (661)

Community Organisations
Community Centre
5 Riz. Voulefton St., 49100   30591
                                        Fax: 31898

Hotels
King Alkinos Hotel   39300

Tourist Sites

Velissariou St.   38802
There was an ancient synagogue and cemetery here, destroyed by the Nazis.

Joannina
Area telephone code (651)

Community Organisations

Community Centre
18 Josef Eliyia St., 45221   25195

Larissa
Area telephone code (41)

Synagogues

29 Kentavron St.   226396

Rhodes (Dodecanese Islands)
Area telephone code (241)

Tourist Sites

1 Simmiou St.   29406
The synagogue built in 1731, is in the old Jewish district. Visitors desiring to see around it should contact the caretaker, Lucia Sulan.

Salonika (Thessaloniki)
Area telephone code (31)

Cultural Organisations

The Israelite Fraternity House
24 Vassileos Irakliou St.   221030
Yad le Zikaron
24 Vassileos Irakliou St.   275701

Synagogues

35 Sigrou, 54630   524968

Libraries

The Centre for Historical Studies of Salonika Jews
24 Vassileos Irakliou St.   223231
Fax: 229069

Trikkala

Synagogues

Odos Diacou   25834

Verria

Synagogues

There is a synagogue in the ancient Jewish quarter.

Volos
Area telephone code (42)

Community Organisations

Community Centre
21b Vassani St., 38333   123079
Enquiries to Raphael Frezis, Community President, 20 Pavliou Mela St.   25640

Tourist Information

20 Parodos Kondulaki
Small Jewish communities are to be found in Cavala & Carditsa. In Hania, the former capital of the island of Crete, there is an old synagogue in the former Jewish quarter, at the above address.

Guadeloupe
see France

Guatemala

GMT – 6 hours
Country calling code (502)

Guatemala City
Area telephone code (2)

Synagogues

Sephardi

Maguen David
7a Av. 3-80, Zona 2   232-0932

Embassy
Embassy of Israel
13 Av. 14-07, Zona 10   371305

Haiti

GMT – 5 hours
Country calling code (509)

Port au Prince

Contact Information

There are 44 Jews in Haiti, all of them living in Port au Prince, the capital. Religious services are held at the home of the Honorary Consul, Mr Gilbert Bigio.

Honduras

GMT – 6 hours
Country calling code (504)

San Pedro Sula

Contact Information   530157

Services Friday and Shabbat at synagogue and community centre.

Embassy

Israel Embassy
Palmira Building, 5th Floor   324232; 325176

Tegucigalpa

Contact Information   315908

Services usually held in private homes. Contact secretary at above number.

Hong Kong

GMT + 8 hours
Country calling code (852)

Community Organisations

Jewish Community Centre
1 Robinson Place, 70 Robinson Road,
Mid-Levels   2801-5440
                        Fax: 2877-0917
A new facility with two kosher restaurants, kosher supermarket and banquet facilities under mashgiach supervision, swimming pool and leisure facilities and library/function facilities. Meals available on Shabbat. Take-away and kosher food delivery available.

Cultural Organisations

Hong Kong Jewish Historical Society
                        2559-2890
                        Fax: 2547-2550
Publishes monographs on subjects of Sino-Judaic interest and maintains an archive. Information from Dennis Leventhal.

Synagogues

Orthodox

Lubavitch in the Far East (Chabad)
18 Kennedy Road, #1A, Mid-Levels 2523-9770
                        Fax: 2845-2772
Holds regular morning services in the Furama Hotel, Room 601. Daily Shacharit at 7:15 am and Mincha-Ma'ariv at 5:50 pm. Shabbat services are followed by Shabbat meals. Due to its popularity and limited space, meals have to be reserved and paid for in advance. Rooms at the Furama Hotel, as well as the Ritz Carlton, can be booked through Chabad at discounted rates. For meals and room reservation, fax requests to the above number. For room reservations, please include your credit card information for guarantee.

Ohel Leah Synagogue
70 Robinson Road, Mid-Levels   2589-2621
                        Fax: 2548-4200
Friday night, Shabbat and weekday services are held.

Shuva Israel Beit Medrash and Community Centre
61 Connaught Road Central, 2/F, Fortune House, Central   2851-6218; 2851-6300
                        Fax: 2851-7482
Sephardi service. Daily minyan during weekdays, Shacharit 7:15 am, Mincha-Maariv, 20 minutes before sunset; Shabbat times, Kabbalat Shabbat at sunset, Shacharit 8 am; Mincha and Seuda Shlishit 30 minutes before sunset.

Shuva Israel Synagogue
16-18 MacDonnel Road, 1-B,
Mid-Levels   2851-6218
                        Fax: 2851-7482
Sephardi service. Shabbat and holidays. A substantial discount can be arranged at a nearby hotel.

Zion Congregation
21 Chatham Road, 4th Floor, Kowloon
                        2366-6364
                        Fax: 2366-6364

Liberal/Reform

United Jewish Congregation of Hong Kong
Jewish Community Centre, Mid-Levels

2523-2985
Fax: 2523-3961
Email: jvujc@hk.super.net

The UJC is the only non-Orthodox community in Hong Kong. It encompasses Jews from Reform, Conservative and Liberal backgrounds. Friday evening services followed by communal Shabbat dinner; periodic Shabbat morning services; holidays.

Embassy

Israel Consulate-General
Admiralty Centre, Tower II, suite 701, 18
Harcourt Road   2529-6091
Fax: 2855-0220

Restaurants

Shalom Grill
61 Connaught Road Central, 2/F, Fortune
House, Central   2851-6218; 2851-6300
Fax: 2851-7482
Email: darvick@chevalier.net

Middle Eastern Glatt Kosher cuisine and grocery. Hours: Breakfast, 8 am to 9 am; Lunch, 12 pm to 2:30 pm; Dinner, 6:30 pm to 9:30 pm.

Cemeteries

The Jewish Cemetery
Located in Happy Valley   2589-2621
Fax: 2548-4200

Hungary

The Jewish population of Hungary is about 100,000, of whom some 80 % live in the capital, Budapest, and the rest mainly in rural areas. (In 1930 the city had a Jewish population of 230,000 – the second largest in Europe). It is probable that Jews lived in this part of Europe in Roman times. The National Tourist Board publishes a brochure on Jewish relics in Hungary.

GMT + 1 hour
Country calling code (36)

Budapest
Area telephone code (1)

Community Organisations
Central Board of the Federation of Jewish Communities in Hungary
VII, Sip utca 12   342-1355

Religious Organisations

Conservative
The Central Rabbinical Council
VII, sip utca 12   142-1180
Rabbi Schweitzer is Chief Rabbi of Hungary and Director of the Rabbinical Seminary.

Synagogues

Orthodox
The Orthodox Central Synagogue
VII, Kazinczy utca 27   132-4331

Heroes Synagogue
VII Wesselenyi utca 5

Mikvaot
VII Kazinczy utca 16

Tourist information
Jewish Information Service   166-5165
                              Fax: 166-5165

Embassy
Embassy of Israel
Fullank Utca 8, II, 1026

Media

Newspapers
Uj Elet (New Life)
Central Board Hotel

Restaurants
Central Kitchen & Food Distribution
IX, Pava utca 9-11
Hannah, VII Dob Utca 35   142-1072
Hours: 11:30 am to 4 pm on weekdays. Cater meals paid in advance for Shabbat. Winter hours may vary.

Bakeries
Kacinczy utca 28
Opening hours and availability are apparently variable.
Dob utca 20

Dairies
The Orthodox Central Synagogue
VII, Kazinczy utca 27
Kosher milk and cheese are available here three mornings a week.

Groceries
Koser Bott, Nyar utcal   322-9276
Osem products, bread etc.

Hotels
King's Hotel
Nagydiofa utca 25-27, 1074   267-9324
                              Fax: 267-9324
Kosher.

Museums

Jewish Museum (formerly Herzl House)
VII Dohany utca 2   142-8949
Open May to October 10am to 3pm.

Tours

Chosen Tours   185-9499
                    Fax: 166-5165
Tours of Jewish sites are provided by Chosen
Tours by telephone arrangement.

Sopron
Area telephone code (99)

Synagogues

Orthodox
Jewish Orthodox
Tomolom utca 22, H-9400   313558

Museums

The Old Synagogue Museum
Uj utca 22-24, H-9400   311327
                    Fax: 311347

A department of the Sopron Museum.
Medieval Synagogue restored as a museum in
1976. Open daily from 9am to 5pm.

Tourist Sites

Uj utca 11
A second medieval Synagogue which formerly
housed the Museum is undergoing restoration
and will reopen in 1997. The ruins of the 1891
synagogue, out of use since 1956, can be seen
at Pap-ret H-9400.

The Neologue Cemetery
Dating from the 19th c. There is a memorial
wall dedicated to the 1600 local victims of the
Holocaust.

There are also Jewish communities in
Debrecen, Györ, Miskolc, Pécs, Szeged,
Szombathely and other cities. The beautiful
Szeged synagogue has recently been restored.

India

Indian Jewry comprises: (1) The Bene Israel, who form about 92 per cent, with the Bombay region as their main centre; (2) the Jews of Cochin and neighbourhood, on the Malabar Coast; (3) Jews from Iraq, as well as Iran, Bokhara and Afghanistan, who first arrived as a small handful of people some 200 years ago. There are altogether about 5,500 Jews in India, of whom some 4,350 live in Bombay. The Bene Israel, according to tradition, arrived in India before the Christian era. The Bene Israel now have more than 20 synagogues in India (19 Sephardi and one Liberal). A monument has been erected in the village of Navgaon where they landed.

Jews from Iraq first arrived in about 1796, escaping persecution. They are to be found chiefly in Bombay, Poona and Calcutta. They have two synagogues in Bombay, one in Poona, and three in Calcutta. Among the more illustrious of their members were the Sassoon, Ezra and Kadoorie families, who established a large number of mills and other business enterprises.

The Jews of Cochin, on the Malabar Coast, arrived as traders about the first century and have records dating as far back as the eighth century. There are only about 200 Jews in the State of Kerala today, the rest having emigrated to Israel and other countries. Diplomatic relations have now been established with Israel.

GMT + 5½ hours
Country calling code (91)

Ahmedabad
Area telephone code (79)

Synagogues
Magen Abraham
Bukhara Mohalla, opp. Parsi Agiari

Bombay
Area telephone code (22)

Synagogues
Beth El Synagogue
Mirchi Galli, Mahatma Gandhi Road, Panvel, 410206

Beth El Synagogue
Rewdanda, Allibag Tehsil, Raigad

Beth Ha-Elohim Syn
Penn

Etz Haeem Prayer Hall
2nd Lane, Umerkhadi, 400009   377-0193

Gate of Mercy (Shaar Harahamim)
254 Samuel Street, Nr Masjid Railway Station, 400003   345-2991
This is the oldest Bene Israel synagogue in India, established in 1796 and known as the Samaji Hasaji Synagogue or Juni Masjid until 1896 when its name was changed to Shaar Harahamim.

Hessed-El Synagogue
Poynad, Alibag Tehsil

Knesseth Eliahu Synagogue
Forbes Street, Fort, 400001   283-1502

Kurla Bene Israel Prayer Hall
275 S. G. Barve Road (Pipe Road), Kurla, West
Bombay, 400070

Magen Aboth Synagogue
Alibag

Magen David Synagogue
opp. Richardson & Cruddas, Byculla, 400008

Magen Hassidim Synagogue
8 Mohammaed Shahid Marg, (formerly
Moreland Road), Agripada, 400011   309-2493

Rodef Shalom Synagogue
Sussex Road, Byculla, 400027

Shaar Hashamaim Synagogue
Tembi Naka, opp. Civil Hospital, Thane,
400601   853-4817

Shaare Rason Synagogue
90 Tantanpura Street, 3rd Road, Don Tad,
Israel Mohalla, Khadak, 400009

Shahar Hatephilla Synagogue
Mhasla

Tifereth Israel Synagogue
92 K. K. Marg, Jacob Circle, 400011   305-3713

Kashrut Information

Pearl Farm, A/1 Ground Floor, Sulabha, Dhobi
Alley, 400601, Maharashtra
Enquiries about the provision of kosher food
can be sent to this address.

Embassy

Israel Consulate
50 Kailash, G. Deshmukh Marg, 26   386-2793

Tour Agents

Tov Tours & Travels (India)
96 Penso Villa, 1st Floor, Dadar, 400028
                                        445-0134
                               Fax: 437-1700
Tours of Jewish India.

Calcutta

Area telephone code (33)

Representative Organisations

Jewish Association of Calcutta
1&2 Old Court House Corner   224861
General inquiries to this telephone number.

Synagogues

Bethel Synagogue
26/1 Pollack Street

Magen David Synagogue
109a Peplabi Rash, Bihari Bose Road, 1,
(formerly Canning Street)

Neveh Shalome Synagogue
9 Jackson Lane, 1

Cochin

Area telephone code (91484)

Synagogues

Chennamangalam
Jew Street, Chennamangalam
Built in 1614 & restored in 1916, this
synagogue has been declared a historical
monument by the Government of India. A few
yards away is a small concrete pillar into
which is inset the tombstone of Sara Bat-
Israel, dated 5336 (1576).

Paradesi, Jew Town, Mattancherry, 2
The only Cochin synagogue that is still
functioning. Built 1568.

Contact Information

Inquiries, Princess Street, Fort   24228; 24988

New Delhi

Area telephone code (11)

Synagogues

Judah Hyam Synagogue
2 Humayun Road, 110003   463-5500

Judah Hyam Synagogue
A/7 Nirman Vihar, Patparganj, 110092
                                        224-3136
The Judah Hyam Annexe houses a library and
centre for Jewish & inter-faith studies.

Pune
Area telephone code (212)

Synagogues
Ohel David Synagogue
Poona Camp (Cantonment), 411001
Succath Shelomo
93 Rasta Peth, 411011
Inquiries to Hon. Sec. 247/1 Rasta Peth, Trupti
Apt., Pune 411011 or Dr S. B. David, 9 Bund
Garden Road, Pune 411001.

Iran

There have never been any reliable statistics on the number of Jews living
in Iran. Today, there are an estimated 28,000. Most live in Tehran. The
Tomb of Daniel is near Ahavaz (Shoush) and that of Mordechai and Esther
is venerated at Hamadan.

GMT + 3½ hours
Country calling code (98)

Isfahan
Area telephone code (31)

Synagogues
Shah Abass Street

Tehran
Area telephone code (21)

Synagogues
Haim, Gavamossaltaneh Street
Meshedi, Kakh Shomali Avenue, opp.
Abrishami School
The Iraqi, Anatole France Street

Tourist Sites
Jewish Quarter of Tehran, Mahalleh, off Sirus
Avenue

Irish Republic

A Sephardi community was established in Dublin in the middle of the seventeenth century. In 1918 the office of Chief Rabbi of Eire was established, the first incumbent being Rabbi Isaac Herzog (who became Chief Rabbi of Israel, and died in 1959). Other holders of the office have included Lord Immanuel Jakobovits. The Jewish population is about 1,200, most of whom live in Dublin.

GMT + 0 hours
Country calling code (353)

Cork

Synagogues
10 South Terrace   (21) 870413
Services: Sat morning 10.30am and Holy-days.

Dublin
Area telephone code (1)

Religious Organisations
The Chief Rabbinate of Ireland
Herzog House, 1 Zion Road, 6   492-3751
Fax: 492-4680
Board of Shechita located here as well.

Synagogues
Dublin Hebrew Congregation
37 Adelaide Road   661-4208
Machzikei Hadass
77 Terenure Road North, Rathfarnham Road
490-8413 or 490-6130
Terenure Hebrew Congregation
Rathfarnham Road, 6, Terenure
The Jewish Home, Denmark Hill, Leinster
Road, West, 6   497-6258
Services are held daily Friday evening at start of Sabbath and Sabbath morning.

Progressive
7 Leicester Avenue, Rathgar, Po Box 3059, 6
490-7605
Services are held on Friday evening at 8.15pm, first Sabbath morning in the month and Sabbath morning at 10.30am

Embassy
Embassy of Israel, Carrisbrook House, 122 Pembroke Road, 4, Ballsbridge

Bakeries
Bretzel, 1a Lennox Street   475-2724
Fax: 298-7944
The bakery is kosher for bread only.

Butchers
B. Erlich
35 Lower Clanbrassil Street   454-2252
Fax: 490-6609
Supervision: Board of Shechita.

Delicatessens
Deli Market
14 Orwell Road, 6, Rathgar   490-9911
Fax: 490-9917
Supervision: Kashrut Commission.

Museums
Irish Jewish Museum
3-4 Walworth Road, 8
676-0737; 475-8388 or 453-1797

Booksellers
Barry's Bookshop
137 Butterfield Avenue, 14   493-4211
Fax: 493-0899

Israel

Fiftieth Anniversary Celebrations: List of Events

The year 1998 celebrates two significant events in Israel's history: fifty years of independence as a State and the centenary of the First Zionist Congress.

The central theme of the fiftieth anniversary events scheduled for this year is 'Hatikvah', which means 'The Hope'. It is the name of Israel's national anthem and is a word that is charged with significance for Jews in Israel and all around the world.

The celebratory events will be spread over an entire year, beginning with the lighting of the first candle of Chanukah on Tuesday, 23 December 1997. All events listed below have been supplied by the Israel Ministry of Tourism, but it must be remembered that these events are tentative and may be subject to change.

Date	Event	Location
23 December 1997 1st night of Chanukah	**The Opening Ceremony** for festivities in Israel and throughout the world	The President's Residence Jerusalem, and 50 points throughout Israel and Jewish communities world wide
12 March 1998	**Disney March**	Tel Aviv
13 March 1998	**Disney March**	Kiryat Shmona to Dimona
April 1998	**International Flower Festival**	Israel Museum, Jerusalem
April 1998	**The Jubilee Jerusalem March**	The route to Jerusalem
29 April 1998	**Main Independence Day Celebration** for tourists, guests, new immigrants, citizens	Ramat Gan Stadium
24 May 1998	**The Fighters' Convention** – a salute to all fighting brigades	Teddy Stadium, Jerusalem
May 1998	**Israel in the Mirror of Fashion** an international fashion show, including the development of the Israeli fashion industry	Eilat
June 1998	**Children's Chain** – 50,000 students holding hands across country	
June 1998	**A Musical Occasion 'Masada'** concert premiere telling of the heroism of Masada, performed by top singers over 3 nights	Foothills of Masada

Date	Event	Location
July 1998	**Special festive concert of the Israel Philharmonic Orchestra and the Cleveland Orchestra,** conducted by Maestro Dohanini	Foothills of Masada
July 1998	**Arts Fair in Caesarea** – works of Israeli and worldwide Jewish artists, in the format of the Biennale in Italy, and exhibiting rare works by Salvador Dali	Caesarea
July 1998	**Folklore Festival**	Carmiel
July 1998	**Gourmet Hospitality** – to take place over a period of one week, with performances by folk dance groups and singers	Kiryat Shmona, Kiryat Malachi, Eilat, Herzlia
August 1998	**Exhibition of the Achievements of the State of Israel** – includes the history of the State, settlement of the land, immigration, security and the Israel Defense Forces, industry, science and technology, tourism, culture. Twelve million balloons to be released on opening evening	The Exhibition Grounds, Tel Aviv
August 1998	**Ethnic Festival** – bands and artists from Turkey, Iran, other third world countries, for 3 days	
August 1998	**Poetry and Songs around the Lake of Galilee** – a two-day event celebrating the history of Hebrew song	Around Lake of Galilee
October 1998	**Standing of 'The Kahal' (The Congregation) in Jerusalem** a ceremony held once every seven years at the height of the Pilgrimage to Jerusalem, on the Festival of Tabernacles	The square in front of the Western Wall, Jerusalem
November 1998	**Jewish Organisations Convention**	

Some General Information

The Ministry of Tourism publishes a *Best of Israel Guide* detailing shops participating in the VAT refund scheme and recommended restaurants; and *Israel: a visitors' companion*. Available at 6 Wilson St., Tel Aviv. Fax: (03) 556-2339.

A visitor's visa is valid for a stay of three months from the date of arrival.

Student Travel to Israel

Throughout the long summer vacation student flights to Israel are operated by ISSTA (Israel Students' Tourist Association), in conjunction with various other national student travel bureaux. In London these are operated by the National Union of Students Travel Dept., 3 Endsleigh St., WC1. Tel: (0171) 387-2184. ISSTA has offices in Haifa, Jerusalem and Tel Aviv. WST Charters, Priory House, 6 Wright's Lane, W8 6TA, Tel: (0171) 938-4362, also specialises in Israel holidays for students and young people.

Individual arrangements for working on a kibbutz for a minimum period of one month can be made for any time of the year, except July and August, through Hechalutz b'Anglia, the Jewish Agency, 741 High Road, Finchley, N12 OBQ, Tel: (0171) 446-1477. Details of other kibbutz schemes are available from Kibbutz Representatives, 523 Finchley Road, London, NW3 7BD, Tel: (0171) 794-5692. Airlines and most shipping lines offer reductions to students.

Disabled Persons

Friends of Yad Sarah, 43 Hanevi'im Street, Jerusalem, 95141, Tel: (02) 624-4242, Fax: (02) 624-4493 (Reg. Charity No. 294801), a volunteer operated home care organisation, lends free, regular and hi-tech medical rehabilitative equipment and provides a spectrum of home care supportive services. Services available to tourists. Head offices, Jerusalem; 77 branches in Israel.

Health Regulations

There are no vaccination requirements for tourists entering Israel.

Traffic Regulations

A valid International Driving Licence is recognised and preferred, although a valid national driving licence is also accepted, provided it has been issued by a country maintaining diplomatic relations with Israel and recognising an Israeli driving licence.

Traffic travels on the right and overtakes on the left. Drivers coming from the right have priority, unless indicated otherwise on the road signs, which are international. Distances on road signs are always given in kilometres (1 km is equal to 0.621 miles).

The speed limit is 50 km (approx. 31 miles) per hour in built-up areas; 80–90 km (approx. 50–56 miles) per hour on open roads.

Climate

With a long Mediterranean coastline, Israel's climate is similar to that of the French and Italian Rivieras. It may also be compared to that of Florida and southern California. Winters are mild and summers warm.

There are differences not only in temperature, but also in rainfall between the northern and southern regions of the country, as well as between the hills and valleys. The rainless summer lasts from April to October. The winter season, November to March, is characterised by bright sunshine with occasional rain. During this period, Tiberias on the Sea of Galilee, Sdom on the Dead Sea and Eilat on the Red Sea are all absolutely ideal for winter holidays.

Hotels and Motels
The Ministry of Tourism abolished the hotel star grading system in 1992. Instead, hotels are to be classified as a 'Listed Hotel' according to minimum requirements covering the business licence, security and fire facilities. Regulations stipulate that prices should be quoted in Shekels and US Dollars.

Kashrut
In Israel, kosher means under official rabbinical supervision. Kosher restaurants, hotels and youth hostels are by law required to display a kashrut certificate.

Hotel Rates
Rates vary slightly from resort to resort according to season.

Youth Hostels
There are 31 youth hostels in Israel for students, youth groups and adults, which are supervised by the Israel Youth Hostels Association (a member of the International Youth Hostels Federation). All hostels offer the standard facilities: dormitories, kosher dining rooms. Most hostels also have a guest house section, with double and family rooms, and private facilities. Most are air-conditioned. Attractive travel packages are offered by the Youth Travel Bureau, P.O.B. 6001, Jerusalem, 91060, Tel: (02) 655-8432.

The Israel Youth Hostels Association offices are at Convention Hall Bldg., P.O.B. 1075, Jerusalem, 91060, Tel: (02) 655-8400.

Shopping, Bank & Office Hours
Shops and offices are open from Sunday to Thursday inclusive, from 8am to 1pm and from 4pm to 7pm. Shopping hours on Friday are from 8:30am to 2pm. In Haifa, most shops are closed on Tuesday afternoons. Banks are open Sunday, Tuesday and Thursday from 8:30am to 12:30pm. Branches of most banks are also open from 4 to 6pm. On Monday and Wednesday, they are open from 8:30am to 12:30pm only. On Friday and the eve of holidays and festivals, they open at 8:30am and close at 12 noon. Government offices are generally open to the public Sunday to Thursday inclusive from 8am to 1pm.

Tours

Regular scheduled tours, using air-conditioned coaches, are operated by Egged and other companies on week-days to all parts of the country, starting from Jerusalem, Tel Aviv and Haifa. Egged's intercity toll-free information number is 177-022-5555.

Among the most important sites visited are the Western Wall; the Old City of Jerusalem; Mount Scopus; the Mount of Olives; Rachel's Tomb in Bethlehem; the Tomb of the Patriarchs (Cave of Machpela) in Hebron; Jericho and the Dead Sea. Tours starting in Jerusalem also visit Beersheba, Masada, Sdom, Ein Gedi and the Galilee.

From Tel Aviv, regular tours go south to the Dead Sea and Elat, and north to the Galilee and the Golan Heights, as far as Banias.

From Haifa, regular tours go north to the Galilee, and south to all places visited by tours from Jerusalem and Tel Aviv.

Air tours, operated by Arkia, Israel's internal airline (Sde Dov airport, Tel Aviv), cover all of Israel. In addition a number of smaller companies operate flights and tours to all parts of the country on a charter basis.

It is now possible to fly to Cairo from Israel, as well as to enter Egypt by land. Full details are available from all Government Tourist Information Offices in Israel and Israel Government Tourist Offices abroad.

Information about coach and air tours inside Israel is available from all Government Tourist Information Offices in Israel.

Transport in Israel

Buses are the most popular means of transport, both for urban and inter-urban journeys.

The Israel Railway runs from Naharia in the north to Beersheba in the south, and fares are lower than on the buses. All passenger trains have a buffet car. Taxis are quick and convenient. All urban taxis have meters, which drivers must use.

Certain taxi companies operate a 'Sherut' service in and between the main cities on weekdays, and some independent taxi owners operate similar services seven days a week. Individual seats are sold at fixed prices, with up to seven people sharing a taxi. In some cities and towns, 'Sherut' taxis follow the main bus routes, charging slightly higher fares than the buses.

Israel Embassy (UK) Travel Information:
http://www.israel-embassy.org.uk/london

Emergencies

Fire: 102; Medical and first aid: 101 (Magen David Adom); Police: 100. Note that the foregoing applies to Haifa, Jerusalem and Tel Aviv only.

Electrical Equipment

Israel's electrical current is 220 volts, A.C., single phase, 50 cycles.

Radio

You can hear the news in English four times a day on Israel Radio at 576, 1170 and 1458 kHz: 7 am; 1 pm; 5 pm; 8 pm. BBC World Service at 1322 kHz.: 1400, 1700 and 2015 GMT. Voice of America at 1260 kHz: 5–6 am and 8–9 am, 5 pm, 5:30 pm, 11 pm.

Average Temperature (Celsius)

	Jerusalem	Tel Aviv	Haifa	Tiberias	Eilat
January	12	15	14	17	17
March	16	18	17	17	22
May	22	22	21	26	29
July	23	24	25	30	35
September	23	26	26	30	32
November	16	19	19	21	21

Rainy Days

	Jerusalem	Tel Aviv	Haifa	Tiberias	Eilat
January	12	14	15	12	1
March	8	8	9	5	2
May	2	1	1	1	0
July	0	0	0	0	0
September	0	1	1	0	0
November	7	8	5	5	1

GMT + 2 hours
Country calling code (972)

Afula
Area telephone code (6)

Restaurants
La Cabania, Ha'atzmaut Square   659-1638
San Remo, 4 Ha'atzmaut Square   652-2458

Akko
Area telephone code (4)

One of the most atmospheric locations in Israel is the old city of Akko (Acre). It boasts old and ancient buildings, mighty ramparts and walls, relics of Crusaders days (a city with a complex of subterranean buildings), a small fishing harbour, a bazaar and the muezzin's repetitive call throughout the day and night. The town has a tumultuous history dating back to 1500 BC according to ancient Egyptian texts. It has been besieged repeatedly by Romans, Arabs, Crusaders, Turks, Napoleon and the British.

Skipping ahead several hunderd years, in May 1948, the Israeli army marched into old Akko and claimed it as part of Israel. Noteworthy is the Citadel, built on the ruins of the Crusaders' city in 1780. During the British mandate it was used as a high-security prison to imprison Jewish resistance fighters pre-1948. The ideological head of the Irgun, Vladimir Jabotinsky, was held prisoner here. In 1947, the Jewish underground fighters orchestrated a mass breakout from the prison to free a number of senior terrorist leaders who had been condemned to death. One of them was Menachem Begin, a member of the Stern Group, who was later to become president of Israel. Leon Uris described the breakout in his popular novel *Exodus*. There is a museum called the Israeli Museum of Heroes which is dedicated to this period in Israeli history.

Tourist Information
Eljazar Street, opposite Mosque   999-1764
   177-022-7764

Restaurants
Amirei Hagalil, Akko-Safed Road, nr. Moshav Amirim, 20115   698-9815/6
Palm Beach   991-2891

Hotels
Kosher
Argaman Motel, Sea Shore   991-6691/7
Palm Beach Club Hotel, Sea Shore   981-5815

Youth Hostels
Acre Youth Hostel   991-1982
   Fax: 991-1982

Museums
Akko Municipal Museum, Old City
Ghetto Fighters' Holocaust & Resistance Museum

Arad
Area telephone code (7)

Arad, the town nearest to the Dead Sea, was founded in 1962 as a base for scientists working in connection with Dead Sea industries and for archaeologists engaged in researching desert and Dead Sea sites. Because there is no pollen in the air and the air is extremely clean, it is suitable for asthmatics. The Margoa Arad Hotel has a clinic catering specifically for them.

For visitors Arad makes an ideal base for touring the northern Negev, the Dead Sea and the wild Judean hills. The Visitor Information Center is well informed on local antiquities and desert walks. Round the edge of the town are several Bedouin encampments where, despite the unrelieved aridity of the area, sheep and goats are somehow grazed. The Bedouin, who have very good relations with the locals, find casual work in the town.

Tel Arad, which is outside of the modern city, was once the settlement of a Canaanite royal family and today is an interesting archaeological site.

Hotels
Arad, 6 Hapalmach Street   995-7040
Margoa, Mo'av Street   995-1222
   Fax: 995-7778
Nof Arad, Moav Street   997-5056/8

Youth Hostels
Blau-Weis, centre of town   995-7150

Ashdod
Area telephone code (8)

As with much of this country, Ashkelon and Ashdod changed hands frequently. There were various Crusader vs Muslim battles over the city and the Crusaders basically destroyed the area in the twelfth century. When Ashdod became resettled in this century, it was initially a hostile Arab village, which housed a British army base; during the 1948 War of Independence, the Egyptians advanced this far into Israel before being forced to retreat. Ashdod is mostly a pretty beachfront with a few modest hotels and a small-town feel to it.

Ashkelon, which is 9 miles south of Ashdod, also has a pleasant beachfront but is more interesting for tourists because of the Ashkelon National Park, a popular picnic area with remnants from several periods. Crusader ruins lie on the sand.

This part of the country is very close to the desert and south and makes a good stopover for day trips.

Tourist Information
4 Haim Moshe Shapira Street, Rova Daled
864-0485/090

Hotels
Kosher
Miami, 12 Nordau Street   852-2085

Avihail

Museums
Bet Hagedudim (History of Jewish Brigade)

B'nei Berak
Area telephone code (3)

Restaurants
Chapanash, 6 Jabotinsky Street

Hotels
Wiznitz, 16 Damesek Eliezer Street   777-1413

Bat Yam
Area telephone code (3)

Hotels
Kosher
Mediterreanean Towers
2 Hayam Street, 59303   555-3666

Beersheba
Area telephone code (7)

The patriarch Abraham settled in Beersheba and purchased a well for the price of seven lambs (be'er sheva means the well of seven and well of the oath). Later, Beersheba was named the southern limit of the land of Israel.

Today it is the fifth-largest city in Israel with 120,000 citizens. The town's most interesting feature is the continuing Bedouin presence. The Bedouin market is held every Thursday but it has been affected negatively by tourism and modernization. Permanent Bedouin encampments can be seen south of town.

Restaurants
Bulgarian, 112 Keren Kayemet St.   623-8504

Hotels
Kosher
Desert Inn   642-4922

Museums
Man in the Desert Museum, 5 miles north-east of the city.
Negev Museum, Ha'atzmaut Street, corner of Herzl Street

Bet Shean

Bet Shean is one of the most important excavation sites in Israel (known to archaeologists as Tel al Husn, the Hill of Strength). Twenty-eight layers of civilization have been uncovered at this spot, including Egyptian, Canaanite, Philistine, Jewish, Hellenistic, Scythian, Roman, Arab and Frankish Crusader settlements. The town gained real importance, however, only when the Romans came in the 2nd century BC and made it into the capital of a ten state federation.

In the middle of the town, a large site contains remnants of a Roman theatre. There are also remains from a well-preserved Byzantine amphitheatre discovered in late 1986. The amphitheatre seated up to 6,000 spectators.

Nearby Mount Gilboa is known throughout the country for its wild flowers. A bit further west is the Bet Alpha synagogue [ruins] which dates back to 518 CE, discovered in 1928. The floor of the synagogue is striking, made up of beautiful mosaics divided into three panels. One depicts religious emblems and the Ark of the Covenant. Another shows a zodiac circle with the astrological signs named in Hebrew, the moon and the stars, four women symbolising the seasons, and a youth riding a horse-drawn chariot. The third represents the sacrifice of Isaac. The work is dated with an Aramaic inscription: 'This floor was laid down in the year of the reign of Emperor Justinus'. Justinus ruled Palestine from 518 to 527 CE.

Museums

Bet Shean Museum, 1 Dalet Street

Caesarea

Area telephone code (6)

Caesarea is an exciting archaeological site with city remains from Herodian, Roman, Byzantine and Crusader periods. In 22 BC Herod built a port, amphitheatre, theatre and hippodrome which could hold up to 38,000 spectators. It surpassed the Colosseum's dimensions in Rome. It has been restored and in the summer hosts a festival of music with live concerts.

South of Caesarea is the Sdot Yam kibbutz which has a small archeological museum and was home to Hannah Sennesh – a young Haganah fighter who parachuted into Nazi Germany in the attempt to save Jews but was caught, tortured and hanged by the Nazis.

The kibbutz also maintains an attractive vacation village with a beach for bathing. Caesarea's Dan Golf Hotel possesses the only 18-hole golf course in Israel.

Restaurants

Caesarean Self Service, Paz Station 633-4609

Hotels

Kosher

Dan Caesarea Golf Hotel   636-2266/268

Dan

The ancient city of Dan, standing on the largest of the three sources of the Jordan River, marked the northern border of the Jews' Biblical Land of Israel. It is now located within a beautiful 100-acre nature preserve with various streams and paths.

Museums

Bet Ussishkin

Dead Sea

The Hebrew name for the Dead Sea is Yam Hamelech or Sea of Salt because the water has an extremely high level of salt that makes life impossible in these waters. The sea is 50 miles (80 km) long and up to 11 miles (18 km) wide, covers a surface area of 390 square miles (1,010 sq. km) and is as much as 1,305 feet deep (399 m). It is so salty that the human body floats like a cork and you can sit in the water reading a newspaper. You travel more than 3,200 feet (1000 m) in altitude along this stretch of road so watch out for ears popping.

There are various spas and mudbaths around the Dead Sea with signs posted directing visitors where to go. Included is the Neve Zohar, a lakeside spa with sulphur baths, the Ein Gedi and En Boqeq resorts with thermal baths that specialize in the treatment of eczema and other skin diseases and, of course, the various high class hotels clustered together in one part of the Sea.

Hotels

Caesar

Contact the Caesar sales office in Tel Aviv for information   (03) 696-8383
Fax: (03) 696-9896

Degania Alef

Museums

Bet Gordon

Eilat

Area telephone code (7)

Israel's southernmost city and its only port on the Red Sea. Eilat is all tourist centre and resort playground, although it is also residential and has both religious and non-religious residents. Founded for its port potential, its main import is mineral oil; in fact it was Egypt's blockade of the Gulf of Eilat on May 22, 1967 that triggered the Six Day War.

A deep blue sea, rich with reefs and exotic fish, surrounded by red granite mountains and a climate warm all year round, the Gulf of Aqaba is a tourist haven which is also one of the most fragile ecosystems in the world. Shared by four nations, Israel, Jordan, Egypt and Saudi Arabia, the Gulf is expected to explode with activity in the next few years as the peace process holds the promise of opening a door for both tourism and industry. Eilat feels like a land apart, separated from the rest of Israel not just by the Negev desert but by attitude. It feels more like a beach town, alive with a taste for pleasure and action.

With the opening of Eilat's Arava border-crossing with Jordan, Petra makes a superb excursion. The amazing desert capital of the Nabateans, with its temples, treasury, tombs, amphitheatre and monastery all cut out of pink sandstone cliffs, can be visited with an overnight stop. Inclusive trips from Eilat are bookable through all hotels.

Trips to the Sinai are also very accessible and cheap.

Restaurants

Arizona, on Main Road to Tel Aviv   667-2710
Bar-B-Que, Hatemarim Blvd.
                   667-3634; 667-5793
Café Royal, King Solomon's Palace Hotel,
North Beach   667-6111
Chinese Restaurant, Shulamit Gardens Hotel,
North Beach   667-7515

Dolphin Baguette, Tourist Centre
Egged, Central Bus Station   667-5161
El Morocco, Tourist Centre
Golden Lagoon, New Lagoona Hotel, North Beach   667-2176
Hakerem, Elot Street, cnr. Hatemarim Blvd.
                    667-4577
Halleluyah, Building 9, Tourist Centre
                    667-5752

Metamei Teman
Hatemarim Blvd., Mini Golf   667-4402
Neve Elat, Hatemarim Blvd., Neviot, North Beach   697-1081
Off the Wharf, King Solomon's Palace Hotel, North Beach   667-9111
Panorama, New Commercial Centre 667-1965

Hotels

Kosher

Americana Eilat
PO Box 27, North Beach   633-3777
Caesar, North Beach   633-3111
                Fax: 633-2624
Carlton Coral Sea, Coral Beach   633-3555
Dalia, North Beach   633-4004
Edomit, New Tourist Center   637-9511
Etzion, Hatmarim Street   637-4131
Galei Eilat, PO Box 1866,   636-7444
North Beach   Fax: 633-0627
Lagoona, North Beach   633-3666
Marina Club, PO Box 4277   633-4191
North Beach   Fax: 633-4206
Moriah Plaza Eilat, North Beach   636-1111
                Fax: 633-4158
Neptune, PO Box 295, North Beach 636-9369
                Fax: 633-3767
Paradise, N.L., 88000, North Beach 633-5050
Queen of Sheba, North Beach   633-4121
Red Rock
PO Box 306, 88102, North Beach   637-3171
Sonesta Suites, N.L., Harava Road   637-6222
Sport, North Beach   633-3333

Youth Hostels

Eilat   637-0088

Museums

Museum of Modern Art
Hativat Hanegev Street

Tours
| Orionia | 667-2902 |
| Pirate | 667-6549 |

Ein Harod

Museums
Bet Sturman & Art Institute

Galilee
Area telephone code (6)

Hotels
Kosher
Kfar Hittim, N.L., DN Galil Tachton   679-5921
Rakefet
N.L., Gush Segev, Western Galilee   980-0403

Youth Hostels
Karei Deshe (Tabgha), Yoram   672-0601
Fax: 672-4818

11 miles north of Tiberias.

Golan Heights
Area telephone code (6)

The Golan Heights rise steeply from the Sea of Galilee to the Mount Avital plataeu.

Hamat Gader
These were thought to be the nicest spa baths in the whole Roman world, according to the Byzantine empress Eudocia. There are impressive ruins including the extensive Roman and Byzantine spa, which served as a grand bathing resort for six centuries, and an ancient synagogue. Four mineral springs and a freshwater spring emerge at Hamat Gader and so it is used today as a modern bathhouse. There is also an alligator farm where dozens of alligators and crocodiles can be seen lazing around.

Restaurants
Hamat Gader Restaurant
Hamat Gader   675-1039

Gush Etzion

The Gush Etzion bloc just celebrated its thirtieth anniversary of Jewish renewal. There are a few historical sites to see here. There is a new Gush Etzion Judaica Center, where a beautiful selection of Judaica is displayed and a Kfar Etzion multi-media programme, an audio-video show that describes the history of the Gush. In addition, 15 minutes from Efrat, the largest settlement in the Gush area with over 2,000 families, is Herodian, King Herod's favorite summer palace with a whole underground tunnel complex built by Bar Kochba to fight the Romans. The tunnels were only discovered recently and are quite fun to walk through although the drive is through Arab villages and should be done either during the holidays like Sukkot and Pesach, when the area is open and well-travelled, or with organised tours.

Restaurants
Pizzeria Efrat
Te'ena Shopping Center, Efrat   (02) 993-1630
Cravings Cafe
Dekel Shopping Center, Efrat   (02) 993-3188
Trocadero, Judaica Center, Gush Etzion Junction   (050) 622-613

Museums
Gush Etzion Museum, Kfar Etzion

Hadera
Area telephone code (6)

Museums
The K'han Museum, 74 Hagiborim Street, POB 3232, 38131   632-2330; 632-4562
Fax: 634-5776
Hours: Sun-Thurs, 8am-1pm; Fri, 9am-12pm; Sun and Tues, 4pm-6pm.

Haifa
Area telephone code (4)

This city is built on three levels, each with its distinctive and highly special character. Mount Carmel (Har Hacarmel), the top level, which offers some magnificent views, is mostly residential and recreational; Hadar Hacarmel, the central level, is also residential, but it also contains the city's main commercial district. The third level contains the port area, Israel's largest, and another business district. Over recent years the beach front to the south of the port has been attractively refurbished.

Like Jerusalem and Tel Aviv, Haifa has a university, and it is also the home of the Technion, Israel's Institute of Technology. The city's theatre and symphony orchestra are well-known, and its array of unusual museums are worth a visit. They include the National Maritime Museum, the Grain Museum, the Mané Katz Museum and the Illegal Immigration Museum. Haifa is also a tourist resort, with miles of bathing beaches and acres of woodland parks and well-tended gardens. It is also the scene of international flower shows, folklore-festivals, conventions and other events.

Tourist Information

106 Sderot Hanassi	837-4010
ISSTA, 28 Nordau Street	866-0411
What's on in Haifa	864-0840

Restaurants

Banker's Tavern
2 Habankim Street   852-8439
Lunch only. Closed Shabbat.

Ben Ezra, 71 Hazayit Street   884-2273

Egged, Central Bus Station   851-5221
Self-service.

Gan Rimon, 10 Habroshim Street   838-1392
Lunch only.

Ha'atzmaut, 63 Derech Ha'atzmaut   852-3829

Hamber Burger
61 Herzl Street   866-6739

Hamidrachov
10 Nordau Street   866-2050

Mac David, 131 Hanassi Boulevard   838-3684

Mac David, 1 Balfour Street

Milky Pinky (Milk Bar)
29 Haneviim Street   866-4166

Paznon, Hof Carmel   853-8181

Rondo, Dan Carmel Hotel, 87 Hanassi Blvd.
                                       838-6211

Technion, Neve Shaanan   823-3011
Self service. Lunch only.

The Chinese Restaurant of Nof
Nof Hotel, 101 Hanassi Blvd.   838-8731

The Second Floor
119 Hanassi Blvd.   838-2020

Tsemed Hemed
Herbert Samuel Square   824-2205

Hotels

Kosher

Dan Carmel, 87 Hanassi Avenue	838-6211
Dan Panorama, 107 Hanassi Ave.	835-2222
Dvir, 124 Yefe Nof Street	838-9131/7
Nesher, 53 Herzl Street	864-0644
Nof, 101 Hanssi Avenue	835-4311
Shulamit, 15 Kiryat Street, 34676	834-2811
	Fax: 825-5206
Yaarot Hacarmel, Mt. Carmel	822-9144/9

Youth Hostels

Carmel	853-1944
	Fax: 853-2516
Shlomi, Hanita Forest	980-8975

Museums

Bet Pinchas Biological Insititute
124 Hatishbi Street   837-2886; 837-2390
                                      Fax: 837-7019
                     Email: biolinst@netvision.net.il
Includes nature museum, zoo and botanical garden. Entrance via Gan Ha'em. Hours: Sunday to Thursday, winter, 8 am to 4 pm, July to August, 8 am to 7 pm; Friday and holiday eves, 8 am to 2 pm; Saturday, 9 am to 5 pm; winter, 9 am to 4 pm.

Dagon Grain Museum
Plumer Square   866-4221
                                      Fax: 866-4211
Tours Sunday to Friday, 10:30am.

Israel Oil Industry Museum, Shemen Factory,
7 Tovim Street, POB 136, 31000   865-4237
                                      Fax: 862-5872

Israel Railways Museum, Haifa Railway Station (east)

Mane Katz Museum, 89 Panorama Road

Moshe Shtekelis Museum of Pre-History
124 Hatishbi Street, Entrance from Gan Ha'em

Museum of Clandestine Immigration & Naval Museum
204 Allenby Road, 35472   853-6249
                                      Fax: 851-2968

Museum of Haifa
26 Shabbtai Levi Street   852-3255
Includes museums of Ancient Art, Modern Art
and Music & Ethnology. Hours: Sunday,
Monday, Wednesday, Thursday, 10am to 4pm;
Tuesday, 4pm to 7pm; Friday and holidays,
10am to 1pm; Saturday, 10am to 2pm.

Reuben & Edith Hecht Museum
Haifa University, 31905   825-7773
                            Fax: 824-0724
        Email: mushecht@research.haifa.ac.il
Hours: Sunday, Monday, Wednesday,
Thursday, 10am to 4pm; Tuesday, 10am to
7pm; Friday, 10am to 1pm; Saturday, 10am to
2pm. Admission free.

**Technoda, National Museum of Science and
Technology,** opp. 15 Balfour Street 867-1372

The National Maritime Museum
198 Allenby Road   853-6622
Hours: Sunday, Monday, Wednesday,
Thursday, 10am to 4pm; Tuesday, 4pm to
7pm; Friday and holidays, 10am to 1pm;
Saturday, 10am to 2pm.

Tikotin Museum of Japanese Art
89 Hanassi Avenue, Mount Carmel   838-3554
Hours: Sunday, Monday, Wednesday,
Thursday, 10am to 4pm; Tuesday, 4pm to
7pm; Friday and holiday eves, 10am to 1pm;
Saturday, 10am to 2pm.

Tours

Guided tours   867-4342
**Mt Carmel, Druse villages, Kibbutz Ben
Oren and Ein Hod artists' colony**
Suns, Mons, Tues, Thurs, Sats, 9.30am

**Bahai shrine and gardens, Druse villages,
Muchraka, the Moslem village of Kabair,
the Carmelite monastery and Elijah's cave**
Weds, 9.30am

Hanita

Museums
Tower & Stockade Period Museum

Haon
Area telephone code (6)

Holiday Villages
Kibbutz Haon, Jordan Valley   675-7555/6

Hazorea

Museums
Wilfrid Israel House of Oriental Art

Herzlia
Area telephone code (9)

Tourist Information
English Speaking Residents Association
PO Box 3132, 46104   958-0632

Restaurants
Dona Flor, 22 Hagalim Blvd.   950-9669
Tadmor Hotel School
38 Basel Street, 46660   957-2321

Hotels
Kosher
Dan Accadia, Herzlia on Sea   959-7070
                            Fax: 959-7092
        Email: danhtls@danhotels.co.il
Holiday Inn, Crown Plaza   954-4444
                            Fax: 954-4675
Tadmor, 38 Basel Street   952-5000
                            Fax: 957-5124
The Sharon, Herzlia on Sea   957-5777
                            Fax: 957-2448

Jaffa

Yaffo or Jaffa, the Arab part of Tel Aviv, in
contrast to Tel Aviv, can look back on 3,000
years of history. It is probably the oldest
working port in the world. Its name is
supposed to date back to Yaphet, the third
son of Noah. Cedar from Lebanon was
shipped here to be used in King Solomon's
temple.

   Its narrow old streets and well-renovated old
town with art galleries, jewellery shops and
excavations have more picturesque charm
than Tel Aviv. In addition, the spectacular view
of the Tel Aviv skyline and the fresh fish
restaurants make the old harbour a very
worthwhile visit.

Museums

Antiquities Museum, 10 Mifratz Shlomo
Street, Old Jaffa, POB 8406, 61083 682-5375
Fax: 681-3624
Hours: Sunday, Monday, Tuesday, Thursday,
9am to 2pm; Wednesday, 9am to 7pm;
Saturday, 10am to 2pm.

Tours

Tel Aviv-Yafo Tourism Association
Clock Square, nr. Yefet Street
Walk takes 2 ½ hours, starting at Clock Square
near Yefet Street, in the centre of Jaffa. Free.

Jerusalem
Area telephone code (2)
To sense the mystery of Jerusalem, start with
Mount Scopus just before dawn. Watch the
red ball of a new day's sun ascend the mists
from behind the Mountains of Moab and set
afire the Judean Desert which laps at the city's
skirts. Near sunset, look down again from near
the same vantage point on the city itself,
when the light catches the gold of the Dome
of the Rock, scattering its rays across
Jerusalem's many hills.

But Jerusalem is also a city of people, a
collection of villages separated by faith and
custom. Enter the Old City by Jaffa Gate and
turn right on to Armenian Patriarchate Road,
where you will find the Cathedral of St. James
and an Armenian community living in its own
little world.

By contrast, spend a Friday morning in Mea
Shearim, the walled city of Ultra-Orthodoxy,
where the ghetto way of life is maintained
with fierce pride. Friday all is abustle.
Youngsters scamper out of school in a babble
of Yiddish. Men, young and old, eyes averted
from the passing tourists, hurry to the mikva,
for here males as well as females take the
ritual cleansing bath.

But also in Jerusalem, you must touch
history, not the spurious history of this tomb
or that stone, but the reality, say, of such as
Hezekiah's Tunnel, hewn by the Judean king's
workmen through the rock of Jerusalem nearly
2,700 years ago so that water would be
available in the city in time of war. The tunnel,
still a conduit for water through which
intrepid Jerusalem explorers frequently wade

for 600 yards of its winding course, starts
close by the spring of Gihon in the Kidron
Valley, on the edge of the ancient City of King
David, south-west of the Old City, with its
excavations.

Jerusalem now has pavement cafes in the
part of Ben-Yehuda Street which is closed to
traffic. There are also many stalls selling a
variety of foods to be enjoyed as one strolls,
and they are well patronised. There is an
enormous variety of national and ethnic foods
available. The many restaurants offer
everything from kosher Chinese to kosher
Argentine.

When night falls, as it does quite early
compared with the slow dusk of the West, it
seems that most of the inhabitants have gone
to bed. Many have, because the day's early
start, despite the traditional afternoon siesta,
dampens any inclination for late nights. But
there is a night-life of sorts.

Religious Organisations
The Young Israel Movement in Israel
20 Strauss Street, 91371 623-1631
Fax: 623-1363

Synagogues
Great Synagogue
260 King George Street
Yeshurun, 44 King George Street (Ashkenazi)

Contact Information
Jewish Student Information Centre
Hebrew University Off-Campus Center,
5/4 Etzel Street, French Hill 581-4939
Ohel Avraham, 1/15 Hameshor'rim Street, Old
City 628-2634
Fax: 628-8338
Email: jseidel@netmedia.net.il

Tourist Information
Ministry of Tourism
24 King George Street 675-4811
The Israel Youth Hostels Association
Convention Hall Building, P.O.B. 1075, 91060
655-8400
ISSTA, 5 Eliashar Street 622-5258
**Tourist Coordinators for the Administered
Territories**, Allenby Bridge Fax: 694-2294
Fax: 624-0571

Restaurants
Meat
Burger Ranch
18 Shlomzion Hamalka Street   622-2392
Burger Ranch, 3 Lunz Street   622-5935
Clafouti, 2 Hasoreg Street   624-4491
Dagrill, 21 King George Street   622-2922
El Gaucho, 22 Rivlin Street   622-6665
El Marrakesh, 4 King David Street   622-7577
El Morocco, 43 Yirmiyahu Street,   500-1670
Centre One   Fax: 538-3496
Supervision: Rabbi Meir Kruyzer.
Feferberg's, 53 Jaffa Road   625-4841
Marvad Haksamim, 16 King George Street
Norman's Steak 'n Burger
27 Emek Refaim Street   566-6603
   Fax: 673-1768
   Web site: www.normans.co.il
Supervision: Jerusalem Rabbinate. American
steakhouse. Reservations recommended. Easy
walking distance from main hotels. Hours:
Sunday to Thursday, 12 pm to 11 pm; Friday,
closed; Saturday, from after Shabbat.
Shaul's Shwarma Centre
14 Ben-Yehuda Street   622-5027
Shemesh, 21 Ben-Yehuda Street   622-2418
Shipodei Hagefen
74 Agrippas Street   622-2367
Yemenite Step
12 Yoel Salamon Street   624-0477
Yo-si Peking
5 Shimon Ben-Shetach Street   622-6893

Dairy
Alumah, 8 Yavetz Street   625-5014
Supervision: Jerusalem Rabbinate, Kosher
Lamehadrin.
Natural food. Take-away available.
Bagel Nash, 14 Ben-Yehuda Street   622-5027
Besograyim, 45 Ussishkin Street   624-5353
Casa Italiana, 6 Yoel Salamon Street
Dagim Beni, 1 Mesilat Yesharim St.   622-2403
Daglicatesse, 1 Rachel Imenu   563-2657
La Pasta, 16 Rivlin Street   622-7687
Mamma Mia   624-8080
38 King George Street, 94262   Fax: 623-3336
Supervision: Jerusalem Rabbinate. Hours:
Sunday to Thursday, 12 pm to midnight,
Friday 12 pm to 4 pm; Saturday, from the end
of Shabbat.

Of Course!, Zion Confederation House,
Emile Botta Street   624-5206
Off The Square
8 Ramban Street
Supervision: Jerusalem Rabbinate, Kosher
Lamehadrin.
Poire et Pomme
The Khan Theatre, 2 Remez Square   671-9602
Primus, 3 Yavetz Street   624-6565
Rimon, 4 Lunz Street   622-2772
Theatre Lounge, Jerusalem Theatre,
20 Marcus Street   566-9351
Ye Olde English Tea Room
68 Jaffa Road   537-6595
Zeze, 11 Bezalel Street   623-1761

Pizzerias
Pizzeria Rimini
15 King George Street   622-6505
Pizzeria Rimini, 7 Paran Street, Ramat Eshkol
Pizzeria Rimini, 43 Jaffa Road   622-5534
Pizzeria Trevi, 8 Leib Yaffe Street   672-4136

Vegetarian
Village Green, 10 Ben-Yehuda Street
Village Green, 1 Bezalel Street

Accommodation Information
Good Morning Jerusalem   623-3459
9 Coresh Street, 94146   Fax: 625-9330
Lists rooms and flats available for tourists.

Hotels
Kosher
Ariel, 31 Hebron Road   671-9222
Caesar, 208 Jaffa Road   500-5656
   Fax: 538-2802
   Email: caesarjm@netvision.net.il
Supervision: Jerusalem Rabbinate.
150 comfortably furnished rooms.
Central, 6 Pines Street   538-4111
   Fax: 5381-480
Four Points Paradise Jerusalem
4 Wilnai Street, 96110   655-8888
   Fax: 651-2266
Supervision: Jerusalem Rabbinate.
Hyatt Regency Jerusalem
32 Lehi Street   533-1234
   Fax: 581-5947
   Email: hyattjrs@trendline.co.il
   Web site: www.intournet.co.il/hyatt/

Israel

Jerusalem Gate,43 Yirmiyahu St.	538-3101
Jerusalem Hilton, Givat Ram	653-6151
Jerusalem Renaissance	
6 Wolfson Street, 91033	652-8111
Jerusalem Tower, 23 Hillel Street	620-9209
King David, 23 King David Street	620-8888
Fax:	620-8880
King Solomon, 32 King David St.	569-5555
Kings, 60 King George Street	620-1201
Fax:	620-1211
Knesset Tower, 4 Wolfson Street	651-1111
Lev Yerushalayim	
18 King George Street	530-0333
Mount Zion, 17 Hebron Road	568-9555
Fax:	673-1425

Supervision: Jerusalem Rabbinate.

Palatin, 4 Agripas Street	623-1141
Radisson Moriah Plaza Jerusalem	
39 Keren Hayesod Street, 94188	569-5695
Fax:	623-2411

Supervision: Jerusalem Rabbinate.

Ramat Rachel Hotel, 90900	670-2555
Fax:	673-3155

Email: resv@ramatrachel.co.il
Web site: www.ramatrachel.co.il
The only kibbutz hotel in Jerusalem.

Reich, 1 Hagai Street, Beit Hakerem	652-3121
Ron, 44 Jaffa Road	622-3122
Fax:	625-0707
Sheraton Jerusalem Plaza	
47 King George Street	629-8683
Fax:	623-1667

Supervision: Jerusalem Rabbinate, Kosher Lamehadrin.

Sonesta Jerusalem, 2 Wolfson Street	652-8221
Windmill, 3 Mendele Street	566-3111
Fax:	561-0964
Zion, 4 Luntz Street	623-2367
Zion, 10 Dorot Rishonim	625-9511
Zion, 47 Lieb Jaffe Street	671-7557

Bed & Breakfasts

A Little House in the Colony
4/a Lloyd George Street, German Colony, 93110   563-7641
Fax: 563-7645
Email: melonit@netvision.net.il
16 rooms, air-conditioning, Israeli breakfast, cafeteria, small garden.

Le Sixteen, 16 Midbar Sinai Street, Givat Hamivtar 97805   532-8008
Fax: 581-9159
Email: le16@virtual.co.il
Web site: www.virtual.co.il/travel/BnB/le16
Member of the Jerusalem Home Accommodation Association. Can provide guest studios with kosher dairy kitchenettes.

Guest Houses

Bet Shmuel
6 Shamma Street, 94101   620-3473; 620-3465
Fax: 620-3467
Single and family guest rooms with a capacity of 240 beds; conference facilities and banquet services; restaurant and coffee shop.

Youth Hostels

Bet Bernstein, 1 Keren Hayesod St.   625-8286
80 rooms.
Davidka, 67 HaNevi'im Street   538-4555
26 rooms.
Ein Karem   641-6282
97 rooms. 10 minutes from the Louise Waterman-Wise Hotel in Bayit Vegan.
Jerusalem Forest   675-2911
140 rooms.
Jerusalem Youth Centre, 9 Shonei Halachot Street   628-5623
Moreshet Yahadut   628-8611
Old city. 75 rooms.

Holiday Villages

Youth Recreation Centre Holiday Village
Yefei Nof, Jerusalem Forest   641-6060

Museums

Ammunition Hill Memorial & Museum, Ramat Eshkol   582-8442
Bible Lands Museum, 25 Granot Street, POB 4670, 91046   561-1066
Fax: 563-8228
The home of one of the most important collections of ancient artifacts displaying rare works of art from the dawn of civilisation to the Byzantine period. Gift shop, weekly lectures and concerts. Hours: Sunday, Monday, Tuesday, Thursday, 9:30am to 5:30pm; Wednesday, April to Oct., 9:30am to 9:30pm, Nov. to March, 1:30pm to 9:30pm; Friday and holiday eves, 9:30am to 2pm; Saturday and holidays, 11am to 3pm. Daily guided tours.

G.U.Y.'s Gallery
12 Hebron Road, 92261   672-5111
       Fax: 672-5166

Herzl Museum, Herzl Blvd., Mount Herzl

Isaac Kaplan Old Yishuv Court Museum
6 Or Hachaim Street, Jewish Quarter, POB
1604, 91016   627-6319
       Fax: 628-4636
The museum is located in the heart of the
Jewish Quarter in the Old City of Jerusalem in
a building built in the sixteenth century. It
displays Ashkenazi and Sephardic life styles
from the beginning of the 19th century.
Hours: Sunday to Thursday, 9 am to 2 pm.

Israel Museum, Hakirya
Includes Bezalel National Museum, Samuel
Bronfman Biblical & Archaeological Museum,
Shrine of the Book & the Rockefeller Museum
in East Jerusalem.

L.A. Mayer Memorial Institute of Islamic Art
2 Hapalmach Street

Museum of Musical Instruments, Rubin
Academy of Music, 7 Smolenskin Street

Museum of Natural History, 6 Mohilever St.

Museum of the History of Jerusalem
Tower of David, Jaffa Gate   628-3273

Nahon Museum of Italian Jewish Art
27 Hillel Street, 94581   624-1610
Founded in 1981, this museum collects and
preserves objects pertaining to the life of the
Jews in Italy from the Middle Ages to the
present day. The main attraction is the ancient
synagogue of Conegliano Veneto, a township
some 60 km from Venice. Hours: Sunday to
Tuesday, 9 am to 2 pm; Wednesday, 9 am to
5 pm; Thursday, 9 am to 1 pm. For guided
tours contact the number above or 625-3480.

S.Y. Agnon's House, 16 Klausner Street,
Talpiot, 93388   671-6498
       Fax: 672-4639
Hours: Sunday to Thursday, 9 am to 1 pm.

Shocken Insititute, 6 Balfour Street

**Siebenberg House of Archaeological
Museum**
6 Hagittit Street, Jewish Quarter   628-2341

Sir Isaac & Lady Wolfson Museum
Hechal Shlomo, 58 King George Street

Tourjeman Post Museum
1 Hel Hahandassa Street   628-1278

Yad Vashem Art Museum, Har Hazikaron, PO
Box 3447, 91034   675-1611
       Fax: 643-3511

Tours

American P'eylim Student Union
10 Shoarim Street   653-2131
Free tours of Jewish Quarter and free
accommodation, in the hostel quarters.

Knesset (Parliament)   654-4111
Sun. & Thurs. between 8.30am and 2.30pm.

**Society for the Protection of Nature in
Israel: Israeli Nature Trails**
13 Helen Hamalka Street, PO Box 930
       624-9567

Katzrin

Area telephone code (4)

This is the largest Jewish town (6,000 Jews
and growing) in the Golan and serves as its
administrative capital. The town makes a good
base for exploring the local antiquities.
Ancient Katzrin was a Talmudic city and,
today, there stands a reconstructed synagogue
and village made to resemble life as it was in
Talmudic times. Gamla, which is 10 km
southeast of Katzrin, is known as the Masada
of the north. Some 9,000 Jewish Zealots had
set up a town in Gamla and were eventually
besieged by the Romans in 67 CE. According
to Josephus Flavius, rather than be captured,
they, like their counterparts in Masada,
committed suicide. The ruined city contains
the remains of an old castle and nearby are
Gamla Falls, a 51 metre waterfall.

The Gamla winery is nearby and offers tours.
Other sites in the area are Gilgal Refa'im
(Ghost's Circle), ancient stone circles 156 m in
diameter, and Khasfin, an abandoned Syrian
village built on the ruins of the Jewish town of
Hisfiyya. It was mentioned in Maccabees as
Kaspin and a church dating back to 400 CE
has been found there.

Restaurants

Lev Hagolan, 30 Dror Street   961-6643
Orcha, Commercial Centre   696-1440

Hotels

Kosher

Ayelet Hashahar, 12200   693-2611
Ein Gedi   659-4222/726
Gesher Haziv, Western Galilee   982-5715
Hagoshrim, Upper Galilee   695-6231

Hagoshrim, Ha'on Camping Village
Sea of Galilee   675-7555/6
Kfar Blum, Upper Galilee   694-3666
Kfar Giladi, Upper Galilee   694-1414/5
                                        Fax: 695-1248
Kiriat Anavim, Judea Hills   534-8999
Lavi, Lower Galilee   679-9450
                                        Fax: 679-9399
Ma'ale Hachamisha, Judea Hills   534-2591

Museums

Golan Archaeological Museum

Kfar Giladi

Museums

Bet Hashomer

Kfar Vitkin

Area telephone code (9)

Youth Hostels

Emer Hefer   866-6032
25 miles north of Tel Aviv.

Kibbutz Hardof

Area telephone code (4)

Restaurants

Vegetarian Restaurant   986-5655

Kibbutz Yotvata

Area telephone code (7)

Near Kibbutz Yotvata, 37 miles north of Eilat,
in the Bibilical Wildlife Reserve Hai Bar Arava,
biologists have settled every breed of animal
that is mentioned in the Bible (guided tours at
9 and 10:30 am, noon and 1:30 pm). Animals
include herds of Somalian wild asses, oryx
antelope, ibex, ostriches, desert foxes, lynx,
hyenas and the last desert leopard in the
Negev, living out her days on the preserve.

Restaurants

Dairy Restaurant   635-7449

Korazim

Area telephone code (6)

Holiday Villages

Amnon Bay Recreation Centre   693-4431
Vered Hagalil Guest Farm   693-5785
                                        Fax: 693-4964

Lod

Tourist Information

Ministry of Tourism
Ben Gurion International Airport(03)971-1485

Maagan

Holiday Villages

Maagan Holiday Village
Sea of Galilee   (06) 675-3753

Maayan Harod

Youth Hostels

Hankin   (06) 658-1660
7 miles east of Afula.

Mahanayim

Tourist Information

Zomet Mahanayim   (06) 693-5016

Metula

Area telephone code (6)

Hotels

Kosher

Arazim   694-4143/5
Hamavri   694-0150
Sheleg Halevanon, P.O.B. 13   694-4015/7

Moshav Shoresh

Hotels

Kosher

Shoresh Apartment Hotel   (02) 533-8338
Harey Yehuda   Fax: (02) 534-0262

Naharia

Area telephone code (4)

Naharia is a fairly modern city, founded in 1934 by Jews fleeing from Germany. It lies 20 miles north of Haifa on the coast and boasts beautiful white beaches. Four miles north of this city, on the Lebanese border, is Rosh Hanikra, which has an extensive system of caves which the sea has washed out of the soft chalk. There is also a lookout point with an adjacent restaurant which reveals a gorgeous panorama of the coast.

Tourist Information

Israel Camping Union, POB 53   992-5392

Restaurants

Cafe Tsafon, 10 Gaaton Blvd.   992-2567

Hotels

Kosher

Astar, 27 Gaaton Blvd.   992-3431
Beit Hava, Shavei Zion, 25227   982-0391
Carlton, 23 Ha'agaaton Blvd   992-2211
Eden, N.L., Meyasdim Street   992-3246/7
Frank, 4 Haaliya Street   992-0278
Panorama, 6 Hamaapilim Street   992-0555
Rosenblatt, 59 Weizmann Street   992-0069

Museums

Naharia Municipal Museum, Hagaaton Blvd

Nazareth

Area telephone code (6)

Restaurants

Iberia, Rassco Centre, Nazareth Elite 655-6314
Nof Nazareth
23 Hacarmel Street, Nazareth Elite   655-4366

Negev

Area telephone code (7)

Making the desert flourish is an old Zionist dream dating back to David Ben-Gurion who tried to push settlement in the south, and who himself went to live on a kibbutz in the Negev after he retired from politics. While it is amazing to see kibbutzim growing produce in the middle of the desert and the pockets of green shock the eye on the drive down south through the arid countryside, it really never became as popular as Ben-Gurion had hoped. Most of landscape is still barren with scorched rock and bare granite mountains surrounded by dry valleys.

Sde Boker (Sede Boqer)

This desert kibbutz was home to Israel's first prime minister David Ben-Gurion and his wife Paula. Every year hundreds of thousands of visitors make their way to his simple wooden hut in the Negev.

Entry to the site is free, as Ben-Gurion stipulated in his will. It is open from 8:30 am to 5 pm in the summer (to 4 pm from October to March), Sunday to Thursday. Fridays and holiday eves it is open from 8:30 am to 2 pm and on Shabbat and holidays from 9 am to 2:30 pm.

En Gedi

En Gedi is the largest oasis in this region. Recreational activities include swimming in the Dead Sea, relaxing in the spa, and hiking in the nearby nature reserves that include hikes in Nahal David and Nahal Arugot. The kibbutz which houses the resort was set up in the 1950s by the children of concentration camp survivors. It is now a beautiful landscape with lush florid greenery startling the visitor with its contrast to the stark, barren red desert rock around it.

Masada

Masada's history and the preservation of the site are fascinating and worth a trip even in the scorching heat of the summer, although then it is advised to either walk up at 4 am or take a cable car.

About 9 miles south of En Gedi, and rising up vertically from the plain 1,440 feet (440 m) on each side, this mighty mountain top has a significant place in Jewish history, to the extent that Israeli soldiers used to be sworn in saying 'Masada shall not fall again'.

Youth Hostels

Bet Noam, Mitzpeh Ramon   658-8433
                                 Fax: 658-8074

Bet Sara, Ein Gedi   658-4165
1.5 m north of Kibbutz Ein Gedi on Dead Sea.

Hevel Katif: Hadarom   684-7597
                                 Fax: 684-7680

Isaac H. Taylor, Masada   658-4349
28 miles from Arad.

Museums

Dimona Municipal Museum
Ramon Crater

Netanya
Area telephone code (9)

Synagogues

Cong. Agudath Achim, 45 Jabotinsky Street
New Synagogue of Netanya
7 MacDonald Street   862-7178
Ohel Shem Civic Auditorium
Cultural Centre, 4 Raziel Street   833-6688
Young Israel of Northern Netanya, cnr.
Shlomo Hamelech, & Yehuda Hanassi Streets

Tourist Information

Kikar Ha'Atzmaut   882-7286

Hotels

Kosher

Arches, 4 Remez Street   882-3322
Bagel Nash, 10 Ha'atzmaut Street 861-6920
Blue Bay
37 Hamelachim Street, 42228   860-3603
                                 Fax: 833-7475
Gal Yam, 46 Dizengoff Street   862-5033
Galei Hasharon
42 Ussishkin Street, 42273   882-5125
Galei Zans, 6 Ha'melachim Street 862-1777
Galil, 18 Nice Blvd.   862-4455
Ginot Yam
9 David Hamelech Street   834-1007
Goldar, 1 Usishkin Street   833-8188
Supervision: Rabbinate of Netanya.
Grand Yahalom
15 Gad Makhnes Street   862-4888

Green Beach, PO Box 230   865-6166
                                 Fax: 835-0075
Hagozal, 95 Herzl Street   833-5301
Jeremy, N.L., 11 Gad Machnes St. 862-2651
King Koresh, 6 Harav Kook Street 861-3555
King Solomon, 18 Hamaapilim St. 833-8444
                                 Fax: 861-1397
MacDavid, 7a Ha'atzmaut Street   861-8711
Margoa (new), 9 Gad Makhnes St. 862-4434
Maxim, 8 King David Street   862-1062
Metropol Grand
17 Gad Makhnes Street   862-4777
Milky Way, 6 Herzl Street   832-4638
Orly, 20 Hamaapilim Street   833-3091
Palace
N.L., 33 Gad Machnes Street   862-0222
                                 Fax: 862-0224
Park, 7 David Hamelech Street   862-3344
Residence, 18 Gad Machnes Street 862-3777
The Seasons Hotel, 1 Nice Blvd   860-1555
                                 Fax: 862-3022
       Email: seasons@netmedia.net.il
Supervision: Rabbinate of Netanya.
Topaz, 25 King David Street   862-4555
Zli-Esh, 6 Shaar Hagai Street   832-4295

Holiday Villages

Green Beach Holiday Village   865-6166
                                 Fax: 835-0075

Museums
Netanya Museum of Biology & Archaeology

Neve Zohar

Museums
Bet Hayotser, Dead Sea area

Petach Tikva
Area telephone code (3)

Museums
Bet Yad Labanim, 30 Arlosov Street

Ra'anana

Area telephone code (9)

Restaurants

Dana, 198 Achuza	790-1452
Lady D, 158 Achuza	791-6517
Limosa, 5 Eliazar Jaffe	790-3407
Pica Aduma, 87 Achuza	791-0508

Ramat Gan

Museums

Bet Emmanuel Museum, 18 Chilbat Zion St.
Pierre Gildesgame Maccabi Museum
Kfar Hamaccabiah

Ramat Hanegev

Tourist Information

Zomet Mashabay Sadeh   (07) 655-7314

Ramat Yohanan

Area telephone code (4)

Youth Hostels

Yehuda Hatzair   844-2976
                                                         Fax: 844-2976

11 miles north-east of Haifa.

Rehovot

Area telephone code (8)

This was home to Zionist leader Chaim
Weizmann (1874-1952), Israel's first president.
In his honour, the world-famous Weizmann
Institute research centre was founded in 1944.
Tours, including the house where he lived and
died, and his garden, can be arranged.

Restaurants

Rehovot Chinese Restaurant
202 Herzl Street   947-1616

Rosh Hanikra

Youth Hostels

Rosh Hanikra   (04) 998-2516
Near the grottos.

Rosh Pina

Rosh Pina, which means cornerstone, is close
to the city of Safed and was settled with
Rothschild funds, by Jews from Safed in 1878.
The original settlement has been preserved
and consists of a main street, restored pioneer
dwellings and the old synagogue. In addition,
many of the old buildings are inhabited by
some 60 artists whose work can be seen and
purchased.

Youth Hostels

Hovevei Hateva   (06) 693-7086
16 miles north of Tiberias.

Safed

Area telephone code (6)

Set at an altitude of more than 2,600 feet in
the midst of magnificent landscapes, Safed is
the fourth holy city of the Talmud after
Jerusalem, Tiberias and Hebron, and was once
the spiritual centre of Jewish mystics and
kabbalists.

Its altitude and purity of air, its completely
restored Old City with its narrow, cobblestone
streets, myriad old synagogues and its large
artist's colony, all combine to make Safed a
popular summer resort. In this town, the
different sects – hassidic and non-relgious,
artistic hippies and newly-religious – all mingle
without the tension felt in larger cities like
Jerusalem. It has a small-town atmosphere.

Tourist Information

50 Jerusalem Street   692-0961/633

Hotels

Kosher

David, Mount Canaan	692-0062
Nof Hagalil, Mount Canaan	692-1595

Pisgah, Mount Canaan   692-0105
Rimon Inn, Artists Colony   692-0665/6
Ron, Hativat Yiftah Street   697-2590

Youth Hostels

Bet Benyamin   692-1086
    Fax: 697-3514
In southern part of town.

Museums

Bet Hameiri Institute (History & Heritage of Safed)
Israel Bible Museum
Museum of Printing Art, Artists' Colony

Tel Aviv

Area telephone code (3)

Tel Aviv (Hill of Spring) started as a Jewish suburb of Arab Jaffa in 1909. Growth was encouraged in the area by the Balfour Declaration in 1917. The anti-Jewish Jaffa riots of 1921 and the advent of Nazism in Germany also encouraged more development of the empty sand dunes. When in 1948 Israel declared independence, Tel Aviv became the temporary site for the provisional government and its population grew by 60 per cent. It is now the second largest city after Jerusalem and the majority of the country's population lives on a narrow strip along the coast, ranging from Ashkelon up to Naharia.

With skyscrapers, crowded streets and traffic and car pollution, Tel Aviv is like any other western metropolis with its upscale shopping districts and poor run-down neighbourhoods. Tel Aviv's outdoor cafes are reminiscent of Europe. Another big draw to the city is its coastline and beaches. There is a five mile stretch of beaches, some of which are only a 10-minute walk from Dizengoff – the main central avenue. There is also a Promenade, paved in swirling patterns, stretching from North Tel Aviv, the border of the yuppified Ramat Aviv, and extending nearly into Yaffo.

Synagogues

Bilu, 122 Rothschild Blvd.
Great, 314 Dizengoff Street
Ihud Shivat Zion, 86 Ben-Yehuda Street
Kedem, 20 Carlebach Street

Main Synagogue, 110 Allenby Road
Ohel Mis'ad, 5 Shadal Street
Tiferet Zvi, Hermann Hacohen Street

Contact Information

Jewish Student Information Centre
Tel Aviv University Off-Campus Center, 82/10 Levanon Street, Ramat Aviv
    Email: jseidel@netmedia.net.il

Tourist Information

Shop # 6108, 6th Floor,   639-5660
New Central Bus Station   Fax: 639-5659
ISSTA, 109 Ben Yehuda Street
The Ministry of Tourism: *Best of Israel Guide*, 6 Wilson Street   556-2339

Restaurants

Hamakom, 1 Lilienbaum Street   510-1823
Hungarian Blintzes
35 Yirmiyahu Street   605-0674
Shaul's Inn, 11 Elyashiv Street, Kerem Hatemanim   517-3303
    Fax: 517-7619
Supervision: Chief Rabbinate of Tel Aviv. Oriental and Yemenite food. Hours: 12 pm to 12 am.
Twelve Tribes, Sheraton Hotel, 115 Hayarkon Street   521-1111

Accommodation Information

Kibbutz Hotels Chain: Head Office
1 Smolanskin Street, P.O.B. 3193, 61031
    524-6161
    Fax: 527-8088
    Email: batya@kibbutz.co.il
    Web site: www.kibbutz.co.il

Hotels

Kosher

Adiv, 5 Mendele Street   522-9141
Ambassador, 56 Herbert Samuel St.   510-3993
Ami, 152 Hayarkon Street   524-9141/5
Armon Hayarkon
268 Hayarkon Street   455-271/3
Avia, Ben Gurion Intl. Airport Area   536-0221
    Fax: 536-0036
Basel, 156 Hayarkon Street   520-7711
Bell, 12 Allenby Street   517-7011

Carlton Tel Aviv, 10 Eliezer Peri St.   520-1818
Fax: 527-1043
City, 9 Mapu Street   524-6253
Dan Panorama, 10 Y. Kaufman St.   519-0190
Dan Tel Aviv, 99 Hayarkon Street   520-2505
Fax: 524-9755
Deborah, 87 Ben-Yehuda Street   544-822
Florida, 164 Hayarkon Street   524-2184
Grand Beach, 250 Hayarkon St.   546-6555
Maxim, 86 Hayarkon Street   517-3721/5
Fax: 517-3726
Metropolitan
11-16 Trumpeldor Street   519-2727
Monopol, N.I. on the promenade, 4 Allenby
Street   655-906
Moriah Plaza Tel Aviv
155 Hayarkon Street   527-1515
Ora, N.L., 35 Ben Yehuda Street   650-941
Ramada Continental
121 Hayarkon Street   527-2626
Ramat Aviv, 151 Derech Namir   699-0777
Fax: 699-0997
Shalom, 216 Hayarkon Street   524-3277
Sheraton Tel Aviv
115 Hayarkon Street   521-1111
The Lobby Lounge serves dairy and
light meals.
Tal, 287 Hayarkon Street   544-2281
Tayelet, N.L. on the promenade, 6 Allenby
Street   510-5845
Tel Aviv Hilton
Independence Park, 63405   520-2222
Yamit Towers, 79 Hayarkon Street   517-1111

Museums

Bet Bialik, 22 Bialik Street
Bet Eliahu-Hahagana
23 Rothschild Blvd., 65122   560-8624
Eretz Israel Museum, 2 Haim Levanon Street,
Ramat Aviv, 69975   641-5244
Fax: 641-2408
**Goldmann Museum of the Diaspora (Beth
Hatefutsoth),** Klausner Street, Ramat Aviv
Haaretz Museums, 17 Ben-Gurion Boulevard
Includes eight smaller museums at Ramat Aviv,
as well as the Israel Theatre Museum.
Helena Rubenstein Pavilion, 7 Tarsat Street
**Independence Hall Museum and Bet
Hatanach,** 16 Rothschild Boulevard

Jabotinsky Institute
38 King George Street   528-7320
Fax: 528-5587
Email: jabo@actcom.co.il
Web site: www.jabotinsky.org
Hours: Sunday to Thursday, 8 am to 4 pm.
Tel Aviv History Museum, 27 Bialik Street
Tel Aviv Museum of Art, 27 Shaul Hamelech
Boulevard, 64283   695-7361
Fax: 695-8099
Hours: Sunday to Thursday, 10 am to 9:30
pm; Friday, closed; Saturday, 10 am to 2 pm
and 7 pm to 10 pm. Parking facilities.

Travel Agencies
Interom Tourism Ltd.   924-6425
Fax: 579-1720

Tiberias
Area telephone code (6)

Tiberias is one of the four cities mentioned in
the Talmud. In 1904 Jewish resettlement
began. By the First World War the tourism
business, which characterises it today, was
already going strong because of its Jewish and
Christian history and its hot springs. During
the War of Independence there was much
fighting over the city, and a memorial garden
was built in the old Jewish quarter of Tiberias
to commemorate the soldiers killed in 1948.

Tourist Information
HaBanim Street, Archaeological Park 672-5666

Hotels
Kosher
Ariston, 19 Herzl Blvd.   679-0244
Astoria, 13 Ohel Ya'akov Street   672-2351/2
Caesar   672-3333
Fax: 679-1013
Carmel Jordan River
Habanim Street   671-4444
Daphna, Ussiskin Street   679-2261/4
Eshel, Tabur Haaretz Street   669-0562
Gai Beach, Derech Hamerchatzaot   679-0790
Galei Kinnereth, 1 Kaplan Street   672-8888
Galilee
Elhadef Street, PO Box 616   679-1166/8

Gan Esther, Hadishon Street	672-9946
Ganei Hamat	
Habanim Street, nr. Hot Springs	679-2890
Golan, 14 Achad Ha'am Street	679-1901/4
Hamat Gader Restaurant	675-1049
Kinar, N.E. Sea of Galilee	673-2670
Lido Kenneret, Gdud Barak Street	672-1538
Moriah Plaza Tiberias	
Habanaim Street	679-2233
Pagoda	
Lido Beach, PO Box 253, 14102	672-5513
Quiet Beach, Gedud Barak Street	679-0125
Ramot-Resort Hotel	
Sea of Galilee	673-2636
Sironit Beach, Hamerchazaot Road	672-1449
Tzameret Inn, Plus 2000 Street	679-4951
Washington, 13 Seidel Street	679-1861/3

Youth Hostels

Taiber	675-0050
	Fax: 675-1628

2.5 miles south of Tiberias.

Museums

Tiberias Hot Springs Lehmann Museum
Hammat Tiberias National Park

Zichron Yaakov

Area telephone code (6)

The road to Haifa is populated with various Rothschild-funded settlements. The largest is Zichron Yaakov, 38 km south-east of Haifa, which was named for James or Jacob Rothschild (1792–1868). It was initially a kibbutz and one of the first Zionist settlements in Israel, having been founded in the mid-1880s. Today it is in the process of rapid growth, its new-found popularity resulting from its proximity to the large Matam industrial park outside of Haifa. Zichron Yaakov is home to the Carmel Oriental Wine Cellars – the second largest in Israel.

West of Zichron Yaakov is Beth Daniel, which affords a wonderful view of the Carmel Coast. It was built as a refuge for musicians by Lillian Friedlander in 1938 in memory of her son Daniel. Concerts are held here and it also has a guest house.

Hotels

Kosher

Baron's Heights & Terraces	
N.L. PO Box 332	630-0333
	Fax: 630-0310

Museums

Nili Museum & Aaronson House
40 Hameyasdim Street

Italy

The Jewish community of Italy, whose history goes back to very early times, increased considerably at the time of the Dispersion in 70 CE. During the Middle Ages and the Renaissance there were newcomers from Spain and Germany. Rich synagogues as well as rabbinical schools, yeshivot and printing houses were set up and gained wide renown.

A decline of Italian Judaism began during the last century: assimilation, concentration in big towns and emigration reduced many once-flourishing centres. During the first years of fascism Italian Jews did not suffer, but after 1938 – under Nazi pressure – racial laws were introduced and, during the German occupation from 1943 to 1945, nearly 12,000 Jews, especially from Rome, were murdered or banished.

There are 35,000 Jews in Italy today, the most important coms. being in Rome (15,000), Milan (9,500), and Turin (1,285), followed by Florence, Trieste and Venice.

Information on Italian Jewry, its monuments and history may be obtained from Unione Comunità Ebraiche Italiane , Lungotevere Sanzio 9, Rome. Tel: (06) 580-3667/3670. Fax: (06) 589-9569.

GMT + 1 hour
Country calling code (39)

Ancona
Area telephone code (71)

Community Organisations
Community Offices
Via Fanti 2 bis   202638

Synagogues
Via Astagno

Mikvaot
Via Astagno

Asti
Area telephone code (141)

Synagogues
Via Ottolenghi 8, Torino

Museums
Via Ottolenghi 8, Torino   539281;-594271

Bologna
Area telephone code (51)

Community Organisations
Comunita Ebraica Bologna
Via Gombruti 9, 40123   232-066
                                Fax: 229-474

Synagogues
Via Mario Finzi

Cafeterias
Comunita Ebraica Bologna
Via Gombruti 9, 40123   232-066
                                Fax: 229-474
Supervision: Rav Moshe Saadoun.
Lunch Sunday to Friday; dinner Friday; closed mid-July and August.

Casale Monferrato
Area telephone code (142)

Synagogues
Community Offices
Vicolo Salomone Olper 44   71807
The synagogue, built in 1500 and rebuilt in
1866, also contains a Jewish museum. Casale-
Monferrato is on the Turin-Milan road, and
can be reached by turning off it about 13
miles beyond Chivasso.

Ferrara
Area telephone code (532)

Community Organisations
Community Offices
Via Mazzini 95   760372

Synagogues
Via Mazzini 95   247004

Mikvaot
Via Mazzini 95   247004

Florence (Firenze)
Area telephone code (55)

Community Organisations
Community Offices
Via Luigi Carlo Farini 4   245252
                                      Fax: 241811

Synagogues
Via Luigi Carlo Farini 4   245252

Mikvaot
Via Luigi Carlo Farini 4   245252 & 243164

Restaurants
Il Cuscussu
Via Farini 2/A   241890

Butchers
Bruno Falsettini
Mercato Coperto di S., Ambrogio   248-0740

Gionvannino
Via Macci 106   248-0734

Museums
Jewish Museum
Via Luigi Carlo Farini 4   234-6654
There is a communal religious & artistic
souvenir shop on these premises.

Genoa
Area telephone code (10)

Community Organisations
Community Offices
Via Bertora 6, 16122

Synagogues
Via Bertora 6   839-1513
                                      Fax: 846-1006
Services every evening & Shabbat morning.
Kosher services available.

Gorizia (Gradicia)
Area telephone code (3831)

Synagogues
Via Ascoli 19   532115

Leghorn (Livorno)
Area telephone code (586)

Synagogues
Community Offices
Piazza Benamozegh 1   -896290

Mikvaot
Piazza Benamozegh 1   896290

Butchers
Corucci, Banco 25, Mercato Centrale   884596

Museums
Jewish Museum, via Micali 21

Mantua (Mantova)
Area telephone code (39376)

Synagogues
Community Offices, via G. Govi 11   321490

Merano
Area telephone code (39473)

Synagogues
Community Offices, via Schiller 14   236127

Museums
Jewish Museum, via Schiller 14   236127

Milan
Area telephone code (2)

Community Organisations
Community Offices
Sally Mayer 2   483-02806
Fax: 483-04660

Synagogues
Via Guastalla 19   551-2029
Fax: 551-92699
Rabbi Dr Laras is the Chief Rabbi.
Beth Shelomo, via Col di Lana 12
Central Synagogue
Via Guastalla 19   551-2101
Merkos L'Inyonei Chinuch
Via Carlo Poerio 35, 20129   953-1213
New Home for Aged
Via Leone XIII   498-2604
Services on Sabbaths and festivals.
New Synagogue, via Eupili 8
Service on Sabbaths and festivals

Sephardi
Via Guastalla 19

Lubavitch
Ohel Yacob
Via Benvenuto Cellini 2   545-5076

Persian
Angelo Donati Beth Hamidrash
Via Sally Mayer 4-6
Angelo Donati Beth Hamidrash
Via Tuberose 14   415-1660
Angelo Donati Beth Hamidrash
Via Montecuccoli 27   415-1660

Mikvaot
Central Synagogue
Via Guastalla 19   551-2101
New Home for Aged
Via Leone XIII   498-2604

Persian
Angelo Donati Beth Hamidrash
Via Sally Mayer 4-6

Tourist Information
Uffizio Nazionale Israeliano del Turismo
Via Podgora 12/b, 20122   760-210-51
Fax: 760-124-77

Embassy
Consulate General
Corso-Europa 12, 20122

Restaurants
Pizzeria Carmel
viale San Gimignano 10   416-368
Supervision: Rav S. Behor.
Hours: 12 pm to 2:30 pm and 5:30 pm to
10:30 pm.
Restaurant Giovannino
Via A. Sciesa 8, 20135   551-95582
Fax: 551-95790
Supervision: Rabbi Garelick, Chief Rabbi of
Milan.
Kosher meals available on 24 hours' notice.

Groceries
Eretz, Largo Scalabrini 5   423-6891
Fax: 423-4753
Hours: 9 am to 7:30 pm.

Documentation Centres
**Contemporary Jewish Documentation
Centre**, via Eupili 8   316338
Fax: 336-02728

Modena

Area telephone code (59)

Synagogues
Community Offices
Piazza Mazzini 26   223978

Butchers
Macelleria Duomo
Mercato Coperto (Covered Market), Stand 25
217269

Naples (Napoli)

Area telephone code (81)

Synagogues
Community Offices
Via Cappella Vecchia 31   764-3480

Ostia Antica

Sites
Here can be found the partially restored excavated remains of a 4th-century synagogue built on the site of another one which stood there 300 years earlier. This is the oldest synagogue in Europe. Ostia Antica is about 40 minutes by train from Rome (Termini or Pyramid stations). To reach the synagogue, cross the footbridge on leaving station. The entrance to the excavations is straight ahead.

Padua (Padova)

Area telephone code (49)

Synagogues
Community Offices
Via S. Martino e Solferino 9   875-1106

Mikvaot
Via S. Martino e Solferino 9   871-9501

Parma

Area telephone code (521)

Synagogues
Community Offices, Vicolo Cervi 4

Perugia

Area telephone code (75)

Synagogues
P. della Republica 77   21250

Pisa

Area telephone code (50)

Synagogues
Community Offices
Via Palestro 24   542580
Services are held on festivals and Holy-days. During the week the resident beadle will be glad to show visitors round the synagogue, which is famed for its beauty. It is very near the Teatro Verdi.

Riccione

Area telephone code (39541)

Hotels
Vienna Touring Hotel: The Hotel Nevada
601245
In the summer, kosher food is obtainable. Provides vegetarian food and particularly welcomes Jewish guests.

Rome

Area telephone code (6)

Representative Organisations
Unione Comunita Ebraiche Italiane (Union of Italian Jewish Communities)
Lungotevere Sanzio 9   580-3667; 580-3670
Fax: 589-9569
Information on Italian Jewry, its monuments and history may be obtained from here.

Religious Organisations
The Italian Rabbinical Council
Headquarters, Lungotevere Sanzio 9
580-3667; 580-3670

Synagogues
Via Catalana 1
Rabbi Dr Toaff is the Chief Rabbi of Rome.

Orthodox
Lungotevere Cenci (Tempio) 9 (Orthodox
Italian service)   684-0061

Orthodox Italian service
Via Balbo 33

Orthodox Sephardi service
Via Catalana
This is the basement of the main synagogue at
Lungotevere Cenci (Tempio) 9.

Orthodox Ashkenazi
Via Balbo 33

Mikvaot
Via Balbo 33
Lungotevere Cenci (Tempio) 9

Embassy
Embassy of Israel
Via Michelle Mercati 14, 00197   322-1541
Embassy of Israel – The Holy See
Rooms 405-8, Hotel Rivoli, Via T. Taramelli 7,
00197

Media
Guides
G. Palombo, Via val Maggia 7
                              810-3716; 993-2074
Ruben E. Popper, 12 Via dei Levii   761-0901
Telephone number is afternoons only.

Newspapers
Shalom, Lungotevere Cenci 9   687-6816
Monthly.

Restaurants
Da Lisa International Restaurant
Via Joscolo 16-18   7049-5456
                                       Fax: 860-3619

Dairy
Zi Fenizia, via Santa Maria del Pianto 64-65,
00186   689-6976

Bakeries
Limentani Settimio, via Portico d'Ottavia 1

Butchers
Massari, Piazza Bologna 11   429120

Sion Ben David, via Filippo Turati 110 733358
Terracina, Via Portico d'Ottavia 1b   654-1364

Bed & Breakfasts
Pension Carmel
via Goffredo Mameli 11, 00153   580-9921
Kosher pension situated in the old district of
Trastevere, ten minutes from the main
synagogue.

Museums
The Jewish Museum, Lungotevere Cenci 9
The main synagogue building contains a
permanent exhibition covering the 2000 year
history of the Italian Jewish community.
Another link with this long history is the Rome
Ghetto almost adjoining. It can be reached by
taking buses 44, 56, 60 or 75, near the
neighbouring Ponte Garibaldi. It is a maze of
narrow alleys dating from Imperial Roman
times, within which, until 1847, all Roman
Jews were confined under curfew. A striking
monument has been erected to the memory
of 335 Jewish and Christian citizens of Rome
who were massacred in 1944 by the Nazis.
names Fosse Ardentine, it lies just outside the
Porta San Paolo, a few yards from the main
synagogue.

Senigallia
Area telephone code (3971)

Synagogues
Via dei Commercianti

Siena
Area telephone code (577)

Synagogues
Vicolo delle Scotte 14   284647
The committee has issued a brochure in
English, giving the history of the synagogue
which dates back to medieval times. The
Synagogue dates from 1750. Services are held
on the Sabbath and High Holy-days. Further
information from Burroni Bernardi, Via del
Porrione. M. Savini, via Salicotta 23. Tel:
283140 (close to the synagogue).

Spezia

Area telephone code (39187)

Synagogues

Via 20 Settembre 165

Trieste

Area telephone code (40)

Community Organisations

Community Offices
Via San Francesco 19   371466

Synagogues

Via Donizetti 2   631898

Tour Information

Smile Service
via Martiri della Liberta' 17, 34134   372-8464
              Fax: 372-6630
This service agency organises tours around the
Jewish sites of Friuli Venezia-Giulia.

Turin (Torino)

Area telephone code (11)

Community Organisations

Community Centre
P.tta Primo Levi 12, 10125   658-585
Synagogue and mikva on premises.

Restaurants

Luna, via C.L. Berthollet 23, 10125   650-2053

Booksellers

Libreria Claudiana
Via Principe Toncmaso 1, 10125   669-2458

Urbino

Synagogues

Via Stretta

Venice

Area telephone code (41)

Hotels

Buon Pesce, S. Nicolo 50   760533
Open Apr. to Oct.

Danieli   26480
Europa & Regina   700477

Community Organisations

Community Offices, Getto Nuovo, 2899
            715012

Synagogues

Chabad, Cannaregio, 2915   716214

Mikvaot

Jewish Rest Home
Ghetto Nuovo, 2874   715118

Restaurants

Beit Chabad
Cannaregio, 2884   716214
            Fax: 716214
Restaurants, books and Judaica available from
here.

Groceries

David's, Ghetto Nuovo, 2880
Jewish articles & religious appurtenances are
available from here.

Guest Houses

Jewish Rest Home, Ghetto Nuovo, 2874
            716002
Very early booking is advised. Kosher meals
and accommodation can occasionally be had
here.

Museums

Jewish Museum
Schola Tedesca, 2902 b   715359
Guided visits to the synagogue (in English)
start every hour from the Museum. There is
also a kosher cafeteria.

Libraries

Jewish Library, Ghetto Nuovo, 2899   718833

Synagogues

Sephardi

Schola Levantina 715012
Sabbath services are held here during winter.

Schola Spagnola
Sabbath services are held here during summer.

Kashrut Information

Ghetto Vecchio, 1189 715118

Groceries

Mordehai Fusetti
Ghetto Vecchio, 1219 714024
Jewish articles & religious appurtenances are
available from here.

Restaurants

Dairy

Gam-Gam, Cannaregio 1122 715-284
Supervision: Rabbi G. Garelick - Lubavitch, R.
Della Rocca - Jewish Community of Venice.
Chalav Yisrael. Shabbat arrangements
available. Open lunch and dinner.

Vercelli

Area telephone code (39161)

Community Organisations

Community Offices
Via Oldoni 20

Synagogues

Via Foa 70

Verona

Area telephone code (45)

Community Organisations

Community Centre
Via Portici 3 800-7112
Fax: 596627
Email: s.i@intesys.it

Synagogues

Via Portici 3

Viareggio

Area telephone code (584)

Contact Information

Mr Sananes, via Pacinotti 172/B 961-025
Private office: Tirreno Tour Srl, 26 Viale
Carducci. Tel: 30777, during daytime.

Sardinia

There is no Sardinian Jewish community today,
but the island is of more than passing Jewish
interest. In 19 C.E. the Emperor Tiberius exiled
Jews to Sardinia. There was a synagogue at
Cagliari, the island's capital, at least as early as
599, for in that year a convert led a riot
against it. Sardinia eventually came under
Aragonese rule, and when the edict of
expulsion of the Jews from Spain was issued
in 1492, the Jews of the island had to leave.
Since then there has been no community
there.

Sicily

Although there are very few Jews in Sicily
today, there is a long and varied history of
Jewish settlement on the island stretching
back to at least the sixth century C.E. and
possibly – according to some scholars – to the
first or second centuries.

By the late Middle Ages, the community
numbered 40,000. In 1282, Sicily passed
under Spanish rule. A century or so later, there
was a wave of massacres of Jews, and another
in 1474. These culminated in the introduction
of the Inquisition in 1479, and the expulsion
of the Jews in 1492.

Jamaica

Jewish settlement in Jamaica, composed in the first instance of fugitives from the Inquisition, goes back to before the period of the British occupation in the mid-seventeenth century. In the eighteenth century there was also a small Ashkenazi influx from England. Jewish disabilities on the island were abolished in 1831.

There were formerly syns. at Port Royal, Spanish Town and Montego Bay. The only one now existing is at Kingston, where the Ashkenazi and Sephardi coms. were combined in 1921. This city contains the majority of the island's 350 Jews.

GMT – 5 hours
Country calling code (1 809)

Kingston
Area telephone code (809)

Synagogues
Shaare Shalom
Duke & Charles Street   927-7948
                              Fax: 978-6240
Services, Friday, 5:30 pm (May to October),

5 pm (November to April). Shabbat, 10 am; festivals, 9 am all year round.

Japan

Taking into account businessmen, students, and other professionals with their families in Japan for 3-5 years the Jewish population can easily run to a couple of thousands at any given time. Exact data on permanent residents are not available and there are very few long-time residents who make Japan their permanent domicile. Conservative estimate: about 600 individuals.

GMT + 9 hours
Country calling code (81)

Hiroshima
Area telephone code (82)

Tourist Sites

Holocaust Education Centre
866 Nakatsuhara, Miyuki, Fukuyama, 720
558001
Fax: 558001
Open Tuesday, Wednesday, Friday and Saturday, 10:30 am to 4:30 pm.

Kobe
Area telephone code (78)

Synagogues

Orthodox
Ohel Shelomoh
12/12 Kitanocho, 4-chome, Ikuta-ku, PO Box 639, M3H 3S4   221-7236
Mikva on premises.

Nagasaki
There are no Jews living in Nagasaki. The old Jewish cemetery is located at Sakamoto Gaijin Bochi. The site of the first synagogue in Japan is Umegasaki Machi.

Okinawa
While there is no native Jewish community on Okinawa, there are normally 200–300 Jews serving with the US military on the island. Regular services are conducted by the Jewish chaplain at Camp Smedley D. Butler, and visitors are welcome.

Tokyo
Area telephone code (3)

Synagogues
Beth David Synagogue, 8-8 Hiroo, 3-chome, Shibuya-ku, 150   3400-2559
Fax: 3400-1827
Services are held Friday eve at 6:30 pm (7 pm during summer); Shabbat morning, 9:30 am; and on Holy-days and festivals. Advance notification requested.

Embassy
Israel Embassy
3 Niban-cho, Chiyodaku   3264-0911

Yokosuka
Area telephone code (468)

Tourist Sites
United States Naval Base
261911 (Ext.6773)
Yokosuka is about 1.75 hours journey south of Tokyo.

Kazakhstan

GMT + 6 hours
Country calling code (7)

Almati
Area telephone code (3272)

Synagogues
Tashkentskaya Street, 1a 480057   306-898

Chimkent

Synagogues
Sephardi
Svobody Street, 47th Lane

Kenya

Jewish settlement in what was British East Africa dates from the beginning of this century. In 1903, when the British Government offered Zionists a territory in Kenya for Jewish settlement, there were already a number of Jews in the capital, Nairobi.

The 'Uganda Plan,' as the offer became known, did not materialise, yet shortly afterwards more Jews settled in the territory. In 1907 the Nairobi Hebrew Congregation was formed, and the foundation-stone for the first synagogue was laid in 1912.

The community was small until 1933, when new immigration started, especially from Central Europe. Today, there are some 500 Jews in the country, including about 400 Israelis. Nearly all live in Nairobi.

GMT + 3 hours
Country calling code (254)

Nairobi
Area telephone code (2)

Community Organisations
Community Centre
Vermont Memorial Hall
Open Mon., Tues., Fri 9am to 1pm; Wed 2.30pm to 5.30pm; Services Friday evening at 6.30pm; Sat morning at 8am. All Festivals. Kosher chickens available.

Synagogues
cnr. University Way & Uhuru Highway, PO Box 40990   222770, 219703
Rosh Kehilla
Vaizman Aharoni

Kyrgyzstan

GMT + 5 hours
Country calling code (996)

Bishkek
Area telephone code (3312)

Synagogues
193 Karpinsky Street

Latvia

GMT + 2 hours
Country calling code (371)

Daugavpils
Area telephone code (54)

Community Organisations
Jewish Community
Saules Street 47   Fax: 24658

Synagogues
Suvorov Street
Gogol Street

Liepaja
Area telephone code (34)

Community Organisations
Jewish Community
Kungu Street 21   25336

Rezhitsa

Synagogues
Kaleru Street

Riga
Area telephone code (2)

Synagogues
6/8 Peitavas Street   21-0827
Fax: 22-4549

Embassy
Embassy of Israel
Elizabetes Street 2, LV1340

Lithuania

GMT + 2 hours
Country calling code (370)

Druskininkai
Community Organisations
Jewish Community, 9/15 Sporto St   54590

Kaunas
Community Organisations
Jewish Community
26 B Gedimino St   (7) 203717

Synagogues
11 Ozheshkienes Street

Klaipeda
Community Organisations
Jewish Community
3 Ziedu Skersqatvis   (6) 93758

Panevezys
Community Organisations
Jewish Community
6/22 Sodu Street, 5300   (54) 68848

Shiauliai
Area telephone code (1)

Community Organisations
Jewish Community
24 Vyshinskio   26795

Vilnius
Area telephone code (2)

Community Organisations
Jewish Community of Lithuania
4 Pylimo, Ground Floor, 2001   61-3003
    Fax: 22-7915

Synagogues
Main Synagogue, 39 Pylimo Street   61-2523
Matzah bakery on premises.

Museums
State Jewish Museum
4 Pylimo, 1st Floor, 2001   63-2951

Luxembourg

GMT + 1 hour
Country calling code (352)

Esch-Sur-Alzette
Synagogues
52 rue de Canal
Minyan services held on Friday evenings.

Luxembourg City
Synagogues
45 Av. Monterery   452914
    Fax: 250430

Kashrut Information
34 rue Alphonse munchen, 2172   452366

Embassy
Consulate General
38 BD Napoleon 1er, L-2210   446-557
    Fax: 453-676

Groceries
Calon, rue de Reins 3

Macedonia

GMT + 1 hour
Country calling code (389)

Skopje
Area telephone code (91)

Community Organisations
Community Offices
Borka Talevski Street 24   237-543

Malawi

GMT + 2 hours
Country calling code (265)

Lilongwe

Embassy
Israel Embassy
PO Box 30319   731-333; 731-789

Malaysia

There are now only three Jewish families in the Malaysian island State of Penang (Pulau Pinang), all resident in the capital of Georgetown. The synagogue is now closed. There is a cemetery in Jalan Yahudi (Jewish St.).

GMT + 8 hours
Country calling code (60)

Malta

There have been a few Jews in Malta since the Roman period. There are about 30 Jewish families in Malta today, both Sephardim and Ashkenazim, at present without a synagogue. Travellers should note there is no kashrut in Malta.

GMT + 1 hour
Country calling code (356)

Mexico

Marrano Jews went to Mexico with the Spaniards at the beginning of the sixteenth century. Sixty years ago the country had about a thousand Jews, most of them coming from the U.S.A., and others from England and Germany. Today's Jewish population is about 48,000. Those in Mexico City (about 40,000) include Ashkenazim and Sephardim.

GMT – 6 hours
Country calling code (52)

Cuernavaca
Area telephone code (73)

Synagogues
Madero 404   20516; 20179

Guadalajara
Area telephone code (36)

Community Organisations
Comunidad Israelita de Guadalajara
Juan Palomar y Arias 651   416-463

Mexico City
Area telephone code (5)

Organisations
Comunidad Monte Sinai
Tennyson 134, Polanco   280-9956
T.O.V., Fuente de Concordia 73, Col.
Tecamachalco   389-8756 or 8766 & 294-6486
                                Fax: 589-9101

Religious Organisations
Comite Central   520-9393; 540-7376
Comunidad Maguen David
                    Email: mdavid@ort.org.mx
Contact for any religious questions.

Synagogues
Agudas Achim
Montes de Oca 32, Condesa

Alianza Monte Sinai
Alejandro Dumas 139, Col. Polanco   531-4932
                                  & 545-8691

Bet Midrash Tecamachalco
Fuente de Marcela 23, Col. Tecamachalco
                                   251-8454

Bircas Shumel
Plinio 311, Polanco   280-2769

Cuernavaca, Prolongacion Antinea Lote 2,
Delicias

Eliahu Elfasi
Fuente de Templanza 13, Col. Tecamachalco
                                   294-9388
Shabbat services only.

Jajam Elfasi
Fuente Del Pescador 168, Col. Tecamachalco
Shabbat services only.

Kolel Aram Zoba
Sofocles 346, Col. Polanco
                     280-2669 & 4886 & 8789

Kolel Maor Abraham
Lafontaine 344, Col. Polanco   545-2482

Midrash Latora
Cerrada de Lod Morales 8, Col. Polanco
                              280-0875 & 3526

Monte Sinai
Fuente de Sulpicio, Tecamachalco

Nidche Israel
Acapulco 70, Condesa   211-0575

Nidche Israel
Acapulco 70, First Floor, Condesa   211-0575

Or Damesek, Seneca 343   280-6281

Ramat Shalom
Fuente del Pescador 35, Tecamachalco
                                   251-3854

Shaare Shalom
Av. de Los Bosques 53, Tecamachalco
                                   251-0973

Mexico

Shuba Israel
Edgar Alan Poe 43, Col. Polanco   545-8061 &
                                    280-1036

Orthodox
Beth Itzhak, Eujenio Sue 20, Polence

Sephardi
Maguen David
Bernard Shaw 110, Polanco   203-9964
Sephardi Synagogue
Monterey 359   564-1197 & 564-1367

Conservative
Bet El, Horacio 1722, Polanco los Morales
                                281-2592
Beth Israel, Virreyes 1140, Lomas   520-8515
English speaking.

Mikvaot
Banos Campeche 58   574-2204
Bernard Shaw 110, Polanco   203-9964
Av. de los Bosques 53, Tecamachalco
                                589-5530
Platon 413   520-9569
Bet Midrash Tecamachalco
Fuente de Marcela 23, Col. Tecamachalco
                                251-8454
Men only.
Shuba Israel
Edgar Alan Poe 43, Col. Polanco   545-8061 &
                                   280-1036
Men only.
Tevila Cuernavaca
Priv. de Antinea 4, Col. Delicias   15 08 41;
                                    18 16 55
Tevila Janet Levy   294-9377

Embassy
Israel Embassy
Sierra Madre 215, PO Box 11000, 10
                                201-1500
                             Fax: 201-1555

Restaurants
Aladinos, Ingenieros Militares 255   395-2949
Buffet, Madero 402, Cuernavaca, Mor.
                                251-3251
Buffet C.D.I.   557-3000
Sundays only.
Centro Social Monte Sinai
Fuente de la Huerte 22   589-8322

Macabim, 5 de Febrero   709-1446
Sabre Kosher
San Jeronimo 726   709-3368
Tauqueria Piny
Ejercito Nacional y Emerson   250-5168
Wendys, Homero & Sofocles, Col. Polanco
                                395-3083

Dairy
Sabrocito, Fuete de Juventud 72   589-0513
Mehadrin.
Shalom, Acapulco 70, 1st Floor   211-1990
Supervision: Rabbi Abraham I. Bartfeld.
This kosher restaurant is above the Nische
Israel Synagogue.
Wendy's, Homero 1507, Col. Polanco
                                395-3083
Mehadrin.
Zahavi Pizza
Pasaje Moliere Loc. 6-1 Polanco   280-5608
Mehadrin.

Butchers
Fuente de Templanza 17, Tecamachalco
Mehadrin.
Carniceria Sary, Santa Ana 64, Tecamachalco
Mehadrin.
Pollos Mugrabi, Platon 133, Polanco
Mehadrin.

Groceries
Casa Amiga
Horacio 1719, Col. Polanco   540-1455
Super Teca Kosher
Acuezunco 15, San Miguel   589-9823,
                             9860 or 3225

Media
Books
Imagen David, La Fontaine 229   203-9964
Revista, La Fontaine 229   203-9964

Newspapers
CDI, Centro Deportivo, Plaza de toros of
Cuatro Caminos   557-3000
Spanish weekly.
Di Shtime, Pedro Moreno 149   546-1720
Yiddish weekly.
Foro de Vida Judia en el Mundo
Aviacion Commercial 16, Col. Polanco, 15700
                                571-1114
Spanish monthly.

Kesher, Ap. Postal 41-969, Lomas de
Chapultepec   203-0517
Spanish monthly.

La Voz de la Kehila
Acapulco 70, 2nd Floor   211-0501
Spanish monthly.

Monterrey
Area telephone code (83)

Community Organisations
Centro Israelita de Monterrey
Canada 207, Nuevo León   461-128

Tijuana
Area telephone code (66)

Synagogues
Tijuanua Hebrew Congregation
Amado Nervo 207, Baja California

Contact Information
JCC Chabad House
Centro Social Israelita de Baja California, Av.
16 Septiembre, 3000, Baja California
                                862-692; 862-693
                                   Fax: 341-532
                        Email: chabadtj@telnor.net
Mikva on premises.

Restaurants
Meat
JCC Chabad House
Centro Social Israelita de Baja California, Av.
16 Septiembre, 3000, Baja California
                                862-692; 862-693
                                   Fax: 341-532
                        Email: chabadtj@telnor.net
Supervision: Rabbi Mendel Polichenco,
Chabad.
For information on services and kosher
products, contact Rabbi Polichenco, Tel: 388-
154.

Moldova

GMT + 2 hours
Country calling code (373)

Cisinau
Area telephone code (2)

Religious Organisations
Yeshiva of Kishinev
Sciusev 5, 277001   264-362; 264-331
Aside from Jewish studies, a mikva and kosher food can be found on premises.

Synagogues
Yakimovsky per. 8, 277000   221-215

Teleneshty

Synagogues
4 28th June Street

Tiraspol
Area telephone code (3)

Contact Information   336-495
Fax: 322-208
Details of the Jewish Community from Dr Vaisman.

Monaco

GMT + 1 hour
Country calling code (377)

Monte Carlo

Synagogues
15 Av. de la Costa, opp. Balmoral Hotel, MC 98000   9330-1646

Services, Friday even. at 6.30pm and Sat. morning at 8.45am and Sat. afternoon at 5.30pm.

Morocco

There is a legend that King Solomon sent emissaries to Morocco to raise funds among Israelites living there towards the building of the Temple in Jerusalem, but it is more likely that the first Jewish settlements in Morocco were established by Jewish slaves who accompanied the Phoenicians there in the 3rd century B.C.E. Hebrew grave markers and the ruins of a synagogue have also been found at the Roman colony of Volubilis.

Today's Jewish community is said to have been founded when a hundred Jewish families, fleeing from Roman persecution in Tripolitania during the first century C.E., sought refuge in the High Atlas. Eventually, the neighbouring Berber tribes converted to Judaism, even establishing Jewish kingdoms, it is said. More Jews went to Morocco with the Expulsion from Spain in 1492.

At its peak in the 1950s the Moroccan Jewish community numbered some 300,000. Today, it has dwindled through emigration to about 8,000.

GMT + 0 hours
County calling code (212)

Agadir
Area telephone code (8)

Organisations
Community Offices
Imm. Arsalane Av. Hassan II　　　　840091
Fax: 822268

Synagogues
Av. Moulay Abdallah, cnr. rue de la Foire
842339

Mikvaot
Av. Moulay Abdallah, cnr. rue de la Foire
842339

Casablanca
Area telephone code (2)

Organisations
Community Offices
rue Abbon Abdullah　　　270976 & 222861
Fax: 266953

Council of Moroccan Jewish Communities
rue Abbon Abdullah

Synagogues
Benisty, 13 rue Ferhat Achad
Bennaroche, 24 rue Lusitania
Em Habanim, 14 rue Lusitania
Hazan, rue Roger Farache
Ne'im Zemiroth
29 rue Jean-Jacques Rousseau
Temple Beth El
61 rue Jaber ben Hayane

Mikvaot

32 rue Officier de Paix Thomas   276688
116 rue Galilee
84 rue des Anglais

Restaurants

Bon Delice, 261 Blvd. Ziraoui, opp. Lycee
Lyautey
La Truffe Blanche
57 rue Taher Sebti   277263
Tradition, Centre 2000   209310

El Jadida

Area telephone code (34)

Organisations

Community Offices
PO Box 59

Essaouira (formerly Mogador)

Area telephone code (47)

Organisations

Community Offices
2 rue Ziri Ben Atyah

Synagogues

2 rue Ziri Ben Atyah

Fez

Area telephone code (5)

Organisations

Community Offices
rue Dominique Bouchery

Synagogues

Beth El, rue de Beyrouth
Sadoun, ruelle 1, blvd. Mohammed V.
Talmud Torah, rue Dominique Bouchery

Mikvaot

Talmud Torah, rue Dominique Bouchery

Restaurants

Community Offices, rue Dominique Bouchery

Hotels

La Boutique, rue de Beyrouth
Mrs Mamane will be pleased to assist all
Jewish visitors.

Kenitra

Area telephone code (7)

Organisations

Community Offices, 58 rue Sallah Eddine

Synagogues

rue de Lyon

Mikvaot

58 rue Sallah Eddine

Marrakech

Area telephone code (4)

Organisations

Community Offices, PO Box 515   448754

Synagogues

Villa Oliviery, Blvd. Zerktouni (Gueliz)
Bitton, rue de Touareg
El Fassines
Mikvah on premises.
Lazama, rue Talmud Torah

Restaurants

Le Viennois, Hotel Mansour Eddabbi, Ave de
France   448222
    Fax: 448168
Supervision: local rabbi.

Meknes
Area telephone code (5)

Synagogues
5 rue de Ghana   21968 or 22549
Tourists will be assisted if telephoning their requests 24 hours in advance.

Mikvaot
5 rue de Ghana   21968 or 22549
Tourists will be assisted if telephoning their requests 24 hours in advance.

Oujda
Area telephone code (68)

Organisations
Community Offices
Texaco Maroc, 36 Blvd. Hassan Loukili

Rabat
Area telephone code (7)

Organisations
Community Offices, 1 rue Boussouni

Synagogues
3 rue Moulay Ismail

Mikvaot
3 rue Moulay Ismail

Safi
Area telephone code (4)

Synagogues
Beth El, rue de R'bat
Mursiand, rue de R'bat

Tangier
Area telephone code (9)

Organisations
Community Centre
1 rue de la Liberte   31633 or 21024

Synagogues
Shaar Raphael, 27 Blvd. Pasteur   231304
Temple Nahon, rue Moses Nahon

Mikvaot
Shaar Raphael, 27 Blvd. Pasteur   231304

Hotels
El Minzah (100), 85 rue de la Liberte
La Grande Villa de France, rue de Belgique
Les Almohade (150), Av. des F. A. R.
Rambrant, Av. Pasteur   378-7071
Rif, Av. d'Espagne

Tourist Sites
rue des Synagogues, off rue Siaghines
There are a number of synagogues in the old part of the town in this street.

Tetuan
Area telephone code (9)

Organisations
Community Offices, 16 rue Moulay Abbas

Synagogues
Benoualid, the old Mellah
Pintada, the old Mellah
Yagdil Torah, Adj. Community Centre

Mozambique

GMT + 2 hours
Country calling code (258)

Maputo
Area telephone code (1)

Organisations
Jewish Community of Maputo
PO Box 232   494413

Myanmar (formerly Burma)

GMT + 6½ hours
Country calling code (264)

Rangoon
Area telephone code (1)

Synagogues
Musmeah Yeshua, 85 26th Street   75062

Embassy
Embassy of Israel
49 Pyay   222-290; 222-709; 222-201
                                    Fax: 222-463

Namibia

Some Jewish settlers came to this territory before the First World War, when it was a German colony. The cemetery at Swakopmund dates from those times. In 1910 a congregation was established at Keetmanshoop. It had a synagogue and cemetery at one time, but is no longer in existence.
In the 1920s and 1930s there were never more than 100 Jewish families in various centres in Namibia. Today, the figure stands at only 11 families. Efforts are made to arrange services for the High Holy-days.

GMT + 2 hours
Country calling code (264)

Windhoek
Area telephone code (61)

Synagogues
Cnr. Tal & Post Streets, PO Box 563

Netherlands

There were some Jews in Holland during the Middle Ages, but Dutch Jewish history effectively began with the settlement of Marranos in Amsterdam at the end of the sixteenth century. Dutch Jewry was given freedom of worship early in the seventeenth century and was formally emancipated in 1796. Holland was the first country in the modern world to admit Jews to Parliament (1797).

In 1940 there were approximately 140,000 Jews in the country, but as the result of the Nazi occupation, not more than 30,000 remain, of whom more than half live in the Amsterdam area, where there is much of Jewish interest to be seen. For information about synagogues, services and kosher food outside Amsterdam, Rotterdam and The Hague, contact Chief Rabbinate of Holland, Tel: 020-6443868.

GMT + 1 hour
Country calling code (31)

Kashrut Information

644-3868

For information on synagogues, services and kosher food outside Amsterdam, Rotterdam and The Hague, contact Chief Rabbinate of Holland.

Amersfoort

Area telephone code (33)

Synagogues

Drieringensteeg 2   472-6204;
                          720943

Amsterdam / Amstelveen

Area telephone code (20)

Organisations

Anne Frank Foundation
Prinsengracht 263-265   556-7100
Ashkenazi Community Offices
van der Boechorststr. 26   646-0046
                          Fax: 646-4357

Community Centre
van der Boechrststr. 26   644-0180

Synagogues

Buitenveldert, van der Boechorststr. 26
Jacob Obrechtplein, Gerard Doustr. 238
Kehilat Jaacow (E. Europe), Lekstr. 61
Kehilat Jaacow (E. Europe), Gerrit v. d. Veenstr. 26
Nieuwe Kerkstraat 149 (E. Europe)
Straat van Messina 10   676-6400
The Portuguese Synagogue
Mr. Visserplein 3   624-5351
                          Fax: 625-4680
This synagogue has been completely restored, and is open April - October: Sun - Fri 10am to 12.30pm and 1pm to 4pm; November to March: Sun 10am to 12pm; Mon.-Thurs. 10am to 12pm and 1pm to 4pm; Fri 10 am to 12.30pm and 1pm to 3pm

Ashkenazi

Ashkenazi Rabbinate of Amsterdam
van der Boechorststr. 26, 1081 BT, PO Box 7967, 10008 AD   644-3868
Maarsen
van der Boechorststr. 26, 1081 BT, PO Box 7967, 10008 AD   644-3868

Sephardi

Portuguese Synagogue & Community Centre
Mr. Visserplein 3   624-5351

Portuguese Synagogue & Community Centre
Texelstr. 82   624-5351

Liberal

Jacob Soetendorpstr. 8, 1079 RM
     644-2619; 642-3562
     Fax: 642-8135

Houses the Judith Druk Library and the Centre for Jewish Studies.

Mikvaot

Mr. Visserplein 3   624-5351
Heinzestr. 3   662-0178

Restaurants

Carmel
Amstelveensewag 224, 1075 XT   675-7636
Hours: 12 pm to 11:30 pm, Sunday to Thursday. Cater Shabbat meals for groups if ordered in advance.

Mrs B. Hertzberger
Plantage Westermanlaan 9, 1018 DK 623-4684
Supervision: Rabbinate of Amsterdam.
5 minutes from Portuguese Synagogue. Friday night and Shabbat meals only. Reservation in advance. Also lunchboxes for groups.

Sandwichshop Sal. Meijer
Scheldestraat 45, 1078 GG   673-1313
     Fax: 642-9020

Students Mensa
Meschibat Nefesh, de Lairessestraat 13, near Concertgebouw   676-7622
Supervision: Amsterdam Rabbinate.
Currently being rebuilt and due to be reopened in early 1998. Kosher meals available. No accommodation is available.

Museum Café, Jewish Historical Museum, Jonas Daniel Meijerplein 2-4   626-9945
Hours: 11 am to 5 pm daily.

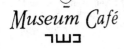

Vegetarian

Bolhoed, Prinzengracht 60   626-1803
Hours: 12 pm to 10 pm daily. Serve vegetarian
and vegan food.

Bakeries

Jerusalem Bakery, Scheldestr. 55	471-1575
Theeboom, Maasstraat 16	662-4827
Theeboom, Bolestein 45-47	642-7003
Tweede, Sweelinckstr. 5	662-7086

Butchers

Marcus Ritueel, Ferd. Bolstr. 44	671-9881
Meyer, Scheldestr. 63	664-0036

Delicatessens

Mouwes Koshere Delicatessan
Kastelenstraat 261, 1082   661-0180

Chocolate Shops

Chocolate shop Bonbon Jeannette

Hall Central Station Amsterdam, Stationsplein
15, 1012 AB   421-5194
Fax: 421-5194
Their bitter and dairy chocolates and bonbons
are kosher and are sanctioned by the Chief
Rabbinate for the Netherlands. Open daily,
8 am to 9 pm.

Chocolate shop Bonbon Jeannette
Europaplein 87, 1078 GZ   664-9638
Fax: 675-6543
Their bitter and dairy chocolates and bonbons
are kosher and are sanctioned by the Chief
Rabbinate for the Netherlands. Hours: Monday
to Friday, 9 am to 6 pm; Sunday, 9 am to
5 pm; closed Mondays in July and August.

Vendors

French Fries
Vootboeg Str. (alleyway off Spuistraat)
This vendor sells only french fries (chips),
cooked in vegetable oil. A variety of sauces are
available and included in the price. The chips
are served in a paper cone.

★★★

A modern hotel in the heart of Amsterdam

All rooms have shower/bath, t.v., telephone.

5 minutes from Central station, main shopping streets and fleamarket, near synagogue, kosher breakfast.

Tel: 020-6388826. Fax: 010-6388726.

Rooms from: single f90,-
double f120,-
triple f150,-

DORIA
HOTEL RISTORANTE

Hotels

Hotel Arsenal
Frans van mierisstr. 97   679-2209
Pre-packed kosher breakfasts available for guests.

Hotel Doria, Damstraat 3   638-8826

Hotel Golden Tulip
Barbizon Centre
Stadhouderskade 7   685-1351

Museums

Anne Frank House
Prinsengracht 263, nr. Westermarkt   556-7100
Several exhibitions, including the original hiding place of Anne Frank, where she wrote her diary. Open weekdays from 9am to 5pm, Suns & Holidays 10am to 5pm.

The Jewish Historical Museum
Jonas Daniel Meijerplein 2-4   626-9945
Housed in a complex of 3 former synagogues. Open daily from 11am to 5pm.

The Resistance Museum, Lekstr. 61
Housed in the Synagogue building.

Tourist Sites

Portuguese Cemetary
Ouderkerk-on-the-Amstel
10 miles south-east of Amsterdam (Manasseh ben Israel is buried here).

Libraries

Bibliothecha Rosenthaliana
Singel 423
A fine collection of Judaica and Hebraica in the university library.

Livraria Montezinos & Ets Haim Library
Mr. Visserplein 3
Open for research only, Mon.-Thurs. 9am to 12.30pm.

Media

Newspapers

"Nieuw Israelitisch Weekblad"
Rapenburgerstr. 109   623-5584

Booksellers

Joachimsthal's Boekhandel
Van Leijenberghlaan 116, 1082 DB   442-0762
           Fax: 404-1843

Samech Books
Gunterstein 69   642-1424

Arnhem

Area telephone code (26)

Synagogues

Pastoorstr. 17a   442-5154

Liberal

Liberal Congregation Inquiries
Regentesselaan 18, Apeldoorn, 7316 AE
           522-2332

Bussum

Area telephone code (36)

Synagogues

Kromme Englaan 1a   691-4882

Delft
Area telephone code (15)

Synagogues
Beth Studentiem
Hillel House, Jewish Students Centre, Technical
University, Koornmarkt 9   212-0300

Eindhoven
Area telephone code (40)

Religious Organisations
Synagogue Inquiries   241-2710

Synagogues
H. Casimirstr. 23   751-1253

Enschede
Area telephone code (53)

Synagogues
Prinsestr. 16   432-3479; 435-3336

Liberal
Liberal Congregation Inquiries
Haaksbergen   435-1330

Groningen
Area telephone code (50)

Synagogues
Folkingestr. 60, Postbus 550, 9700 AN
                                       312-3151

Haarlem
Area telephone code (23)

Synagogues
Kenaupark 7   332-6899; 324-2051

Hilversum
Area telephone code (35)

Synagogues
Laanstr. 30   621-2044
Inter-Provincial Chief Rabbinate also based at
this address. Rabbi's J. S. Jacobs, S. Evers and
A. L. Heintz. Tel: 035-623-9238.

Leiden
Area telephone code (71)

Organisations
Jewish Students Centre
Levendaal 8   513-0382

Synagogues
Levendaal 16   512-5793

Maastricht
Area telephone code (43)

Synagogues
Capucijnengang 2
Est. 1840.

Rotterdam
Area telephone code (10)

Synagogues
A. B. N. Davidsplein 4   466-9765
Mikva on premises.

Liberal
Molenhoek Hillegersberg   644-2619
Inquiries to Secretary on 461-3211.

Butchers
Piket, Walen-burgerweg 97   467-2856
Wednesdays only. Kosher groceries available
Wednesday and Thursday pm.

The Hague
Area telephone code (70)

Synagogues
Corn. Houtmanstr., 11 Bezuidenhout
347-3201
Mikva on premises.
Beis Jisroel
Doorniksestraat 152, 2587 AZ   358-6363
Fax: 347-9002
For catering under supervision of the
Rabbinate.

Liberal
Liberal Synagogue
Prinsessegracht 26   365-6893
Fax: 360-3883

Embassy
Embassy of Israel
Buitenhof 47, 2513 AH

Tourist Sites
Spinoza House
Paviljoensgracht
Spinoza House is of special interest, as is the
18th c. Portuguese Synagogue in the
Prinsessegracht, which is now used by the
Liberal congregation.

Tilburg
Area telephone code (70)

Synagogues
Liberal Synagogue Brabant   365-6893
Inquiries to 013-467-5566

Utrecht
Area telephone code (30)

Synagogues
Springweg 164   231-4742
Liberal
Liberal Synagogue   644-2619
Inquiries to 603-9343.

Bakeries
De Tarwebol, Zadelstr. 19   231-4887

Delicatessens
Milk and Honey, Poorstr. 93   273-3114

Zwolle
Area telephone code (38)

Synagogues
Samuel Hirschstr. 8, Postbox 1468, 8001 BL
211412

Netherlands Antilles

GMT – 4 hours
Country calling code (599)

Aruba

Synagogues
Adrian Laclé Blvd, Oranjestad   23272
Services Friday, 8 pm.

Curaçao
Area telephone code (9)

Organisations
Israel Consulate
Blauwduifweg 5, PO Box 3058, Willemstad
    365088
    Fax: 370707

Synagogues

Ashkenazi Orthodox
Congregation Shaarei Tsedek
Leliweg 1a, PO Box 498   375738

Sephardi, Reconstructionist
United Netherlands Portuguese Congregation
PO Box 322   611067
    Fax: 611214
Sabbath & Holy-day services are Friday at 6.30pm (second Friday in the month is a family service), Saturday at 10am

Kashrut Information
There is no kosher restaurant in Curacao, but kosher food is available at some out-of-town supermarkets.

Travel Agencies
S. E. L. Maduro & Sons, Inc.
Maduro Plaza, Dokweg 19   376700
    Fax: 376131

New Zealand

New Zealand boasts a small but vibrant Jewish community of 5,000 (out of a total population of 3.5 million), most of whom live in Auckland and Wellington. The community pre-dates the establishment of British sovereignty in 1840. The first two mayors of Auckland were Jewish, and Jews have occupied a number of prominent offices including Administrator, Prime Minister and Chief Justice.

The community is growing in both strength and number, thanks in part to immigration from South Africa.

Kadimah college in Auckland is considered one of the country's best primary schools and will be opening a secondary school this year. There are a variety of active youth and student movements, Zionist organisations, Jewish social and welfare groups, with adult education programmes running through the year. A full range of Jewish facilities operate in the principal cities, including mikvaot and kosher shops attached to the shuls.

The Auckland community produces a 'Kosher Kiwi Guide' with regular updates. Visitors are welcome to contact the Auckland Hebrew Congregation for further information and to arrange Shabbat meals and hospitality.

GMT + 12 hours
Country calling code (64)

Auckland
Area telephone code (9)

Representative Organisations
Auckland Jewish Council
PO Box 4315   309-9444
                            Fax: 373-2283

Synagogues

Orthodox
Auckland Hebrew Congregation
108 Greys Avenue, PO Box 68-224   373-2908
                            Fax: 303-2147

Progressive
Temple Shalom
180 Manukau Road, Epsom 3   524-4139

Bakeries
Manhattan Bagels   309-9098

Caterers
Shelleys Catering
13 Collingswood Street, Freemans Bay
                                360-2989
                            Fax: 486-0158

Christchurch
Area telephone code (3)

Representative Organisations
Christchurch Jewish Council   358-8769

Synagogues
406 Durham Street   365-7412

Dunedin

Area telephone code (3)

Synagogues

Progressive Congregation
cnr. George & Dundas Streets

Wellington

Area telephone code (4)

Representative Organisations

Wellington and New Zealand Regional Jewish Council
54 Central Terrace, 5   475-7622

Community Organisations

Wellington Jewish Community Centre
80 Webb Street   384-5081
                                    Fax: 384-5081
There are no kosher restaurants in Wellington. Visitors who want kosher meals & kosher food should contact the centre office of the Community Centre.

Synagogues

Orthodox

Beth-El Synagogue
80 Webb Street   384-5081
                                    Fax: 384-5081

Progressive

Temple Sinai
147 Ghuznee Street   385-0720
                                    Fax: 385-0572

Mikvaot

Wellington Jewish Community Centre
80 Webb Street   384-5081
                                    Fax: 384-5081

Embassy

Israel Embassy
D.P. Tower, 111 The Terrace, PO Box 2171
                                         472-2368
                                    Fax: 499-0632

Media

Newspapers

New Zealand Jewish Chronicle
PO Box 27-211   384-4229
                                    Fax: 384-4229
Edited by Mike Regan, this monthly is the official publication of the Zionist Federation of New Zealand.

Delicatessens

Dixon Street Delicatessen   384-2436
                                    Fax: 384-8692
Not kosher but provides kosher bagels, bread rolls and challahs.

Groceries

Kosher Co-op, 80 Webb Street   384-3136

Norway

Norway's Jewish com. is one of Europe's youngest and smallest. Jews first arrived in the country in 1851, but it was not until 1881 that comparatively large-scale Jewish immigration began. The community was founded in 1892. By the beginning of the Second World War, in 1939, there were 1,800 Jews in Norway.

Half of the Norwegian Jewry were killed in Auschwitz, the other half saved by the Norwegian resistance in Sweden. In 1947 the Government invited 500 D.P.s to settle in the country. The Jewish population is now about 1,400, of whom 950 live in Oslo.

GMT + 1 hour
Country calling code (47)

Oslo

Synagogues

Bergstien 13-15, 0172   2269-6570

Embassy

Embassy of Israel
Drammensveien 82c, 2   2244-7924

Restaurants

Kosher Food Centre
Waldemar Thranesgt., 0171   2260-9166
Supervision: Rabbi Michael Melchior.
Open 4 pm to 6 pm Tuesday and Thursday,
and 12 pm to 2 pm on Friday. Closed
Shabbat.

Vegetarian

Frisksport Vegeta Vertshus
Munkedamsveien 3b, 0161
                          2283-4020; 2283-4232
Hours: 11 am to 11 pm, 7 days a week. Large
salad and hot dish buffet all day. Lacto-ovo-
vegetarian food, no animal fat.

Tourist Sites

Ostre Gravlund Cemetary
There is a Jewish war memorial erected here.

Trondheim

Synagogues

Ark. Christiesgt. 1

Panama

GMT – 5 hours
Country calling code (507)

Panama City

Organisations

Consejo Central Comunitario Hebrew de
Panama
Apt. 3309, 4 · · · · · · · · · · · · 263-8411
Fax: 264-7936
Jewish Centre Centro Cultural Hebreo De
Beneficiencia
Calle 50 Final, PO Box 7166, 5 · · · 226-0455
Fax: 226-0869
Restaurant open daily for lunch and supper.
Closed Saturdays.

Religious Organisations

Chief Rabbi Sion Levy
Calle 44-40, Bella Vista 85,
Apartado, 6222, 5 · · · · · · · · · · 227-2828

Synagogues

Sephardi Orthodox
Sociedad Israelita Shevet Ahim
Calle 44-27 · · · · · · · · · · · · · 225-5990
Fax: 227-1268

Daily services.

Ashkenazi
Beneficiencia Israelita Beth El
Calle 58E, Urb., Obarrio · · · · · · 223-3383

Reform
Koll Sherit Israel
Av. Cuba 354-16 · · · · · · · · · · 225-4100

Mikvaot
Beneficiencia Israelita Beth El
Calle 58E, Urb., Obarrio · · · · · · 223-3383
Sociedad Israelita Shevet Ahim
Calle 44-27 · · · · · · · · · · · · · 225-5990
Fax: 227-1268

Contact Information
PO Box 6629, 5 · · · · · · · Fax: 228-6796

Embassy
Israel Embassy
Edificio Grobman, Calle Manuel Maria Icaza,
5th Floor, apdo 6357, 5 · · · · · · 264-8022
Fax: 642-706

Restaurants
Candies Bazaar
Via Argentina, 155 L-2 · · · · · · · 269-4857
Pita Pan, Plaza Bal Harbour, Paitilla 264-2786

Butchers
La Bonbonniere
Calle Juan XXIII, Paitilla · · · · · · 264-5704
Shalom Kosher
Plaza Bal Harbour, Paitilla · · · · · 264-4411
Super Kosher
Calle San Sebastian, Paitilla · · · · 236-5254;
235-5253

Chocolatier
Chocolatier
Calle 53, Urb., Marbella · · · · · · 264-4712

Paraguay

GMT – 5 hours
Country calling code (507)

Asuncion
Area telephone code (21)

Organisations
Consejo Representativo Israelita de Paraguay
General Diaz, 657, PO Box 756   41744

Synagogues
General Diaz, 657

Embassy
Israel Embassy
Calle Yegros No. 437 C/25 de Mayo, Edificio San Rafael, Piso 8, PO Box 1212
495-097; 496-043; 496-044
Fax: 496-355

Peru

GMT – 5 hours
Country calling code (51)

Lima
Area telephone code (14)

Organisations
Asociacion Judia de beneficencia y Culto de 1870
Jose Galvez 282, Miraflores, 18
451089 or 445-5148
Fax: 445-5148

Religious Organisations
Chief Rabbi 424-505
Rabbi Benhamu is the Chief Rabbi of Peru.

Synagogues
Beit Jabad, Salverry 3095, San Isidro, 27
264-6060
Fax: 442-9441

Orthodox
Centro Social y Cultural Sharon
Av. 2 de Mayo 1815, San Isidro, 27   440-0290
Sociedad de Beneficencia Israelita Sefardi
Enrique Villar 581, Santa Beatriz, 1   442-4505;
471-7230
Union Israelita del Peru
Jose Quinones 290, Miraflores 18   441-3461
Services are held at the Centro Sharon.

Mikvaot
Union Israelita
Ave. Gral. Juan A. Pezet 1472, San Isidro, 27
264-2187
Sociedad Israelita Sefardi
Beit Jabad

Kashrut Information
Rabbinate
Av. de Mayo 1815, San Isidro, 27   264-0678
There is no kosher restaurant in Lima. Visitors who want kosher meals should contact Rabbi Kraus.

Embassy
Israel Embassy
Natalio Sanchez 125 6 Piso, Santa Beatris, apartado 738   433-4431
Fax: 433-8925

Caterers
Salon Majestic
965 Pueblo Libre, 21   463-0031
Fax: 461-8912
Supervision: Rabbi Abraham Benhamu and Rabbi Yaacov Kraus.
Catering for special groups and parties by prior arrangement only.

Groceries
Minimarket Kasher
Av. Gral. Juan A. Pezet 1472, San Isidro, 27
264-2187
Supervision: Rabbi Kraus.
Pharmax
Kosher items available.
Santa Isabel
Kosher items available.
Wong
Kosher items available.

Hotels
Hostal Regina
Av. 2 de Mayo 1421, San Isidro, 27
441-2541; 442-8870
Fax: 421-2044
Shabbat observers may wish to stay here as there is only a short walk to the Centro Sharon.
Hotel Libertador
Los Eucaliptos 550, San Isidro, 27   421-6666
Fax: 442-3011
Shabbat observers may wish to stay here as there is only a short walk to the Centro Sharon.

Museums

Museum of the Inquisition
Junin 548
Dungeon and torture chamber of the
headquarters of the Inquisition for all Spanish
South America. In front of the Congress.

Tourist Sites

Pilatos House
Ancash 390
17th c. private mansion, now used by the
National Institute of Culture. On the 2nd floor
was the synagogue of the Marrano Jews.

Media

Newspapers

J.T.A. - Publicationes Memora S. A.
Psje. Malvas 135, Brena, 5   424-0534
Daily publication.
Shofar, Husares de Junin 163, Jesus Maria, 11
                                                    241412, 312410
Monthly.

Philippines Republic

GMT + 8 hours
Country calling code (63)

Manila

Area telephone code (2)

Synagogues

**Jewish Association of the Philippines (Beth
Yaacov Synagogue)**
H. V. de la Costa Street, Salcedo Village,
Makati, Metro Manila, 1200   815-0263, 0265
                                          Fax: 818-9990
Services: Fri at 6.30pm, Sat at 9.30am.

Mikvaot

**Jewish Association of the Philippines (Beth
Yaacov Synagogue)**
H. V. de la Costa Street, Salcedo Village,
Makati, Metro Manila, 1200   815-0263, 0265
                                          Fax: 818-9990
Kosher requirements by arrangement.

Embassy

Israel Embassy
Tratalgar Plaza 23 Floor, 105 H.V. dela Costa
Street, Saleeldo Village, Makati, Metro Manils
                                    892-5329/30/31/34
                                          Fax: 894-1027
Postal address: POB 374, Makati Metro,
Manila 1299.

Poland

Jews settled in Poland in the ninth century, coming from Germany, Bohemia and Russia. The first documentary evidence of Polish Jews is dated 1185, and there is also evidence on coins: Jews were in charge of Polish coinage in the twelfth century, and coins bore Hebrew inscriptions.

The Kalisz Statutes of 1264, granted by Duke Boleslaw the Pious, were a charter of Jewish rights. Casimir the Great, the last Polish king of the Piast dynasty (1303–1370), was a protector of the Jews and was, according to legend, married secretly to a Jewess, Esther. Jewish learning flourished from the sixteenth century onwards. Mystic Chasidism, based on the Cabbala, had its wonder-rabbis. Famous Talmudic scholars, codifiers of the ritual, and other eminent men of learning were produced by Polish Jewry.

Of the 3,500,000 Jews in Poland in 1939, about three million were exterminated by Hitler. Many put up a heroic fight, like those of the Warsaw Ghetto in 1943. Fewer than half a million fled to the West and to the Soviet Union. After the Second World War there were several waves of emigration, the last of which was in 1968. Today's ageing Jewish population numbers an estimated 6,000.

Synagogues and Social Cultural Societies (TSZK) are known to exist in the following towns: Biala, Bielsko, Bytom, Czestochowa, Dzierzoniów, Gliwice, Katowice, Legnica, Lublin, Milejczyce, Sosnowiec, Swidnica, Szczecin, Tarnów, Tykocin, Walbrzych, Wloclawek, Wroclaw, Zamosc, Zary k/Zag, Zgorzelec.

Foreign tourists are advised to address all their queries and requests to the Foreign Tourists' Office, Krakowskie Przedmiescie St., Warsaw 13, Tel: 26-16-68.

GMT + 1 hour
Country calling code (48)

Bielsko-Biala
Area telephone code (2)

Organisations
Elzbieta Wajs, Ul Mickiewicza 26, 43-300
22438

Bytom
Area telephone code (3)

Organisations
Ul Smolenia 4, 41902　　813510

Cracow
Area telephone code (12)

Organisations
Zwiakzek Wyznania Mojzeszowego
Ul Skawinska 2　　662347

Synagogues
Remuh, Ul Szeroka 40

Restaurants
Ariel Café, 17 Szeroka Street, Miodowa 41, Restaurant at no. 18

Meat

Na Kazimierzu
ul. Szeroka 39, 31-053   229-644
                                         Fax: 219-909
Billed as the 'only kosher restaurant in Cracow
and the south of Poland'. Hours: 12 pm to
12 am every day. Traditional Shabbat courses
are available on Shabbat.

Galleries

Hadar, 13 Florianska Street   218992

Booksellers

Jordan, 2 Szeroka Street, Miodowa 41 217166

Gliwice

Area telephone code (32)

Contact Information

Ul Dolnych Walow 9, 44100   314797

Katowice

Area telephone code (32)

Contact Information

Ul Mlynska 13, 40098   537742

Legnica

Area telephone code (76)

Contact Information

Ul Chojnowska 37, 59220   22730

Lodz

Area telephone code (42)

Organisations

Jewish Chabad   331221, 336825
Jewish Congregation
Zachodnia 78   335156

Lublin

Area telephone code (81)

Contact Information

Ul Lubartowska 10, 20080   22353

Rzeszów

Two synagogues face each other in ul. Bonicza
at the edge of pl. Ofiara Getta.

Szczecin

Area telephone code (91)

Contact Information

Ul Niemcewicza 2, 71553   221674

Warsaw

Area telephone code (22)

Organisations

The Jewish Historical Institute
3/5 Tlomackie Street, 00090   271530
This establishment has a remarkable collection
of Judaica. It includes a library of documents
on the manuscripts stolen by the Germans
from all over Europe.
Zwiazek Religijny Wyznania Mojzeszowego
Ul Krajowej Rady Narodowej 6   204324

Synagogues

Vadd Hakehilla, 6 Twarda Street   204324

Embassy

Embassy of Israel, Ul I Kryzwickiego 24

Restaurants

Ekologica Restaurant
Rynek 13, Nowy Miasto
Menora, Plac Grzybowski 2   203754
Panorama, Al Witsoa 31   642-0666
Salad Bar, Ul Tamka 37   635-8463

Tours

Shalom Tours   220-3037
                                         Fax: 220-0559

Wrocklaw

Area telephone code (71)

Museums

Historical Museum, Slezna Street 37   678236

Portugal

GMT + 0 hours
Country calling code (351)

Algarve
Area telephone code (82)

Community Organisations
Jewish Community of Algarve
Rua Infante Dom Henrique 12, 3°B, 8500,
Portimão   416-710
                                    Fax: 416-515

Belmonte
Area telephone code (75)

Organisations
Jewish Community of Belmonte
Apt. 18, Bairo de Santa Maina,
6250 Belmonte   912465
                                    Fax: 912465

Faro
Area telephone code (89)

Museums
Faro Jewish Cemetery and Museum
1838-1932. Only remaining vestige of the first
post-Inquisition Jewish presence in Algarve.
Open weekday mornings from 9:30 am to
12:30 pm. Situated opposite entrance to Faro
Hospital. Enquiries to Ralf Pinto, Jewish
Community of Algarve.

Lisbon
Area telephone code (1)

Organisations
Communal Offices
Rua Alexandre Herculano 59-1250   385-0604
                                    Fax: 388-4304
Services on Fri. eve. & Sat. morning.

Jewish Club & Centre
Rua Rosa Araujo 10   572041

Synagogues
Rua Alexandre Herculano 59-1250   385-0604
                                    Fax: 388-4304
Services on Fri. eve. & Sat. morning.

Ashkenazi
Avenida Elias Garcia, 100-1'-1050

Embassy
Embassy of Israel
Rua Antonio Enes 16, 1000
          570-251; 570-145; 570-374; 570-478

Kosher Meals
Mrs R. Assor
Rua Rodrigo da Fonseca 38.1°D   386-0396
Kosher meals are obtainable if prior notice is
given. She can also supply delicatessen. For
kosher meats, contact the communal offices.

Oporto
Area telephone code (2)

Synagogues
Rua Guerra Junqueiro 340

Ponta Delgada
Capital of the island of Sao Miguel, in the
Azores, a group of Atlantic islands owned by
Portugal synagogue, Rua do Brum 16.

Tomar
The ancient synagogue in Rua de Joaquim
Jacinto (built 1492–1497) has been re-opened
as a museum. A Marrano. Luis Vasco. is the
custodian and guide. Tomar is north of Lisbon,
near Fatima.

Madeira

Area telephone code (91)

During the war most Gibraltar Jews were evacuated to Madeira, but only a few Jews live there now. There is no organised Jewish community.

Hotels

Hotel Madeira Palacio (260)
PO Box 614, Funchal   30001
Madeira-Sheraton Hotel (292)
Largo Antonio Nobre, Funchal   31031
Reid's Hotel, Funchal
Savoy, Funchal
Vegetarian and fish meals can be eaten in all the above listed hotels.

Puerto Rico

GMT – 4 hours
Country calling code (1 787)

San Juan-Santurce

Area telephone code (787)

Synagogues

Shaare Zedeck
903 Ponce de Leon Av., Santurce, 00907
                                                        724-4157

Reform

Temple Beth Shalom
San Jorge Av. & Loiza St., Santurce, 00907

Kashrut Information

Some major hotels provide kosher-style meals in the winter season. Frozen kosher poultry and delicatessen are available at some Pueblo supermarkets.

Romania

There have been Jews in the territory that is now Romania since Roman times. The country's Jewish population today is some 14,000, of whom about 6,500 live in Bucharest. There are 70 functioning synagogues, 4 of them in Bucharest, including two at the two homes for the aged. There are Talmud Torah classes in 24 communities throughout the country.

GMT + 2 hours
Country calling code (40)

Arad

Area telephone code (57)

Organisations

Community Offices
10 Tribunal Dobra Street   281310
Home for the Aged
22, 7 Episcopei Street

Synagogues

Muzeul Judetean
Piata George Enescu 1   280114
Neologa, 10 Tribunal Dobra Street
Talmud Torah
10 Tribunal Dobra Street

Orthodox
12 Cozia Street

Restaurants

Ritual, 22, 7 Episcopei Street   280731

Hotels

Hotel Astoria, Revolutiei 79-81   281-990
Hotel Parc, Bd. Dragulina 25   280-820

Bacau

Area telephone code (34)

Organisations

Community Offices
11 Alexandru cel Bun Street   134714

Synagogues

Avram A. Rosen Synagogue
31 V. Alecsandri Street
Cerealistilor, 29 Stefan cel Mare Street

Restaurants
11 Alexandru cel Bun Street

Borsec

Synagogues
Transylvania Hotel – see below

Hotels

Kosher
Transylvania Hotel
c/o Interom Tours   972-3-924-6425
                          Fax: 972-3-579-1720

Botosani

Area telephone code (31)

Organisations

Community Offices
220 Calea Nationala   0315-14659

Synagogues

Great, 1a Marchian Street
Mare, 18 Muzicantilor Street
Yiddish, 10 Gh. Dimitrov Street

Mikvaot
67 7 Aprilie Street

Restaurants
69 7 Aprilie Street 0315-15917

Brasov
Area telephone code (68)

Organisations
Community Offices
27 Poarta Schei Street 143532

Synagogues
27 Poarta Schei Street

Restaurants
27 Poarta Schei Street 144440

Bucharest
Area telephone code (1)

Representative Organisations
Federation of Romanian Jewish
Communities
24 Popa Rusu Street 211-8080
The Federation publishes a bi-monthly, 'Revista
Realitatea Evreiasca'.

Community Organisations
Jewish Community of Bucharest
Strada Sf. Vineri 9 613-1782

Religious Organisations
Chief Rabbi of Romania
Strada Sf. Vineri 9 613-2538
Fax: 312-0869

Synagogues
Choral Temple
Strada Sf. Vineri 9 147-257
Talmud Torah on premises.

Credinta, 48 Vasile Toneanu Street

Ieshua Tova
9 Nikos Beloiannis Street 659-5675
Near the Lido and Ambassador hotels.

Sephardi
Great Synagogue
9-11 Vasile Adamache Street 615-0846

Mikvaot
5 Negustori Street

Embassy
Embassy of Israel
6 Burghelea Street 613-2634/5/6

Restaurants
Jewish Community
18 Popa Soare Street 322-0398
This restaurant is operated by the Jewish
Community.

Museums
Museum of the Jewish Community in
Romania
3 Mamoulari Street 615-0837
Hours: Wednesday and Sunday, 9 am to 1 pm.

Documentation Centres
Romanian Jewish History Research Centre
12 Juliu Barasch Street 323-7246

Theatres
Jewish State Theatre 323-4530

Cluj Napoca
Area telephone code (64)

Organisations
Community Offices
25 Tipografiei Street 11667

Synagogues
Beth Hamidrash Ohel Moshe
16 David Fransisc Street

Sas Hevra, 13 Croitorilor Street

Templul Deportatilor
21 Horea Street

Mikvaot
16 David Fransisc Street

Restaurants
5-7 Paris Street   11026

Constanta
Area telephone code (41)

Organisations
Community Office
3 Sarmisagetuza Street   611598

Synagogues
Great Temple
2 C. A. Rosetti Street
Small, 3 Sarmisagetuza Street
Talmud Torah
3 Sarmisagetuza Street

Dorohoi
Area telephone code (31)

Organisations
Community Office
95 Spiru Haret Street   611797

Synagogues
Great, 4 Piata Unirii Street

Restaurants
14-18 Dumitru Furtuna Street

Galati
Area telephone code (36)

Organisations
Community Office
9 Dornei Street   413662

Synagogues
Meseriasilor
11 Dornei Street

Restaurants
9 Dornei Street   413662

Iasi (Jassy)
Area telephone code (32)

Organisations
Community Office
15 Elena Doamna Street   114414

Synagogues
Great, 7 Sinagogilor Street
Schor, 5 Sf. Constantin Street

Mikvaot
15 Elena Doamna Street

Restaurants
15 Elena Doamna Street   1117883

Oradea
Area telephone code (59)

Organisations
Community Office
4 Mihai Viteazu Street   134843

Synagogues
Great, 4 Mihai Viteazu Street
Neolog, 22 Independentei Street
Sas Hevra, 4 Mihai Viteazu Street

Mikvaot
5 Mihai Viteazu Street

Restaurants
5 Mihai Viteazu Street   131383

Piatra Neamt
Area telephone code (33)

Organisations
Community Office
7 Petru Rares Street   623815

Synagogues
Leipziger, 12 Meteorului Street

Old Baal Shem Tov
7 Meteorului Street
Old historical monument.

Radauti
Area telephone code (30)

Organisations
Community Office
11 Aleea Primaverii, Block 14, Apt.1   461333

Synagogues
Great, 2, 1 Mai Street
Vijnitzer, 49 Libertatii Street

Satu Mare
Area telephone code (61)

Organisations
Community Office
4 Decebal Street   743783

Synagogues
Great, 4 Decebal Street

Sighet
Area telephone code (62)

Organisations
Community Office
8 Basarabia Street   511652

Synagogues
Great, 8 Basarabia Street

Suceava
Area telephone code (30)

Organisations
Community Office
8 Armeneasca Street   213084

Synagogues
Gah Chavre, 4 Dimitrie Onciu Street

Timisoara
Area telephone code (56)

Organisations
Community Office
5 Gh. Lazar Street   132813

Synagogues
Cetate, 6 Marasesti Street
Fabric, 2 Splaiul Coloniei
Iosefin, 55 Resita Street

Mikvaot
55 Resita Street

Restaurants
10 Marasesti Street   136924

Tirgu Mures
Area telephone code (65)

Organisations
Community Office
10 Brailei Street   115001

Synagogues
21 Aurel Filimon Street

Tushnad

Hotels
Kosher
Olt Hotel, c/o Interom Tours 972-3-924-6425
Fax: 972-3-579-1720

Vatra Dornei
Area telephone code (30)

Organisations
Community Office
54 M Eminescu Street   371957

Synagogues
Vijnitzer, 14 Luceafarul Street

Russian Federation

A selection of information provided by the Commission on Jewish Education in the Republics of the former Soviet Union has been used as a first step in increasing coverage of these areas now that Jewish communal life is beginning to burgeon again.

The latest Soviet census, taken in 1989, gave the Jewish population of the USSR as 1,450,000. Emigration and Aliyah in the past five years has hastened the lowering of this figure.

In Moscow alone there were estimated to be about 250,000 Jews.

The list of synagogues given below is not complete.

GMT + 2 to 12 hours
Country calling code (7)

Astrakhan

Synagogues
30 Babushkin Street

Birobidjan

Synagogues
9 Chapaev Street, Khabarovsk Krai

Bryansk

Klintsy

Synagogues
82 Lermontov Street

Daghestan

Buynaksk

Synagogues
Narodov Vostoka Street

Derbent

Synagogues
94 Tagi-Zade Street

Makhachkala

Synagogues
111 Yermoshkin Street

Ekaterinburg *(formerly Sverdlov)*
Area telephone code (3432)

Synagogues
18/2 Kirov Street
14 Kuibyshev Street

Irkutsk
Area telephone code (3952)

Synagogues
17 Karl Liebknecht Street

Kursk
Area telephone code (71)

Synagogues
3 Bolshevitskaya Street

Moscow
Area telephone code (095)

Synagogues
2nd Korenyovsky Lane, Moscow Oblast, Malakhovka

Mar'ina Roshcha
5a Viacheslavsky Lane   289-2325

Moscow Choral Synagogue
Bolshoi Spasoglinishchevsky per. (Arkhipova St)
10   924-2424

Poliakoff Synagogue, Chabad Centre,
Bolshaya Brennaya 6   202-7696
                                    Fax: 202-7645

Contact Information
Rabbi Pinchas Goldschmidt
Chief Rabbi of Moscow   923-4788; 924-2424

Embassy
Embassy of Israel
Bolshaya Ordinka 56

Restaurants
Meat
King David Club
Bolshoi Spasoglinishchevsky per. (Arkhipova St)
6, door code 77   925-4601
                                    Fax: 924-4243
                          Email: ail@ail.msk.ru
Supervision: Rabbi Pinchas Goldschmidt, Chief
Rabbi of Moscow.
This Kosher Food Centre serves as a glatt
kosher restaurant and a mini hotel. Catering
services are available as are lunchboxes.

Museums
Poliakoff Synagogue
Bolshaya Brennaya 6

Nalchik

Synagogues
73 Rabochaya Street, cnr. Osetinskaya

Novosibirsk
Area telephone code (3832)

Synagogues
23 Luchezarnaya Street

Penza

Synagogues
15 Krasnaya Street

Perm
Area telephone code (3422)

Synagogues
Kuibyshev Street
Pushkin Street

Rostov-On-Don
Area telephone code (8632)

Synagogues
18 Gazetnaya Lane

Sachkhere

Synagogues
145 Sovetskaya Street
105 Tsereteli Street

Samara *(formerly Kuibyshev)*
Area telephone code (8462)

Synagogues
3 Chapaev Street

Saratov

Synagogues
Posadskov Street
2 Kirpichnaya Street

St Petersburg
Area telephone code (812)

Representative Organisations
St Petersburg Jewish Association
Ryleev St, 29-31, a/b 103   272-4113

Synagogues
2 Lermontovsky Prospekt   114-1153
This is the second street past the Kirov Opera
& Ballet Theatre.

Mikvaot
2 Lermontovsky Prospekt   113-8974

Restaurants
Dining Room at Shamir School
Ligovskiy Prospekt 161-8   116-1003

Tour Information
Zekher Avoteinu
Jewish Tourist and Genealogical Agency, Pr.
Strachek 212, #46, 198262   184-1248
                                    Fax: 184-1248
The agency has prepared an exciting
programme to inform visitors about Jewish
history and life in St Petersburg.

Tula
Area telephone code (872)

Synagogues
15 Veresaevskaya Street

Vladikavkaz *(formerly Ordzhonikidze)*

Synagogues
Revolutsiya Street

Senegal

GMT + 0 hours
Country calling code (221)

Dakar
Area telephone code (8)

Contact Information
Mr C. Politis
13 rue San Diniery, Po Box 449   232784 or
235174
Fax: 233330
Will be pleased to receive overseas visitors.

Singapore

The Jewish community of Singapore, numbering about 240, dates from 1840. The street in which Jewish divine service was first held in a house is now known as Synagogue Street. The first building to be erected as a synagogue was Maghain Aboth, opened in 1878. This was rebuilt and enlarged in 1925. Another synagogue, Chesed-El, was built in 1905. The community is mainly Sephardi (of Baghdad origin).

GMT + 8 hours
Country calling code (65)

Representative Organisations
Jewish Welfare Board
Robinson Road, PO Box 474

Synagogues
Orthodox
Chesed-El
2 Oxley Rise, S-0923   732-8832
Services, Monday only, Shacharit and Mincha/Maariv.

Maghain Aboth
24 Waterloo Street   336-0692
Mikva on premises. Daily and Shabbat services held, except for Monday. Because Singapore has equatorial times, Mincha/Maariv falls between 6:30 and 6:45 pm throughout the year. Shacharit: weekdays, 7 am; Shabbat, 9 am. Every Shabbat lunch is served for the community. Breakfast is currently served every morning after services.

Reform
United Hebrew Congregation (Singapore)
65 Chulia Street, OCBC Centre, #31-00 East Lobby, 049513   536-8300
Established in 1995, the congregation's members are mostly Ashkenazi from English-speaking countries. The congregation conducts a full set of High Holy Day services with a rabbi and cantor, celebrations for other holidays, monthly Shabbat dinners and services, and educational and social events.

Contact Information
David Miller   Email: dlmiller@singnet.com.sg
Rabbi Abergel
Email: mordehai@singnet.com.sg

Embassy
Israel Embassy
58 Dalvey Road, S-1025   235-0966
Fax: 733-7008

Slovak Republic

GMT + 1 hour
Country calling code (421)

Bratislava (Pressburg)
Area telephone code (7)

Representative Organisations
Union of Jewish Communities in Slovakia
Kozia 21/II, 81447   312167
                              Fax: 311106

Synagogues
Heydukova 11-13
Services held Mon. Thurs. - Sat.

Mikvaot
Zamocka 13   312642
Kosher food is obtainable here as well. (Open
for lunch only.)

Restaurants
Chez David, Zamocka 13 531-3824; 531-6943
                          Fax: 531-2642
Supervision: Rabbi Baruch Myers, the Jewish
Religious Community.

Bed & Breakfasts
Chez David, Zamocka 13 531-3824; 531-6943
                          Fax: 531-2642
Supervision: Rabbi Baruch Myers, the Jewish
Religious Community.

Museums
The Museum of Jewish Culture
Zidovska Street
Underground Mausoleum
Contains the graves of 18 famous rabbis,
including the Chatam Sofer. The key is
available from the community offices.

Galanta

Synagogues
Partizanska 907, daily services held.

Mikvaot
Partizanska 907

Kosice (Kaschau)
Area telephone code (95)

Synagogues
Puskinova Ul 3
Beth Hamidrash
Zvonarska Ul 5
Daily services held.

Restaurants
Community Centre
Zvonarska Ul 5, 04001   622-1047

Piestany

Synagogues
Hviezdoslavova 59
Shabbat and festival services held.

Cemeteries
Old Cemetery, Janosikova Ul 606

Presov
Area telephone code (91)

Community Organisations
Community Centre
Sverthova 32   31271
                                   Fax: 31271
Synagogue and museum on premises.

Trnava

Synagogues
Kapitulska Ul 7

Monument
Monument to Deportees
Halenarska Ul 32
In the courtyard of the former synagogue.

Slovenia

The newly independent Republic of Slovenia has a tiny Jewish community of 78 members. There is no synagogue and no kosher restaurant. The nearest synagogue is in Trieste, Italy. Services are also held at the Jewish community office in Zagreb, Croatia. Appointments with Exec. Cttee. members of the Jewish community of Ljubljana by writing only.

The Jewish community of Ljubljana takes care of Jewish cemeteries in Ljubljana, Lendava, Murska Sobota and Rozhna dolina (Nova Gorica). There are monuments to victims of fascism at the Ljubljana and Lendava cemeteries. The Rozhna dolina (Nova Gorica) cemetery is protected as a historic monument. The old synagogue in Maribor, 1429, is currently being renovated by the municipality of Maribor as a historic monument.

GMT + 1 hour
Country calling code (386)

Ljubljana
Area telephone code (61)

Community Organisations
**Jewish Community of Slovenia and
Ljubljana**
PO Box 569, 61101   315884

South Africa

The Jewish community began as an organised body in Cape Town in 1841, although individual Jews had settled there much earlier. The organisation of religious life varies with the density of the Jewish population (which totals about 100,000). In all, there are about 200 organised communities, most of which have their own synagogues.

The major supermarket chains – Pick and Pay, and Checkers – stock a large range of kosher items.

GMT + 2 hours
Country calling code (27)

Cape Province

Cape Town

Area telephone code (21)

Representative Organisations

South African Jewish Board of Deputies Cape Council
Leeusig House, 3rd floor, 4 Leeuwen Street, 8001   232-320
Fax: 232-615

Religious Organisations

Union of Orthodox Synagogues Cape Council
191 Buitenkant Street, 8001   461-6310
Fax: 461-8320
Beth Din located at same address.

Synagogues

Orthodox
Arthur's Road
31 Arthur's Road, 8001, Sea Point   452-239
Fax: 452-259
Camps Bay, 23 The Cheviots, Camps Bay
438-8082
Fax: 461-8320
Cape Town Hebrew Congregation
84 Hatfield Street, Gardens   451-405
Chabad House
21 Avenue Protea, Fresnaye
434-3740; 434-2821

Claremont Hebrew Congregation
16 Carisbrook Avenue, Claremont   619-007
Fax: 683-3011
Constantia
21 Abbotsford Avenue, 7800, Claremont
752-520
Fax: 753-110
Green & Sea Point Hebrew Congregation
Marais Road, Sea Point   439-7543
Fax: 434-3760
Milnerton
29 Fitzpatrick Road, 7441, Cambridge Estate
697-1913
Fax: 461-8320
Muizenberg, Camp Road, Muizenberg
788-1488
Rondebosch, Stuart Road, Rondebosch
614-069
Fax: 461-8320
Schoonder Street Shul
10 Yeoville Road, Vredehoek   452-239
Fax: 461-1510
Sephardi Hebrew Congregation
18 Kei Apple Road, Sea Point   439-1962
Fax: 439-9620
Wynberg Hebrew Congregation
5 Mortimer Road, 7800, Wynberg   797-5029
Fax: 761-4669

Reform
Temple Israel
Upper Portswood Road, Green Point 434-9721
Temple Israel, Salisbury Road, Wynberg
797-3362

South Africa

Mikvaot

Arthur's Road, Sea Point 434-3148; 525-684;
082-452-5757

Restaurants

Meat

Garden of Eden
359a Main Road, 8001, Sea Point 439-1632
Supervision: Cape Beth Din and permanent
mashgiach. Deli and take-away service
available. Hours: Sunday to Thursday, 9:30 am
to 11:30 pm; Friday, to 4 pm; Motzei Shabbat.

Kaplan Student Canteen
University of Cape Town 650-2688
Supervision: Cape Beth Din.
Lunches, take-away and orders. Meat and
pareve. Open Monday to Friday. Closed
December/January for varsity holidays and
during summer vacation.

Marrakesh
315 Main Road, 8001, Sea Point 434-0455
Fax: 434-0829
Supervision: Cape Beth Din.
Upmarket restaurant with full liquor license.
Situated in the centre of Cape Town's Jewish
area, within walking distance to all major
hotels, guest houses and four synagogues. All
meat glatt kosher. Open 6 days a week for
lunch and dinner.

The Pie Works
15 Regent Road, Sea Point 439-4484
Supervision: Cape Beth Din. Hours: Sunday to
Thursday, 8:30 am to 9 pm; Friday, to 4 pm.

Dairy

Dovidil's Pizza
74 Regent Road, 8001, Sea Point 434-1267
Fax: 439-7280
Supervision: Cape Beth Din. Delivery service.
Hours: Sunday to Thursday, 11 am to 11 pm;
Friday, to 3 pm; Saturday night after Shabbat.

The Pickle Barrel
Dean Street Arcade, Dean Street, Newlands
686-3633
Supervision: Cape Beth Din.
Deli and take-away also available. Pre-packed
cold meat available for take-away. Hours:
Monday to Wednesday, 8 am to 6 pm;
Thursday, to 10:30 pm; Friday, to 4 pm;
Sunday, 10 am to 11 pm.

Butchers

Checkers
Sea Point, 8001, Sea Point 439-6159
Fax: 439-5630
Supervision: Cape Beth Din. Also bakery.

Claremont Kosher Butchers
Marine Drive, Paarden Eiland, Claremont
683-2920
Supervision: Cape Beth Din.
Also serve light lunches, Monday to Friday,
9 am to 3 pm (meat).

Pick 'N Pay
Sea Point, 8001 438-2049
Supervision: Cape Beth Din. Also bakery.

Pick 'N Pay, Constantia 794-5690
Supervision: Cape Beth Din.

Pick 'N Pay, Claremont 683-2900
Supervision: Cape Beth Din.

Shoprite, Rondebosch 689-4563
Supervision: Cape Beth Din.

Delicatessens

Goldies, 64 Regent Road, Sea Point
439-3008; 434-1116
Supervision: Cape Beth Din.
Sit-down deli and take-away. Meat and
pareve. Hours: Sunday to Thursday, 7 am to
8 pm; Friday, to 5 pm.

Reingold's Deli & Butchery, Plumstead
762-8093
Supervision: Cape Beth Din.

Hotels

Kosher

Belmont Hotel
Holmfirth Road, 8001, Sea Point 439-1155
Supervision: Cape Beth Din.

Cape Sun, Strand Street 238-844
Supervision: Cape Beth Din. Breakfast only.

Bed & Breakfast

Dinah's Guest House, 6 Molteno Road, 8001,
Oranjezicht 241-568
Fax: 241-598
Supervision: Cape Beth Din.
SA Tourism Board accredited kosher guest
house. Six en-suite bedrooms, bed & breakfast
(with other meals on request), walking
distance to Gardens Synagogue (Orthodox),
close to city centre, with 'meet and greet'
facility from airport.

Museums
Jewish Museum
84 Hatfield Street, Gardens   451-546
Sunday, 10 am to 12:30 pm; Tuesday &
Thursday, 2 pm to 5 pm.

Libraries
Jacob Gitlin Library
Leeusig House, Ground floor, 4 Leeuwen
Street, 8001   245-020

East London
Area telephone code (431)

Synagogues
Orthodox
Shar Hashomayim
56 Park Avenue, 5201   430-181

Kimberley
Area telephone code (531)

Synagogues
United Hebrew Institutions
20 Synagogue Street, 8301   825-652

Oudtshoorn
Area telephone code (443)

Synagogues
United Hebrew Institutions
291 Buitenkant Street   223-068
There is a Jewish section in the C.P. Nel
Museum.

Paarl
Area telephone code (2211)

Synagogues
New Breda Street   24087
Community centre and Talmud Torah at same
address.

Port Elizabeth
Area telephone code (41)

Synagogues
Orthodox
**Port Elizabeth Hebrew Congregation United
Synagogue**
55 Roosevelt Street, 6001, Gledinningvale
          331-332
          Fax: 333-293

Progressive
Temple Israel
Upper Dickens Street   336-642

Museums
Raleigh Street Synagogue   554-458

Natal

Durban
Area telephone code (31)

Representative Organisations
Council of KawZulu-Natal Jewry
44 Old Fort Road   372-581
          Fax: 379-600

Community Organisations
Durban Jewish Club, 44 Old Fort Road, PO
Box 10797, Marine Parade, 4056   372-581

Synagogues
Orthodox
Durban Hebrew Congregation
cnr. Essenwood & Silverton Roads, PO Box
50044, Musgrave Road, 4062   214-755
          Fax: 211-964

Progressive
Temple David, 369 Ridge Road   286-105

Butchers
Pick 'N Pay
Musgrave Centre, Berea, 4001   214-208
Bakery as well.

Umhlanga

Contact Information
Chabad of Umhlanga
POBox 474, 4320   562-487
                              Fax: 561-5845

Orange Free State

Bloemfontein

Area telephone code (51)

Representative Organisations
O.F.S. & Northern Cape Zionist Council
Community Centre, 2 Fairview, PO Box 564,
9300   480-817
                              Fax: 480-104

Religious Organisations
United Hebrew Institutions, Community
Centre, 2 Fairview, POB 1152, 9300   312-207
Mornings.

Synagogues *(Orthodox)*
United Hebrew Synagogue
16 Waverley Road   436-7609
                              Fax: 436-6447

Transvaal

Benoni

Religious Organisations
United Hebrew Institutions
32 Park Street   (11) 845-2850

Brakpan

Religious Organisations
United Hebrew Institutions
11 Heidelberg Road, Parkdene   744-4822

Germiston

Religious Organisations
United Hebrew Institutions
President Street   825-2202

Johannesburg

Community Organisations
Chabad House
33 Harley Street, 2198, Yeoville   648-1133
                              Fax: 648-1139

Religious Organisations
The Southern African Union for Progressive
Judaism
357 Louis Botha Avenue, Highlands North
                                   640-6614
Union of Orthodox Synagogues of South
Africa
Goldberg Centre, 24 Raleigh Street, Yeoville
                                   648-9136
                              Fax: 648-4014
The Office of the Chief Rabbi as well as the
Beth Din are located here. Beth Din fax: 648-
2325. There are more than 50 Orthodox
synagogues in Johannesburg alone. Contact
these offices for more details.

Mikvaot
Goldberg Centre, 24 Raleigh Street, Yeoville
                                   648-9136
Beth Harer (Glen Hazel Area Hebrew
Congregation)
PO Box 28836, Sandringham, 2131, Glenhazel
                                   640-5061

Kashrut Information
Kashrut Hotline   648-9136
                              Fax: 648-2325

Media

Magazines
Jewish Affairs
Building 1, Anerley Office Park, 7 Anerley
Road, Parktown   486-1434
                              Fax: 646-4940
Quarterly journal of the South African Jewish
Board of Deputies.

Jewish Heritage
PO Box 3 7179, 2015, Birnham Park 880-1830
Jewish Tradition
24 Raleigh Street, PO Box 27701, 2143,
Yeoville   648-9136
                              Fax: 648-4014
Publication of the Union of Orthodox
Synagogues.
South African Jewish Observer
PO Box 29189, 2131, Sandringham 640-4420
                              Fax: 640-4442
Publication of the Mizrachi organisation of
South Africa.
The South African Jewish Times, Publico
House, 30 Andries Street, Wynberg 887-6500
                              Fax: 440-5364

Restaurants

Aviv, 444b Louis Botha Avenue, 2192,
Highlands North   640-4572
                              Fax: 640-4081
Supervision: Beth Din.
Food store on premises as well. Hours: Sunday
to Thursday, 9 am to 11 pm; Friday, to
4:30 pm; Motzei Shabbat, to 1 am.
Haifa Haktanah
576 Louis Botha Avenue, Gresswold 440-1563
                              Fax: 887-1059
Supervision: Beth Din. Hours: Monday to
Thursday, 10 am to 10 pm; Friday, to 4 pm;
Motzei Shabbat, 1 hour after Shabbat till late.
King Solomon
Gallaghers Corner, cnr. Louise Botha Avenue &
9th Street, Orange Grove   728-3000
                              Fax: 728-3305
Supervision: Beth Din.
Hours: Monday, 4:30 pm to late; Tuesday to
Thursday and Sunday, 11:30 am to 2:30 pm,
5:30 pm to late; Motzei Shabbat, late.
MacDavids, Northfield Shopping Centre,
Northfield Avenue, Glenhazel   440-2214
Supervision: Beth Din.
On The Square
Cradock Avenue, 2196, Rosebank   880-4153
Supervision: Beth Din. Hours: Sunday to
Thursday, 10 am to 3 pm; 6 pm to 10 pm;
Saturday, 1 hour after Shabbat to 12 am.
Shula's
173 Oxford Road, 2196, Rosebank   880-6969
                              Fax: 880-6605
Supervision: Beth Din. Pareve and milk. Hours:
Sunday to Thursday, 7 am to 11 pm; Friday, to
4 pm; Motzei Shabbat to 1 am.

Delicatessens & Bakeries

D.J.'s Delicatessen
Shop No. 121, Balfour Park Shopping Centre,
2090, Balfour Park   887-8906
Supervision: Beth Din.
Feigel's Kosher Delicatessen
Bramley Gardens Shopping Centre, shop 1,
280 Corlett Drive   887-9505/6
Supervision: Beth Din. Hours: Friday, 7:30 am
to 4:30 pm; Sunday, 8 am to 1 pm; Monday
to Thursday, 10 am to 5 pm.
Feigel's Kosher Delicatessen
Shop 3, Queens Place, Kingswood Road, 2192,
Glenhazel   887-1364
Supervision: Beth Din.
Kosher King
74 George Avenue, Sandringham   640-6234
Supervision: Beth Din.
Hours: Monday to Thursday, 8:30 am to 5 pm;
Friday, 8 am to 3 pm; Sunday, 9 am to 1 pm.
Mamale's Deli
Shop No 38, Morning Glen Shopping Centre,
Bowling, 2052, Gallo Manor Ave.   804-2068
Supervision: Beth Din.
Neil's Bakery
Fairmount Shopping Centre, 10 Bradfield
Drive, Fairmount   640-2686
Supervision: Beth Din.
Hours: Monday to Thursday, 7:30 am to 5 pm;
Friday, to 2:30 pm; Sunday, to 1 pm.
Pick 'N Pay, cnr. Grant Avenue & 6th Street,
Norwood   483-3357
Supervision: Beth Din.
Closed on Shabbat and Yom Tov.
Saveways Spar Supermarket, Fairmount
Shopping Centre, cnr. Livingston St & Sandler
Avenue, 2192, Fairmount   640-6592; 3056
Supervision: Beth Din.
Hours: Monday to Thursday, 8 am to 6 pm;
Sunday and public holidays, 8 am to 1 pm.
Shirley's Bakery & Deli, 442 Louis Botha
Avenue, 2192, Highlands North   640-2629
Supervision: Beth Din.
Shoshana's Bakery, 1 Glenstar Centre,
Kingswood Avenue, Glenhazel   885-1039
Supervision: Beth Din.
Shula's, 42 Kenmere Road, cnr. Hunter Street,
Yeoville   487-1072
Supervision: Beth Din.

The Pie Works, Shop 35 Greenhill Road, 2195, Emmarentia   486-1502
            Fax: 486-0580
Supervision: Beth Din. Hours: weekdays, 8 am to 5 pm; Friday, to 4 pm; Sunday, to 2 pm.
The Pie Works, 74 George Avenue, 2192, Sandringham   485-2447
Supervision: Beth Din.
Hours: weekdays, 8 am to 5 pm; Friday, to 4 pm; Sunday, to 2 pm.

Butchers

Bolband Poultry Shoppe, 74-76 George Avenue, 2192, Sandringham   640-4080
            640-4170
Supervision: Beth Din.
Checkers
Emmerentia, Balfour Park, 2196   880-6962
Supervision: Beth Din.
Gardens Kosher
Braides Avenue, 2052   483-3357
         Fax: 728-3660
Supervision: Beth Din.
Kinneret Butchery
Saveways, Fairmount Shopping Centre, Sandringham   640-6592
Supervision: Beth Din.
Maxi Discount Kosher Butcher, 74 George Avenue, 2192, Sandringham 485-1485/86
         Fax: 485-2991
Supervision: Beth Din.
Nussbaums, 434 Louis Botha Avenue, 2192, Highlands North   485-2303
Supervision: Beth Din.
Pick 'N Pay, Gallo Manor
Supervision: Beth Din.
Rishon Butchery
Balfour Park Shopping Centre, Atholl Road, 2090, Balfour Park   786-5396
Supervision: Beth Din.
Segell's Butchery, 578 Louis Botha Avenue, Gresswold (Savoy), 2090   885-2459
Supervision: Beth Din.
Yumpolski's
5 Durham Street, 2192, Raedene 485-1045
         Fax: 485-1082
Supervision: Beth Din.

Hotels

Courtleigh Hotel
38 Harrow Road, Berea   487-1577
Supervision: Beth Din. Meat and dairy.

Libraries
Kollel Library
22 Muller Street, 2198, Yeoville   648-1175

Tour Information
Distinctive Tours
PO Box 357, 2037, Highlands North 887-5262
         Fax: 885-3097
    Email: celpro@hixnet.co.za
The company specialises in kosher tours to South Africa, for people needing kosher food and Shabbat arrangements.
Israel Government Tourist Office
5th Floor, Nedbank Gardens, 33 Bath Avenue, PO Box 52560, 2132, Rosebank   788-1700
         Fax: 447-3104

Booksellers
Chabad House Books
Fairmount Shopping Centre, George Street, Fairmount   485-1957
         Fax: 648-1139
Kollel Bookshop
Pick n Pay Norwood Hypermarket Shop 8a, rant & 6th Street, Norwood cnr. 728-1822
         Fax: 128-1813
Ohr Someyach Books
Northfield Shopping Centre, Northfield Avenue, Glenhazel   887-1437
         Fax: 887-1437

Krugersdorp

Religious Organisations
United Hebrew Institutions, Cilliers Street, Monument, PO Box 1008, 1740   954-1367
         Fax: 953-4905

Pretoria
Area telephone code (012)

Synagogues
Adath Israel, 441 Sibelius Street, Lukasrand, 0181   344-1511
         Fax: 343-0287
Pretoria United Hebrew Congregation
Great Synagogue, 717 Pretorius Street, Arcadia   344-3019

Progressive

Temple Menorah
315 Bronkhorst Street, New Muckleneuk, PO
Box 1497   467-296

Kashrut Information

Pretoria Council of BOD   344-2372
                              Fax: 344-2059

Embassy

Israel Embassy & Consulate-General
3rd Floor, Dashing Centre, 339 Hilda Street,
Hatfield   421-2227

Restaurants

JAFFA Old Age Home
42 Mackie Street, Baileys Muckleneuk, 0181
                                     346-2006
Hotel as well. Prior booking necessary.

Groceries

One Stop Superliner
217 Bronkhorst Street, Baileys Muckleneuk, L
Brooklyn, 0181   463-211

Museums

Sammy Marks Museum
Swartkoppies Hall   833-239

Springs

Religious Organisations

United Hebrew Institutions
First Avenue   648-1133; 363-1202
                            Fax: 648-1139

South Korea

There are about 100 families in the Capital, Seoul, including U.S. military personnel and their families.

GMT + 9 hours
Country calling code (82)

Seoul
Area telephone code (2)

Synagogues

South Post Chapel
Building 3702, Youngsan Military Reservation
793-3728
Fax: 796-3805
Civilians welcome to participate in all Jewish activities, inc. kosher le-Pesach sedarim, meals and services.

Spain

There are about 12,000 Jews in Spain: 3,000 in Barcelona, 3,500 in Madrid, 1,500 in Malaga, 1,000 in Marbella, 800 in Ceuta (North Africa), 950 in Melilla (North Africa), and the rest in Alicante, Benidorm, Seville, Valencia and the Balearic and Canary Islands. Newcomers continue to arrive, especially from Morocco and South America. Small communities existed in Seville, Barcelona and Madrid before the Second World War, founded by Sephardim from Morocco, Turkey and Greece, and by Ashkenazim from Eastern and Central Europe.

Today, Spanish Jewry is flourishing, consolidating its communal organisations, and expanding its synagogues and newly created day schools. The various communities have enjoyed full official recognition as religious associations since June, 1967.

GMT + 1 hour
Country calling code (34)

Alicante
Area telephone code (6)

Organisations
Communidad Israelita
Apdo. 189, Playa de San Juan, 03540
515-1572

Synagogues
Avda Santander, 3, Playa de San Juan

Avila
The Mosen Rubi Church, cnr. Calle Bracamonte and Calle Lopez Nunez, was originally a synagogue, built in 1462.

Barcelona
Area telephone code (3)
The ancient community of the city lived in the area of the Calle el Call. The cemetery was in Montjuich (Mountain of the Jews). Most of the tombstones are in the Provincial Archaeological Museum.

Organisations
Community Centre
Calle de l'Avenir 24, 08071   200-6148, 8513

Synagogues
Calle Porvenir 24   200-6148, 8513
The first synagogue to be built in Spain since the Inquisition.

Mikvaot
Calle de l'Avenir 24, 08071   200-6148, 8513

Embassy
Consulate General
Avenida Diagonal 474, 5-2, 08006

Restaurants

Vegetarian
Calle Canuda 41
Closed during August.

Travel Agencies
Jewish Travel Agency
Viajes Moravia, Consejo de Ciento 380
246-0300

Bembibre

The synagogue here was converted into a church.

Benidorm

Area telephone code (6)

Kashrut Information   522-9360

Besalu

The Juderia is by the River Fluviá. A mikva was recently discovered there.

Burgos

The Juderia was in the area of the Calle Fernan Gonzalez.

Caceres

Part of the Juderia still exists. The San Antonio Church on the outskirts of the town is a 13th-century former synagogue.

Ceuta (N. Africa)

Area telephone code (56)

Kashrut Information

Calle Sargento Coriat 8

Cordoba

Area telephone code (57)

Tourist Sites

Calle de los Judios 20
This is an ancient synagogue (declared as a monument). Near by, a statue of Maimonides has been erected in the Plazuela de Maimonides. The entrance to the ancient Juderia is near the Almodovar Gate.

El Escorial

The library of the San Lorenzo Monastry contains a magnificent collection of medieval Hebrew Bibles and illuminated manuscripts. On the walls of the Patio of Kings, in the Palace of Philip II, are sculpted effigies of the six Kings of Judah.

Estella

The Santa Maria de Jus Castillo Church was once a synagogue.

Girona

Area telephone code (7)

The Jewish quarter of Girona, known as the Call, is located in the heart of the old town. Its main street exists today, and it is known as Carrer de la Força. The Jewish Quarter of Girona is one of the best-preserved to be found in Europe today.

During the Middle Ages, the Jewish community of Girona achieved considerable importance. It was there that the most important Cabbala school in Western Europe was developed, largely under the guidance of Rabbi Mossé ben Nahman, or Ramban, perhaps its best known representative.

The Bonastruc ça Porta Center houses the Museum of Catalan-Jewish Culture and the Nahmanides Institute for Jewish Studies, on the site where the 15th- century synagogue was located.

In the municipal archives there is an important collection of fragments of Hebrew manuscripts dating from the 13th and 14th centuries. The Archaeological Museum contains more than 20 medieval gravestones with Hebrew inscriptions, found in the old Jewish cemetery.

Since January 1995, Girona has held the status of Secretary of the Red de Juderías de España, a network of towns and cities within Spain whose common aim is to foster popular knowledge and awareness of Jewish culture in Spain.

Organisations

Bonastruc ça Porta Center
c/ Sant Llorenc s/n, 17004   221-6761
                      Fax: 221-6761
Opening hours; Winter 10am to 6pm. Summer 10am to 9pm; Sundays and Holidays 10am to 2pm.

Granada

The Juderia ran from the Corral del Carlon to Torres Bermejas.

Hervas

This village in the Gredos Mountains, 150 miles west of Madrid, has a well-preserved Juderia, declared a national monument. Its main street has beenm renamed Calle de la Amistad Judeo Cristiana.

Madrid

Area telephone code (1)

Organisations

Community Centre
Calle Balmes 3   445-9843, 9835

Synagogues

Calle Balmes 3   445-9843, 9835
The capital's first synagogue since the Expulsion of Jews in 1492 was opened in December 1968. The building also houses the Community Centre, as well as Mikvah, Library, Classrooms, an assembly Hall and the office of the community. Nearest underground station: Metro Iglesias.

Lubavitch Synagogue
Chabad House, Calle Jordan 9, Apt. 4 Dcha., 28010   445-9629

Mikvaot

Calle Balmes 3   445-9843, 9835

Tourist Information

Ogicina Nacional Israeli de Turismo
Gran via 69, Ofic 801, 28013   559-7903
                      Fax: 542-6511

Embassy

Embassy of Israel
Calle Velasquez 150, 7th Floor, 28002
                      411-1357

Restaurants

Community Centre
Calles Balmes 3   446-7847
For groups only.

Museums

Museo Arquelogico, Calle de Serrano 13
See casts of Hebrew inscriptions from medieval buildings.

Libraries

Calle Balmes 3   445-9843, 9835

Souvenir Shops

Sefarad Handicrafts
Jose Antonio Av. 54   548-2577, 547-6142
Jewish religious articles and Spanish handicrafts are on sale here.

Malaga

Area telephone code (5)

Synagogues

Calle Duquesa de Parcent 8, 3°, 29001
                      221-4041

Mikvaot

Calle Somera 12, 29001

Butchers

Carmiceria Kosher
Calle Somera 14, 29001   260-4201

Marbella

Area telephone code (5)

Organisations

Community Centre
Paseo Maritima

Synagogues

Beth El, 21 Calle Jazmines, Urbanizacion El Real, Km. 184   277-4074, 0757 or 282-4983 About 2 miles from the town centre to the east. Services held at the following times; Friday eve. (winter) 7.00pm (summer) 8.30pm; Shabbat morn. & all festivals 10am.

Mikvaot

Beth El, 21 Calle Jazmines, Urbanizacion El Real, Km. 184   277-4074, 0757 or 282-4983

Bakeries

La Tahona   282-2781

Groceries

Joelle Kanner   277-4074 Kosher poultry and wine.

Media

Publications

"Edificio Marbella 2000", Paseo Maritima **"Focus"**, PO Box 145, 29600 Community Journal.

Melilla (N. Africa)

Area telephone code (5)

Synagogues

Yamin Benarroch, Calle Lopez Moreno 8 **Isaac Benarroch**, Calle Marina 7 **Jacob Almoznino**, Calle Luis de Sotomayor 4 **Salama**, Calle Alfonso XII 6 **Solinquinos**, Calle O'Donnell 13 There are nine other synagogues in the Barrio Poligono. These are open on festivals and High Holy-days only.

Kashrut Information

Calle General Mola 19

Montblanc

The Jewish quarter was in the Santa Clara district, where the church was once a synagogue.

Santiago de Compostela

The cathedral has 24 statues of Biblical prophets framed in the so-called 'Holy Door'.

Segovia

The Alcazar contains the 16-century 'Tower of the Jews'. Calle de la Juderia Vieja and Calle de la Juderia Nueva are the sites of the medieval Jewish quarters, where the former synagogue now houses the Corpus Christi Convent.

Seville

Area telephone code (5)

The old synagogue, now the church of Los Venerables Sacerdotes, is the Barrio de Santa Cruz. Seville Cathedral preserves in its treasures two keys to the city presented to Ferdinand III by the Jews. The Columbus Archives (Archives of the Indies), 3 Queipo de Llano Av., preserve the account books of Luis de Santangel, financier to King Ferdinand and Queen Isabella. Arco & Torreon of the Juderia, in the old Calle de la Juderia, was the gate connecting the Alcazar and the Jewish quarter. There is a Jewish cemetery in part of the city's Christian burial ground in the Macarena district.

Synagogues

Comunidad Israelita de Sevilla Calle Bustos Tavera 8, 41003 Mr Hassan's private telephone number is 4 45 74 34. There is no phone at the synagogue.

Tarazona

The Juderia is near the bishop's palace.

Tarragona

Tarragona Cathedral, Calle de Escribanias Viejas, has in its cloister a seventh-century stone inscribed in Latin and Hebrew. Some very old coins are preserved in the Provincial

Archaeological Museum. The gate to the medieval Juderia still stands at the entrance to Calle de Talavera.

Toledo

Though it now has no established community, Toledo is the historical centre of Spanish Judaism. Well worth a visit are two ancient former synagogues. One is the El Transito (in Calle de Samuel Levi), founded by Samuel Levi, the treasurer of King Pedro I, in the 14th century. It has been turned by the Spanish Government into a museum of Sephardi culture. The other, now the Church of Santa Maria la Blanca, is the oldest Jewish monument in Toledo, having been built in the 13th century. It stands in a quiet garden in what was once the heart of the Juderia, not far from the edge of the Tagus River. Also of interest is the house of Samuel Levi, in which El Greco, the famous painter, lived. The house is now a museum of his works.

Plaza de la Juderia, half-way between El Transito and Santa Maria la Blanca, was part of the city's two ancient Jewish quarters, where many houses and streets are still much as they were 500 years ago.

Torremolinos
Area telephone code (5)

Synagogues
Beth Minzi, Calle Skal La Roca 13 383952
Calle Skal La Roca is a small street at the seaward end of the San Miguel pedestrian precinct, almost opposite the Police Station. Sephardi and Ashkenazi services are held on Sabbath morning at 9.30am and Friday evening services are held at 6.30pm in winter and 8.30pm in summer.

Tortosa
The Museum of Santo Domingo Convent preserves the sixth-century gravestone of 'Meliosa, daughter of Judah of blessed memory'.

Tudela
The remains of the Juderia are near the cathedral. There is a memorial stone to the great Jewish traveller, Benjamin of Tudela.

Valencia
Area telephone code (6)

Synagogues
Calle Asturias 7-4 334-3416
Services: Friday eve. & festivals.
Office, Av. Professor Waksman 9 339901

Vitoria
The monument on the Campo de Judizmendi commemorates the ancient Jewish cemetery.

Zaragoza
This city was once a very important Jewish centre. A mikva has been discovered in the basement of a modern building at 126–132 Calle del Coso.

Canary Islands

La Palmas De Gran Canaria
Area telephone code (28)

Synagogues
Calle Leon y Castillo 238, 1st Floor 248497

Tenerife
Area telephone code (22)

Organisations
Comunidad Israelita de Tenerife
247296, 247246

Kashrut Information

General Mola 4, Santa Cruz, 38006   274157
Welcomes all Jewish visitors

Majorca

Area telephone code (71)

Palma Cathedral contains some interesting Jewish relics, including a candelabrum with 365 lights, which was originally in a synagogue. In the 'Tesoro' room are two unique silver maces, over 6 feet long, converted from Torah 'rimonim'. The Santa Clara Church stands on the site of another pre-Inquisition synagogue. The Montezion Church was, in the 14th century, the Great Synagogue of this capital. In Calle San Miguel is the Church of San Miguel, which also stands on the site of a former synagogue. It is not far from the Calle de la Plateria, once a part of the Palma Ghetto.

Majorca's Jewish population today numbers about 300, although fewer than 100 are registered with the community. Founded in 1971, it was the first Jewish community to be officially recognised since 1435. The Jewish cemetery is at Santa Eugenia, some 12 miles from Palma.

Synagogues

Calle Monsenor Palmer   700243
This synagogue was dedicated to the community in June 1987. Services are held on Fridays and Holy-days. A communal Seder is also held.

Kashrut Information   283799

Sri Lanka

GMT + 5½ hours
Country calling code (94)

Colombo
Area telephone code (1)

Kashrut Information

82 Rosemead Place, 7	695642
	Fax: 698091

Surinam

GMT – 3 hours
Country calling code (597)

Paramaribo
Area telephone code (692)

Organisations
Jewish Community
PO Box 1834   11998

Synagogues

Ashkenazi
Neveh Shalom
Keizerstr. 82
Services are held every Shabbat in each
synagogue alternately.

Sephardi
Sedek Ve Shalom
Herenstr. 20

Kashrut Information

Commewijnestr. 21	400236
	Fax: 71154

Tourist Sites
Sights to see include Joden Savanah (Jewish
Savanah) one of the oldest Jewish settlements
in the Americas.

Sweden

In 1775 the first Jew was granted the right to live in Sweden – Aaron Isaac, of Germany, who founded the Stockholm cong. In 1782 Jews were admitted to Gothenburg and Norrköping, and the com. in Kariskrona was founded not long afterwards. After Sweden's Jews were emancipated in 1870, coms. were founded in Malmö and several other towns. There are some 16,000 Jews in Sweden. About half of them are former victims of the Nazis, and some 2,000 settled in Sweden from Poland after 1968.

GMT + 1 hour
Country calling code (46)

Boras
Area telephone code (33)

Organisations
Jewish Community of Boras & Synagogue
Varbergsvagen 21, Box 46, 50305   124892
Email: s. rytz@vertextrading.se

Gothenburg
Area telephone code (31)

Organisations
Jewish Community Centre and Community Offices
Ostra Larmgatan 12, 41107   177245
Fax: 7119360

Synagogues
Orthodox
Storgatan 5

Conservative
Ostra Larmgatan 12   177245

Groceries
Dr. Allardsgata 4   824-051

Media
Radio
Thursdays at 9pm on 94.4 MHz.

Helsingborg
Area telephone code (42)

Organisations
Jewish Centre
Springpostgranden 4

Lund
Area telephone code (46)

Organisations
Community Centre & Students Club (Jusil)
Winstrupsgatan 1   148052
Institute for Jewish Culture
Winstrupsgatan 1   148052

Synagogues
Orthodox
Winstrupsgatan 1   148052
Services on festivals and High Holy-days only.

Malmö
Area telephone code (40)

Organisations
Jewish Community Centre
Kamrergatan 11   118460, 118860
Also houses old-age home and Community offices.

Sweden

Synagogues

Orthodox
Foreningsgatan

Mikvaot
Kamrergatan 11   118860

Stockholm
Area telephone code (8)

Organisations

Community Centre
Judaica House, Nybrogatan 19, PO Box 5053,
10242   663-6566, 662-6686

Jewish Community of Stockholm
Wahrendorffsgatan 3, PO Box 7427, 10391
    679-2900

Synagogues

Orthodox
Adas Jeshrun
Riddergatan 5, PO Box 5053, 10242 611-9161

Adas Jisroel
St. Paulsgatan 13   644-1995

Conservative
Great, Wahrendorffsgatan 3b   679-2900
Services: Mon., Thurs., Fri eves. & Sat.
morning. Open to tourists Mon. - Fri from
10 am till 2pm.

Mikvaot
Community Centre
Judaica House, Nybrogatan 19, PO Box 5053,
10242   663-6566, 662-6686

Kashrut Information
Community Centre, Judaica House, Nybrogatan
19, PO Box 5053, 10242   663-6566
There are no kosher restaurants in Stockholm,
but lunches are under the Rabbi Edelmann's
supervision at the Community Centre during
the summer. Dinners can be arranged at the
Community Centre for groups.   679-2900

Tourist Information
Israeliska Statens Turistbyra
Sveavagen 28-30, 4 tr., Box 7554, 10393
Stockholm 7   21-3386/7
    Fax: 21-7814

Embassy
Embassy of Israel
Torstenssongatan 4, 11456, PO Box 14006,
10440-14   663-0435

Bakeries
Kosher Bakery, Nybrogatan 7   678-8128
Has a full range of cakes, bread, sandwiches,
salads and dairy meals. Restaurant on
premises. Take-away can be arranged.

Delicatessens
Kosher Deli, Riddargatan 7   678-8127
Has an extensive range of kosher meats,
poultry and delicatessen as well as cheeses,
salads and provisions. Meat sandwiches. Take-
away can be arranged. Kosher Deli also caters
for any function and arranges Shabbat meals
for tourists.

Caterers
Community Centre, Nybrogatan 19, 10242
Coffee, cakes and sandwiches (dairy) are
available at the Community Centre during
opening hours. The Community Centre can
also arrange catering for visiting groups. Also
houses the Kosherian and Judaica House cafés.

Hillelschool Kitchen   662-3948
During school term time, dairy and vegetarian
lunch is available at the school lunch room.

SAS, Scandinavian Airlines
Serving kosher meals on all flights leaving
Swedish airports for abroad, if advance notice
of this requirement is given to SAS offices in
Sweden or to a Swedish travel agency. Only
new crockery and cutlery used.

Museums
Jewish Museum
Halsingegatan 2   310143

Libraries
Wahrendorffsgatan 3, PO Box 7427, 10391
    679-2900
Raoul Wallenberg Room also on premises,
named after the Swedish diplomat who saved

scores of thousands of Hungarian Jews from the Nazis, was arrested by the Russians in Budapest in 1945 and disappeared.

Travel Agencies

Menorah
PO Box 5053, 10242   667-6770
                                  Fax: 663-7676

Booksellers

Community Centre
Judaica House, Nybrogatan 19, PO Box 5053, 10242   663-6566, 662-6686

Souvenir Shops

Menorah: Community Centre Shop
Nybrogatan 19, 11439   663-6566

Uppsala
Area telephone code (8)

Organisations

Jewish Students Club
Dalgatan 15   125453

Switzerland

The Jews were expelled from Switzerland in the fifteenth century, and it was not until the beginning of the seventeenth century that they were permitted to settle in Lengnau and Endingen. Both villages have old synagogues. In 1856 immigration increased, chiefly from Germany, Alsace and eastern Europe. The Jewish population, 3,150 in 1850, is now about 17,600. Zurich, Basel and Geneva have the largest communities.

GMT + 1 hour
Country calling code (41)

Arosa
Area telephone code (81)

Hotels
Levin's Hotel Metropol   377-4444
                                  Fax: 377-2100
Mikva on premises. Own Kosher bakery.

Baden
Area telephone code (56)

Synagogues
Parkstrasse 17   271-5128
Services on Friday nights, Sabbaths and festivals at 8.30am.

Restaurants
Take-Away
Kosher pre-packed meals are available at Schweizerhof, Verenahof and Blume hotels.

Basel
Area telephone code (61)

Synagogues
Israelitische Gemeinde Basel
Leimenstrasse 24   272-9850
Rabbi Dr. I.M. Levinger: 271-6024

Israelitsche Religionsgemeinschaft
Ahornstrasse 14   301-4898
Rabbi B. Snyders: 302-5391

Mikvaot
Eulerstr. 10, 4051   301-6831
Thannerstrasse 60, 4054   301-2200;
                                       272-9548

Restaurants
Juedisches Restaurant Topas
Leimenstrasse 24, 4051   271-8700
                                  Fax: 271-8701
Supervision: Rabbi Dr I.M. Levinger, Basel Jewish Community.
Hours: 11:30 am to 2 pm, 6:30 pm to 9 pm; closed Wednesday. Friday night, Shabbat lunch and holidays by reservation before 2 pm of the preceding day.

Take-Away
Hess Kosher sausage-king   272-8835
Offers kosher meals on request at Hotel Euler.

Bakeries
Bakery Schmutz
Austrasse 53   272-4765
IGB & IRG   272-6365

Butchers
Genossenschaftsmetzgerei
Friedrichstrasse 26   301-3493
H. Hess, Leimenstrasse 41   272-8835

Hotels
Basel Lodge
Leimenstrasse 24, 4051   271-8700/01
Hotel Drei Konige   261-5252
                                  Fax: 261-2153

Offers kosher meals on request.

Hotel Euler 272-4500
Fax: 271-5000
Offers kosher meals on request.

Hotel Metropol 271-7721
Fax: 271-7882

Museums

Jewish Museum of Switzerland
Kornhausgasse 8, 4051 261-9514
Hours: Monday and Wednesday, 2 pm to
5 pm; Sunday, 11 am to 5 pm. Free entrance.

Media

Newspapers

Judische Rundschau Maccabi
Leonhardstrasse 37 272-8589

Booksellers

Victor Goldschmidt
Mostackerstrasse 17 261-6191

Berne

Area telephone code (31)

Synagogues

Synagogue & Community Center
Kapellenstrasse 2 381-4992
Rabbiner Michael Dick: 381-7303.

Embassy

Embassy of Israel
Alpenstrasse 32, 3006 351-1042

Biel/Bienne

Area telephone code (32)

Synagogues

Rüschlistrasse 3 331-7251

Bremgarten/Aargau

Synagogue

Luzernstr. 1

Contact Information

Ringstr. 37, 5620 633-6626

Davos

Area telephone code (81)

Synagogues

Etania Rest Home
Richtsattweg 3, 7270 416-5404
Mikva on premises. Rooms and kosher meals
available.

Endingen

Area telephone code (56)

Contact Information

J. Bloch, Buckstr. 2, 5304 242-1546
Can arrange visits to the old synagogues and
cemetery.

Engelberg

Area telephone code (41)

Hotels

Hotel Marguerite 94-2522
Supervision: Agudas Achim, Zurich.
Mikva on premises.

Fribourg

Area telephone code (26)

Synagogues

9 avenue de Rome 322-1670

Geneva

Area telephone code (22)

Synagogues

The Geneva Synagogue (Ashkenazi)
11 Place de la Synagogue
Hekhal Haness (Sephardi)
54 ter route de Malagnou 736-9632

Machsike Hadass (Orthodox)
2 place des Eaux Vives   735-2298
12 Quai du Seujet (Liberal)   732-3245

Mikvaot   786-4671

Embassy
Permanent Mission of Israel to the United Nations
9 Chemin Bonvent, 1216, Cointrin

Restaurants
Le Jardin, 10, rue St-Leger   317-8910
                                  Fax: 317-8990
Arrangements can be made so that lunches
and dinners can be delivered to any hotel
downtown.

Meat
Heimishe Kitchen
Avenue de Miremont 1, 1206   346-0892
                                  Fax: 346-0830
Supervision: Machsike Hadass.
This is located on the first floor of an
apartment building and there is no sign
outside the building.

Butchers
Boucherie Kosher
Biton 21, rue de Montchoisi   736-3168

Media
Newspapers
Shalom European Jewish Times
rue St Leger 10, 1205   347-8088

Grindelwald
Area telephone code (36)

Hotels
Wagner-Kahn's Hotel Silberhorn   53-2822
                                  Fax: 53-4822
Mikva on premises. Open mid-December until
after Succot.

Kreuzlingen
Area telephone code (71)
Oratory: Hafenstr. 42   671-1630

Contact Information
Louis Hornung, Schustr. 7   671-1630

La Chaux-De-Fonds
Area telephone code (32)

Synagogues
63 rue du Parc   913-0477

Lausanne
Area telephone code (21)

Community Organisations
Communauté Israélite de Lausanne
3 avenue de Georgette, case postale 336,
1001   312-6733
                                  Fax: 320-9383

Synagogues
1 avenue Juste-Olivier   320-9911
Corner of J. Olivier and av. Florimont

Mikvaot
1 avenue Juste-Olivier   729-9820

Restaurants
Community Centre
3 avenue de Georgette, 1003   312-6731
Serves lunch only, from 12 pm to 2 pm.

Groceries
Kolbo Shalom
7 avenue Juste-Olivier   312-1265

Lengnau
Area telephone code (56)

Contact Information
For visits to the old synagogue and cemetery
                                       241-1203

Lucerne
Area telephone code (41)

Synagogues
Bruchstrasse 51   240-6400

Mikvaot
Bruchstrasse 51   320-4750

Butchers
Judische Metzgerei
Bruchstrasse 26   240-2560

Lugano
Area telephone code (91)

Synagogues
Via Maderno 11
Rabbi B.Z. Rabbinowitz: 932-6134

Mikvaot
Via Maderno 11

Kashrut Information
via Olgiati 1   922-9955
Mon.-Thurs. 5.30pm-7pm.

Hotels
Hotel Dan, Via Fontana 1   985-7030

Montreux
Area telephone code (21)

Synagogues
25 avenue des Alpes

St Gallen
Area telephone code (71)

Synagogues
Frongartenstrasse 18   223-5923

St Moritz-Bad
Area telephone code (81)

Hotels
Bermann's Hotel Edelweiss   833-5533
                       Fax: 833-5573
Mikva on premises.

Solothurn
Area telephone code (32)

Contact Information
R. Dreyfus, Grenchenstr. 8   623-2327

Vevey
Area telephone code (21)

Synagogues
3 blvd. Plumhof   923-5354

Restaurants
Les Bergers du Leman   923-5355/54
Serve kosher meals.

Winterthur
Area telephone code (52)

Synagogues
Rosenstrasse 5   232-8136

Yverdon
Area telephone code (24)

Contact Information
Dr Maurice Ellkan, 1400 Cheseaux-Noréaz
                       425-1851

Zug

Restaurants
Restaurant Glashof
Baarerstr. 41, 6301   (42) 221-248
Prepared kosher meals are available.

Zurich

Area telephone code (1)

Synagogues

Manessestrasse 198, 8045	202-8784
Lowenstrasse - Ecke, cnr. Nüschelerstrasse	
	281-1479
Freigutstrasse 37	201-4998

Judische Gemeinde Agudas Achim
Erikastrasse 8, 8003

Minjan Wollishofen
Chabad Lubavitch, Etzelstrasse 6, 8038
201 1691

Mikvaot

Telephone before 8.30 am.	201-4022
Freigutstrasse 37	201-7306
Telephone between 9 am & 11am.	

Tourist Information

Offizielles Israelisches Verkehrsbureau
Lintheschergasse 12, 8021   211-2344/5
                                    Fax: 212-2036

Media

Periodicals

Jewish City Guide of Switzerland
Spectrum Press International, Im Tannegg 1,
Friesenbergstrasse 221, 8055
462-6411; 462-6412
Published quarterly in English and German, a
guide to Jewish communities throughout
Switzerland.

Restaurants

Fein & Schein
Schontalstrasse 14, Corner/Ecke Hallwylstrasse
241-3040
Fax: 241-2112

Kosher Restaurant Schalom
Lavaterstrasse 33   201-1476
                                   Fax: 201-1496

Bakeries

Ruben Bollag	242-8700

Butchers

Adass/Metzgerei   211 5210
Supervision: Israelitische Religionsgesellschaft
Zurich Ashkenas.

Taam/Metzgerei   463-9094
Supervision: Judische Gemeinde Agudas
Achim.

Groceries

Chaimson	463-0440

Hotels

Hotel International   311-4341
Offers kosher meals on request.

Booksellers

Morasha
Seesatrasse 11, 8002   201-1120
Hours: Monday to Thursday, 9 am to 12 pm,
2 pm to 6:30 pm.

Taiwan

There are more than 30 families in Taiwan, most of them living in the capital, Taipei.

GMT + 8 hours
Country calling code (886)

Taipei
Area telephone code (2)

Organisations
Taiwan Jewish Community Centre
No 1, Lane 61, Teh Hsing East Road, Shihlin
396-0159
Fax: 396-4022
Services are held on most Friday evenings at 7.30pm. Visitors to check in advance. All holydays and major festivals are celebrated.

Synagogues
Orthodox
Ritz Hotel, 41 Min Chuan East Road 597-1234
Shabbat and festival services are held here.

Restaurants
Meat
Y.Y.'s Steakhouse
Chungshan North Road, Section 3, cnr. The Huei St.
There are no kosher restaurants in Taipei, but this Steakhouse has a separate kitchen and dining room, where kosher meat meals are served on separate crockery, with separate cutlery. No milk products are available in this section.

Tajikistan

GMT + 5 hours
Country calling code (7)

Dushanbe
Area telephone code (3772)

Synagogues
Ashkenazi
Proletarsky Street

Bokharan
Nazyina Khikmeta Street 26

Shakhrisabz
Synagogues
23 Bainal Minal Street

Thailand

The Jewish community of Thailand numbers about 250. Only a handful are Thai nationals, and they are of European and Asian origin.

GMT + 7 hours
Country calling code (66)

Bangkok
Area telephone code (2)

Organisations

Jewish Community of Thailand Community Centre
Beth Elisheva Building, 121 Soi Sai, Nam Tip 2 (Soi 22), Sukhumvit Road 252-7809, 252-2809

Ohr Menachem - Chabad
Kaosarn Road, 108/1 Ramburthi Road, Banglampoo 282-6388
Fax: 282-6388
Daily services. Friday evening services.

Synagogues

Beth Elisheva
121 Soi Sai, Nam Tip 2 (Soi 22), Sukhumvit Road 258-2195
Fax: 663-0245

Orthodox

Even Chen Synagogue
Bossotel Inn, 55/12-14 Soi Charoenkrung, 42/1 New Road (Silom Road) 630-6120
Fax: 237-3225
Synagogue club and kosher restaurant under supervision of Rabbi Y. Kantor. Daily morning & evening minyan. Regular Friday evening & Shabbat morning, afternoon and evening services. Light kosher meal after services, by advance reservation.

Kashrut Information 318-1577
237-1697
234-0606

Embassy

Israel Embassy
'Ocean Tower II' 25th floor, 75 Sukumvit Soi 19, 10110 260-4854/9
Fax: 260-4860

Tunisia

The Jewish population of Tunisia is approximately 2,000, most of whom live in Tunis. There are also some small communities, mainly in Jerba, Sfax, Sousse and Nabeul.

GMT + 1 hours
Country calling code (216)

Jerba

There are Jews in two villages on this small island off the Tunisian coast. There is also a magnificent synagogue, El Ghriba, many hundreds of years old, in the village of Er-Riadh (Hara Sghira). Jewish silversmiths are prominent in Hournt souk on rue Bizerte.

Sfax

Area telephone code (4)

Synagogues

Azriah, 71 rue Habib Mazoun
Near the Town Hall.

Tunis

Area telephone code (1)

Organisations

Community Offices
15 rue de Cap Vert   282469, 287153

Synagogues

Beth Yacob, 3 rue Eve, Nohelle   348964
Grande, 43 Av. de la Liberte
Lubavitch Yeshiva
73 rue de Palestine   791429

Kashrut Information

26 rue de Palestine   282406; 283540

Turkey

After the Expulsion of the Jews from Spain in 1492, at a time when Jews were not tolerated in most of the Christian countries of Western Europe, what was then the Ottoman (Turkish) Empire was their principal land of refuge. In -1992 they celebrated the 500th anniversary of the establishment of the community. Under the national constitution, their civil rights were reconfirmed. In recent years, many Jews have emigrated to Israel, Western Europe and the United States, and Turkey's Jewish population today numbers about 25,000, of whom 23,000 live in Istanbul.

GMT + 2 hours
Country calling code (90)

Ankara
Area telephone code (312)

Synagogues
Birlik Sokak, Samanpazari   311-6200
This Synagogue is not easy to find. Off Anafartalar Caddesi in Samanpazari, there is a stairway down at the right of the TC Ziraat Bankasi. The synagogue is several buildings along the street on the left, behind a wall. Services every morning Sabbath morning services begin at 7 or 7.30am depending on the time of year.

Embassy
Embassy of Israel
Mahatma Gandhi Sok 85, Gaziosmanpasa

Bursa
Area telephone code (224)

Synagogues
Gerush Synagogue
Kurucesme Caddesi   368-636
Services on Friday evening, Shabbat morning and festivals. This Synagogue is in the old Jewish quarter. There are 180 Jews in this town.

Istanbul
Area telephone code (21)

Community Organisations
Buyuk Hendek
Sokak No 61, Galata   293-7566
Secretary General: Lina Filiba

Religious Organisations
Chief Rabbinate
Yemenici Sokak 23, Beyoglu, 80050, Tunel
293-8794/5
Fax: 244-1980

Synagogues
Askenazi Synagogue
Yuksekkaldinm Sok No 37, Galata   243-6909
Saturdays only.

Beth Israel
Efe Sok No 4, Sisli   240-6599
Every day.

Caddesbostan Synagogue
Tasmektep Sok, Goztepe   356-5922
Every day.

Etz Ahayim Synagogue
Muallim Naci Cad No 40 & 41, Ortakoy
260-1896
Every day.

Hemdat Israel Synagogue
Izettin Sok No 65, Kadikoy   336-5293
Every day.

Hesed Leavraam Synagogue
Pancur Sok No 15, Buyukada 382-5788
June-September including High Holy days.

Italian Synagogue
Sair Ziya Pasa Yokusu No 29, Galata 293-7784
Saturdays only.

Neve Shalom Buyuk
Hendek Sok, No 61, Galata 293-7566
Saturdays only.

Kashrut Information

Chief Rabbinate
Yemenici Sokak 23, Beyoglu, 80050, Tunel
293-8794/5
Fax: 244-1980

Embassy

Consulate General
Valikonag Caddesi No 73 255-1045
Weekly publication: Salom (Turkish and Ladino).

Hotels

Merit Antique
Ordu Cad 226, Lalelil 513-9300
Fax: 512-6390
With kosher restaurant.

Izmir

Area telephone code (232)

Community Organisations

Jewish Community Council
Azizler Sokak 920/44, Guzelyurt 123-708

Synagogues

Beth Israel
265 Mithatpasa Street, Karatas

Shaar Ashamayan
1390 Sokak 4/2, Bikur Holim, Esrefpasa
Caddesi, Alsancak

Butchers

Kosher Meat 148-395
Tuesday and Thursday or inquire at the synagogue.

Ukraine

Pilgrimage to the graves of the Chassidic leaders and their landmarks are now increasingly underway. Further details of access and contacts in such places as Ampoli, Berdichev, Hadich, Medzhibuzh, Peremishlani, Pogrebisheh, Polonnoye, Shepebovka and Uman are required.

GMT + 2 hours
Country calling code (380)

Berdichev

Area telephone code (4143)

Synagogues

4 Dzherzhinskaya Street   23938 / 20222
Kosher kitchen on premises.

Mikvaot

4 Dzherzhinskaya Street   23938 / 20222

Tourist Information

The grave of Levi Isaac ben Meir is in Berdichev.

Beregovo

Synagogues

17 Sverdlov Street

Bershad

Synagogues

25 Narodnaya Street

Chernigov

Synagogues

34 Kommunisticheskaya Street

Chernovtsy

Area telephone code (3722)

Synagogues

24 Lukyana Kobylitsa Street   54878

Chmelnitsy

Synagogues

58 Komminnestnaya Street

Kharkov

Area telephone code (57)

Synagogues

48 Kryatkovskaya Street

Orthodox

Orthodox Union Project Reunite
Surnskaya 45   408-378
     Fax: 439-209

Kiev

Area telephone code (44)

Synagogues

29 Shchekovichnaya Street   416-2442/4430

Reform

Reform Congregation
7 Nemanskaya Street   295-6539

Embassy
Embassy of Israel
Lesi Ukrainki 34, GPE-S, 252195

Korosten
Synagogues
8 Shchoksa Street

Kremenchug
Synagogues
50 Sverdlov Street

Lviv
Area telephone code (32)

Synagogues
4 Brativ Mikhnovskykh Street, 290018

330-524

Fax: 333-536
Kosher kitchen available: 333-535.

Odessa
Area telephone code (48)

Synagogues
3 Lesnaya Street
Gazovy Lane, Moskovskaya Street
Matzah bakery on premises.

Slavuta
Area telephone code (4479)

Synagogues
Kuzovskaya Street 2   25452
The first edition of Tanya was printed here by the Shapira family whose tombs are in the cemetary.

Zhitomir
Area telephone code (41494)

Synagogues
59 Lubarskaya Street   373-468
Reb Ze'ev Wolf, disciple of Dov Baer, is buried *in the Smolanka cemetery.

United Kingdom

England

Greater London

Well over half the 300,000 (1991) Jews of Britain live in London. Numbering about 210,000, they are spread throughout the metropolis, with the largest concentration in north-western districts like Golders Green, Hendon, Edgware and Hampstead Garden Suburb. There are also large communities in North London (Stamford Hill) and in the East (Redbridge). Once it was in Stepney that the biggest part of London Jewry lived and, in spite of many changes there, Aldgate and Whitechapel should be visited, not only for the many reminders of their Jewish heyday, but also for the bustling life which is still to be seen there.

The City

There are many historically interesting sites in the City, that square mile of Central London which adjoins the East End. The Bank of England, with its Underground station of the same name, is a useful starting point.

One of the numerous streets which converge on this busy hub is Poultry, leading quickly to Cheapside. The first street on the right is Old Jewry. Here, and in the neighbourhood, the earliest community lived before England expelled all its Jews in 1290. There were synagogues in this street and in Gresham and Coleman Streets, not far from historic Guildhall, which is itself a 'must' for tourists.

Inside the Royal Exchange, situated opposite the Bank of England in Threadneedle Street, there is a series of murals including one by Solomon J. Solomon, R.A., of 'Charles I Demanding the Five Members', and a portrait of Nathan Mayer Rothschild, who founded the London house of the famous banking firm. There was a time when the south-east corner of the Royal Exchange was known as 'Jews' Walk'.

The Rothschild headquarters is not far away, in St. Swithin's Lane. To reach this handsome building (which has in its entrance-hall more Rothschild portraits, as well as a large tapestry of Moses striking the rock), cross carefully from the Royal Exchange to the Lord Mayor's Mansion House and then turn left into King William Street.

Cornhill, which stretches eastwards from the Bank, leads to Leadenhall Street and its shipping offices and, after a short walk, to Creechurch Lane and the Cunard building, on the back of which is an interesting plaque. 'Site of the First Synagogue after the Resettlement 1657–1701. Spanish and Portuguese Jews' Congregation' is the inscription. Here the post-Expulsion Jews whom Oliver Cromwell welcomed to England set up their house of prayer. In 1701 they built a synagogue in Bevis Marks (close by), modelling it on the famous Portuguese Synagogue in Amsterdam. It has been scheduled by the Royal Commission on Ancient Historical Monuments as 'a building of outstanding value', and is considered one of the most beautiful pieces of synagogue architecture extant. In it are some benches from the Creechurch Lane Synagogue.

London's chief Ashkenazi place of worship, the Great Synagogue, stood, until it was bombed during the Second World War, in Duke's Place, which adjoins Bevis Marks. The 'Duke's Place Shool' (as it was called) was the country's best-known synagogue, the scene of many great occasions and a popular choice for weddings. On the wall of International House, which has replaced it, there is a plaque informing the visitor that the synagogue stood there 'from 1690 and served the community continuously until it was destroyed in September, 1941'.

After the Second World War and until the 1970s, the Great Synagogue was in Adler Street, named after the two Chief Rabbis of that name, Rabbi Nathan Marcus Adler and his son, Rabbi Dr. Hermann Adler. Duke's Place leads to Aldgate High Street where, on the opposite side, Jewry Street marks another centre of the pre-Expulsion community. At the time of Richard I's coronation many Jews, escaping from rioting mobs, moved here from Old Jewry.

The East End

Further eastwards, along Aldgate High Street, is Middlesex Street, which becomes the crowded Petticoat Lane every Sunday morning. The cheerful and cheeky language of the stall-holders has made 'The Lane' famous throughout the world. On week-days an offshoot, Wentworth Street continues the market.

Eastwards again, to Whitechapel, which has changed almost out of all recognition since the days before the Second World War, when it had a teeming Jewish population. Just beyond Aldgate East Underground station two familiar spots remain: Whitechapel Art Gallery and Whitechapel Library.

The library's extensive Yiddish collection has been transferred to the Taylorian Library, Oxford University's modern-language library. The next turning on the left is Osborne Street, which leads to Brick Lane. A large and sombre building in Brick Lane (at the corner of Fournier Street) represents more than anything else the changes that have taken place in the East End over the years. The Huguenots built it as a church, the Jews turned it into a synagogue (the Machzike Hadass), and now the Bengalis, who have replaced the Jews, have converted it into a mosque.

The former synagogue in Princelet Street (No. 19) is being converted into a museum by the Spitalfields Trust, which is collaborating with the Jewish Museum to develop the building to show the history of the different immigrant groups which have inhabited the Spitalfields area during the past 300 years. For further information about activities at the Princelet Street Building, contact the Jewish Museum.

In Brune Street, it is possible to see the building of the former Soup Kitchen for the Jewish Poor that was established in 1902. Its work of distributing food to the small elderly Jewish community still resident in the area is now undertaken by Jewish Care, the largest Jewish social service organisation in Britain.

Further along Whitechapel Road, outside Whitechapel Underground station, stands a drinking fountain. It was erected in 1911 'in Loyal and Grateful Memory of Edward VII Rex et Imperator from subscriptions raised by Jewish inhabitants of East London'.

Next to the former offices of the Federation of Synagogues in the former Synagogue Community Centre is the Kosher Luncheon Club. This establishment maintains a strong Jewish tradition and still caters for local as well as business people who require a wholesome dairy meal at lunchtime. This is provided in an informal atmosphere and visitors can learn from the clientele something of the former glories of the East End.

Brady Street is the site of an old cemetery, opened for the New Synagogue in 1761 and subsequently used also by the Great Synagogue. The cemetery became full in the 1790s, and it was decided to put a four-foot-thick layer of earth over part of the site, using this for further burials. This created a flat-topped mound in the centre of the cemetery. The cemetery is perhaps the only one where, because of the two layers, the headstones are placed back to back. Among those buried here are: Solomon Hirschel, who was Chief Rabbi from 1802 to 1842, and Nathan Meyer Rothschild (1777–1836), the banker. To view the cemetery, contact the United Synagogue Burial Society (0181-343 3456).

In Mile End there are three more old cemeteries: two Sephardi and one Ashkenazi. Behind 253 Mile End Rd., where the Sephardi Home for the Aged (Beth Holim) was located before moving to Wembley, is the first Resettlement cemetery, the oldest existing Anglo-Jewish cemetery, opened in 1657.

Abraham Fernandez Carvajal, regarded as the founder of the modern

Anglo-Jewish community, is buried here, and also Haham David Nieto, one of the greatest of Sephardi spiritual leaders. At 329 Mile End Road, the Nuevo Beth Chaim, opened in 1725, contains the grave of Haham Benjamin Artom. This is among the 2,000 graves remaining on the site. Some 7,500 were transferred to a site in Brentwood, Essex, during the 1970s. The earliest Ashkenazi cemetery, acquired in 1696, is in Alderney Road, and here the founders of the Duke's Place Synagogue, Moses and Aaron Hart and others, and also the 'Baal Shem of London' (the Cabbalist, Haim Samuel Falk), lie buried. In Beaumont Grove, on the south side of Mile End Road, is the Stepney B'nai B'rith Clubs and Settlement, managed in co-operation with Jewish Care, which caters primarily for the needs of the 7,500 Jews still living in the East End.

In Commercial Road, Hessel Street, another Jewish market centre, is now occupied by Bengali traders. Henriques Street is named after Sir Basil Henriques, a leading welfare worker and magistrate, and founder of the Bernhard Baron St. George's Jewish Settlement, who died in 1961. On the same side, three turnings along, is Alie Street. At the Jewish Working Men's Club here in July, 1896, Theodor Herzl addressed a meeting which was effectively the launching of the Zionist movement in Britain.

West Central
Chief Rabbi Hermann Adler (1891–1911) is honoured at the Central Court, the Old Bailey (Underground station: St. Paul's), where a mural over the entrance to Court No. 1, entitled 'Homage to Justice,' includes the figure of Dr. Adler. By the City Boundary High Holborn is the Royal Fusiliers City of London Regiment Memorial. The names of the 38th, 39th and 40th (Jewish Batallions) are inscribed on the monument together with all other batallions which served in the First World War. At the western edge of the City, Chancery Lane Station, Holborn, is a useful centre for several points of interest. To the east, Furnival Street has the *Jewish Chronicle* office. Northward, Gray's Inn Road leads to Theobald's Road. There, at No. 22, a plaque on the wall recalls that it is the birthplace of Benjamin Disraeli. Further to the north is Great Russell Street, which runs along part of the south side of the British Museum. When visiting the Museum, one should certainly see its collection of illuminated *haggadot*, in particular its copy of the fifteenth century Ashkenazi Haggadah. No. 77 Great Russell Street was the headquarters of the Zionist organisations from 1919 to 1964. Westward, in Chancery Lane, the Public Record Office has in its vast collection many documents of Jewish historical value, including the petitions to Cromwell.

Commonwealth House, 1-19 New Oxford Street, is the new centre of

British Jewry's communal activities, housing the Board of Deputies and a range of other offices.

B'nai B'rith-Hillel House, the student centre, is at 1-2 Endsleigh Street, in Bloomsbury, at the heart of the University neighbourhood, and the Council of Christians and Jews in Gordon Street is close by. In the building of University College in Gower Street, the Jewish Studies Library houses the Altmann, Mishcon and Mocatta Libraries and the Margulies Yiddish Collection. The School of Oriental and African Studies in the University precinct includes Judaica and Israelitica in its library.

West End

A permanent art collection has been accumulated by the Ben Uri Art Society.

In the Marble Arch district, in the part of Hyde Park known as 'The Dell', a Holocaust Memorial Garden was dedicated in June 1983. The garden plot was given over by the British Government to the Board of Deputies, which commissioned Mr. Richard Seifert to design the memorial centre-piece rocks bearing a quotation from the Book of Lamentations. Also in the Marble Arch area, you will find an important associate of the United Synagogue (the recently amalgamated Western and Marble Arch Synagogues in Great Cumberland Place), the West End Great, as well as the West London (Reform) Synagogue (Upper Berkeley Street) and the magnificent Victorian New West End Synagogue in St. Petersburg Place, just off Bayswater Road. The Jewish Memorial Council and Bookshop is in Enford Street.

The British Zionist Federation was inaugurated at the Trocadero Restaurant in Piccadilly Circus in January 1899. At 175 Piccadilly was the London bureau of the Zionist Organisation, set up in August 1917. Here, Dr. Chaim Weizmann and other Zionist leaders worked, and here, in November 1917, the Balfour Declaration was delivered by Lord Rothschild. The Westminster Synagogue in Rutland Gardens, Knightsbridge, houses the Czech Memorial Scrolls Centre, where there is a permanent exhibition telling the story of the salvaging from Prague in 1964 of 1,564 Torah Scrolls confiscated by the Nazis during the Second World War, and of their restoration and the donation of many to communities throughout the world. The exhibition is open from 10 am to 4 pm on Tuesdays and Thursdays, and at other times by appointment.

In St. John's Wood are three more interesting synagogues: the New London (Abbey Road) and the St. John's Wood (Grove End Road), where the Chief Rabbi, who lives in near-by Hamilton Terrace, generally worships. The third synagogue of great interest in St. John's Wood is the

Liberal Jewish, opposite Lord's Cricket Ground recently rebuilt and renovated.

Stamford Hill

Of London's many synagogues, one remarkable group is the series of Chasidic 'shtiblech' in Stamford Hill (and the yeshivot which are attached to some of them). Cazenove Road contains several of these, and it is here and in the vicinity that the long coats and wide hats of *chasidim* and the curled sidelocks of their children are to be seen. The Lubavitch Foundation headquarters and the Yesodey Hatorah Schools are in Stamford Hill.

AJEX House at East Bank, Stamford Hill houses an interesting military museum. In this district, also, are North African, Adeni, Indian and some Persian Jews and their synagogues.

North-East

The migration of the Jews from the East End took many of them eventually to the London borough of Redbridge where today the greatest density of London's Jews reside. To obtain a flavour of this large Jewish community one should visit the Redbridge Youth and Community Centre, Sinclair House, Woodford Bridge Road, Ilford, Essex. Sinclair House is a large modern, purpose-built Jewish community centre and it is the base for a number of organisations and the focal point of many Israeli and Zionist communal events. It also houses the Clayhall Synagogue, the Redbridge Jewish Programmes Material Project and community representative councils.

North-West

The Jewish Museum has moved from Woburn House and recently opened at new premises in Albert Street, Camden Town. It houses Britain's major collection of ritual articles and Anglo-Judaica.

The starting point for visiting North-West London is Golders Green. Jews first settled here during the First World War, and the Golders Green Synagogue (United) in Dunstan Road, was opened in 1922. Walk down Golders Green Road from the Underground station for half a mile or so, and you will come to Broadwalk Lane on the right-hand side, where the Lincoln Institute is. This is the home of Ohel David, a congregation of Indian Jews, many of whom came to England when India was partitioned in 1947. Their forebears went to India from Baghdad.

On the opposite side of the road, at the end of a short turning called The Riding, is the Golders Green Beth Hamedrash – formerly known as 'Munk's' after its founder in the 1930s, Rabbi Dr. Eli Munk. This very Orthodox congregation, mainly of German origin, adheres to the religious principles of Rabbi Samson Raphael Hirsch. There are many other strictly Orthodox congregations in Golders Green, including chasidic groups.

Any of the buses travelling along Golders Green Road away from the Underground station will take you to Bell Lane, in Hendon. A few hundred yards down on the left-hand side is Albert Road, where you will find Jews' College – established in 1855 as an Institute of Higher Education and associated with London University for many years. A group of Persian Jews holds Shabbat morning services there. Its 70,000-volume library is open to the public.

Also in Hendon in Egerton Gardens, a turning opposite Barnet Town Hall in The Burroughs, 10–15 minutes walk from Bell Lane, is Yakar, which provides a wide variety of adult educational and cultural programmes and has a lending library. Several minyanim are held here on Shabbat and festivals. Further information is available on (0181) 202 5552.

Return to Golders Green Underground station from Hendon Central, either by Underground or by bus. Once there, take a bus northwards along Finchley Road for two miles or so, getting off at East End Road, which is more or less opposite the bus stop. On the right-hand side is the Sternberg Centre, the largest Jewish community centre in Europe. The Georgian former manor house contains Leo Baeck College, with its library of 18,000 books, which trains Reform and Liberal rabbis; the offices of the Reform Synagogues of Great Britain, and the London Museum of Jewish Life, now the second centre of the Jewish Museum. In addition to permanent displays, the museum also mounts special exhibitions and runs walking tours and educational programmes. There is a Holocaust memorial, as well as a biblical garden and a bookshop and a dairy snack bar.

GMT
Country calling code (44)

Religious Organisations

Orthodox

Federation of Synagogues, 65 Watford Way, Hendon, NW4 3AQ   (0181) 202-2263
Burial: (0181) 202-3903
Fax: (0181) 203-0610

Spanish and Portuguese Jews Congregation, Vestry Office, 2 Ashworth Road, Maida Vale, W9 1JY   (0171) 289-2573
Fax: (0171) 289-2709

Union of Orthodox Hebrew Congregations
140 Stamford Hill, Stamford Hill, N16 6QT
(0181) 802-6226/7

United Synagogue, 735 High Road, Finchley, N12 0US   (0181) 343-8989
Fax: (0181) 343-5262
The **London Beth Din** is also located at this address.   (0181) 343-6270
Fax: (0181) 343-6257

Masorti (Conservative in the USA)

Assembly of Masorti Synagogues, 1097 Finchley Road, NW11 0PU   (0181) 201-8772
Fax: (0181) 201-8917
Email: Masorti.uk@ort.org

Reform

Reform Synagogues
The Sternberg Centre for Judaism, 80 East End Road, N3 2SY   (0181) 349-4731
Fax: (0181) 343-0901

Liberal

Union of Liberal and Progressive Synagogues
The Montague Centre, 21 Maple Street, W1P 6DS   (0171) 580-1663
Fax: (0171) 436-4184

With more than 200 synagogues in the London area alone, not counting independent synagogues and *shtieblach*, we recommend that you contact one of the above organisations to find the synagogue of your choice nearest you, along with minyan times.

Kashrut Information

Joint Kashrus Committee-Kedassia (Union of Orthodox Hebrew Congregations)
140 Stamford Hill, Stamford Hill, N16 6QT   (0181) 800-6833
Fax: (0181) 809-7092

Federation Kashrus Board, 65 Watford Way, Hendon, NW4 3AQ   (0181) 202-2263
Fax: (0181) 203-0610

London Beth Din, 735 High Road, Finchley, N12 0US   (0181) 343-6255
Fax: (0181) 343-6254
Web site: www.kosher.org.uk
Kashrut hotline: 343-6259
Publishes *The Really Jewish Food Guide*, which contains a list of all the establishments it certifies as well as guidance for the shopper in buying general consumer products.

London Board for Shechita, 401-405 Nether Street, Finchley, N3 1YR   (0181) 349-9160
Fax: (0181) 346-2206

Sephardi Kashrut Authority, 2 Ashworth Road, Maida Vale, W9 1JY   (0171) 289-2573
Fax: (0171) 289-2709

Contact Information

JCi (Jewish Community information)
B'nai B'rith Hillel House, 1-2 Endsleigh Court, WC1H 0DS   (0171) 383-3272
Fax: (0171) 387-8014
A comprehensive service of communal information is under development between the Board of Deputies and B'nai B'rith.

Tourist Information

Israel Government Tourist Office, 18 Great Marlborough St., W1V 1AE   (0171) 434-3651
Fax: (0171) 437-0527

Visitorcall – The Phone Guide to London
London Tourist Board, 26 Grosvenor Gardens, Victoria, SW1W 0DU   123-456
Features over 30 lines of recorded information services.

Embassy

Embassy of Israel, 2 Palace Green, Kensington, W8 4QB   (0171) 957-9500

Israeli Consulate-General
15a Old Court Place, Kensington, W8
Web site: www.israel-embassy.org.uk/london
Nearest tube station: High Street Kensington.
Consular office hours: Monday to Thursday, 10 am to 1 pm; Friday, 10 am to 12 pm.

Media

Visitors to London and tourists in the UK should be aware of the following newspapers, magazines and listings of Jewish interest.

Newspapers

Essex Jewish News
900 Eastern Avenue, Newbury Park, Ilford,
Essex, IG2 7HH   (0181) 599-8866
                    Fax: (0181) 599-0984
Quarterly publication serving East London and
Essex.

Jewish Chronicle
25 Furnival Street, EC4A 1JT   (0171) 405-9052
                    Fax: (0171) 405-9040
Established 1841. Weekly publication serving
the United Kingdom.

London Jewish News, 28 St Albans Lane,
NW11 7QE   (0181) 731-8814
                    Fax: (0181) 731-8815
Fortnightly publication serving the greater
London community.

Magazines

New Moon, 28 St Albans Lane,
NW11 7QE   (0181) 731-8088

Listings

Board of Deputies
Commonwealth House, 1-19 New Oxford
Street, WC1A 1NF   (0171) 543-5421/5422

London Diary of Jewish Events
12 Holne Chase, N2 0QN   (0181) 458-2466
                    Fax: (0181) 458-5457

Directories

Jewish Year Book, Vallentine Mitchell, 900
Eastern Avenue, Newbury Park, Ilford, Essex,
IG2 7HH   (0181) 599-8866
                    Fax: (0181) 599-0984

Internet

Brijnet
11 The Lindens, Prospect Hill, Waltham Forest,
Walthamstow, E17 3EJ   520-8331
          Email: rafi@brijnet.org
Website: http://shamash.org/ejin/brijnet

Radio

Jewish Spectrum Radio, 558 AM, PO Box
12591, NW2 2ZP   (0181) 905-5533
                    Fax: (0181) 209-1565

The mikvaot, kosher food, accommodation
and Jewish interest listings have been broken
down for convenience into Central, East,
North, Northwest, South and West London. In
some of these instances they include parts of
other regions which fall under the umbrella of
Greater London.

Central London

Area telephone code (0171)

Restaurants

Deli at West London Synagogue
33 Seymour Place, W1   723-4404

Hillel Restaurant
Yoffi's, B'nai B'rith-Hillel Foundation, 1-2
Endsleigh Street, WC1H 0DS   388-0801
                    Fax: 916-3973
                    Email: hillel@ort.org
Supervision: London Beth Din.
Hours: Monday to Thursday, 12 pm to
2:30 pm; Friday night Shabbat meal available
if booked and paid in advance by Thursday
11 am. Please phone for details of summer
months opening. Re-opens for students and
all other visitors mid-September.

Rabins Salt Beef Bar
28 Great Windmill Street, W1   434-9913

Reubens
79 Baker Street, W1M 1AJ   486-0035
                    Fax: 486-7079
Supervision: Sephardi Kashrut Authority.
Open daily except for Shabbat; open Friday
until two hours before sundown.

Stars Restaurant
11 Soho Square, W1V 5DB   467-6525 or 9535

The Noshery
12-13 Grenville Street, EC1   242-1591

Bakeries

M & D Grodzinski
53 Goodge Street, W1   636-0561
Supervision: London Beth Din.

Taboon Continental Bakery
204 Preston Road, E1 7TD   247-7079
Supervision: London Beth Din.

Butchers

Gold Bros.
222 Jubilee Street, E1   790-1572
Supervision: London Board of Shechita.

Delicatessens

DD's Kosher Dairy Sandwich Bar
41 Greville Street, EC1   242-5487
Supervision: London Beth Din.

Hotels

Andrews Hotel, 12 Westbourne Street, Hyde

Park, W2 2TZ   723-4514
     Fax: 706-4143
Hebrew spoken. Kosher, but no supervision. Walking distance to all synagogues in this area, airbus A2 from Heathrow, tube stations: Lancaster Gate and Paddington. For budget travellers.

Museums

Ben Uri Art Society & Gallery, 4th Floor, 21 Dean Street, W1V 6NE   437-2582
The aim of the Society, which is a registered charity founded in 1915, is to promote Jewish art as part of the Jewish cultural heritage. The gallery provides a showcase for exhibitions of contemporary art as well as for the Society's own collection of over 700 works by Jewish artists, including David Bomberg, Mark Gertler, Jacob Epstein, Reuven Rubin and Leon Kossof. Open Monday to Thursday, 10 am to 5 pm, Sunday afternoons during exhibitions, 2 to 5 pm. Closed Jewish Holy-days and Bank Holidays.

Jewish Museum
Raymond Burton House, 129-131 Albert Street, Camden, NW1 7NB   284-1997
The Jewish Museum holds a Ceremonial Art collection of world importance and a major collection on the history of the Jews in Britain. Hours: Sunday to Thursday, 10 am to 4 pm; Closed Friday, Saturday, Jewish Festivals and Bank Holidays. Groups by previous arrangement with Secretary.

Libraries

Institute for Contemporary History and Weiner Library
4 Devonshire Street, W1N 2BH   636-7247
     Fax: 436-6248
     Email: lib@wl.u-net.com
With 50,000 books and periodicals, and over 1,000,000 press cuttings, etc., the library serves as a research institute and reference centre for twentieth century history (especially German), modern Jewish history and antisemitism, minorities, refugees, fascism, etc. Hours: Monday to Friday, 10 am to 5:30pm.

The Jewish Studies Library
University College London Library, Gower Street, WC1E 6BT   387-7050
     Fax: 380-7373
In addition to materials purchased for the College's Department of Hebrew Studies it

incorporates the Mocatta Library, Altmann Library, William Margulies Yiddish Library and the Library of the Jewish Historical Society of England. Applications to use or view the collections should be made in advance in writing to the Librarian.

Travel Agencies

Goodmos Tours, Dunstan House, 14a St Cross Street, EC1N 8XA   430-2230
     Fax: 405-5049

Booksellers

Jewish Memorial Council and Bookshop
25 Enford Street, W1H 2DD   724-7778
     Fax: 706-1710

East London

Mikvaot

Ilford Mikvah Federation of Synagogues
463 Cranbrook Road, Ilford   (0181) 554-2551
     Evenings: (0181) 554-8532
Correspondence to: 367 Cranbrook Road.

Bakeries

Galillee Bakery
388 Cranbrook Road, Ilford   (0181) 518-3567
Supervision: London Beth Din.

J. Goide (caterers) Ltd
4 Stepney Green, Stepney, E1 (0171) 790-3449
Supervision: London Beth Din.

Mr Bagels Factory, 1 Kings Yard, Carpenters Road, E15 2HD   (0171) 533-7553
Supervision: Sephardi Kashrut Authority.

Butchers

C. Solomons, 646 Cranbrook Road, Barkingside   (0181) 554-6562
Supervision: London Board of Shechita.

Ilford Kosher Meats
7 Beehive Lane, Ilford, IG2   (0181) 554-3238
Supervision: London Board of Shechita.

La Boucherie, 145 High Street, Barkingside, IG6 2AJ   (0181) 551-9215
     Fax: (0181) 551-9977
Supervision: London Board of Shechita.

N. Goldberg, 12 Claybury Broadway, Redbridge   (0181) 551-2828

Supervision: London Board of Shechita and Kedassia.

Stanley Cohen, 93b Upper Clapton Road, Clapton, E5   (0181) 806-5035
Supervision: London Board of Shechita.

Groceries

Brownsteins Delicatessen, 24a Woodford Avenue, Gants Hill, IG2 6XG   (0181) 550-3900
Selection of groceries and delicatessen sold are under the supervision of various religious authorities. Hours: Mon. to Thurs., 7:30 am to 6 pm; Fri. and Sun., 7 am to 2 pm.

Hotels

Kadimah Hotel, 146 Clapton Common, Clapton, E5 9AG   800-5960; 800-1716
                                         Fax: 800-6237
Supervision: London Beth Din.
Within easy reach of tourist attractions.

Menorah Hotel & Caterers, 54-54a Clapton Common, Clapton, E5   806-4925; 6340

Bed & Breakfasts

Harold Godfrey Hillel House
25 Louisa Street, Stepney, E1 4NF
Summer accommodation in London at affordable prices. 20 rooms, kosher, dairy only kitchens, easy access to London tourist attractions and theatre. Enquiries and bookings to: Evelyn Bacharach, Kingscliffe, 1a Antrim Grove, London NW3 4XS, Tel: (0171) 722-0420, Fax: (0181) 203-8727.

Travel Agencies

Longwood Holidays, 182 Longwood Gardens, Ilford, IG5 0EW   (0181) 551-4494
Open Sundays 10 am to 2 pm.

North London

Area telephone code (0181)

Mikvaot

Adath Yisroel Synagogue Mikvah, 40a Queen Elizabeth's Walk, cnr. 28 Gazebrook Rd., Stamford Hill, N16 0HH   802-2554
Craven Walk Mikvah, 72 Lingwood Road, Stamford Hill, N16   800-8555
                                    Evenings: 809-6279

Reform Mikvah
The Sternberg Centre, 80 East End Road, Finchley, N3 2SY   349-2568
Satmar Mikvah
62 Filey Avenue, Stamford Hill, N16 806-3961
Stamford Hill and District Mikvah
Margaret Road, Stamford Hill, N16   806-3880
                                     809-4064
                                     800-5119

Restaurants

Morry's Milk Bar Restaurant
4 Windus Road, Stamford Hill, N16
Tasti Pizza
23 Amhurst Parade, Amhurst Park, Stamford Hill, N16 5AA   802-0018; 455-0004
Supervision: London Beth Din and Kedassia.
Uncle Shloime's, 204 Stamford Hill, Stamford Hill, N16   802-9355
Supervision: Kedassia.

Bakeries

Marlene's Kosher Bakery and Delicatessen
6 Hendon Lane, Finchley, N3   349-1674

Parkway Patisseries Ltd., 326-328 Regents
Park Road, Finchley, N3   346-0344
Supervision: London Beth Din and Kedassia.
Hours: Sunday, 7:30 am to 1:30 pm; Monday
to Thursday, to 5:30 pm; Friday, to 1 hour
before Shabbat.

Rensow Patisserie Ltd.
Unit a, 8-10 Timber Wharf Road, Stamford
Hill, N16 6DB   800-2525
          Fax: 880-2023
Supervision: London Beth Din and Kedassia.

Butchers

A. Perlmutter
1-2 Onslow Parade, Hampden Square,
Southgate, N14 5JN   361-5441/2
Supervision: London Board of Shechita.

D. Gilbert
880 High Road, Finchley, N12 9RH   445-2224
Supervision: London Board of Shechita.

Greenspans
9-11 Lyttelton Road, N2 0DW
          455-9921; 455-7709
          Fax: 455-3484
Supervision: London Board of Shechita.

Jack Schlagman
112 Regents Park Road, Finchley, N3 346-3598
Supervision: London Board of Shechita.

Mehadrin Meats, 25a Belfast Lane, Stamford
Hill, N16   806-7686; 806-3002
Supervision: Kedassia.

Miss G. Ismach, 230 Regents Park Road,
Finchley, N3   346-6554
Supervision: London Board of Shechita.

Groceries

The World of Kosher
25 Station Parade, Cockfosters Road,
Cockfosters, EN4 0DW   441-3621
Supervision: Federation of Synagogues.

Hotels

Eshel Hotel
Stamford Hill, N16   800-1445

Bed & Breakfasts

Pension Strom, 22 Rookwood Road, Stamford
Hill, N16 6SS   800-1151
Breakfast only. Other meals to order.

Museums

**Jewish Military Museum and Memorial
Room,** AJEX House, East Bank, Stamford Hill,
N16 5RT   800-2844; 802-7610
          Fax: 800-1117
Memorabilia, artefacts, medals, letters,
documents, pictures and uniforms all
illustrating British Jewry's contribution to the
Armed Forces of the Crown from the Crimea
to the present day. By appointment, Sunday
to Thursday, 11 am to 4 pm.

London Museum of Jewish Life
The Sternberg Centre, 80 East End Road,
Finchley, N3 2SY   349-1143
Permanent exhibitions traces history London
Jewry with reconstructions of a tailoring
workshop, an immigrant home and East
London bakery. Also organises temporary
exhibitions, educational programmes and
guided tours of Jewish London. Hours:
Monday to Thursday, 10:30 am to 5 pm;
Sunday (except during August and Bank
Holiday weekends), 10:30 am to 4:30 pm.
Closed Friday, Saturday and Jewish festivals,
public holidays and 25 December to 5 January.

Travel Agencies

Peltours, 11-19 Ballards Lane, Finchley, N3
1UX   346-9144
          Fax: 343-0579

Northwest London

Area telephone code (0181)

Mikvaot

Edgware & District Communal Mikvah
Edgware United Synagogue Grounds, 22
Warwick Avenue Drive, Edgware   958-3233

Kingsbury United Synagogue, Kingsbury
Road, Kingsbury, NW9 8XR   204-6390

North West London Communal Mikvah
10a Shirehall Lane, Hendon, NW4   202-1427
          Evenings: 202-8517/5706

Restaurants

Fish

Croft Garden Restaurant
44 Ravenscroft Avenue, Golders Green, NW11
8AY   458-3331
          Fax: 455-9175

Supervision: Kedassia.

Folman's, 134 Brent Street,
Hendon, NW4   202-1339; 202-5592
Supervision: Federation Kashrus Board.
Kosher fish restaurant and take-away.

Meat

Amor, 8 Russell Parade,
Golders Green, NW11   458-4221
Supervision: Kedassia.

Blooms World-Famous Kosher Restaurant
130 Golders Green Road, Golders Green,
NW11 8HB   455-1338
Supervision: London Beth Din.
Free delivery service, air conditioned.

Catskills
1-4 Belmont Parade, Finchley Road, Temple
Fortune, NW11   458-1999
Supervision: London Beth Din.
Kosher deli, diner, restaurant. Open Motzei
Shabbat in winter.

Dizengoff
118 Golders Green Road, Golders Green,
NW11 8HB   458-7003
                                 458-9958
                             Fax: 381-4902
Supervision: Sephardi Kashrut Authority.
Grilled meat our specialty. Hours: Sunday to
Thursday, 11 am to midnight; Friday, to 4 pm;
Saturday night, winter only.

Erez
239 Golders Green Road, Golders Green,
NW11 9PN   458-0444
Supervision: Federation Kashrus Board.
Glatt kosher Lebanese and Iranian restaurant.
Take-away service available.

Kaifeng
51 Church Road, Hendon, NW4 4DU 203-7888
                             Fax: 203-8263
          Web site: www.kaifeng.co.uk
Supervision: London Beth Din.
Luxury Chinese restaurant with take-away and
delivery service. Weekday lunches, 50% off
menu prices. Free delivery with minimum
order of £25. Hours: Sunday to Thursday,
12:30 pm to 2:30 pm, 6 pm to 11 pm; Open
Saturday evening, September to April.

Marcus's
5 Hallswelle Parade, Finchley Road, Golders
Green, NW11 0DL   458-4670
Supervision: London Beth Din.

Sami's Restaurant
157 Brent Street, Hendon, NW4 4DJ 203-8088
                             Fax: 203-1040
Supervision: Federation Kashrus Board.

Glatt kosher middle eastern cuisine.
Mashgiach temidi.

Solly's
148a Golders Green Road, Golders Green,
NW11   455-0004
Supervision: London Beth Din.

Solly's Exclusive
146-150 Golders Green Road, Golders Green,
NW11   455-2121
Supervision: London Beth Din.

The White House Kosher Restaurant
10 Bell Lane, Hendon, NW4   203-2427
                             Fax: 203-2527
Supervision: London Beth Din.

Dairy

Café on the Green
122 Golders Green Road, Golders Green,
NW11 8HB   209-0232
Supervision: London Beth Din.
Chalav Yisrael. Open Motzei Shabbat in
winter.

Cassit, 225 Golders Green Road, Golders
Green, NW11   455-8195
Supervision: Federation Kashrus Board.
0181 455 0379 for home delivery service.
Delivery times: Sunday to Thursday, 12:30 pm
to 11 pm. Delivery areas: NW3, NW4, NW11,
N3. Minimum delivery order, £10.

Milk n' Honey, 124 Golders Green Road,
Golders Green, NW11   455-0664
Supervision: London Beth Din.

Old Jaffa
27 Finchley Lane, Hendon, NW4   203-0750
Supervision: Sephardi Kashrut Authority.

Tasti Pizza
252 Golders Green Road, Golders Green,
NW11   209-0023
Supervision: London Beth Din and Kedassia.

Bakeries

Carmelli Bakery
128 Golders Green Road, Golders Green,
NW11   455-2074
Supervision: London Beth Din and Kedassia.

Cousins Bagel Bakery
109 Golders Green Road, Golders Green,
NW11   201-9694
Supervision: Sephardi Kashrut Authority.

Creme de la Creme
5 Temple Fortune Parade, Bridge Lane, Golders
Green, NW11 1QN   458-9090
Supervision: London Beth Din.

Daniel's Bagel Bakery
12-13 Hallswelle Parade, Finchley Road,
Golders Green, NW11   455-5826
Supervision: London Beth Din.
Hours: Sunday to Wednesday, 7 am to 9 pm;
Thursday, to 10 pm; Friday, to 1½ hours
before Shabbat.

David Bagel Bakery
38 Vivian Avenue, Hendon, NW4   203-9995
Supervision: Kedassia.

Dino's Bakery, 11 Edgwarebury Lane,
Edgware, HA8 8LH   958-1554
                        Fax: 958-2554
Supervision: London Beth Din.

Dino's Bakery, 106 Brent Street, Hendon,
NW4 2HH   202-1155
Supervision: London Beth Din.

Hendon Bagel Bakery
55-57 Church Road, Hendon, NW4   203-6919
                        Fax: 203-8843
Supervision: Kedassia.

Keene's Patisserie
Unit 6, Mill Hill Ind. Est., Flower Lane, Mill Hill,
NW7 2HU   906-3729
Supervision: London Beth Din.

M & D Grodzinski, 6 Edgwarebury Lane,
Edgware, HA8   958-1205
Supervision: London Beth Din.

M & D Grodzinski, 9 Northways Parade,
Hampstead, NW3   722-4944
Supervision: London Beth Din.

M & D Grodzinski Hot Bread Shop
223 Golders Green Road, Golders Green,
NW11   458-3654
                        Fax: 905-5382
Supervision: London Beth Din and Kedassia.
Hours: Sunday to Thursday, 6 am to 10 pm;
Tuesday, to 9 pm; Friday, to ¾ hour before
Shabbat.

Parkway Patisserie Ltd., 30a North End Road,
Golders Green, NW11   455-5026
Supervision: London Beth Din and Kedassia.
Hours: Sunday, 7:30 am to 1:30 pm; Monday
to Thursday, to 5:30 pm; Friday, to 1 hour
before Shabbat.

Taboon Continental Bakery
17 Russell Parade, Golders Green Road,
Golders Green, NW11   455-7451
Supervision: Sephardi Kashrut Authority.

The Cake Company, Basement, 2-4 Sentinel
Square, Hendon, NW4 2EL   202-2327
Supervision: London Beth Din.

Toast 'n' Roll Sandwich Bar, 9 Golders Green
Road, Golders Green, NW11   455-2232
Supervision: Sephardi Kashrut Authority.

Woodberry Down Bakery
47 Brent Street, Hendon, NW4   202-9962
Supervision: London Beth Din.

Butchers

Frohwein's, 1095 Finchley Road
Temple Fortune, NW11   455-9848
Supervision: Kedassia.

H. Gross & Son
6 Russell Parade, Golders Green Road, Golders
Green, NW11   455-6662
Supervision: London Board of Shechita.

Ivor Silverman, 4 Canons Corner, London
Road, Stanmore   958-8682/2692
                        Fax: 958-1725
Supervision: London Board of Shechita.

Ivor Silverman, 358 Uxbridge Road,
Hatch End, HA4 4HP   428-6564
Supervision: London Board of Shechita.

J.M. Glass, 100 High Road, Bushey 420-4443
Supervision: London Board of Shechita.

L. Botchin, 423 Kingsbury Road, Kingsbury,
NW9   204-2236
Supervision: London Board of Shechita.

La Boucherie
4 Cat Hill, East Barnet, EN4 8JB   449-9215
                        Fax: 441-1848
Supervision: London Board of Shechita.

Louis Mann, 23 Edgwarebury Lane, Edgware,
HA8   958-3789
Supervision: London Board of Shechita.

Menachem's
15 Russell Parade, Golders Green Road,
Golders Green, NW11   201-8629
Supervision: London Board of Shechita.

R. Wolff, 84 Edgware Way,
Edgware, HA8 8JS   958-8454
Supervision: London Board of Shechita.

Fishmongers

Leveyuson
47a Brent Street, Hendon, NW4   202-7834
Supervision: London Board of Shechita.

Sam Stoller
28 Temple Fortune Parade, Finchley Road,
Golders Green, NW11   455-1957; 458-1429
Supervision: Sephardi Kashrut Authority.
76 High Road, Bushey   421-8168
Supervision: Sephardi Kashrut Authority.

CROFT COURT HOTEL
CROFT GARDEN RESTAURANT

44 Ravenscroft Avenue, London NW11 8AY
Telephone: 0181 458 3331 Fax: 0181 455 9175

The hotel is situated in Golders Green and is well positioned for easy access into the West End. All rooms have en suite facilities and are equipped with direct dial telephone, tea/coffee facilities, colour television and hairdryer. Safe and fax facilities are available.

We serve a cooked breakfast and traditional Shabbat meals are glatt kosher.

The Restaurant, which is under the highest Rabbinical supervision "**Kedassia**" is fortunate to have a first class chef who not only creates the most delicious food, but ensures the presentation is as tempting. The menu is centred on French inspired cuisine, various fish and vegetarian dishes to suit the most discerning diners.

We also have facilities to cater for **private parties**, Barmitzvah, Batmitzvah, Anniversary, Sheva Berachot, Engagements, Weddings.

The restaurant is open on Sundays from 12 noon and weekdays from 6pm.

Contact 0181-458 3331 for reservations.

United Kingdom

Groceries

B Kosher
91 Bell Lane, Hendon, NW4   202-1711
Opposite Vincent Court.

Carmel Fruit Shop
40 Vivian Avenue, Hendon, NW4   202-9587
Fresh fruit and vegetables as well as a good
supply of kosher products, cakes and biscuits.

Kosher King, 235 Golders Green Road,
Golders Green, NW11   455-8329/1429

Kosher Paradise, 10 Ashbourne Parade,
Temple Fortune, NW11   455-2454

Maxine's
20 Russell Parade, Golders Green Road,
Golders Green, NW11   458-3102

Pelter Stores
82 Edgware Way, Edgware, HA8   958-6910
Supervision: Federation Kashrus Board.

Yarden, 123 Golders Green Road, Golders
Green, NW11   458-0979
Free delivery on orders over £25. Hours:
Sunday, Wednesday, Thursday, 8 am to 10
pm; Monday, Tuesday, 8 am to 9 pm; Friday,
8 am.

Hotels

13 Brook Avenue,
Edgware, HA8 9XF   958-4409

Central Hotel, 35 Hoop Lane, Golders Green,
NW11 8BS   458-5636
                    Fax: 455-4792
Private bathrooms and parking. Credit cards
accepted.

Croft Court Hotel
44 Ravenscroft Avenue, Golders Green, NW11
8AY   458-3331
          Fax: 455-9175
Supervision: London Beth Din.
Twenty rooms. Meals need to be pre-booked.

Golders Green Hotel
147-149 Golders Green Road, Golders Green,
NW11 9BN   458-7127/9

Hampstead House Residential Hotel
12 Lyndhurst Gardens,
Hampstead, NW3 5NR   794-6036

Woodstock Guesthouse
68 Woodstock Avenue, Golders Green, NW11
9RJ   209-0637; 455-4120

Bed & Breakfasts

3 Elm Close, Hendon, NW4 2PH   202-0642
Breakfast only. Other meals by arrangement.

26 Highfield Avenue, Golders Green, NW11
9ET   455-7136

Kacenberg's, 1 Alba Gardens, Golders Green,
NW11 9NS   455-3780
                    Fax: 381-4250
Shabbat meals available. Strictly Orthodox.

Travel Agencies

Peltours, 240 Station Road, Edgware, HA8
7AU   958-1144
                    Fax: 958-5515

Sabra Travel Ltd., 9 Edgwarebury Lane,
Edgware, HA8 8LH   958-3244-7

Travelink
50 Vivian Avenue, Hendon NW4   931-8000
Specialise in chartered flights to Israel.

Booksellers

J. Aisenthal, 11 Ashbourne Parade, Finchley
Road, Temple Fortune, NW11 0AD   455-0501

Joseph's Bookstore
2 Ashbourne Parade, Finchley Road, Temple
Fortune, NW11 0AD   731-7575

Torah Treasures, 4 Sentinel Square, Brent
Street, Hendon, NW4 2EL   202-3134
                    Fax: 202-3161

South London

Area telephone code (0181)

Mikvaot

South London Mikvah, 42 St Georges Road,
Wimbledon, SW19 4ED   944-7149

Butchers

L. Kelman
49 Streatham Hill, Streatham, SW2   674-3626
Supervision: London Board of Shechita.

S. Samuels, 30 Red Lion Street,
Richmond   940-3060; 940-6282
Supervision: London Board of Shechita.

Libraries

British Library, Oriental & Indian Collections
197 Blackfriars Road,
SE1 8NG   (0171) 928-9531 ext:262
The Hebrew section contains 70,000 printed
books and 13,000 manuscripts and fragments.
Hours: daily, 9:30 am to 4:45 pm; Saturday,
9:30 am to 12:45 pm.

West London

Area telephone code (0181)

Bakeries

Keene's Patisserie
192 Preston Road, Wembley   904-5952
Supervision: London Beth Din.

Parkway Patisserie Ltd.
204 Preston Road, Wembley   904-7736
Supervision: London Beth Din and Kedassia.
Hours: Sunday, 7:30 am to 1:30 pm; Monday
to Thursday, to 5:30 pm; Friday, to 1 hour
before Shabbat.

Butchers

J. Kelman, 198 Preston Road,
Wembley, HA9 9NQ   904-7625
          Fax: 904-0897
Supervision: London Board of Shechita.

M. Lipowicz
9 Royal Parade, Ealing, W5   997-1722
Supervision: London Board of Shechita.

Travel Agencies

Magic of Israel
47 Shepherds Bush Green, Shepherds Bush,
W12 8PS   743-9000

Regions

Aldershot (Hampshire)

Contact Information

**Inquires to Senior Jewish Chaplain H.M.
Forces,** 25 Enford Street, London, W1H 2DD
          (0171) 724-7778
          Fax: (0171) 706-1710

Basildon (Essex)

Contact Information

Inquires to M. Kochmann
3 Furlongs, SS16 4BW   (01268) 524947

Birmingham (West Midlands)

Area telephone code (0121)

This Jewish community is one of the oldest in
the Provinces, dating from at least 1730.
Birmingham was a centre from which Jewish
pedlars covered the surrounding country week
by week, returning home for Shabbat.

The first synagogue of which there is any
record was in The Froggery in 1780. There was
a Jewish cemetery in the same neighbourhood
in 1730, and Moses Aaron is said to have been
born here in 1718. The synagogue of 1780
was extended in 1791, 1809 and 1827. A new
and larger synagogue, popularly known as
'Singers Hill', opened in 1856. Today's Jewish
population stands at about 2,300.

Representative Organisations

**Representative Council of Birmingham &
Midland Jewry**
37 Wellington Road, B15 2ES   236-1801
          Evenings: 440-4142
          Fax: 236-9906

Synagogues

Birmingham Hebrew Congregation
Singer's Hill, Ellis Street, B1 1HL   643-0884

Central Synagogue, 133 Pershore Road, B5
7PA   440-4044

New Synagogue
11 Park Road, B13 8AB   449-3544

Progressive Synagogue
4 Sheepcote Street, B16 8AA   643-5640

Mikvaot

133 Pershore Road, B5 7PA   440-5853

Kashrut Information

Shechita Board
Singers Hill, Ellis Street, B1 1HL   643-0884

Contact Information

Lubavitch Centre
95 Willows Road, B12 9QF   440-6673
Bookshop on premises.

Tourist Information

Israel Information Centre & Bookshop
Singers Hill, Blucher Street, B1 1QL   643-2688

Delicatessens

A. Gee
75 Pershore Road, B6 7NX   440-2160
Kosher butcher, baker and deli.

Caterers

B'tayavon, 20 Hampton Court, George Road,
B15 1PU   456-2172
Golda, 125 Salisbury road, B13 8LA   449-2261
    440-1925

Blackpool

Area telephone code (01253)

Synagogues

Orthodox
United Hebrew Congregation
Synagogue Chambers, Leamington Road, FY1
4HD   28164

Reform

Reform Jewish Congregation, 40 Raikes
Parade, FY1 4EX   23687

Delicatessen

Lytham Delicatessen
53 Warton Street, Lytham St. Annes   735861

Bournemouth (Dorset)

Area telephone code (01202)
The Bournemouth Hebrew Congregation was established in 1905, when the Jewish population numbered fewer than 20 families. Today, the town's permanent Jewish residents number 3,500 out of a total population of some 151,000. During the holiday season, however, there are many more Jews in Bournemouth, for it is an extremely popular resort with kosher hotels, guest houses and other holiday accommodation.

Representative Organisations

**Bournemouth Jewish Representative
Council**   762-101

Synagogues

Orthodox
Bournemouth Hebrew Congregation
Synagogue Chambers, Wootton Gardens, BH1
1PW   557-433

Reform
Bournemouth Reform Synagogue, 53
Christchurch Road, BH1 3PN   557-736

Delicatessens

Louise's Deli
164 Old Christchurch Road, BH1 1NU 295-979
Supervision: Kedassia.
Stocks kosher meat, groceries, challot.

Hotels

Grove House Hotel
61 Grove Road, BH1 3AT   554-161

Kosher

New Ambassador Hotel
Meyrich Road, East Cliff, BH1 3DP   555-453
Supervision: London Beth Din.
112 rooms, all with bathroom en suite.

Normandie Hotel, Manor Road, E. Overcliff
Drive, BH1 3HL   552-246
                              Fax: 291-178
Supervision: Kedassia.
71 rooms.

Bradford (Yorkshire)

Area telephone code (01274)
The Jewish community, although only about
140 years old, has exercised much influence
on the city's staple industry: wool. Jews of
German descent developed the export trade of
wool yarns and fabrics.

Synagogues

Orthodox

Bradford Hebrew Congregation
Springhurst Road, Shipley, BD18 3DN 728925
Services 10am monthly on Shabbat
Mevarchim, High holy-days & certain festivals.

Reform

Bradford Synagogue, Bowland Street,
Manningham Lane, BD1 3BW   544420

Brighton and Hove (Sussex)

Area telephone code (01273)
The first known Jewish resident of Brighton
lived there in 1767. The earliest synagogue
was founded in Jew Street in 1789. Henry
Solomon, vice-president of the congregation,
was the first Chief Constable of the town. He
was murdered in 1844 by an insane youth. His
brother-in-law, Levi Emanuel Cohen, founded
the *Brighton Guardian*, and was twice elected

president of the Newspaper Society of Great
Britain. Other nineteenth-century notables
living in Brighton and Hove included Sir Isaac
Lyon Goldsmid and numerous members of the
Sassoon family. The town's Jewish population
today is about 8,000.

Community Organisations

Hillel House
18 Harrington Road, BN1 6RE   503450
Closed during summer vacation. Friday
evening meals available.

Lubavitch Chabad House
15 The Upper Drive, BN3 6GR   21919

Synagogues

Brighton & Hove Hebrew Congregation
Middle Street Synagogue, 66 Middle Street,
BN1 1AL   327785

West Hove Synagogue, 31 New Church Road,
Hove, BN3 4AD   776170

Hove Hebrew Congregation, 79 Holland
Road, Hove, BN3 1JN   732085

Reform

New, Palmeira Avenue, BN3 3GE 735343

Progressive

Progressive Synagogue
6 Landsdowne Road, BN3 1FF   737223

Mikvaot

Prince Regent Swimming Pool Cmplx., Church
Street, BN1 1YA   21919

Religious Organisations

Brighton & Hove Joint Kashrus Committee,
5 The Paddock, The Droveway, Hove   506574

Media

Sussex Jewish News, PO Box 1623   504455

Delicatessens

Cantor's of Hove
20 Richardson Road, Hove, BN3 5BB 723-669

Caterers

Angela Samuels Catering
5 St Keyne Avenue, Hove, BN3 4PN 422-224
Supervision: Brighton & Hove Kashrus
Committee.

Bristol (Avon)

Area telephone code (0117)

Bristol was one of the principal Jewish centres of medieval England. Even after the Expulsion from England in 1290 there were occasional Jewish residents or visitors. A community of Marranos lived here during the Tudor period. The next Jewish settlement in Bristol was around 1754 and its original synagogue opened in 1786. The present building dates from 1871 and incorporates fittings from the earlier building. The Jewish house at Clifton College (known as Polack's House) was founded in 1878 and is the only remaining Jewish house in a public school.

Organisations

Hillel House
45 Oakfield Road, Clifton, BS8 2BA   946-6589

Polack's House, Clifton College   973-7634

Synagogues

British Hebrew Congregation
9 Park Row, BS1 5LP   925-5160
Synagogue has kosher delicatessen, alternate Sundays, 10 am.

Progressive

Bristol & West Progressive Jewish Congregation, 43 Bannerman Road, Easton, BS5 0RR   954-1937
Judaica shop on premises.

Restaurants (Vegetarian)

Cherries
122 St Michaels Hill, BS2 8BU   929-3675

Millwards Vegetarian Restaurant, 40 Alfred Place, Kingsdown, BS2 8HD   924-5026

Cambridge (Cambridgeshire)

Area telephone code (01223)

Synagogues

Student Centre
3 Thompsons Lane, CB5 8AQ   68346
                                354783
Daily morning and evening service during term time. Shabbat morning during vacations, other services by arrangement.

Beth Shalom Reform Synagogue   365614

Kosher Food

There is a kosher canteen during term time serving lunch most weekdays and Friday night and Shabbat meals.   352145

Canterbury (Kent)

Area telephone code (01227)

Synagogues

The Old Synagogue, King Street
The Old Synagogue, an Egyptian-style building of 1847, stands in King Street and is now used by the Kings School for recitals.

Restaurants (Vegetarian)

Teapot Mother Earth
34 St Peter's Street, CT16 1BK   463-175

Cheltenham

Area telephone code (01242)

The congregation was established in 1824 and the present synagogue opened in 1839. However, after two generations, the congregation declined and the synagogue was closed in 1903. At the outbreak of the Second World War, the synagogue was re-opened following the influx of Jewish newcomers to the town. The congregation has its own cemetery on Elm Street, purchased in 1824.

Synagogues

St James Square   525032

Restaurant (Vegetarian)

The Barleycorn
317 High Street, GL50 3HN   241070

Chigwell (Essex)

Synagogues

Limes Avenue, Limes Farm Estate, IG7 5NT

Coventry (West Midlands)

Area telephone code (01203)

The Jewish presence in Coventry dates back to 1775, if not earlier.

Synagogues
Coventry Hebrew Congregation
Barras Lane, CV1 3BW   220168
Coventry Jewish Reform Community 672027

Eastbourne (Sussex)

Synagogues
22 Susans Road, BN21 3HA   (01435) 866928
                            Fax: (01435) 865783

Exeter (Devon)

Area telephone code (01392)

In pre-Expulsion times, Exeter was an important Jewish centre. The synagogue was built in 1763, while the cemetery in Magdalen Road dates from 1757.

Synagogues
Synagogue Place,
Mary Arches Street, EX4 3BA   51529

Restaurants *(Vegetarian)*
Brambles
31 New Bridge Street, EX4 3AH   74168
Herbies
15 North Street, EX4 3QS   58473

Gateshead (Tyne & Wear)

Area telephone code (0191)

A community with many schools, *yeshivot* and training institutions.

Synagogues
180 Bewick Road, NE8 1UF   477-0111
Mikva on premises. For appt: 477-3552

Bakeries
Stenhouse
215 Coatsworth Road, NE8 1SR   477-2001

Butchers
K.L. Kosher Butcher
83 Rodsley Avenue, NE8   477-3109
Kosher.

Booksellers

J. Lehmann
28-30 Grasmere Street, NE8 1TS   477-3523
Also has wholesale and mail order, 20
Cambridge Terrace, NE8 1RP   490-1692
Fax: 477-5955

Grasmere (Cumbria)

Hotels

Lancrigg Vegetarian Country House Hotel
Easedale, LA22 9QN   (015394) 35317

Grimsby (Humberside)

Synagogues

Sir Moses Montefiore Synagogue
Heneage Road, DN32 9DZ   (01472) 342579

Guildford (Surrey)

Synagogues

Guildford & District Synagogue, York Road,
GU1 4DR   (01483) 576470

Tourist Sites

Enquiries about the recent discovery of a
medieval synagogue in the town may be
addressed to the Guildford Museum.

Harlow (Essex)

Synagogues (Reform)

Harberts Road, CM19 4DT   416138

Harrogate (Yorkshire)

Synagogues

St Mary's Walk, HG2 0LW   (01423) 871713

Guest Houses

Amadeus Vegetarian Hotel
115 Franklin Road, HG1 5EN   (01423) 505151
Totally vegetarian and non-smoking. Meals for
resident guests only. 10 minutes walk from
railway station.

Hastings (Sussex)

Includes Bexhill, Battle, Rye and St Leonards.

Contact Information

Hastings District Jewish Society, c/o Mrs Ilse
Eton, 6 Gilbert Road, St Leonards-on-Sea, E.
Sussex, TN38 0RH   (01424) 436551

Hotels

Tower House Hotel
26-28 Tower Road West, St Leonards On Sea,
TN38 0RG   (01424) 42717

Hemel Hempstead
(Hertfordshire)

Synagogues

Morton House
Midland Road, HD1 1RP   (01923) 232007

Hornchurch (Essex)

Synagogues

Elm Park Synagogue, Woburn Avenue, Elm
Park, RM12 4NG   (01708) 449305

Hull (Humberside)

Area telephone code (01482)

In Hull, as in other English port towns, a
Jewish community was formed earlier than in
inland areas. The exact date is unknown, but it
is thought to be the early 1700s. There were
enough Jews in Hull to buy a former Roman
Catholic chapel, damaged in the Gordon Riots
of 1780, and turn it into a synagogue. A
cemetery is believed to have been acquired in
the late 1700s. Hull was then the principal
port of entry from northern Europe, and most
Jewish immigrants came through it. In 1851
the Jewish community numbered about 200.
Today, it numbers some 350 families. Both the
Old Hebrew Synagogue in Osborne Street and
the Central Synagogue in Cogan Street were
destroyed in air raids during the Second World
War. The two Orthodox congregations merged
in 1994 and moved to the new Pryme Street
building in the western suburbs, where most
of the community now live.

United Kingdom

Synagogues

Hull Hebrew Congregation
30 Pryme Street, Anlaby, HU10 6SH   653398
Reform Synagogue, Great Gutter Lane,
Willerby, HU10 7JT   656469

Kashrut Information

Board of Shechita, Mr E. Pearlman   653398

Museums

Hull Synagogue Museum
Linnaeus Street, HU3 2PD   26848
Fax: 568756
Correspondence: 771 Anlaby Road, HU3 2PD.

Lancaster (Lancashire)

Bed & Breakfast

Lancaster University Jewish Society,
Interfaith Chaplaincy Centre,
University of Lancaster, Bailrigg Lane, LA1
4YW   (01524) 65201, ext. 4075
Jewish rooms and kosher kitchen.
Fairview, 32 Hornby Road, Caton, LA2 9QS
(01524) 770118

Leeds (Yorkshire)

Area telephone code (0113)
The Leeds Jewish community is the second
largest in the provinces, and numbers about
12,000. The community dates only from 1804,
although a few Jews are known to have lived
there in the previous half-century. The first
synagogue was built in 1860, when there
were about 60 Jewish families.

Representative Organisations

Leeds Jewish Representative Council
c/o Shadwell Lane Synagogue   269-7520
Fax: 237-0851
Publishes Year Book.

Community Organisations

The Club, Lubavitch Centre, 168 Shadwell
Lane, LS17 8AD   266-3311
Fax: 237-1130
Supervision: Leeds Kashrut Authority/Beth Din.
A community centre. Restaurant on premises
which is currently not open. Call to see if it
has re-opened.

Synagogues

Orthodox

Beth Hamedrash Hagadol, 399 Street Lane,
LS17 6HQ   269-2181
Chassidishe, c/o Donisthorpe Hall, Shadwell
Lane, LS17 6AW
Etz Chaim
411 Harrogate Road, LS17 7BY   266-2214
Shadwell Lane Synagogue
(United Hebrew Congregation), 151 Shadwell
Lane, LS17 8DW   269-6141
Fax: 237-0851
Shomrei Hadass
368 Harrogate Road, LS17 6QB   268-1461

Reform

Sinai, Roman Avenue, off Street Lane, LS8
2AN   266-5256

Religious Organisations

Beth Din   269-6902
Fax: 237-0893
Information about kosher food and
accommodation may be obtained here.

Mikvaot

411 Harrogate Road, LS17 7BY   237-1096
(answerphone)
368 Harrogate Road, LS17 6QB   268-1461
at rear of Shomrei Hadass shul.

Bakeries

Chalutz Bakery
378 Harrogate Road, LS17 6PY   269-1350
Supervision: Leeds Kashrut Commission.
Hours: Monday to Thursday, 8 am to 6 pm;
Friday, to 1 hour before Shabbat; Saturday,
from 1 hour after Shabbat to 2 pm Sunday.

Butchers and Delicatessens

Fisher's Deli
391 Harrogate Road, LS17 6DJ   268-6944
Supervision: Leeds Beth Din.
Gourmet Foods
Sandhill Parade, 584 Harrogate Road, LS17
8DP   268-2726
Supervision: Leeds Beth Din.
The Kosherie
410 Harrogate Road, LS17 6PY   268-2943
Supervision: Leeds Beth Din.

Hotels

Beegee's Guest House
18 Moor Allerton Drive, off Street Lane,
Moortown, LS17 6RZ   293-5469
                                      Fax: 275-3300
Near all synagogues.

Hansa's
72 North Street, LS2 7PN   244-4408
Vegetarian restaurant as well.

Libraries

Jewish Library
Porton Collection; Central Library, Municipal
Buildings, LS1 3AB   246-2016

Media

Jewish Telegraph
1 Shaftesbury Avenue, LS8 1DR   266-6000

Leicester (Leicestershire)

Area telephone code (0116)
There has been a Jewish presence here since
the Middle Ages, but the first record of a
'Jews' Synagogue' dates from 1861 in the
Leicester Directory.

Synagogues

Community Centre
Highfield Street, LE2 0NQ   270-6622
Mikva on premises.

Progressive Jewish Congregation 283-2927

Restaurants *(Vegetarian)*

Blossoms
17b Cank Street, LE1 5YP   253-9535

The Ark, St Martins Square   262-0909

The Chaat House
108 Belgrave Road, LE4 5AT   266-0513

The Good Earth
19 Free Lane, LE1 1JX   262-6260

Groceries

Tesco's, Beaumont Leys
A limited range of kosher delicatessen is now
stocked here.

Libraries

Jewish Library and Bookshop, Community
Hall, Highfield Street, LE2 0NQ   273-7620

Lincoln (Lincolnshire)

Lincoln was one of the centres of medieval
Jewry. One of England's oldest stone houses
in the city is known as Aaron the Jew's House.
The site of the old Jewry is remembered now
at Jews' Court. In the cathedral is a recent
token of ecclesiastical apology for the
thirteenth-century incidence of the blood libel
retold in Chaucer. Jews returned to the area in
the nineteenth century. The current
community is of very recent date.

Community Organisations

Lincolnshire Jewish Community, c/o Edna
Creed, Plot 62, Hales Lane, Chapel Heath,
Navenby, LN5 0TP

Liverpool (Merseyside)

Area telephone code (0151)
There is evidence of an organised community
before 1750, believed to have been composed
of Sephardi Jews and to have had some
connection with the West Indies or with
Dublin, although some authorities believe they
were mainly German Jews. This small
community, which was known to John Wesley,
the religious reformer, declined at first, but
was reinforced by a new wave of settlers,
mostly from Europe in about 1770. The largely
Ashkenazi Jews were to some degree
intending emigrants for the USA and the West
Indies who changed their minds and stayed in
Liverpool. By 1807 the community had a
building in Seel Street, the parent of today's
synagogue in Princes Road, one of the
handsomest in the country.

Representative Organisations

Merseyside Jewish Representative Council
433 Smithdown Road, L15 3JL   733-2292

Synagogues

Orthodox

Allerton, cnr. Mather & Booker Avenues, L18
9TB   427-6848

Childwall Hebrew Congregation, Dunbabin
Road, L15 6XL   722-2079

Greenbank Drive Hebrew Congregation
Greenbank Drive, L17 1AN   733-1417

Old Hebrew Congregation
Princes Road, L8 1TG   709-3431

Ullet Road Hebrew Congregation
101 Ullet Road, L17

Progressive
Liverpool Progressive Synagogue
28 Church Road North, L15 6TF   733-5871

Mikvaot
Childwall Hebrew Congregation
Dunbabin Road, L15 6XL   722-2079

Kashrut Information
Liverpool Kashrut Commission (inc. Liverpool Shechita Board), c/o Shifrin House, 433 Smithdown Road, L15 3JL   733-2292

Media

Newspapers
Jewish Telegraph, Harold House, Dunbabin Road, L15 6XL   475-6666
Fax: 475-2222

Restaurants
Harold House
Dunbabin Road, L15 6XL   475-5825
Kosher.

JLGB Centre   475-5825; 475-5671
Open Sun, Tues., Thurs. 6.30-11.00pm. Licensed bar. Out-of-town visitors welcome. Also take-away service.

Vegetarian
Munchies Eating House
Myrtle Parade   709-7896

Caterers
Elaine Marco
20 Beauclair Drive, L15 6XG   722-1536
M&E Stoops Catering
23 Montclair Drive, L18   722-7459

Self-catering
Student Accommodation
Conference Office, Liverpool Uni. Halls of Resids., PO Box 147, L69 3BX   794-6440
Containing more than 2,000 single bedrooms. These are available during vacations for conferences, student groups, tourists, etc. No kosher catering facilities available, however. Also available, self-catering flats.

Booksellers
Liverpool Jewish Resource Centre, Harold House, Dunbabin Road, L15 6XL   722-3514
Fax: 475-2212
Large range of audio-visual and printed materials for sale or hire. Hours: Monday to Thursday, 2:30 pm to 5 pm; Sunday, 11 am to 1 pm. Answerphone.

Loughton (Essex)

Synagogues
Loughton, Chigwell & District Synagogue
Borders Lane, IG10 1TE   (0181) 508-0303
Fri Even. 8pm; Sat Morn. 9.30am.

Luton (Bedfordshire)

Synagogues
PO Box 215, LU1 1HW   (01582) 25032
Fri night and Sabbath morn. services. Office open 9.30am to 12.30pm on Sundays.
Chiltern Progressive Synagogue
39 Broadacres, LU2 7YF   (01234) 21837

Maidenhead (Berkshire)

Maidenhead is a growing Jewish area. The synagogue, membership 500+ families, covers the Berkshire and Buckinghamshire areas.

Synagogues (Reform)
9 Boyn Hill Avenue, SL6 4ET   (01628) 73012
Services; Fri 8.30pm; Sat 10.30am.

Manchester

Area telephone code (0161)

The Manchester Jewish community is the second largest in the United Kingdom, numbering about 35,000. There was no organised community until 1780. A cemetery was acquired in 1794. The present Great Synagogue claims with justice to be the direct descendant of this earliest community. The leaders of Manchester Jewry in those early days had without exception come from the neighbouring relatively important Jewish community of Liverpool. After the Continental revolutions of 1848, the arrival of 'liberal' Jews began. One of them, a Hungarian rabbi and soldier of the Revolution, Solomon Schiller-Szinessy, became minister of a Reform synagogue established in 1856. In 1871 a small Sephardi group from North Africa and the Levant drew together and formed a congregation, which extended to fill two handsome synagogues. However, one has now been turned into a Jewish museum.

Greater Manchester

Synagogues

Orthodox

Adass Yeshurun, Cheltenham Crescent., Salford, M7 0FE   792-1233

Adath Yisroel Nusach Ari, Upper Park Road, Salford, M7 0HL   740-3905

Bury Hebrew Congregation, Sunnybank Road, Bury, BL9 8EP   796-5062

Central & North Manchester (incorporating Hightown Central and Beth Jacob), Leicester Road, Salford, M7 4GP   740-4830

Cheetham Hebrew Congregation, 453-5 Cheetham Hill Road, M8 9PA   740-7788

Congregation of Spanish and Portuguese Jews, 18 Moor Lane., Kersal, Salford, M7 0WX   773-2954

Hale & District Hebrew Congregation, Shay Lane, Hale Barns, Ches., WA15 8PA   980-8846

Heaton Park Hebrew Congregation, Ashdown, Middleton Road, M8 6JX   740-4766

Higher Crumpsall & Higher Broughton, Bury Old Road, Salford M7 4PX   740-1210

Higher Prestwich, 445 Bury Old Road, Prestwich, M25 1QP   773-4800

Hillock Hebrew Congregation, Ribble Drive, Whitefield, M45   766-1162

Holy Law South Broughton Congregation, Bury Old Road, Prestwich, M25 0EX 792-6349
                                           721-4705

Kahal Chassidim, 62 Singleton Road, Salford M7 0LU   740-1629

Machzikei Hadass, 17 Northumberland Street, Salford, M7 0FE   792-1313

Manchester Great & New Synagogue, Stenecourt, Holden Road, Salford, M7 4LN   792-8399

North Salford
2 Vine St., Salford, M7 0NX   792-3278

Ohel Torah, 132 Leicester Road, Salford, M7 0EA   740-6678

Prestwich Hebrew Congregation, Bury New Road, M25 9WN   773-1978
                                      Fax: 773-7015

Sale & District Hebrew Congregation, 14 Hesketh Road, Sale, M33 5AA   973-2172

Sedgley Park (Shomrei Hadass), Park View Road, Prestwich, M25 5FA   773-6092

Sha'are Sedek Synagogue & Talmud Torah, Old Lansdowne Road, W. Didsbury, M20 8NZ   445-5731

South Manchester, Wilbraham Road, Fallowfield, M14 6JS   224-1366
                                      Fax. 225-8033

United Synagogue
Meade Hill Road, M8 4LR   740-9586

Whitefield Hebrew Congregation, Park Lane, Whitefield, M45 7PB   766-3732
                                      Fax: 767-9453

Withington Congregation of Spanish & Portuguese Jews, 8 Queenston Road, West Didsbury, M20 2WZ   445-1943
                                      Fax: 434-8094

Yeshurun Hebrew Congregation, Coniston Road, Gatley, Cheshire, SK8 4AP   428-8242

Reform

Cheshire Reform Congregation
Menorah Synagogue, Altrincham Road, M22 4RZ   428-7746

Manchester Reform Synagogue, Jackson's Row, M2 5NH   834-0415

Sha'arei Shalom, North Manchester Reform Congregation, Elms Street., Whitefield, M45 8GQ   796-6736

Mikvaot

Manchester & District Mikva, Sedgley Park Road, Prestwich   773-1537; 773-7403

Manchester Communal Mikvah
Broome Holme, Tetlow Lane, Salford, M7 0BU   792-3970
Appointments for Friday and Yom Tov evenings   740-4071; 740-5199.

Naomi Greenberg South Manchester Mikvah, Hale Synagogue, Shay Lane, Hale Barns   904-8296
Use is by appointment only.

Whitefield Mikvah
Park Lane, Whitefield, M45 7PB   796-1054
Ansaphone   Evenings: 792-0306
Use is by appointment only.

Religious Organisations

Machzikei Hadass, 17 Northumberland Street, Salford, M7 0FE   792-1313

Media

Newspapers

Jewish Telegraph
Telegraph House, 11 Park Hill, Bury Old Road, Prestwich, M25 0HH   740-9321
   Fax: 740-9325

Kashrut Information

Manchester Beth Din
435 Cheetham Hill Road, M8 0PF   740-9711
   Fax: 721-4249
They certify *all* the following restaurants, bakeries, butchers, delicatessens, caterers, groceries and hotels. Contact them to ensure that the establishment is still certified.

Restaurants

Antonio's, JCLC, Corner Bury Old Road & Park Road   795-8911

J.S. Kosher Restaurant, 7 Kings Road, Prestwich, M25 0LE   798-7776
Glatt kosher.

Bakeries

Brackman's
43 Leicester Road, Salford, M7   792-1652

Broughton Bakery
18 Trafalgar Street, Cambridge Industrial Area, Salford, M7   839-5224

Crusty Corner
24 Bury New Road, Prestwich   773-7997

Jack Maurer Patisserie
70 St James' Road, Salford, M7   792-3751

State Fayre Bakeries
Unit 1, Empire Street, M3   832-2911

Swiss Cottage Patisserie
118 Rectory Lane, Prestwich   798-0897

Vera Issler Patisserie
3 Waterpark Road, Salford, M7   792-2778

Butchers

A1 Kosher Meats
445 Bury New Road, Prestwich   773-6601

Hymark Kosher Meat Ltd, 39 Wilmslow Road, Cheadle, Cheshire   428-3400

J.A. Hyman (Titanic) Ltd
123/9 Waterloo Road, M8   792-1888

Sells groceries as well.

Joseph Halberstadt
55 Leicester Road, Salford, M7   792-1109

Kosher Foods
49 Bury New Road, Prestwich   773-1308
Sells groceries as well.

Lloyd Grosberg (J. Kreger)
102 Barlow Moor Road, M20   445-4983

Meat at Abramsons
61 Bury Old Road, Prestwich   773-2020

Park Lane Kosher Meats
142 Park Lane, Whitefield   766-5091

Vidal's Kosher Meats
75 Windsor Road, Prestwich   740-3365

Delicatessens

Cottage Deli
83 Park Lane, Whitefield   766-6216

Deli King
Kings Road, Prestwich, M25 8LQ   798-7370
   Fax: 798-5654
Hours: Sunday to Friday, 8:30 am to 6 pm.

Haber's, 8 Kings Road, Prestwich   773-2046

Hyman's Delicatessen, 41 Wilmstow Road, Cheadle, Cheshire   491-1100

Jehu Delis and Take Away
5 Parkhill, Bury Old Road, Prestwich   740-2816

Caterers

Celia Clyne Banqueting
54 Chapeltown Street, M1 2NN   273-8888
   Fax: 273-8890

I&M Kosher Banqueting Caterers
Unit 17, Cambridge Industrial Estate, Salford, M7   832-2167

Renée Hodari Specialist Kosher Caterers
36 Brooklawn Drive, Withington, M20 9GZ   445-7170

Sheila Mendelson Catering, 81-87 Silverdale Road, Gatley, SK8 4QR   428-1477

Simon's Catering
105 Leicester Road, Salford, M7   740-3905

Groceries

S. Halpern
59 Leicester Road, Salford, M7   792-1752

State Fayre
77 Middleton Road, M8   740-3435

State Fayre
53 Bury Old Road, Prestwich   773-7630

Hotels

Fulda's Hotel, 144 Old Bury Road, Salford,
M7 4QY   740-4748
                                    Fax: 740-4551
Four star hotel open all year. Glatt kosher.
Within easy access of motorways, and
uniquely placed in the heart of the
Manchester Jewish community in Broughton
Park. Within easy walking distance of
numerous synagogues and shopping facilities.

Museums

Manchester Jewish Museum, 190 Cheetham
Hill Road, M8 8LW   834-9879; 832-7353
Exhibitions, heritage trails, demonstrations
and talks. Calendar of events available on
request. Educational visits for schools and
adult groups must be booked in advance.
Open Mon.-Thurs., 10.30am to 4pm Sundays
10.30am to 5pm Admission charge.

Libraries

Central Library
St Peter's Square, M2 5PD   234-1983; 1984
Large collection of Jewish books for reference
and loan, including books in Hebrew. Contact
the Social Sciences Library.

Travel Agencies

Goodmos Tours
23 Leicester Road, Salford, M7 0AS   792-7333
ITS: Israel Travel Service
546-550, Royal Exchange, Old Bank Street, M2
7EN   839-1111
                                    Fax: 839-0000
Peltours Ltd
27-29 Church Street, M4 1QA   834-3721
                                    Fax: 832-9343

Booksellers

B. Horwitz
20 Bury Old Road, Prestwich, M8   740-5897
B. Horwitz
2 Kings Road, Prestwich, M25 0LE   773-4956
                                    Fax: 740-5897
                                    Email: broom49@aol.com
Hasefer Book Store
18 Merrybower Road, Salford, M7   740-3013
J. Goldberg, 11 Parkside Avenue, Salford, M7
0HB   740-0732
Jewish Book Centre, 25 Ashbourne Grove,
Salford, M7 4DB   792-1253

Hours: Sunday to Thursday, 9 am to 9 pm;
Friday, to 1 am.

Margate (Kent)

Synagogues

Godwin Road,
Cliftonville, CT9 2HA   (01843) 223219

Middlesbrough (Cleveland)

Synagogues

Park Road South, TS5 6LE   (01642) 819034

Restaurants (Vegetarian)

Filberts
47 Borough Road, TS1 4AF   (01642) 245-455

Milton Keynes (Middlesex)

Synagogues

Milton Keynes & District Reform Synagogue
Tinkers Bridge Meeting Place (01908) 569-661

Butchers

Gilbert's Kosher Foods, Kestrel House, Mount
Avenue, MK1 1LJ   (01908) 646-787
                                 Fax: (01908) 646-788
Supervision: London Board of Shechita.

Newark (Nottinghamshire)

Museums

Beth Shalom Holocaust Memorial Centre
Laxton, NG22 0PA   (01623) 836-627
                                 Fax: (01623) 836-647

Newcastle (Tyne & Wear)

Area telephone code (0191)
The community was established before 1831,
when a cemetery was acquired. Jews have
lived in Newcastle since 1775. There are about
1,200 Jews in the city today.

Representative Organisations

Representative Council of North-East Jewry
24 Adeline Gardens, Gosforth,
NE3 4JQ   285-1253

Synagogues

United Hebrew Congregation, Graham Park
Road, Gosforth, NE3 4BH   284-0959
Mikva on premises.

Newcastle Reform Synagogue, The Croft, off
Kenton Road, Gosforth, NE3 4RF   284-8621

Kashrut Information

Kashrus Committee
Lionel Jacobson House, Graham Park Road,
Gosforth, NE3 4BH   285-2593

Media

Newspapers

The North-East Jewish Recorder

Restaurants

G. Lurie
32 St. Mary's Place, NE1 7PS   261-0577
                                 285-7928
Kosher.

Vegetarian

The Red Herring, 3 Studley Terrace, Fenham,
NE4 7PG   272-3484

Groceries

Zelda's Delicatessen, Unit 7 Kenton Park
Shopping Centre, NE3 4RU   213-0013
Supervision: Newcastle Kashrus Committee,
Rabbi Yehuda Black.
Delicatessen, fresh meat, poultry and bread
also sold here. Closed Mondays.

Northampton

(Northamptonshire)

Synagogues

Overstone Road, BB1 3JW   (01604) 33345
Services on Friday night.

Norwich (Norfolk)

The present community was founded in 1813,
Jews having been resident in Norwich during
the Middle Ages, and connected with the
woollen and worsted trade, for which the city
was at that time famous. A resettlement of
Jews is believed to have been completed by
the middle of the eighteenth century. Today's
congregation serves a large area, having
members in Ipswich, Great Yarmouth,
Lowestoft and Cromer.

Synagogues

3a Earlhan Road, NR2 3RA   (01603) 503434

Progressive Jewish Community of East Anglia
c/o Frimette Carr   (01603) 714162

Restaurants *(Vegetarian)*

Eat Naturally
11 Wensum Street, NR3 1LA   (01603) 660-838
The Treehouse
15 Dove Street, NR2 1DE   (01603) 660-838

Nottingham (Nottinghamshire)

Area telephone code (0115)

Jews settled in Nottingham as early as
medieval times, and centres of learning and
worship are known to have existed in that
period. The earliest known record of an
established community dates from 1822 when
a grant of land for burial purposes was made
by the Corporation; in 1825 the then Chief
Rabbi appointed the community's first
shochet. The community grew apace as a
result of the late nineteenth century pogroms
in eastern Europe and during the 20 years
preceding and following the Second World
War, growing to some 1,700 by the 1950s.
Today the known Jewish population is
estimated at 1,00, about two-thirds of whom
are members of the Orthodox synagogue.

Synagogues

Shakespeare Street, NG1 4FQ   947-2004
Nottingham Progressive Jewish Congregation
Lloyd Street, Sherwood, NG5 4BP   962-4761

United Kingdom

Restaurants (Vegetarian)

Krisha Restaurant, 144 Alfreton Road,
Redford, NG7 3NS   970-8608

Maxine's Salad Table, 56 Upper Parliament
Street, NG1 2AG   947-3622

Rita's Café
15 Goosegate, Hockley, NG1 1FE   948-1115

The Vegetarian Pot, 375 Alfreton Road,
Redford, NG7 5LT   970-3333

Oxford (Oxfordshire)

Area telephone code (01865)

There was an important medieval community,
and the present one dates back to 1842. The
Oxford Synagogue and Jewish Centre, opened
in 1974, serves both the city and the
university. It is available for all forms of Jewish
worship.

Community Organisations

L'Chaim Society
Albion House, Little Gate   794-462

The Synagogue and Jewish Centre
21 Richmond Road, OX1 2JL   553-042
Call for information about services. A kosher
meals service operates during term time.

Plymouth (Devon)

The congregation was founded in 1752 and a
synagogue erected ten years later. This is now
the oldest Ashkenazi synagogue building in
England still used for its original purpose. It is
a scheduled historical monument. In 1815
Plymouth was one of the four most important
provincial centres of Anglo-Jewry.

Synagogues

Catherine Street, PL1 2AD   612-281
Services: Fri., 6pm; Sat., 9:30am. The
congregation offers free use of minister's
modern flat as holiday accommodation in
return for conducting Orthodox Friday evening
and Saturday morning services.

Restaurants (Vegetarian)

**Plymouth Arts Centre Vegetarian
Restaurant**
38 Looe Street, PL4 0EB   202-616
Hours: lunch, Monday to Saturday, 12 pm to

2 pm; dinner, Tuesday to Saturday, 5 pm to
8 or 9 pm.

Libraries

Holcenberg Collection, Plymouth Central
Library, Drake Circus, PL4 8AL
A Jewish collection of fiction and non-fiction
books, mainly lending copies.

Portsmouth & Southsea
(Hampshire)

The Portsmouth community was founded in
1746. Its first synagogue was in Oyster Row,
but the congregation moved to a building in
White's Row which it continued to occupy for
almost two centuries. A new building was
erected in 1936. The cemetery is in a street
which was once known as Jews' Lane. It is the
oldest in the provinces still used for the
interment of Jews.

Synagogues

Synagogue Chambers, The Thicket, Southsea,
PO5 2AA   (01705) 821494

Ramsgate (Kent)

Synagogues

Montefiore Endowment, Hereson Road
**Visitors wishing to see the Montefiore
Mausoleum & Synagogue**   (01843) 862507
Thanet and District Reform Synagogue,
293A Margate Road, CT12 6TA   (01843) 851164

Reading (Berkshire)

Jewish settlement began in 1886. The
Orthodox synagogue was opened in 1900 and
has been in continuous use since. This
flourishes today and has the distinction of
being the only Orthodox synagogue in
Berkshire.

Synagogues

Goldsmid Road, RG1 7YB   (01734) 571018
     Email: secretary@rhc.datanet.co.uk
**Thames Valley Progressive Jewish
Community,** 6 Church Street   (01734) 867769

Rochester (Kent)

Synagogues

Magnus Memorial Synagogue
366 High Street, ME1 1DJ   (01634) 847665
Grade 2 listed building known as The Chatham
Memorial Synagogue.

Romford (Essex)

Synagogues

25 Eastern Road

Ruislip (Middlesex)

Synagogues

Shenley Avenue, Ruislip Manor,
HA4 6BP   (01895) 632934

St Albans (Hertfordshire)

Synagogues

Oswald Road, AL1 3AQ
St Albans Masorti Synagogue
PO Box 23   (01727) 760891

St Annes On Sea (Lancashire)

Synagogues

Orchard Road, FY8 1PJ   (01253) 721831
Services 7.30am and 8pm

Sheffield (Yorkshire)

Synagogues

Sheffield Jewish and Congregation Centre
Wilson Road, S11 8RN   (0114) 266-3567
**Sheffield & District Reform Jewish
Congregation**   (0114) 230-1054

Solihull (West Midlands)

Synagogues

Solihull & District Hebrew Congregation
3 Monastery Drive, St Bernards Road,
B91 3HN   (0121) 707-5199
Services Friday evening; Sat 9.45am, Sun 9am.

Southampton (Hampshire)

Synagogues

Moordaunt Road, The Inner Avenue, SO2 0GP
Services Sat. morn 10am.
Southampton & District Jewish Society,
Hillel House, 5 Brookvale Road, Portswood,
SO2 1QN
Hartley Library, University of Southampton,
houses both the Parkes Library and the Anglo-
Jewish Archives.

Southend/Westcliff (Essex)

Area telephone code (01702)

Jews began settling in the area in the late
nineteenth century, mainly from the East End
of London. The first temporary synagogue was
built in 1906. The Jewish population is 4,500.

Representative Organisations

Southend & District Representative Council
343192

Synagogues

**Southend and Westcliff Hebrew
Congregation,** Finchley Road, Westcliff, SS0
8AD   344900
Southend Reform Synagogue, 851 London
Road, Westcliff   75809

Delicatessens

Westcliff Kosher Bagel, Hamlet Court Road,
Westcliff   435678
Supervision: Southend & Westcliff Kashrut
Commission.

Hotels

Archery's Hotel
27 Grosvenor Road   353323; 334001
Cobham Lodge Hotel
2 Cobham Road, SS0 8EA   346438

Guests can be reached on 332-377.
Unsupervised. Telephone for brochure and
tariffs.

Embassy Hotel, 35-41 Grosvenor Road, SS0
8EP   (Bookings) 335803
                                          (Visitors) 341175

Redstone's Hotel
Pembury Road, SS0 8DS   348-441

Booksellers

Dorothy Young
21 Colchester Road, SS2 6HW   331218
Religious articles, Israeli giftware, etc., also
stocked. Jewish software ordered. Call for
appointment.

Southport (Merseyside)

Representative Organisations
Jewish Representative Council (01704) 538276

Synagogues
Southport Hebrew Congregation
Arnside Road, PR9 0QX   (01704) 532964
Mikva on premises.

New (Reform) Synagogue, Portland Street,
PR8 1LR   (01704) 535950

Groceries
Tesco, Town Lane, Kew
Kosher bread range only.

Staines (Middlesex)

Includes Slough and Windsor Synagogue.

Synagogues
Staines & District Synagogue, Westbrook
Road, South Street, TW18 4PR (01784) 254604

Stoke On Trent (Staffordshire)

Synagogues
Birch Terrace, Hanley, ST1 3JN (01782) 616417

Sunderland (Tyne & Wear)

Synagogues
Sunderland Hebrew Congregation, Ryhope
Road, SR2 7EQ   (0191) 522-7560

Mikvaot
Contact Mrs Zahn   (0191) 565-0224

Contact Information
Rabbi S. Zahn.
11 The Oaks East, SR2 8EX   (0191) 565-0224

Torquay (Devon)

Covering also Brixham and Paignton.

Synagogues
Old Town Hall, Abbey Road,
TQ1 1BB   (01803) 607724
Services first Shabbat of every month and
festivals 10:30am.

Bed & Breakfasts
Brookesby Hall Hotel, Hesketh Road,
Meadfoot Beach, TQ1 2LN   (01803) 292194
Strictly vegetarian/vegan. 14 rooms.

Wallingford (Oxfordshire)

Community Organisations
Carmel College
Mongewell Park, OX10 8BT   (01491) 837505
Kosher meals available in term time (except on
Shabbat), provided Bursar is telephoned in
advance.

Watford (Hertfordshire)

Covers also Carpenders Park, Croxley Garden,
Garston, King's Langley and Rickmansworth.

Synagogues
16 Nascot Road, WD1 3RE   (01923) 222755

Welwyn Garden City
(Hertfordshire)

Synagogues
Barn Close, Handside Lane, AL8 6ST   762829

Whitley Bay (Tyne & Wear)

Synagogues

2 Oxford Street   daytime: (01670) 367053
         evening: (0191) 252-1367
Visitors required for services.

Wolverhampton (West Midlands)

Synagogues

Fryer Street, WV1 1HT
Established over 150 years ago. Membership 15 families.

York (Yorkshire)

Tours

Yorkwalk
3 Fairway, Clifton, YO3 6QA   (01532) 622-303
         Fax: (01532) 656-244
Introduced new walk called 'The Jewish Heritage Walk', recalling the Jewish contribution to York's history. The tour includes the Minster with its magnificent religious art. The walk finishes at Clifford's Tower, the site of a dreadful Jewish massacre in 1190.

Channel Islands

Alderney

Memorials

On the Corblets Road at Longy, there is a memorial to the victims of the Nazis during their occupation of the English Channel Islands during the Second World War. It bears plaques in English, French, Hebrew and Russian.

Jersey

Synagogues

Jersey Jewish Congregation
La Petite Route des Mielles, St Brelade, JE3 8FY
Shabbat morning service, 10:30 am; Holy days, 7 pm and 10 am.

Contact Information

Mr. Stephen Regal
Armon, 3 Clos des Chataigniers, Rue de la Croix, St Ouen, JE3 2HA
Honorary secretary of the Jersey Jewish Congregation.

Isle of Man

There are more than 70 Jews on the Island.

Douglas

Synagogues

Hebrew Congregation   (01624) 24214

Northern Ireland

Belfast

Area telephone code (01232)
There were Jews living in Belfast in the year 1652, but the present community was founded in 1869.

Organisations

Vegetarian Society of Ulster
66 Ravenhill Gardens, BT6 8QG   457888

Synagogues

49 Somerton Road, BT15 3LH   777974
Services: Sat., Sun., Mon., & Thurs.; am

Restaurants

Jewish Community Centre
49 Somerton Road, BT15 3LH   777974
Open Sunday 6:30 pm to 9:30 pm.

Scotland

Aberdeen

Area telephone code (01224)

Synagogues
74 Dee Street, AB1 2DS   582135

Restaurants (Vegetarian)
Jaws Wholefood Café
5 West North Street, AB1 3AT   645676

Dundee

Synagogues
St Mary Place, DD1 5RB   (01382) 223557

Dunoon

Synagogues
Argyll & Bute Jewish Com.   (01369) 705118

Edinburgh

Area telephone code (0131)

The Town Council and Burgess Roll minutes of 1691 and 1717 record applications by Jews for permission to live and trade in Edinburgh. Local directories of the eighteenth century contain Jewish names.

Synagogues
4 Salisbury Road, EH16 5AB   667-3144

Kashrut Information
3 Hallhead Road, EH16 5QT   667-1521

Restaurants (Vegetarian)
Anna Purna, 45 St Patrick Sq.   662-1807
Black Bo's, Blackfriars Street   557-6136
Henderson's
94 Hanover Street, EH2 1DR   225-2131
                                              Fax: 220-3542
Kalpna Restaurant
2 St Patrick Sq., EH8 9EZ   667-9890
Pierre Lapin
West Nicholson Street   668-4332

Bakeries
William Innes Wood
84 E. Crosscauseway, EH8 9HQ   667-1406
Supervision: Edinburgh Hebrew Congregation.
Kosher bread and bakery products.

Butchers
3 Hallhead Road, EH16 5QT   667-1521
Regular deliveries from suppliers in Glasgow and Manchester.

Glasgow

Area telephone code (0141)

The Glasgow Jewish community dates back to 1823. The oldest synagogues building is the Garnethill Synagogue, now also the home of the Scottish Jewish Archives, which opened in 1879. The community grew rapidly from 1891 with many Jews settling in the Gorbals. In recent years the community has gradually spread southwards and is now mainly situated in the Giffnock and Newton Mearns areas.

Representative Organisations
Glasgow Jewish Representative Council, 222 Fenwick Road, Giffnock, G46 6UE   620-1700
                                              Fax: 638-2100

Synagogues
Orthodox
Garnethill, 127 Hill Street, G3 6UB   332-4151
Giffnock & Newlands, Maryville Avenue, Giffnock, G46 7NE   638-6600
Langside
125 Niddrie Road, G42 8QA   423-4062
Lubavitch   638-6116
Netherlee & Clarkston, Clarkston Road at Randolph Drive, G44   637-8206
Newton Mearns, 14 Larchfield Court, G77 5BH   639-4000
Queen's Park
Falloch Road, G42 9QX   632-1743

Reform
Glasgow New Synagogue, 147 Ayr Road, Newton Mearns, G77 6RE   639-4083

Mikvaot
Giffnock & Newlands Synagogue   621-0021
                                              620-3156

Media
Newspapers
Jewish Telegraph
43 Queen Sq., G41 2BD   423-9200

Restaurants
Kaye's Restaurant, Maccabi Youth Centre,
May Terrace, G46   620-3233

Delicatessens
Giffnock Kosher Deli
200 Fenwick Road, G46   638-8267
    632-2313

Marilyn's Kosher Deli
2 Burnfield Road, G46 7QB   638-4383
Michael Morrison and Son
52 Sinclair Drive, G42 9PY   632-0998

Hotels
Forres Guest House
10 Forres Avenue, G46 6L   638-5554
    Mobile: 0410 864-151
    Email: june.d@ukonline.co.uk

Guest House
26 St Clair Avenue, G46 7QE   638-3924
Kosher, but not supervised.

Booksellers
J & E Levingstone
47 & 55 Sinclair Drive, G42 9PT   649-2962
Well of Wisdom, Giffnock Syn.   638-2030

St Andrews

Contact Information
Jewish Students' Society, c/o Sec., Students' Union, University of St Andrews, KY16 9UY

Wales

Cardiff
Area telephone code (01222)

Synagogues
Orthodox
Cardiff United Synagogue, Brandreth Road,

Penylan   473728
    491795
Reform
Cardiff New Synagogue, Moira Terrace, CF2 1EJ   614915

Mikvaot
Wales Empire Pool Building, Wood Street, CF1 1PP   382296

Restaurants (Vegetarian)
Munchies Wholefood Co-op
60 Crwys Road, Cathays, CF2 4NN   399677

Self-catering
210 Lake Road East, CF2 5NR   758614

Llandudno

Synagogues
28 Church Walks, LL30 2HL   (01492) 572549
No resident minister, but visiting ministers during summer months.

Newport

Synagogues
Newport Mon Hebrew Cong., 3 Queens Hill Crescent, NP9 5HH   (01633) 262308

Swansea
Area telephone code (01792)

Synagogues
Ffynone   473333

Contact Information
Dr N.H. Saunders, 95 Cherry Grove, Sketty, SA2 8AX   20210
Dr L. Mars
70 Gabalfa Road, Sketty, SA2 8NE   20526
Both are willing to help and advise students coming to Univeristy College.

Restaurants (Vegetarian)
Chris's Kitchen
The Market, SA1 3PE   64345

United States of America

GMT – 5 to 11 hours
Country calling code (1)

Kashrut Information

As there is no unified Jewish ecclesiastical control in America, or a Chief Rabbinate as exists in other countries of the world, there is little 'official' supervision of kashrut. Instead, there are a proliferation of hashgachot by individual rabbis and companies who engage in kashrut supervision on a commercial level. More than 170 such symbols and organisations are known to exist in the US today. They tend to have differing degrees of reliability. The 'big three' national symbols are OU, Kof-K and Circle-K. 'K' alone is an unregistered trademark and unreliable as a mark of proper kosher supervision. Travellers are recommended to check with a local rabbi or religious organisation to learn the local reliable supervising bodies.

Agudat Israel (address and phone number below) will provide, free of charge, a list of people in most major US cities who can provide reliable information about kashrut.

Religious Organisations

Although most of these organisations are based in New York, they can provide you with information about their constituent synagogues and the relevant details (addresses, phone numbers, minyan times) across the country.

Orthodox

Agudat Israel World Organization, 84 William Street, NY, NY 10273   (212) 797-9600
Lubavitch Movement, 770 Eastern Parkway, Brooklyn, NY, 11213   (718) 221-0500
Fax: (718) 221-0985

National Council of Young Israel
National Office, 3 West 16th Street, NY, NY, 10011   (212) 929-1525
Southern Regional Office, 1035 NE 170th Terrace, Miami, FL, 33162   (305) 770-3993
email:ncyi.south@youngisrael.org

Washington, DC Office, 1101 Pennsylvania Avenue, Suite 1050, Washington, DC, 20004
(202) 347-4111
Fax. (202) 347-8341
West Coast Regional Office, 1050 Indiana Avenue, Venice, CA 90291   (310) 396-3935
Fax: (310) 581-0904
email: ncyi.west@youngisrael.org
Union of Orthodox Jewish Congregations of America, 333 Seventh Avenue, NY, NY, 10001
(212) 563-4000
Fax: (212) 613-8333

Conservative

United Synagogue of America, 155 Fifth Avenue, NY, NY, 10010   (212) 533-7800
World Council of Synagogues can be found at the same location.

Reform

Union of American Hebrew Congregations
838 Fifth Ave, NY, NY, 10021   (212) 249-0100

Progressive

World Union for Progressive Judaism, 838 Fifth Ave, NY, NY, 10021
(212) 249-0100, ext 502
Fax: (212) 517-3940

Sephardic

Union of Sephardic Congregations, 8 West 70th Street, NY, NY, 10023   (212) 873-0300

Alabama

Birmingham

Area telephone code (205)

Community Organisations

Birmingham Jewish Federation
3966 Montclair Road, 35213   803-0416
                                    Fax: 803-1526

Synagogues

Orthodox
Knesseth Israel
3225 Montevallo Road, 35223   879-1464

Conservative
Beth-El
2179 Highland Avenue, 35205

Reform
Emanu-El
2100 Highland Avenue, 35205

Mikvaot

Beth-El
2179 Highland Avenue, 35255
Knesseth Israel
3225 Montevallo Rd, 35213   879-1464

Contact Information

Rabbi Meir Rosenberg
3225 Montevallo Road, 35213   879-1464
Visitors requiring information about kashrut,
temporary accommodation, etc., should
contact Rabbi Rosenberg.

Delicatessens

Browdy's, 2607 Cahaba Rd, 35223   879-6411

Libraries

Hess Library, 3960 Montclair Road, 35213

Huntsville

Synagogues

Conservative
Etz Chayim, 7705 Bailey Cove Road, 35802

Mobile

Synagogues

Reform
Spring Hill Avenue Temple
1769 Spring Hill Avenue, 36607

Montgomery

Area telephone code (205)

Community Organisations

Jewish Federation
PO Box 20058, 36120   277-5820

Synagogues

Orthodox
Etz Ahayem (Sephardi)
725 Augusta Road, 36111

Conservative
Agudath Israel, 3525 Cloverdale Road, 36111
Mikvah attached.

Reform
Beth Or, 2246 Narrow Lane, 36106
Maxwell Air Force Base
Building 833, Chaplain's School

Alaska

Anchorage

Area telephone code (907)

Synagogues

Orthodox
Congregation Shomrei Ohr, 1210 E. 26th,
99508   279-120€

Reform
Beth Sholom, 7525 E. Northern Lights Blvd,
99504   338-183€
                                    Fax: 357-401.
                 Email: http//Alaska.Not/Sholon
This has the only Jewish pre-school in the
state.

Arizona

Area telephone code (602) except where shown

Mesa

Synagogues

Conservative

Beth Sholom Congregation
316 Le Seuer Street, 85204   964-1981

Phoenix

Community Organisations

Jewish Federation of Greater Phoenix
32 W. Coolidge, Suite 200, 85013   274-1800

Tri-Cities Jewish Community Center
1965 E. Hermosa Temp, AZ, 85282   897-0588

Valley of the Sun Jewish Community Center
1718 W. Maryland Avenue, 85015   249-1832

Synagogues

Orthodox

Chabad-Lubavitch Center
2110 E. Lincoln Drive, 85020   944-2753

Congregation Beth Joseph
515 E. Bethany Home Road, 85012   277-7479

Congregation Shaarei Tzedek   944-1133

Young Israel of Phoenix
745 E. Maryland Avenue, 85014   265-8888

Conservative

Congregation Beth El
1118 W. Glendale, 85021   944-3359

Reform

Temple Beth Ami, 4545 N. 36th Street, 211,
85018   956-0805

Temple Chai
4645 E. Marilyn Avenue, 85032   971-1234

Temple Kol Ami
15030 N. 64th Street, 204, 85254   951-9660

Kashrut Information

Rabbi David Rebibo, 515 E. Bethany Home
Rd., 85012   277-7479
Visitors requiring kashrut information should
contact Rabbi Rebibo.

Restaurants

J.J.'s Kosher
1331 E. Northern Av., 85015   371-0999

Segal's Kosher Foods
4818 North 7th Street, 85014   285-1515
Fax: 277-5760
Supervision: Greater Phoenix Vaad Hakashrut.
Strictly kosher full service restaurant serving
lunch and dinner Monday through Thursday
and Shabbat take-out on Friday. Kosher bakery
within premises.

Museums

Plotkin Judaica Museum
3310 North 10th Avenue, 85013   264-4428
Fax: 264-0039
Hours: Sunday 12-3 p.m., Tuesday-Thursday
10-3, Friday evenings after services. Advanced
notice required for groups of 10 or more.

Media

Newspapers

Greater Phoenix Jewish News
1625 E. Northern 106, 85020   870-9470

Shalom Arizona
32 W. Coolidge, Suite 200, 85013   274-1800

Scottsdale

Synagogues

Conservative

Beth Emeth of Scottsdale
5406 E. Virginia Avenue, 85254   947-4604

Beth Joshua Congregation
6230 E. Shea Blvd., 85254   991-5404

Har Zion
5929 E. Lincoln Drive, 85253   991-0720

Reform

Temple Solel
6805 E. MacDonald Drive, 85253   991-7414

Restaurants

Cactus Kosher, 8005 E. Indian School Road,
85251   970-8441
Supervision: Greater Phoenix Vaad Hakashrut.
Delicatessen which also offers take-out and
catering for area hotel delivery.

Sierra Vista

Synagogues

Temple Kol Hamidbar
228 North Canyon Drive   458-8637
(Ans. phone only)

Solomonsville

The town was founded by Isador E. Solomon, a friend of the Indians, in 1876.

Synagogues

Beth Sholom of Mesa, 316 LeSeuer Street, 85204   964-1981

Har Zion, 5929 E. Lincoln Drive, Paradise Valley, 85253   991-0720

Sun City/Sun City West

Synagogues

Conservative
Beth Emeth of Sun City, 13702 Meeker Blvd., Sun City West, 85373   584-1957

Reform
Beth Shalom of Sun City, 12202 101st Avenue, Sun City, 85351   977-3240

Tempe

Community Organisations

Tri-City Jewish Community Center
1965 E. Hermosa Drive, 85282   897-0588

Synagogues

Orthodox
Chabad-Lubavitch Center
23 W. 9th Street, 85281   966-5163

Reform
Temple Emanuel
5801 Rural Road, 85283   838-1414

Tucson

Area telephone code (520)

Community Organisations

Jewish Federation of Southern Arizona
3822 E. River Road, 85718   577-9393

Synagogues

Orthodox
Congregation Chofetz Chayim
5150 E. 5th Street, 85711
Young Israel of Tucson
2443 E. 4th Street, 85710   326-8362

Conservative
Congregation Bet Shalom
3881 E. River Road, 85718

Anshei Israel, 5550 E. 5th Street, 85711

Reform
Temple Emanuel
225 N. County Club Road, 85716

Groceries

Feig's Kosher Foods
5071 E. 5th Street, 85711   325-2255
Supervision: Rabbi A. Oleisky.
Fresh glatt beef, lamb and veal, full service deli, groceries. Hours: Monday to Thursday, 8 am to 5:45 pm; Friday, to 3:45 pm; Sunday, to 1:45 pm.

Arkansas

El Dorado

Synagogues

Reform
Beth Israel, 1130 E. Main Street

Helena

Synagogues

Temple Beth-El, 406 Perry Street, 72342
Founded 1875.

Hot Springs

Synagogues

House of Israel, 300 Quapaw St., 71901
Hot Springs is known for its curative waters.
The Leo Levi Memorial Hospital (for joint
disorder, such as arthritis) was founded by
B'nai B'rith, as was the adjacent Levi Towers, a
senior citizen housing project.

Little Rock

Area telephone code (501)

Community Organisations

Jewish Federation of Arkansas
2821 Kavanaugh, Garden Level, 72205-3868
663-3571

Synagogues

Orthodox
Agudath Achim, 7901 W. 5th St., 72205
Mikva on premises. The only orthodox
synagogue in the state open all year round.

Reform
B'nai Israel, 3700 Rodney Parham Rd., 72212

Bakeries
Andre's, 11121 Rodney Parham Rd, 72212

California

As the general population of California
continues to increase, the Jewish community is
growing as well. Places of worship abound,
from Eureka in the north to San Diego in the
south, but the major part of the community
lives in the Los Angeles metropolitan area.

Alameda

Synagogues

Reform
Temple Israel, 3183 Mecartney Road, 94501

Anaheim

Synagogues

Conservative
Temple Beth Emet, 1770 W. Cerritos Avenue,
92804   (714) 772-4720

Arcadia

Synagogues

Conservative
Congregation Shaarei Torah, 550 S. 2nd
Avenue, 91006   (818) 445-0810

Arleta

Synagogues

Reform
Temple Beth Solomon of the Deaf, 13580
Osborne Street, 91331   (818) 899-2202
(TDD) (818) 896-6721

Bakersfield

Synagogues

Conservative
B'nai Jacob, 600 17th Street, 93301

Reform
Temple Beth El, 2906 Loma Linda Dr., 93305

Berkeley

Area telephone code (510)
See also Oakland.

Synagogues

Orthodox
Beth Israel, 1630 Bancroft Way, 94703
Chabad House, 2643 College Avenue, 94704

Conservative
Netivot Shalom, 1414 Walnut Street

Reform
Temple Beth El, 2301 Vine Street, 94708

Egalitarian
Hillel Foundation, 2736 Bancroft Way, 94704
845-7793
Traditional egalitarian services on Friday evening.

Mikvaot
Mikvah Taharas Israel
2520 Warring Street, 94707   848-7221

Museums
Judah L. Magnes - Jewish Museum of the West, 2911 Russell St., 94705   549-6950
Fax: 849-3650
Among the latest institutions of its kind west of New York. It includes the Western Jewish History Center & the Blumenthal Library. Open Sun-Thurs. 10-4.
Lehrhaus Judaica, 2736 Bancroft Way, 94704

Beverly Hills
Area telephone code (310)
Note: Beverly Hills, Hollywood and Los Angeles are contiguous communities and in many cases have overlapping bodies.

Synagogues
Orthodox
Beth Jacob, 9030 Olympic Blvd, 90211
Young Israel of Beverly Hills
8701 W. Pico Blvd, 90035   275-3020

Reform
Temple Emanuel, 8844 Burton Way, 90211

Burlingame
Synagogues
Reform
Peninsula Temple Sholom, 1655 Sebastian Drive, 94010   (415) 697-2266
Fax: (415) 697-2544

Carmel
Synagogues
Reform
Congregation Beth Israel, 5716 Carmel Valley Road, 93923   (408) 624-2015

Castro Valley
Synagogues
Reform
Shir Ami
4529 Malabar Avenue, 94546   (415) 537-1787

Costa Mesa
Area telephone code (714)

Community Organisations
Jewish Federation of Orange County
250 E. Baker Street, 92626   755-5555
Fax: 755-0307

Delicatessens
The Kosher Bite, 23595 Moulton Parkway, Laguna Hills, 92653   770-1818

Daly City
Synagogues
Conservative
B'nai Israel
1575 Annie Street, 94015   (415) 756-5430

Davis
Synagogues
Reform
Davis Jewish Fellowship, 1821 Oak Avenue, 95616

Downey

Synagogues

Reform
Temple Ner Tamid, 10629 Lakewood Blvd,
90241   (310) 861-9276

Eureka

Synagogues

Reform
Beth El, Hodgson & T Streets, PO Box 442,
95502   (707) 444-2846

Fremont

Synagogues

Reform
Temple Beth Torah, 42000 Paseo Padre Pkwy,
94539   (415) 656-7141

Fresno

Community Organisations
Jewish Federations Office
1340 W. Herndon, Suite 103, 93711

Synagogues

Orthodox
Chabad House, 6735 N. ILA, 93711

Conservative
Beth Jacob, 406 W. Shields Avenue, 93705
Reform
Temple Beth Israel, 6622 N. Maroa Avenue,
93704
This temple has its own etrog tree, planted
from a sprig brought to the USA from Israel.

Gardena

Synagogues

Conservative
Southwest Temple Beth Torah, 14725 S.
Gramercy Place, 90249

Greater East Bay
See Oakland.

Hollywood
Area telephone code (818)

Synagogues

Conservative
Hollywood Temple Beth El, 137 N. Crescent
Heights Blvd,

Kashrut Information
Kosher Information Bureau
15365 Magnolia Blvd, Sherman Oaks, 91403
                                        762-3197

Long Beach
Area telephone code (562)

Community Organisations
**Jewish Federation of Greater Long Beach &
W. Orange County**
3801 E. Willow St., 90815   426-7601

Synagogues

Orthodox
Cong. Lubavitch, 3981 Atlantic Ave, 90807
Young Israel of Long Beach
4134 Atlantic, 90807   527-3163

Conservative
Beth Shalom, 3635 Elm Avenue, 90807
Cong. Shalom of Leisure World, 1661
Golden Rain Road, Northwood Clubhouse No.
3, Seal Beach, 90740
Temple Beth Zion Sinai, 6440 Del Amo Blvd,
90713

Reform

Temple Beth David, 6100 Hefley Street, Westminster

Temple Israel, 338 E. 3rd Street, 90812

Mikvaot

3847 Atlantic Avenue, 90807

Media

Newspapers

Jewish Community Chronicle
3801 E. Willow St., 90815 1791

Los Alamitos

Area telephone code (714)

Bakeries

Fairfax Kosher Market & Bakery
11196-98 Los Alamitos Blvd, 90720   828-4492

Los Angeles

Los Angeles is America's, and the world's, second largest Jewish metropolis, with a Jewish population of around 600,000. Fairfax Avenue and Beverly Blvd together form the crossroads of traditional Jewish life while a growing Orthodox enclave centres around Pico and Robertson Blvds.

Important note: Area telephone codes have recently been split to 310 and 213 for central Los Angeles. We have endeavored in all cases to correct our information, but cannot guarantee the veracity of those who did not send in updates.

Community Organisations

Jewish Federation of Greater Los Angeles
6505 Wilshire Blvd, 90048   (310) 852-7758
                        Fax: (310) 852-8723

Los Angeles Jewish Community Buildings
6505 Wilshire Blvd, 90048

Los Angeles West Side Community Center
5870 W. Olympic Blvd., 90036
This address also houses the Jewish Center's Association of Los Angeles and includes a 'hands-on' museum for children.

Synagogues

Orthodox

B'nai David Congregation, 8906 W. Pico Blvd., 90035

Breed St. Shule, 247 N. Breed St., 90033
This synagogue is of historical interest.

Chabad House, 741 Gayley Avenue, W. Los Angeles, 90025

Etz Jacob, 7659 Beverly Blvd., 90036

Mogen David, 9717 W. Pico Blvd., 90035

Ohel David, 7967 Beverly Blvd.

Ohev Shalom, 525 S. Fairfax Avenue, 90036

Young Israel of Century City
9317 West Pico Blvd, 90035   (310) 273-6954

Young Israel of Hancock Park
225 South La Brea   (213) 931-4030

Young Israel of Los Angeles, 660 N. Spaulding Avenue, 90036   (213) 655-0300/22

Orthodox Sephardi

Kahal Joseph, 10505 Santa Monica Blvd. 90025

Magen David, 322 N. Foothill, Beverly Hills, 90210

Temple Tifereth Israel, 10500 Wilshire Blvd., 90024

Conservative

Adat Shalom, 3030 Westwood Blvd., 90034

Beth Am, 1039 S. La Cienega Blvd., 90035

Sinai Temple, 10400 Wilshire Blvd., 90024

Reform

Beth Chayim Chadishim, 6000 W. Pico Blvd, 90035

Leo Baeck Temple, 1300 N. Sepulveda Blvd., 90049

Stephen S. Wise Temple, 15500 Stephen S. Wise Dr., Bel Air, 90024

Temple Akiba, 5249 S. Sepulveda Blvd., Culver City 90230

Temple Isaiah, 10345 W. Pico Blvd., 90064

University Synagogue, 11960 Sunset Blvd., 90049

Wilshire Blvd. Temple, 3663 Wilshire Blvd., 90010

Reconstructionist

Kehillath Israel, 16019 Sunset Blvd., Pacific Palisades, 90272

Mikvaot
Los Angeles Mikva, 9548 W. Pico Blvd, 90035

Kashrut Information
Board of Rabbis of Southern California
6505 Wilshire Blvd,   (310) 852-7710
Suite 511, 90048   (310) 852-1234
Kosher Information Bureau (818) 792-3197
                        Fax: (818) 980-6908
Rabbi Bukspan
6407 Orange Street, 90048   (310) 653-5083
Rabbinical Council of California, 1122 S.
Robertson Blvd, 90035   (310) 271-4160
                        Fax: (310) 271-7147

Embassy
Consulate General
Suite 1700, 6380 Wilshire Blvd, 90048

Media
Newspapers
Heritage Southwest Jewish Press
Weekly publication, coming out on Fridays.
Israel Today
Jewish Calendar Magazine
Jewish Journal, Weekly, published on Fridays.
Jewish News
Jewish News, Published monthly.
Yisrael Shelanu

Restaurants
Berookhim Royal Catering
6170 Wilbur Ave   (310) 458-9993
Berookhim Royal Catering
324 Marguerita Ave   (310) 458-9993
Beverly Hills Cuisine
9025 Wilshire Blvd   (310) 247-1239
Supervision: RCC.
Beverly/Fairfax & Downtown
7231 Beverly Blvd   (310) 936-1653
Classic Restaurant
1420 Westwood Blvd   (310) 234-9191
Supervision: RCC.
Coffee Brake
1507 S. Robertson Blvd   (310) 277-6741
Cohen Restaurant
316 E. Pico Blvd   (213) 742-8888
Supervision: RCC.
Grill at the Beverly Carlton
9400 W. Olympic   (310) 282-0945

Habayit Restaurant
11921 W. Pico Blvd   (310) 488-9877
Haifa Restaurant
8717 W. Pico Blvd   (310) 550-2704
Hillel Restaurant
108 E. 8th St   (213) 488-9939
Supervision: RCC.
Judy's, 129 N. La Brea Avenue (213) 934-7667
Supervision: RCC.
Mosaique, 8146 W. Third St. (310) 951-1133
Nessim's, 8939 W. Pico Blvd (310) 204-5334
Supervision: RCC.
New York Sandwich
600 W. 9th St.   (310) 623-4623
Rib Tickler
533 N. Fairfax Ave.   (310) 655-6333
Rimini Restaurant
9400 W. Olympic Blvd   (310) 552-1056
Supervision: RCC.
Sharon's II, 306 E. 9th Street (213) 622-1010
Supervision: RCC.
Shula & Esther
5519 N. Fairfax Ave   (310) 951-9651
Simone, 8706 W. Pico Blvd   (310) 657-5552
Supervision: RCC-Mehadrin.

Meat
Chick'N Chow
9301 W. Pico Blvd, 90035   (310) 274-5595
                        Fax: (310) 274-9693
Supervision: Kehillah of Los Angeles.
Glatt kosher eat in, take out, delivery. Hours:
11:30 am to 10 pm.
Dizengoff Restaurant
8103 1/2 Beverly Blvd   (213) 651-4465
Supervision: Kehillah of Los Angeles.
Sit down or take out.
Elat Burger
9340 W. Pico Blvd   (310) 278-4692
Supervision: RCC.
Elite Cuisine
7119 Beverly Blvd   (213) 930-1303
Supervision: Kehillah of Los Angeles.
Sit down or take out.
Glatt Hut, 9303 W. Pico Blvd (310) 246-1900
Supervision: RCC.
Grill Express
501 N. Fairfax Ave.   (213) 655-0649
Supervision: RCC.
Kabob & Chinese Food
11330 Santa Monica   (310) 914-3040
Supervision: Kehillah of Los Angeles.

Kabob & Chinese Food
9180 W. Pico Blvd   (310) 274-4007
Supervision: Kehillah of Los Angeles.

La Gondola Ristorante Italiano
6405 Wilshire Blvd, 90048   (213) 852-1915
                            Fax: (213) 852-0853
            Web site: www.thegondola.com
Supervision: Kehillah of Los Angeles.
Use all Lubavitch meats. Hours: Monday to
Thursday, 11:30 am to 3 pm, 5 pm to 10 pm;
Sunday, 5 pm to 10 pm; Saturday night after
Shabbat in the winter. Located next to Beverly
Hills, there is a delivery service to the hotels.

Magic Carpet Restaurant
8566 W. Pico Blvd   (310) 652-8507
Supervision: Kehillah of Los Angeles.

Motty's Place
7308 Beverly Blvd   (213) 935-8087
Supervision: Kehillah of Los Angeles.

Museum Cafeteria
9760 W. Pico Blvd, 4th Floor   (310) 553-9036
Supervision: Kehillah of Los Angeles.
Pareve and meat.

Nagila Meating Place
9407 W. Pico Blvd   (310) 788-0119
Supervision: Kehillah of Los Angeles.

Olé, 7912 Beverly Blvd   (213) 933-7254
Supervision: Kehillah of Los Angeles.
Hours: 12 pm to 9 pm, five days a week;
closed Friday and Saturday.

Pat's, 9233 W. Pico Blvd   (310) 205-8705
Supervision: Kehillah of Los Angeles.
Sit down restaurant and catering.

Shalom Hunan Restaurant
5651 Wilshire Blvd   (213) 934-0505
Supervision: RCC.

Simon's La Glatt
446 N. Fairfax   (213) 658-7730
Supervision: RCC.

Westside Grille
9411 W. Pico Blvd   (310) 843-9829

Yiddishe Mama
9216 W. Pico Blvd   (310) 385-0101
Supervision: Kehillah of Los Angeles.

Dairy

Café Elite, 7115 Beverly Blvd   (213) 936-2861
Supervision: Kehillah of Los Angeles.
Chalav Yisrael.

Fish Grill, 7226 Beverly Blvd   (213) 937-7162
Supervision: Kehillah of Los Angeles.
Chalav Yisrael. Sit down or take out.

Milk N'Honey
8837 W. Pico Blvd   (310) 858-8850
Supervision: RCC.

Milky Way, 9108 W. Pico Blvd (310) 859-0004
Supervision: Kehillah of Los Angeles.
Chalav Yisrael.

Smoothie Queen
8851 W. Pico Blvd   (310) 273-3409
Supervision: Kehillah of Los Angeles.
Chalav Yisrael.

Fish

Tami's Fish House
553 B, Fairfax Avenue   (310) 655-7953

The Fishing Well, W. Pico Blvd (310) 859-9429
Supervision: RCC.

Pizzerias

Kosher Pizza Nosh
8644 W. Pico Blvd   (310) 276-8708

Nagila Pizza
9016 W. Pico Blvd   (213) 550-7735
Supervision: Kehillah of Los Angeles.
Chalav Yisrael.

Pizza Delight
435 N. Fairfax Ave.   (213) 655-7800
Supervision: Kehillah of Los Angeles.
Chalav Yisrael.

Pizza Mayven, 140 Labrea Ave (310) 847-0353

Pizza World
365 S. Fairfax Avenue, 90036   (213) 653-2896
Supervision: Kehillah of Los Angeles. Chalav
Yisrael. Italian/Mexican dairy restaurant.

Rami's Pizza
17736 1/2 Sherman Way   (818) 342-0611
Supervision: RCC.

Shalom Pizza
8715 W. Pico Blvd   (310) 271-2255
Supervision: RCC.

Bakeries

Aviv Bakery
15030 Ventura Blvd   (818) 789-3176
Supervision: RCC.

Back East Bialy Bakery
8562 W. Pico Blvd   (310) 276-1531
Supervision: Kehillah of Los Angeles.

Beverly Hills Patisserie
9100 W. Pico Blvd   (310) 275-6873
Supervision: RCC.

BH International Bakery
7113 Beverly Blvd   (213) 939-6497
Supervision: Kehillah of Los Angeles.

BH International Bakery
9211 W. Pico Blvd   (310) 859-8927
Supervision: Kehillah of Los Angeles.

BH International Bakery
7304 1/4 Santa Monica   (213) 874-7456
Supervision: Kehillah of Los Angeles.
All three locations have both pareve and dairy
and are Chalav Yisrael.

Eilat Bakery
457 1/2 N. Fairfax Avenue   (213) 653-5553
Supervision: Kehillah of Los Angeles.
Chalav Yisrael.

Eilat Bakery #2
9233 W. Pico Blvd   (310) 205-8700
Supervision: Kehillah of Los Angeles.
Chalav Yisrael.

Famous Bakery
350 N. Fairfax Avenue   (213) 933-5000
Supervision: Kehillah of Los Angeles.
Chalav Yisrael.

Le Palais, 8670 W. Pico Blvd   (310) 659-4809
Supervision: RCC.

Noah's New York Bagels   (800) 931-NOAH
                    Email: noah@noahs.com
Supervision: RCC. All stores in Southern
California are under RCC supervision; for the
location of a store near you, call the above
number.

Renaissance Bakery
22872 Ventura Blvd   (818) 222-0110
Supervision: RCC.

Schwartz Bakery
8616 W. Pico Blvd   (310) 854-0592
Supervision: RCC.

Schwartz Bakery
441 N. Fairfax   (213) 653-1683
Supervision: RCC.

Yummy Pita Bakery
1437 S. Robertson Blvd   (310) 557-2122
Supervision: Kehillah of Los Angeles.
Restaurant as well. Chalav Yisrael.

Butchers

City Glatt, 7667 Beverly Blvd   (213) 933-4040
Supervision: Kehillah of Los Angeles.
Sells Kehillah brand meats.

Doheny Kosher Meats
9213 W. Pico   (310) 276-7232
Supervision: RCC. Non-glatt.

Elat Market, 8730 W. Pico   (310) 659-7070
Supervision: RCC.
Non-glatt meat, deli and fish only.

Kosher Club
4817 W. Pico Blvd   (213) 933-8283
Supervision: RCC. Market as well.

Royal Palate Foods
960 E. Hyde Park Blvd   (310) 330-7700
Supervision: RCC.

Roz Kosher Meat
12422-24 Burbank Blvd   (818) 760-7694
Supervision: RCC. Market as well.

Star Meats
12136 Santa Monica Blvd   (310) 447-1612
Supervision: RCC.

Valley Glatt
12450 Burbank Blvd   (818) 766-4530
Supervision: Kehillah of Los Angeles.
Sells Kehillah brand meats.

Fishmongers

Fairfax Fish
515 N. Fairfax Avenue   (213) 658-8060
Supervision: Kehillah of Los Angeles.

Kosher Kitchens

Cedars Sinai Hospital
8700 Beverly Blvd   (310) 855-4797
Supervision: RCC.

Delicatessens

Micheline's
2627 S. LaCienega Blvd   (310) 204-5334
Supervision: RCC. Catering and take out.

Pico Kosher Deli
8826 W. Pico Blvd, 90035   (310) 273-9381
                    Fax: (310) 273-8476
Supervision: RCC.
Hours: Sunday to Thursday, 10 am to 9 pm;
Friday, 9 am to 3 pm; Shabbat, closed.

Caterers

Simon's Gourmet Glatt Caterers, 10505 S.
Monica Blvd, 90025   (310) 474-4011
                           888-4-SIMON-1
                    Fax: (310) 474-8026
Supervision: RCC. Glatt kosher caterers serving
southern California and the United States
since 1980. Catering at all 5 star hotels in the
US available.

Groceries

Kotlar's Pico Market
8622 W. Pico Blvd   (310) 652-5355
Supervision: RCC. Market, fish and butcher.

La Brea Kosher Market
410 N. La Brea Avenue (213) 931-1221
Supervision: Kehillah of Los Angeles.

Little Jerusalem
8917 W. Pico Blvd (310) 858-8361
Supervision: RCC.
Market, fish and butcher.

Pico Glatt Kosher Mart
9427 W. Pico Blvd (310) 785-0904
Supervision: Kehillah of Los Angeles.

PS Kosher Food Services
9760 W. Pico Blvd, 90035 (310) 553-8804
Fax: (310) 553-8989
Email: psfood@juno.com
Kitchens located at Yeshiva University.

Western Kosher Market
444 N. Fairfax Avenue (213) 655-8870
Supervision: Kehillah of Los Angeles.

Museums

Museum of Tolerance (Beit Hashoah)
9786 West Pico Blvd, 90035 (310) 553-9036
Fax: (310) 553-4521
Web site: www.wiesenthal.com

High-tech, hands-on museum that focuses on two themes through interactive exhibits: the dynamics of racism and prejudice, and the history of the Holocaust – the ultimate example of man's inhumanity to man.

Booksellers

House of David, 9020 W. Olympic Blvd, Beverly Hills, 90211 (310) 276-9414
Probably the most complete selection of books of Jewish interest can be found here.

North Beverly Hills

Synagogues

Orthodox
Young Israel of North Beverly Hills
9350 Civic Center Drive, 90210 203-0170

Northridge
Area telephone code (818)

Synagogues
Young Israel of Northridge
17511 Devonshire Street, 91324   368-2221

Oakland *(Greater East Bay)*
See also Berkeley

Community Organisations
Berkeley/Richmond JCC, 1414 Walnut St.,
Berkeley 94709
Contra Costa JCC, 2071 Tice Valley Blvd.,
Walnut Creek 94595
Jewish Federation of the Greater East Bay
401 Grand Avenue #500, 94610

Synagogues

Orthodox
Beth Jacob, 3778 Park Blvd., 94610

Conservative
Beth Abraham, 327 MacArthur Blvd., 94610
Beth Sholom, 642 Dolores, San Leandro,
94577
B'nai Shalom, 74 Eckley Lane, Walnut Creek,
94596

Reform
B'nai Tikvah, 25 Hillcroft Way, Walnut Creek,
94596
Beth Hillel, 801 Park Central, Richmond,
94803
Beth Emek, PO Box 722, Livermore, 94550
Temple Isaiah, 3800 Mt Diablo Blvd.,
Lafayette, 94549
Temple Sinai, 2808 Summit, 94609

Independent
B'nai Israel of Rossmoor, c/o Fred Rau, 2601
Ptarmigan #3, Walnut Creek, 94595
Beth Chaim, PO Box 23632, Pleasant Hill,
94523

Jewish Renewal
Aquarian Minyan, c/o Goldfarb, 2020 Essex,
Berkeley, 94703
Kehilla, PO Box 3063, Berkeley, 94703

Mikvaot
Beth Jacob Synagogue   (510) 482-1147

Delicatessens
Oakland Kosher Foods, 3256 Grand Avenue,
94610
Holy Land Restaurant
677 Rand Avenue, 94610   (510) 272-0535
Glatt kosher.

Palm Springs
Area telephone code (619)

Community Organisations
**Jewish Federation of Palm Springs Desert
Area**
611 S. Palm Canyon Drive, 92264   325-7281

Synagogues

Orthodox
Desert Synagogue, 1068 N. Palm Canyon
Drive, 92262   327-4848

Conservative
Temple Isaiah, 332 W. Alejo Road, 92262
Jewish community centre at this location too.

Restaurants

Dairy
New York Sandwich
125 E. Tahquitz   323-7883

Palo Alto
Area telephone code (415)

Community Organisations
Albert L. Schultz Community Center
655 Arastradero Road, 94306   493-9400

Synagogues

Orthodox
Congregation Chabad, 3070 Louis Road,
94308   429-8444
Palo Alto Orthodox Minyan, 260 Sheridan
Avenue, 94306   948-7498

Groceries

Garden Fresh, 1245 W. El Camino Road,
Mount View, 94040 961-7795

Mollie Stone's Markets
164 South California Avenue 323-8361
Near Stanford University.

Sacramento

Area telephone code (916)

Community Organisations

Jewish Federation of Sacramento
2351 Wyda Way, 95825 486-0906

Synagogues

Orthodox
Kenesset Israel Torah Center, 1024 Morse
Avenue, 95864 481-1159

Conservative
Mosaic Law
2300 Sierra Blvd, 95825 488-1122

Reform
B'nai Israel
3600 Riverside Blvd, 95818 446-4861

Beth Shalom
4746 El Camino Avenue, 95608 485-4478

Restaurants

Farah's Catering & Fine Foods
2319 El Camino Avenue, 95821 971-9500
Supervision: Rabbi Rosen, Kenesset Israel.

Groceries

Bob's Butcher Block & Deli
6436 Fair Oaks Blvd, Carmichael, 95608

San Bernardino

Synagogues

Emanu El, 3512 N. E Street, 92405 886-4818
This congregation is the oldest in southern
California.

The 'Home of Eternity' cemetery, 8th St. &
Sierra Way, presented by the Mormons, is one
of the oldest Jewish cemeteries in western US.

San Carlos

Area telephone code (650)

Accommodation Information

Jewish Travel Network
PO Box 283, 94070 368-0880
Fax: 599-9066
Email: jewishtn@aol.com
International hospitality exchange. Bed and
breakfast and home exchanges.

San Diego Area

Area telephone code (619)

Community Organisations

**United Jewish Federation of San Diego
County,** 4797 Mercury St, 92111 571-3444
Fax: 571-0701

Jewish Travel Network
International Hospitality Exchange

Travel while enjoying the warmth and hospitality of a Jewish home.
Host Jewish travelers from around the world.

Bed & Breakfast and Home Exchanges

Address: P.O. Box 283, San Carlos, CA 94070 USA
Tel: (650) 368-0880 **Fax:** (650) 599-9066 **Email:** jewishtn@aol.com

Synagogues

Orthodox

Beth Jacob Congregation, 4855 College
Avenue, 92115   287-9890

Beth Eliyahu Torah Center, 5012 Central
Avenue, Bonita, 91902   472 2144

Chabad House, 6115 Montezuma Road,
92115   265-7700

Chabad of La Costa, 1980 La Costa Avenue,
Carlsbad, 92009   943 8891

Chabad of La Jolla, 3232 Governor Drive,
Suite N, 92122   455-1670

Chabad of Rancho Bernardo, 16934 Old
Espola Road, Poway, 92064   451-0455

Congregation Adat Yeshurun
8950 Villa La Jolla Drive, Suite 1224, La Jolla,
92037   535-1196

Young Israel of San Diego, 7920 Navajo
Road, Suite 102, 92119   589-1447

Conservative

Adat Ami, 123 Camino de la Reina, Suite
N100, 92108   220-8888

Beth Am, 525 Stevens Avenue, Solana Beach,
92075   481-8454

Beth El
8660 Gilman Drive, La Jolla, 92037   452-1734

Beth Tefilah
4967 69th Street, 92115   463-0391

Ner Tamid
16981 Via Tazon, Suite G, 92127   592 9141

Temple Beth Sholom, 208 Madrona Street,
Chula Vista, 91910   420-6040

Temple Judea
1527 Roma Drive, Vista, 92083   724-8318

Tifereth Israel, 6660 Cowles Mountain Blvd.,
92119   697-6001

Reform

Beth Israel
2512 3rd Avenue, 92103   239-0149

Etz Chaim
PO Box 1138, Ramona, 92065   789 8117

Temple Adat Shalom, 15905 Pomerado Road,
Poway, 92064   451-1200

Temple Emanu-El
6299 Capri Drive, 92120   286-2555

Temple Solel, 552 S. El Camino Real,
Encinitas, 92024   436-0654

Reconstructionist

Dor Hadash, 4858 Ronson Court, Suite A,
92111   268-3674

Mikvaot

5170 La Dorna   287-6411
Call to arrange an appointment.

Restaurants

City Delicatessen, 6th Avenue & University
Avenue, 92103   295-2747
                           Fax: 295-2129
Kosher style restaurant and bakery featuring
Jewish specialties. Open late.

Croce's Restaurant-Jazz Bar
802 5th Avenue (at "F" St.), 92101   233-4355

Lang's, 6165 El Cajon Blvd, 92115   287-7306
                          800-60-LANGS
                           Fax: 582-1545
Kosher pareve bakery, dairy deli and foods.

Shmoozers Vegetarian & Pizzeria
6366 El Cajon Blvd, 92115
Supervision: Vaad HaRabbanim of San Diego.
Hours: Sunday to Thursday, 11:30 am to 9
pm; Friday, to 2 pm; Saturday, Motzei
Shabbat to 11 pm.

Western Glatt Kosher & N.Y. Deli, 7739 Fay
Avenue, La Jolla, 92037   454-6328

Delicatessens

D.Z. Akin's Deli
6930 Alvardo Road, 92120   265-0218

Eva's Fresh & Natural
6717 El Cajon Blvd, 92115   462-5018
Supervision: Vaad of San Diego.
Dairy and vegetarian food.

Media

Directories

Jewish Directory
4797 Mercury Street, 92111-2101   571-3444
                           Fax: 571-0701

Newspapers

Heritage
3443 Camino Del Rio S., Suite 315, 92108
                                 282-7177

San Diego Jewish Times
4731 Palm Avenue, La Niesa, 91941   463-5515

Tourist Sites

Balboa Park, the largest public park in San Diego, includes the House of Pacific Relations, which comprises 30 cottages for various ethnic groups. These include the Cottage of Israel, which mounts exhibitions throughout the year, portraying the history and traditions of the Jewish people, biblical and modern Israel. Open Sun. 1:30 pm to 4:30 pm, except on Holy-days and major festivals.

San Fernando Valley

Area telephone code (818)
The Valley is about 12 miles from Hollywood.

Community Organisations

North Valley Center, 16601 Rinaldi Street, Granada Hills, 91344
Valley Cities Center, 13164 Burbank Blvd., Van Nuys, 91401
West Valley Center, 22622 Vanowen Street, West Hills, 91307

Synagogues

Orthodox

Adat Ari El Synagogue, 5540 Laurel Canyon Blvd., N. Hollywood, 91607
There are eleven beautiful stained-glass windows, designed by Mischa Kallis, depicting significant dates in the religious calendar.
Chabad House, 4917 Hayvenhurst, Encino, 91346
Shaarey Zedek, 12800 Chandler Blvd., N. Hollywood, 91607

Conservative

Beth Meier Congregation, 11725 Moorpark, Studio City
Ner Maarev Temple, 5180 Yarmouth Avenue, Encino, 91316
Temple Aliyah, 24400 Aliyah Way, Woodland Hills, 91367
Shomrei Torah
Valley Circle, West Hills   346-0811
Temple B'nai Hayim, 4302 Van Nuys Blvd., Sherman Oaks
Temple Emanu-El, 1302 N. Glenoaks Avenue, Burbank, 91504
Temple Ramat Zion, 17655 Devonshire Avenue, Northridge

Valley Beth Shalom, 15739 Ventura Blvd., Encino, 91316

Reform

Beth Emet, 320 E. Magnolia Blvd., Burbank, 91502
Temple Ahavat Shalom, 11261 Chimineas Avenue, Northridge
Temple Judea, 5429 Lindley Avenue, Tarzana
Shir Chadash, 17000 Ventura Blvd., Encino

Mikvaot

Teichman Mikvah Society, 12800 Chandler Blvd, N. Hollywood, 91607   506-0996

Kashrut Information

The Kashrus Information Bureau, 12753 Chandler Blvd, N. Hollywood, 91607 762-3197

Restaurants

Apropo Falafel, 6800 Reseda Blvd   881-6608
Drexler's Kosher Restaurant
12519 Burbank Blvd, N. Hollywood 984-1160
Falafel Express, 5577 Reseda Blvd   345-5660
Falafel Village, 16060 Ventura Blvd 783-1012
Supervision: RCC.
Flora Falafel
12450 Burbank Blvd, N. Hollywood   766-6567
Supervision: RCC.
Golan, 13075 Victory Blvd   763-5375
Supervision: RCC.
Hadar Restaurant and Catering
12514 Burbank Blvd   762-1155
Supervision: RCC.
Orly Dairy Restaurant & Pizza
12454 Magnolia Blvd   508-5570
Sharon's
18608 1/2 Ventura Blvd, Tarzana   344-7472
Supervision: RCC.
Sportsman Lodge, Sherman Oaks   984-0202
Tiberias, 18046 Ventura Blvd   343-3705
Supervision: RCC.

Pizzerias

La Pizza, 12515 Burbank Blvd   760-8198
Pacific Kosher Pizza
12460 Oxnard   760-0087

Bakeries

Continental Kosher Bakery
12419 Burbank Blvd   762-5005

Sam's Kosher Bakery
12450 Burbank Blvd, Suite H   769-8352
Supervision: RCC.

Groceries

Ventura Market
18357 Ventura Blvd   873-1240
Supervision: RCC. Butcher, market and deli.

Ice Cream Parlors

Carvel's Ice Cream
25948 McBean Parkway, Valencia   259-1450
Supervision: KOF-K.

San Francisco

Area telephone code (415)

Community Organisations

**Jewish Com. Fed. of San Francisco, the
Peninsula, Marin & Sonoma Counties**
121 Steuart St., 94105   777-0411
                              Fax: 495-6635
Publishes 'Resource guide to the Bay Area' and
'Resource guide to Jewish life in Northern
California'.

Synagogues

Orthodox

Adath Israel
1851 Noriega Street, 94122   564-5665

Anshey Sfard
1500 Clement Street, 94118   752-4979

Chabad House
11 Tillman Place, 94108   956-8644

Chevra Thilim
751 25th Avenue, 94121   752-2866

Keneseth Israel, Suite 203, 655 Sutter Street,
94102   771-3420
A downtown synagogue offering meals over
Shabbat.

Magain David (Sephardi), 351 4th Avenue,
94118   752-9095

Torat Emeth
768 27th Avenue, 94121   386-1830

Young Israel of San Francisco
1806 A Noriega Street, 94122   387-1774

Conservative

Beth Sholom, 14th Avenue & Clement Street,
94118   221-8736

B'nai Emunah
3595 Taraval Street, 94116   664-7373

Ner Tamid
1250 Quintara Street, 94116   661-3383

Beth Israel-Judea, 625 Brotherhood Way,
94132   586-8833

Reform

Sha'ar Zahav
220 Danvers Street, 94114   861-6932

Sherith Israel
2266 California Street, 94118   346-1720

Emanu-El
Arguello Blvd. & Lake Street, 94118   751-2535

Mikvaot

3355 Sacramento Street, 94118   921-4070

Tourist Information

Jewish Com. Information & Referral Service
121 Steuart St, 94105   777-4545

Embassy

Consulate General
Suite 2100, 456 Montgomery Street, 94104

Restaurants

Lotus Garden
532 Grant Avenue, 94108   397-0130

Sabra, 419 Grant Avenue   982-3656
                              Fax: 982-3650
Supervision: Vaad Hakashrus of Northern CA.
Bishul Yisrael, Pat Yisrael and Mashgiach
Temidi. Free delivery to the financial district
for groups of 10 or more. Catering available.

This Is It, 430 Geary Street, 94210   749-0201
Middle Eastern cuisine.

Groceries

Gourmet Kosher Meals, Cong. Adath Israel,
1851 Noriega Street, 94122
Supervision: Orthodox Rabbinical Council.

Grill Middle Eastern Cuisine
430 Geary Street   749-0201

Jacob's Kosher Meats
2435 Noriega Street, 94122   564-7482

Jerusalem
420 Geary (at Mason), 94108   776-2683
Supervision: Cong. Thilim.

Kosher Meats Israel & Cohen Kosher Meats
5621 Geary Blvd, 94121   752-3064

Kosher Nutrition Kitchen, Montefiore Senior Center, 3200 California Avenue
Supervision: Orthodox Rabbinical Council.

Tel Aviv Strictly Kosher Meats
2495 Irving Street, 84122   661-7588
Supervision: Orthodox Rabbinical Council.

Museums

Jewish Community Museum
121 Steuart Street 94105   543-8880

Libraries

Holocaust Library & Research Center
601 14th Avenue, 94118   751-6040

San Jose

Area telephone code (408)

Community Organisations

Jewish Federation of Greater San Jose
14855 Oka Road, Los Gatos, 95030 358-3033
                          Fax: 356-0733

Synagogues

Orthodox

Ahavas Torah, 1537-A Meridian Avenue,
95125   266 2342

Almaden Valley Torah Center, 1281 Juli Lynn
Drive, 95120   997 9117

Congregation Am Echad, 1504 Meridian
Avenue, 95125   267 2591

Conservative

Congregation Beth David, 19700 Prospect
Road, Saratoga, 95070   257 3333

Congregation Emeth, P. O. Box 1430, Gilroy,
95021   847-4111

Traditional

Congregation Sinai, 1532 Willowbrae
Avenue, 95125   264 8542

Reform

Congregation Shir Hadash, 16555 Shannon
Road, Los Gatos, 95032   358-1751

Temple Beth Sholom, 2270 Unit D, Canoas
Garden Avenue, 95153   978-5566

Temple Emanu-El, 1010 University Avenue,
95126   292 0939

Restaurants

White Lotus, 80 North Market St.   977-0540

Delicatessens

Willow Glen Kosher Deli
1185 Lincoln Avenue, 95125   297-6604
Under Orthodox Rabbinical supervision. Glatt
kosher.

Booksellers

Alef Bet Judaica, 14103-0 Winchester Blvd,
Los Gatos, 95030   370-1818

San Rafael (Marin County)

Synagogues

Reform

Rodef Sholom, 170 N. San Pedro Rd., 94903

Santa Barbara

Synagogues

Orthodox

Young Israel of Santa Barbara
1826 C Cliff Drive, 93109   (805) 966-4565

Reform

Cong. B'nai B'rith, 900 San Antonio Creek
Road, 93111

Santa Monica

Area telephone code (213)

Synagogues

Orthodox

Chabad House, 1428 17th Street, 90404

Young Israel of Santa Monica
21 Hampton Avenue   399-8514
Mailing address is: PO Box 5725, 90405

Reform

Beth Sholom, 1827 California Avenue, 90403

Santa Rosa
Area telephone code (707)

Synagogues

Conservative
Beth Ami, 4676 Mayette Av., 95405   545-4334
Dairy kitchen on premises.

Reform
Shomrei Torah, Services at United Methodist Church, 1717 Yulupa Av., 95405   578-5519

Saratoga

Synagogues *(Conservative)*
Cong. Beth David, 19700 Prospect Rd. at Scully, 95070-3352   (408) 257-3333

Stockton

Stockton is one of the oldest communities west of the Mississippi River, founded in the days of the California Gold Rush. Temple Israel was founded as Congregation Ryhim Ahoovim in 1850 and erected its first building in 1855.

Synagogues
Reform
Temple Israel, 5105 N. El Dorado St., 95207

Thousand Oaks
Synagogues
Conservative
Temple Etz Chaim, 1080 E. Janss Rd., 91360. Kosher catering.   (805) 497-6891
Fax: (805) 497-0086
Synagogue contains unique artistic Aron Kodesh and Holocaust memorial.

Tiburon

Synagogues *(Conservative)*
Cong. Kol Shofar, 215 Blackfield Dr., Tiburon 94920   (415) 388-1818

Tustin

Synagogues *(Conservative)*
Cong. B'nai Israel
655 S. "B" St., 92680   (714) 259-0655

Vallejo

Synagogues
Cong. B'nai Israel (unaffiliated), 1256 Nebraska St., 94590   (707) 642-6526

Venice
Area telephone code (310)

Synagogues
Orthodox
Jewish Pacific Center, 505 Ocean Front Walk & 720 Rose Avenue, 90291   392-8749
Mikva and an elementary day school with summer camp facilities for visitors. It also offers a full range of kosher food, bakery products and meat, as well as accommodation.
Young Israel Torah Learning Center of Venice, 949 Sunset Avenue, 90021   450-7541

Conservative
Mishkon Tephilo, 206 Main Street, 90291

Ventura

Community Organisations
Jewish Community Centre
259 Callens Road   (805) 658-7441

Synagogues *(Reform)*
Temple Beth Torah, 7620 Foothill Road, 93004   (805) 647-4181

Walnut Creek

Synagogues
Conservative
Cong. B'nai Shalom, 74 Eckley Lane, 94595

Contra Costa Jewish Com. Center, 2071 Tice Valley Blvd., 94595

Reform
Cong. B'nai Tikvah, 25 Hillcroft Way, 94595

Whittier

Synagogues *(Conservative)*
Beth Shalom Syn. Center, 14564 E. Hawes Street, 90604 (310) 914-8744

Colorado

Boulder

Area telephone code (303)

Community Organisations
Hillel Foundation, 2795 Colorado Avenue, University of Colorado 442-6571

Synagogues
Orthodox
Lubavitch of Boulder County
4900 Sioux Drive, 80303 494-1638
Offering home hospitality.

Conservative
Congregation Bonai Shalom
1527 Cherryvale Rd, 80303 442-6605
Offering home hospitality.

Reform
Congregation Har Hashem
3950 Baseline Road, 80303 499-7077
Jewish Renewal Community of Boulder,
5001 Pennsylvania, 80303 271-3541
Meets third Friday each month.

Colorado Springs
Area telephone code (719)

Synagogues
Orthodox
Chabad House
3465 Nonchalant Circle, 80909 596-7330

Conservative & Reform
Temple Shalom
1523 E. Monument Street, 80909 634-5311

Denver
Area telephone code (303)

Community Organisations
Allied Jewish Federation of Colorado
300 S. Dahlia Street, 80222 321-3399
Fax: 322-8328

Community Center
4800 E. Alameda Avenue, 80222

Synagogues
Orthodox
Bais Medrash Kehillas Yaakov, 295 S. Locust Street, 80222 377-1200
Congregation Zera Abraham
1560 Winona Court, 80204 825-7517
E. Denver Syn., 198 S. Holly, 80222 322-7943

Traditional
B.M.H. Cong., 560 S. Monaco Pkwy, 80222

Conservative
Hebrew Educational Alliance (HEA)
6445 East Ohio#200, 80224 331-6950
Rodef Shalom, 450 S. Kearney, 80224

Reform
B'Nai Chaim
P.O.Box 621303, Littleton, 80162 281-8789
Congregation Emanuel
51 Grape Street, 80220 388-4013
Temple Miacah
2600 Leyden Street, 80207 388-4239
Temple Sinai
3509 South Glencoe Street, 80237 759-1827

Reconstructionist
B'Nai Havurah
6445 East Ohio Avenue, 80224 388-4441
B'nai Torah
P.O. Box 5488, Arvada, 80006 692-5234
Beth Shalom, 2280 East Noble Place, Littleton, 80121 794-6643

Mikvaot

Mikvah of Denver
1404 Quitman, 80204   893-5315

Religious Organisations

Rocky Mountain Rabbinic Council
6445 East Ohio Avenue, 80224   388-4441

Synagogue Council of Greater Denver
PO Box 102732, 80250   759-8484

Kashrut Information

Rabbi Mordecai Twerski
295 South Locust Avenue, 80224   377-1200

Vaad Hakashrus, 1350 Vrain, 80204
                                              595-9349

Restaurants

Elegance by Andrew
745 Quebec Street, 80220   322-2298

Dairy

Mediterranean Health Cafe
2817 East 3rd Avenue, 80206   399-2940
Supervision: Vaad Hakashrus of Denver.
Kosher/dairy/vegetarian food. Chalav Yisrael
and Pat Yisrael available. Hours: Sunday, 12
pm to 8 pm; Monday to Thursday, 11 am to 8
pm; Friday, to 2 pm.

Pizzerias

Johnny's Pizza, 9345 Monaca Pkwy 399-6666

Bakeries

Bagel Shop
2412 East Arapahoe Road, 80122   220-5101

Einstein's
700 Colorado Blvd, Unit D, 80206   322-5166

Einstein's, 200 Fillmore, 80206   399-7448

Einstein's, 6460 East Yale, 80222   744-2605

Finster Brothers Bagel Bakery
5709 East Clofax, 80220   377-2088

Heidi's Bagels
3130 Lowell Blvd, 80211   477-2605

Jacob's Bagelry
290 South Downing, 80209   744-6028

Moe's Broadway Bagel
2650 Broadway, Boulder, 80302   444-3252

New York Bagel Boys
6449 E Hampden Avenue, 80231   388-2648

The Bagel Store
942 South Monaco, 80224   388-2648

Delicatessens

900 Auraria Parkway (Tivoli Centre) 572-3354

East Side Kosher Deli
5475 Leetsdale Drive, 80222   322-9862
Supervision: Vaad Hakashrus of Denver.

New York Deli News
7105 East Hampden   759-4741

The Bagel Deli
6217 East 14th   322-0350

The Bagel Deli
6439 East Hampden   756-6667

The New York Deli
1117 Pearle Street, Boulder   449-5161

Zaidy's Deli
112 Adams, 80206   333-5336

Groceries

The following stores have kosher sections.

Cub Foods
1985 Sheridan Blvd, Edgewater   232-8972
4600 Leetsdale Drive   232-1110

King Soopers
6470 East Hampden Avenue   758-1210
890 S.Monaco Pkwy   333-1535

Safeway
7150 Leetsdale drive (& Quebec)   377-6939
6460 E. Yale (& Monaco)   691-8870

Media

Newspapers (weekly)

Intermountain Jewish News
1275 Sherman Avenue, 80203   861-2234
                                   Fax: 832-6942

Littleton

Synagogues (Conservative)

Beth Shalom
2280 E. Noble Place, 80121   (303) 794-6643

Pueblo

Synagogues

Conservative

United Hebrew Congregation
106 W. 15th Street, 81003

Reform
Temple Emanuel, 1325 Grand Avenue, 81003

Connecticut

Bridgeport

Area telephone code (203)

Community Organisations
Jewish Federation of Greater Bridgeport
4200 Park Avenue, 06604   372-6504
Serving Bridgeport, Easton, Fairfield, Monroe,
Shelton, Stratford and Trumball.

Religious Organisations
Bridgeport Va'ad, 1571 Stratfield Road,
Fairfield, 06432   372-6529

Synagogues

Orthodox
Agudas Achim, 85 Arlington Street, 06606
Ahavath Achim, 1571 Stratfield Road,
Fairfield, 06432
Bikur Cholim, Park & Capitol Avenues, 06604
Shaare Torah Adath Israel, 3050 Main Street,
06606

Conservative
B'nai Torah, 5700 Main St., Trumbull, 06611
Cong. Beth El, 1200 Fairfield Woods Rd.,
Fairfield, 06430
Rodeph Sholom, 2385 Park Avenue, 06604

Reform
Temple B'nai Israel, 2710 Park Ave, 06604

Reconstructionist
Cong. Shirei Shalom, POB 372, Monroe, 06468

Mikvaot
Mikveh Israel, 1326 Stratfield Rd., Fairfield,
06432

Restaurants
Brooklawn Bakery & Pizza Shop
1718 Capitol Avenue   384-0504
Supervision: Vaad Hakashrus of Fairfield
County. Separate pareve and dairy sections.

Cafe Shalom
c/o Abel, Community Center   372-6567

Bakeries
Carvel Ice Cream Bakery, 1838 Black Rock
Turnpike, Fairfield   384-2253
Supervision: Vaad Hakashrus of Fairfield
County. All products in the store are under
supervision, except for those Snapple drinks
not marked with an OK.
The Original Bagel King of Fairfield, 22670
Black Rock Turnpike, Fairfield   368-3365
Supervision: Vaad Hakashrus of Fairfield
County. Wide variety of bagels and challah.
The uncut bagels and uncut challah are
supervised.

Delicatessens
Chai Café at the JCCS
4200 Park Avenue   374-5556
Supervision: Vaad Hakashrus of Fairfield
County. Glatt kosher deli.

Media

Newspapers
Bridgeport Jewish Ledger, c/o Jewish
Federation, 4200 Park Avenue   372-6504

Radio
WVOF Radio   254-4111
Jewish public affairs show Sun, 7pm on
88.5FM.

Danbury

Area telephone code (203)

Community Organisations
Jewish Federation
105 Newtown Road, 06810   792-6353
                                  Fax: 748-5099
Issues monthly publication.

Synagogues

Conservative
Cong. B'nai Israel, 193 Clapboard Ridge
Road, 06811   792-6161

Reform
United Jewish Center, 141 Deer Hill Avenue,
06810   748-3355

Hamden

Restaurants
Abel's
2100 Dixwell Avenue, 06514

Hartford

Area telephone code (860)

Community Organisations
Jewish Federation of Hartford
333 Bloomfield Avenue, 06117   232-4483
Publishes 'All Things Jewish'.

Synagogues

Orthodox
Agudas Achim, 1244 N. Main St., W.
Hartford, 06117
Beth David
20 Dover Rd., W. Hartford, 06119   236-1241
Chabad House of Greater Hartford, 798
Farmington Av., W. Hartford, 06119
Contact for kosher meal & Shabbat
arrangements.
Teferes Israel, 27 Brown St., Bloomfield,
06002
United Synagogue of Greater Hartford, 840
N. Main St., W. Hartford, 06117
Young Israel of Hartford
1137 Troutbrook Drive, 06119   523-7804
Young Israel of West Hartford, 2240 Albany
Avenue, W. Hartford, 06117

Conservative
Beth El, 2626 Albany Avenue, W. Hartford
06117
Beth Tefilah, 465 Oak St., E. Hartford, 06118
B'nai Sholom, 26 Church St., Newington,
06111
Temple Emanuel, 160 Mohegan Dr., W.
Hartford, 06117

Reform
Beth Israel, 701 Farmington Av., W. Hartford,
06119
Temple Sinai, 41 W. Hartford Rd., Newington,
06011

Mikvaot
61 Main Street, 06119

Kashrut Information
Kashrut Commission
162 Brewster Road, 06117   563-4017

Booksellers
Israel Gift Shop Hebrew Book Store
262 S. Whitney Street, 06105   232-3984

Manchester

Synagogues (Conservative)
Temple Beth Sholom, 400 Middle Turnpike
E., 06040   (860) 643 9563

Meriden

Synagogues (Conservative)
B'nai Abraham, 127 E. Main St., 06450

Middletown

Synagogues (Conservative)
Adath Israel, 48 Church St., 06457

New Britain

Synagogues

Orthodox
Tephereth Israel, 76 Winter Street, 06051

Conservative
B'nai Israel, 265 W. Main St., 06051

New Haven

Area telephone code (203)

Community Organisations
Jewish Federation of Greater New Haven
360 Amity Road,
Woodbridge Ct, 06525   387-2424

Synagogues

Orthodox

Beth Hamedrosh Westville, 74 West Prospect
Street, 06515   389-9513

Young Israel of New Haven
292 Norton Street, 06511   776-4212
            Web site: www.youngisrael.org/yinh

Conservative

Beth-El Keser Israel, 85 Harrison Street,
06515   389-2108

Mikvaot

86 Hubinger Street, 06511   387-2184

Contact Information

Young Israel House at Yale University
    Web site: www.yale.edu/hillel/orgs/yihy.html

Bakeries

Westville Kosher Bakery
1460 Whalley Avenue, 06515   397-0839

Delicatessens

Fox's Deli
1460 Whalley Avenue, 06515   387-2214

Zackey's
1304 Whalley Avenue, 06515   387-2454

Groceries

Westville Kosher Meat Market
95 Amity Road, 06525   389-1723

New London

Organisations

Jewish Federation of Eastern Conneticut
28 Channing Street, 06320   (203) 442-8062

Norwalk

Community Organisations

Jewish Federation of Greater Norwalk
Shorehaven Road, 06855   (203) 853-3440

Bakeries

The Original Bagel King of Norwalk
250 Westport Avenue   (203) 846-2633
Supervision: Vaad Hakashrus of Fairfield
County. Wide variety of bagels and challah.
The uncut bagels and uncut challah are
supervised.

Norwich

Synagogues (Orthodox)

Brothers of Joseph, Broad & Washington
Aves., 06360   (203) 887-3777
Mikva attached.

Stamford

Area telephone code (203)

Organisations

United Jewish Federation
1035 Newfield Avenue, 06905   321-1373

Synagogues

Orthodox

Young Israel of Stamford
69 Oak Lawn Avenue, 06905   348-3955

Bakeries

Carvel Ice Cream Bakery
810 East Main Street   324-0944
Supervision: Vaad Hakashrus of Fairfield
County. All products in the store are under
supervision, except for those Snapple drinks
not marked with an OK.

Cerbone Bakery
605 Newfield Avenue   348-9029
Supervision: Vaad Hakashrus of Fairfield
County.

Delicatessens

Delicate-Essen at the JCC
1035 Newfield Avenue, 06902   322-0944
                              Fax: 322-5160
Supervision: Vaad Hakashrus of Fairfield
County. Glatt kosher sit down café serving hot
and cold sandwiches, soups and grilled items.
Hours: Monday to Thursday, 9 am to 8 pm;
Friday, to 2 pm; Sunday, to 4 pm.

Nosherye, JCC Building, 1035 Newfield Ave, 06905   321-1373

Groceries
Delicate-Essen
111 High Ridge Road, 06905   316-5570
       Fax: 316-5573
Supervision: Vaad Hakashrus of Fairfield County. Full selection of grocery items. Glatt kosher butcher and take-out products available. Open six days a week.

Media
Magazines
United Jewish Federation
39 Regent Court, 06907   322-2840

Waterbury

Community Organisations
Jewish Federation of Greater Waterbury
73 Main Street, South Woodbury, 06798   (203) 263-5121

Bakeries
Ami's Hot Bagels
111 Tomaston Avenue   596-9020
Supervision: Vaad Hakashrus of Fairfield County. Bagels, sandwiches and spreads are all supervised. All products are dairy.

Westport
Area telephone code (203)

Synagogues
Young Israel of Westport & Norwalk
215 Post Road West, 06880   226-6901

Woodbridge

Restaurants
Center Cafe & Jewish Libraries
JCC of Greater New Haven, 360 Amity Road, 06525   387-2424
Kosher dairy café offering breakfast, lunch and light snacks.

Delaware

Dover

Synagogues
Cong. Beth Sholom of Dover, POB 223, 19903

Newark

Synagogues
Temple Beth El, 101 Possum Pk. Rd., 19711

Wilmington

Community Organisations
Jewish Community Center, 101 Garden of Eden Road, 19803   (302) 478-5660
       Fax: (302) 478 6068

Synagogues
Orthodox
Adas Kodesh Shel Emeth, Washington Blvd. & Torah Dr., 19802

Conservative
Beth Shalom, 18th St. and Baynard Blvd., 19802

Reform
Beth Emeth, 300 W. Lea Blvd., 19802.

District of Columbia

Washington
Area telephone code (202)

Organisations
Jewish Com. Council of Greater Washington
American Israel Public Affairs Com., 500 N. Capitol St., N.W., Suite 412, 20001
Jewish Historical Society of Greater Washington
701 3rd Street NW, 20001-2624   789-0900

Synagogues

Temple Micah, 2829 Wisconsin Avenue N.W., 20007   342-9175

Kashrut Information

Rabbinical Council of Greater Washington
7826 Eastern Avenue, 20012

Eruv Information

Eruv in Georgetown   338-ERUV

Embassy

Embassy of Israel
3514 International Drive, 20008

Restaurants

Nuthouse Pizza   942-5900

Delicatessens

Hunan Deli, "H" Street   833-1018
Posins Bakery & Deli
5756 Georgia Avenue   726-4424
Bakery is under Conservative hashgacha.

Off Licence

Potomac Wines & Spirits
3057 M Street   333-2847

Hotels

St James Suites
950 24th Street, NW   457-0500
Gives discounts to Kesher Israel guests.

Museums

B'nai B'rith Museum, Klutznick Exhibit Hall, 1640 Rhode Island Av., 20036
Jewish War Veterans, Usa National Memorial
1811 R. Street N.W., 20009   265-6280
John F. Kennedy Center, 2700 "F" Street
Israeli lounge donated by the people of Israel.
Lillian & Albert Small Museum
3rd & "G" Sts. N.W., 20008
Housed in Washington's oldest synagogue building, Adas Israel, built in 1876.
Smithsonian Institute, The Natural History Building, 10th & Constitution Avs. NW, 20001
Contains a collection of Jewish ritual articles.
The Isaac Polack Building
2109 Pennsylvania Av. N.W.

Built in 1796, The Isaac Polack Building was the home of the first Jew to settle in Washington
United States Holocaust Memorial Museum
2000L Street, #717, 20036-4907   822-6464

Libraries

Jewish War Veteran, USA Memorial
1811 R. Street N.W., 20009   265-6280
Has a large collection of Judaica.
The National Archives
Pennsylvania Av. at 8th Street N.W.
Containing historical Jewish documentation.

Media

Newspapers
The Jewish Week, 1910 "K" Street, 20006

Booksellers

B'nai B'rith Museum
1640 Rhode Island Avenue, 20036

Florida

Aventura

Synagogues (Orthodox)

Young Israel of Aventura, 2956 Aventura Blvd, 2nd Floor, 33180   (305) 931-5188

Belle Glade

Area telephone code (202)

Synagogues (Conservative)
Temple Beth Sholom
224 N.W. Avenue, "G", 33430   996-3886

Boca Raton

Area telephone code (407)

Community Organisations
Jewish Federation of South Palm Beach County
9901 Donna Klein Blvd, 33428   852-3100

Synagogues

Orthodox

Young Israel of Boca Raton
7200 Palmetto Circle Blvd, 33433   391-5509

Mikvaot

Boca Raton Synagogue Mikveh, 7900
Montoya Circle South, 33433   538-0070

Restaurants

Eilat Cafe, Delmar Shopping Village, 7158 N.
Beracasa Way, 33434   368-6880

Falafel Armon
22767 State Road 7, 33428   477-0633

Orchids Garden
9045 La Fontana Blvd, #B-9, 33434   482-3831
   Fax: 482-5951
Supervision: ORB.
Hours: Monday to Thursday, 11:30 am to 9
pm; Sunday, 3 pm to 9 pm.

The Cafe, Cultural Arts Building, 9901 Donna
Klein Blvd, 33428-1788   852-3204

Delicatessens

Deli Maven
8208 Glades Road, 33434   477-7008

Clearwater

Area telephone code (813)

Community Organisations

Jewish Federation of Pinellas County, 13191
Starkey Road, Suite 8, 34643-1438   530-3223
   Fax: 531-0221

Synagogues

Orthodox

Young Israel of Clearwater
2385 Tampa Road, Suite 1, 34684   789-0408

Conservative

Beth Shalom
1325 S. Belcher Road, 34624   531-1418

Reform

B'nai Israel
1685 S. Belcher Road, 34624   531-5829

Temple Ahavat Shalom, 1575 Curlew Road,
Palm Harbor, 34683   785-8811

Daytona Beach

Area telephone code (407)

Community Organisations

**Jewish Federation of Volusia & Flagler
Counties,**
733 S. Nova Road, Ormond Beach, 32174
   672-0294

Synagogues

Conservative

Temple Israel
1400 S. Peninsula Drive, 32118   252-3097

Reform

Temple Beth El, 579 N. Nova Road, Ormond
Beach, 32174   677-2484

Deerfield Beach

Area telephone code (954)

Synagogues

Orthodox

Young Israel of Deerfield Beach
1880 H West Hillsboro Blvd, 33112   698-0328

Delray Beach

Area telephone code (904)

Synagogues

Anshei Emuna
16189 Carter Road, 33445   499-9229

Conservative

Temple Anshei Shalom of West Delray
Oriole Jewish Center, 7099 W. Atlantic
Avenue, 33446   495-1300

Temple Emeth
5780 W. Atlantic Avenue, 33446   498-3536

Reform

Temple Sinai
2475 W. Atlantic Avenue, 33445   276-6161

Restaurants

Mandarin, 5046 West Atlantic Avenue, (Pines
Plaza), 33484   496-6278

Groceries

Meat Market, Oriole Kosher Market, 7345 West Atlantic Ave, 33446

Fort Lauderdale

Area telephone code (305)

Community Organisations

Jewish Federation of Greater Fort Lauderdale
8358 W. Oakland Park Blvd, 33321   748-8400
Fax: 748-6332

Synagogues

Orthodox
Young Israel of Hollywood-Ft. Lauderdale
3291 Stirling Road, 33312   966-8870

Restaurants

David Shai King, 5599 N. University Drive, Lauderhill, 33321   572-6522

Delicatessens

East Side Kosher Restaurant & Deli
6846 W. Atlantic Blvd, Margate, 33063

Fort Meyers

Synagogues *(Reform)*

Temple Beth El, 16225 Winkler Road Ext, 33908   (941) 433-0018

Fort Pierce

Synagogues *(Reform)*

Temple Beth-El Israel
4600 Oleander Drive, 34982   (407) 461-7428

Hollywood & Vicinity

Area telephone code (305)

Community Organisations

Jewish Federation of South Broward
2719 Hollywood Blvd, 33020   921-8810

Synagogues

Orthodox
Chabad Ocean Syn., 4000 S. Ocean Dr., Hallandale

Chabad of Southwest Broward, 11251 Taft St., Pembroke Pines

Congregation Ahavat Shalom, 315 Madison St., Hollywood

Cong. Levi Yitzchok-Lubavitch, 1295 E. Hallandale Beach Blvd., Hallandale

Young Israel of Hollywood/Ft. Lauderdale, 3291 Stirling Rd., Ft. Lauderdale

Young Israel of Pembroke Pines, 13400 S.W. 10 St., Pembroke Pines

Conservative
B'nai Aviv, 200 Bonaventure Blvd., Weston

Century Pines Jewish Center, 13400 S.W. 10 St., Pembroke Pines

Hallandale Jewish Center, 416 N.E. 8 Av., Hallandale

Temple Beth Ahm Israel, 9730 Stirling Rd.

Temple Beth Shalom, 1400 N. 46 Avenue, Hollywood

Temple Judea of Carriage Hills, 6734 Stirling Rd., Hollywood

Temple Sinai, 1201 Johnson St., Hollywood

Reform
Temple Beth El, 1351 S. 14 Av., Hollywood

Temple Beth Emet, 10801 Pembroke Rd., Pembroke Pines

Temple Solel, 5100 Sheridan St., Hollywood

Sephardi
B'nai Sephardim, 3670 Stirling Rd., Ft. Lauderdale

Restaurants

Pita Plus, 5650 Stirling Rd, 33021   985-8028

Pizzerias

Jerusalem Pizza II
5650 Stirling Road, 33021   964-6811

Media

Newspapers
The Jewish Community Advocate of South Broward
2719 Hollywood Blvd, 33020   922-8603

Jacksonville

Area telephone code (904)

Community Organisations

Jacksonville Jewish Federation
8505 San Jose Blvd, 32217 448-5000

Kosher Nutrition Center
5846 Mt. Carmel Terrace, 32216 737-9075

Synagogues

Etz Chaim
10167 San Jose Blvd, 32257 262-3565
Mikva on premises.

Kendall

Area telephone code (305)

Synagogues *(Orthodox)*

Young Israel of Kendall
7880 SW 112th Street, 33156 232-6833

Key West

Synagogues

Conservative
B'nai Zion
750 United Street, 33040-3251 294-3437

Lakeland

Synagogues

Temple Emanuel, 600 Lake Hollingsworth
Drive, 33803 (813) 682-8616

Miami / Miami Beach

Area telephone code (305)

Community Organisations

Greater Miami Jewish Federation
4200 Biscayne Blvd, 33137 576-4000
Fax: 573-8115
Has information and referral service, ext. 283.

Religious Organisations

Young Israel Southern Regional Office
1035 NW 170th Terrace, 33162 770-3993
Fax: 770-3993
Email: ncyi.south@youngisrael.org

Synagogues

Orthodox
Young Israel of Greater Miami
990 NE 171st Street, North Miami Beach,
33162 651-3591

Young Israel of Miami Beach
4221 Pine Tree Drive, 33140 534-3206

Young Israel of Sky Lake
1850 NE 183rd Street, North Miami Beach,
33179 945-8712/8715

Conservative
Beth Raphael
1545 Jefferson Avenue, 33139 538-4112
Dedicated to the six million martyrs of the
Holocaust. On an outside marble wall, a large
six-light menorah burns every night. Six
hundred names have been inscribed on the
marble. There is also a notable Holocaust
Memorial at Dade and Meridian Avenues.

Mikvaot

Adas Dej Mikveh
225 37th Street, 33140 538-0070

**B'nai Israel & Greater Miami Youth
Synagogue Mikveh,** 16260 S. W. 288th
Street, Naranja, 33033 264-6488

Daughters of Israel
2530 Pinetree Drive, 33140 672-3500

Mikveh Blima of North Dade, 1054 N.E.
Miami Gardens Drive, 33179 949-9650

Embassy

Consulate General
Suite 1800, 100N Biscayne Blvd, 33132

Restaurants

Aviva's Kitchen
16355 W. Dixie Hwy., 33160 944-7313

Bagel Time
3915 Alton Road, 33140 538-0300
Supervision: Star-K. Eat in or take out. Hours:
Sunday to Friday, 6:30 am to 4 pm.

Beethoven Restaurant, Sasson Hotel, 2001
Collins Ave., 33139 531-0761

China Kikor Tel Aviv
5005 Collins Avenue, 33140   866-3316

Crown Buffet & Dairy Bar, Crown Hotel,
4041 Collins Ave., 33140   531-5771

Embassy Peking Tower Suite, 4101 Pinetree
Drive, Tower 41, 33140   538-7550

Gitty's Hungarian Kitchen
6565 Collins Avenue, Sherry Frontenac Hotel,
33141   865-4893

Jerusalem Peking
4299 Collins Avenue, 33140   532-2263

Ocean Terrace Restaurant & Grille
4041 Collins Avenue, 33140   531-5771

Pinati Restaurant
2520 Miami Gardens Drive, 33180   931-8086

Pita King, 343 East Flagler, 33131   358-0386

Pita Plus
20103 Biscayne Blvd, 33180   935-0761

Shalom Haifa
1330 N.E. 163 Street, 33162   945-2884

South Beach Pita
Washington Avenue, 33139   534-3706

The Noshery (Seasonal dairy), Saxony Hotel,
3201 Collins Ave., 33140   538-6811

Wing Wan II
1640 N.E, 164 Street, 33162   945-3585

Pizzerias

Jerusalem Pizza
761 N.E. 167th Street, 33162   653-6662

Sarah's Kosher Pizza
2214 N.E. 123 Street, 33181   891-3312

Sarah's Kosher Pizza
1127 N. E. 163 Street, 33162   948-7777

Shemtov Kosher Pizza
514 - 41st Street, 33140   538-2123

Yonnie's Kosher Pizza
19802 W. Dixie Hwy., 33180   932-1961

Accommodation Information

Some of the following hotels are open all year
round. The others close for varying lengths of
time between the end of Pesach and
November.

The following hotels offer kosher catering
and Passover facilities, but visitors are advised
to check before booking.

Hotels

Alexander, 5225 Collins Avenue, 33140

Carriage House, 5401 Collins Avenue, 33140

Crown Hotel, Ocean Front Block 40-41 Street,
33140   531-5771
Supervision: OU.

Doral, 4833 Collins Avenue, 33140

Eden Roc, 4525 Collins Avenue, 33140

Embassy
1051 N. Miami Beach Blvd, 33168   538-7550
Under Kashrut supervision.

Fountainbleau-Hilton
4441 Collins Avenue, 33140

Harbor House Hotel Apartments
10275 Collins Avenue, 33154

Marco Polo
19201 Collins Avenue, 33160

Sans Souci Hotel, 31st Street & Collins
Avenue, 33140   531-8261
Under Kashrut supervision.

Sasson Ocean Resort
2001 Collins Avenue, 33139   531-0761
Under Kashrut supervision.

Shawnee Beach Resort
4343 Collins Avenue, 33140

Sheraton Bal Harbor
9701 Collins Avenue, 33154

Sherry Frontenac
6565 Collins Avenue, 33141   866-1637
Under Kashrut supervision.

Museums

Jewish Museum of Florida
301 Washington Avenue, Miami Beach,
33139-6965   672-5044

Media

Directories
Jewish Life in Dade County
4200 Biscayne Blvd, 33137   576-4000
Fax: 573-8115

Tours

Jewish Travel and Education Network - JTEN
931-1782
Offers organised tours of Miami and Miami
Beach.

Orlando

Area telephone code (407)

Community Organisations

Jewish Federation of Greater Orlando
851 N. Maitland Avenue, 32751   645-5933

Synagogues

Orthodox

Ahavas Yisroel
708 Lake Howell Road, Maitland, 32741

Conservative

Congregation Beth Shalom, 13th & Center
Streets, Leesburg, 32748   742-0238
Congregation Ohev Shalom
5015 Goddard Avenue, 32804   298-4650
Congregation Shalom (Williamsburg), c/o
Sydney Ansell, 11821 Soccer Lane, 32821
Congregation Shalom Aleichem
PO Box 424211, Kissimmee, 34742-4211
Southwest Orlando Jewish Congregation
11200 S. Apopka-Vineland Road, 32836
Temple Israel, 4917 Eli St, 32804   647-3055

Reform

Congregation of Liberal Judaism
928 Malone Drive, 32810   645-0444

Restaurants

Kinneret Kitchens
517 South Delany   422-7205
Senior Citizens dining room. Meals: Mon.-Fri
at 5pm. Call at least 24 hours in advance to
reserve a meal.
The Lower East Side at Catalonia Inn Hotel
      648-4830
Glatt kosher.

Delicatessens

Market Place Deli, Hyatt Orlando
6375 W. Irlo Bronson Highway   396-1234
Has frozen kosher food only.

Groceries

Amira's Catering and Specialty, 1351 E.
Altamonte, Altamonte Springs   767-7577
Cold cuts, side dishes, frozen meals, groceries.
Kosher Korner
8464 Palm Parkway, 32836   238-9968

Complete kosher grocery and takeout.
Packaged frozen glatt meat. Will deliver to
hotels.

Hotels

Catalina Inn – Lower East Side Restaurant
3401 MacLeod Road, 32805   648-4830
Supervision: OU.

Palm City

Synagogues

Conservative

**Treasure Coast Jewish Center-Congregation
Beth Abraham,** 3998 S.W. Leighton Farms
Avenue, 34990   287-8833

Palm Coast

Synagogues

Temple Beth Shalom, 40 Wellington Drive,
POB 350557, 32135-0557   (904) 445-3006

Pensacola

Synagogues

Conservative

B'nai Israel, 1829 N. 9th Avenue, 32503

Reform

Beth El, 800 N. Palafox Street, 32501

Rockledge

Community Organisations

Jewish Federation of Brevard
108A Barton Avenue   (407) 636-1824

Sarasota

Community Organisations

Sarasota-Manatee Jewish Federation
580 S. McIntosh Road, 34232   (813) 371-4546

St Augustine

Synagogues
First Sons Of Israel, 161 Cordova St, 32084

St Petersburg
Area telephone code (813)

Synagogues

Conservative
B'nai Israel, 301 59th Street N., 33710
Beth Shalom, 1844 54th Street S., 33707

Reform
Beth-El
400 Pasadena Avenue S., 33707   347-6136

Groceries
Jo-El's Specialty Foods
2619 23rd Avenue N., 33713   321-3847
Also has delicatessen and butcher shop.
Hours: Monday to Thursday, 9 am to 5 pm;
Friday, to 4 pm; Sunday, to 1 pm.

Surfside

Synagogues
The Shul of Bal Harbor, Bay Harbor &
Surfside
9540 Collins Avenue, 33154   (305) 868-1411

Tampa
Area telephone code (813)

Community Organisations
Tampa Jewish Federation, 13009 Community
Campus Drive, 33625-4000   264-9000
960-1840
Fax: 265-8450

Synagogues

Orthodox
Hebrew Academy
14908 Penington Road, 33624   963-0706
Young Israel of Tampa
3721 W Tacon Street, 33629   832-3018

Conservative
Kol Ami, 3919 Moran Rd., 33618   962-6338
Rodeph Shalom
2713 Bayshore Blvd., 33629   837-1911
Temple David
2001 Swann Avenue, 33606   254-1771

Reform
Schaarai Zedek
3303 Swann Avenue, 33609   876-2377

Mikvaot
Bais Tefilah
14908 Pennington Road, 33624   963-2317

Vero Beach
Area telephone code (407)

Synagogues
Reform
Temple Beth Shalom, 365 43rd St. 569-4700

West Palm Beach
Area telephone code (407)

Community Organisations
Jewish Federation of Palm Beach County
4601 Community Drive, 33417   478-0700
Chabad House
4800 23rd St. N, 33407   640-8111

Georgia

Athens

Synagogues *(Reform)*

Congregation Children of Israel
Dudley Drive, 30606   (404) 549-4192

Atlanta

Area telephone code (404)

Community Organisations

Jewish Federation, 1753 Peachtree Road, NE
30309   873-1661
Fax: 874-7043
Publishes an annual community guide.

Synagogues

Orthodox
Young Israel of Toco Hills
2074 La Vista Road, 30329   636-4818

Beth Jacob
1855 La Vista Road, 30329   633-0551
Mikva on premises.

Kashrut Information

Atlanta Kashrut Commission
1855 La Vista Road, N.E., 30329   634-4063
A non-profit organisation dedicated to
promoting kashrut through education,
research and supervision. Publishes a monthly
kashrut newsletter.

Embassy

Consulate General, Suite 440, 1100 Spring
Street, NW, 30309-2823

Restaurants

Broadway Café
2166 Briarcliff Road, 30329   329-0888
Supervision: Atlanta Kashrut Commission.

Quality Kosher
5942 Roswell Road, Hammond Square, 30342
Supervision: Atlanta Kashrut Commission.

Wall Street Pizza
2470 Briarcliff Road, N.E., 30329   633-2111
Supervision: Atlanta Kashrut Commission.
Delivery available.

Bakeries

Bernie the Baker, 3015 N. Druid Hills Road,
N.E., 30329   633-1986
Supervision: Atlanta Kashrut Commission.
Pat Yisrael.

Kg's Bakery & Stuff
2088 Briarcliff Road, 30329   321-1166
Supervision: Atlanta Kashrut Commission.
Pat Yisrael.

Delicatessens

Harris Teeter, 1799 Briarcliff Road, 2nd level,
30329   607-1189
Supervision: Atlanta Kashrut Commission.
Kosher fish, meat and deli.

Kroger Kosher Fish, Meat & Deli
2205 La Vista Road, N.E., 30329   633-8694
Supervision: Atlanta Kashrut Commission.
Select departments only.

Quality Kosher
2153 Briarcliff Road, 30329   636-1114
Supervision: Atlanta Kashrut Commission.
Glatt and non-glatt butcher, deli and grocery.

Caterers

Bijan Catering
3130 Raymond Drive, N.E., 30360   457-4578
Supervision: Atlanta Kashrut Commission.

Bed & Breakfasts

Bed & Breakfast Atlanta, 1801 Piedmont
Avenue, Suite 208, 30324   875-0525
Fax: 875-9672
Providing kosher and Shomer Shabbat
accommodation.

Augusta

Synagogues *(Orthodox)*

Adas Yeshuron
935 Johns Road, Walton Way, 30904

Bakeries

Sunshine Bakery, 1209 Broad Street, 30902

Delicatessens

Parti-Pal, Daniel Village, 30904
Strauss, 965 Broad Street, 30902

Columbus

Synagogues

Conservative
Shearith Israel, 2550 Wynnton Road, 31906

Reform
Temple Israel
1617 Wildwood Avenue, 31906

Macon

Synagogues

Conservative
Sherah Israel, 1st & Plum Streets, 31201

Reform
Beth Israel, 892 Cherry Street, 31201

Savannah

Community Organisations
Jewish Federation
51111 Abercorn Street, 31405   355-8111

Synagogues

Orthodox
B'nai B'rith Jacob
5444 Abercorn Street, 31405

Conservative
Agudath Achim, 9 Lee Blvd., 31405

Reform
Mickve Israel, Bull & Gordon Sts., 31401
The oldest synagogue in Georgia, having been
founded before 1790.

Contact Information
Rabbi Avigdor Slatus
5444 Abercorn Street, 31405
Visitors requiring information about kashrut,
temporary accommodation, etc., should
contact Rabbi Slatus.

Hawaii

Hilo

Synagogues *(Unaffiliated)*
Temple Beth Aloha
POB 96720   (808) 969-4153

Honolulu
Area telephone code (808)

Community Organisations
Jewish Federation of Hawaii
44 Hora Lane, 96813   941-2424

Synagogues

Orthodox
Chabad of Hawaii
4851 Kahala Ave   735-8161

Conservative
Congregation Sof Ma'arav, 2500 Pali
Highway, 96817   373-1331; 923-5726

Groceries
Down To Earth, King's Street, Near University
Avenue
Foodland Supermarket Beretania
cnr. Kalakana

Bed & Breakfasts
Bed & Breakfast Honolulu (Statewide)
3242 Kaohinani Drive, 96817   595-753
                    800-288-466
                    Fax: 595-2036
          Email: BnBsHI@aloha.ne
Web site: http://planet-hawaii.com/bnb-honolulu
Not kosher, but within walking distance of
Orthodox services for the High Holy Days.

Kihei

Synagogues
Jewish Congregation of Maui   243-249

Reform
Congregation Gan Eden
P.O. Box 555, Kihei Road, 96753   879-922

Kona

Synagogues
Kona Beth Shalom Kailua-Kona   322-9144

Waikiki

Synagogues
Chabad, Alana Hotel, Park Plaza, 1956 Ala
Moana Blvd.   735-8161

Idaho

Boise

Synagogues *(Conservative)*
Ahavath-Beth Israel, 1102 State St, 83702

Illinois

Champaign-Urbana

Community Organisations
Champaign-Urbana Jewish Federation, 503
E. John St, Champaign, 61820 (217) 367-9872

Synagogues *(Reform)*
Sinai Temple, 3104 Windsor Road,
Champaign, 61821   (217) 352-8140

Chicagoland

Chicagoland (Greater Chicago) consists of the
City of Chicago and the collar counties of
Cook, Dupage, Kane, Lake and McHenry
Counties. The Jewish community is spread
throughout Chicagoland, with the main
concentrations being in West Rogers Park (City
of Chicago), Skokie (Cook County), Buffalo
Grove and Highland Park (Lake County).

Greater Chicago has a Jewish population of
about 261,000. For a history of the Jews of
Chicago see: I. Cutter: *The Jews of Chicago:
from Shtetl to Suburbs.*

Entries in this section are arranged in the
sequence that Chicagoland residents think of
the area. There are three basic divisions in
Chicagoland:

a. City of Chicago (telephone area code 312
and 773) includes West Rogers Park and the
California/Dempster Avenue areas

b. North and Northwest Suburbs (includes
Cook, Lake and McHenry counties; telephone
area codes 773, 815 and 847) includes Buffalo
Grove, Deerfield, Evanston, Highland Park,
Northbrook, and Skokie.

c. South and West Suburbs (includes DuPage
and Kane counties' telephone area codes 630
or 708) includes Flossmoor and Olympia
Fields.

City of Chicago

Community Organisations
Jewish Federation of Metropolitan Chicago
1 S. Franklin Street, 60606   (312) 346-6700
Chicago Board of Rabbis (multi-
denominational) is located here as well.

Religious Organisations
Chicago Mikva Association
3110 W. Touhy Avenue, 60645
Chicago Rabbinical Council
3525 W. Peterson Avenue, Suite 315, 60659
                             (312) 588-1600
                        Fax: (312) 588-2141
Information about kashrut and related matters
may be obtained from the Council, which
issues an annual directory.

Synagogues

Orthodox
Young Israel of Chicago
4931 North Kimball Street, 60625
Young Israel of West Rogers Park
2716 West Touhy Avenue, West Rogers Park,
60645   (773) 743-9400

Embassy
Consulate General
Suite 1308, 111 East Wacker Drive, 60601

Media

Newspapers

Chicago Jewish News
2501 West Peterson Avenue, 60659

JUF News
1 S. Franklin Street, 60606   (312) 346-6700

Restaurants

Meat

Great Chicago Food & Beverage Co.
3149 W. Devon, 60659   (773) 465-9030
Supervision: Chicago Rabbinical Council.

Jeweler's Club
5 S. Wabash, 60603   (312) 849-9898
Supervision: Chicago Rabbinical Council.

Mi Tsu Yun
3010 W. Devon, 60659   (773) 262-4630
Supervision: Chicago Rabbinical Council.

Dairy

Dunkin Donuts
3132 W. Devon, 60659   (773) 262-4561
Supervision: Chicago Rabbinical Council.

Jerusalem Kosher Restaurant
3014 W. Devon, 60659   (773) 262-0515
Supervision: Chicago Rabbinical Council.

Tel Aviv Kosher Pizza & Dairy Restaurant
6349 N. California, 60659   (773) 764-3776
Supervision: Chicago Rabbinical Council.

Bakeries

Gitel's Bakery
2745 W. Devon, 60659   (773) 262-3701
Supervision: Chicago Rabbinical Council.

North Shore Bakery
2919 W. Touhy, 60645   (773) 262-0600
Supervision: Chicago Rabbinical Council.

Tel Aviv Bakery
2944 W. Devon, 60659   (773) 764-8877
Supervision: Chicago Rabbinical Council.

Butchers

Jacob Miller & Sons
2727 W. Devon, 60659   (773) 761-4200
Supervision: Chicago Rabbinical Council.

Romanian Kosher Sausage
7200 N. Clark, 60625   (773) 761-4141
Supervision: Chicago Rabbinical Council.

Delicatessens

Good Morgan Fish
2948 W. Devon, 60645   (773) 764-8115
Supervision: Chicago Rabbinical Council.

Kosher Karry
2828 W. Devon, 60659   (773) 973-4355
Supervision: Chicago Rabbinical Council.
Sells groceries as well.

Moshe's New York Kosher
2900 W. Devon, 60659   (773) 338-3354
Supervision: Chicago Rabbinical Council.
Sells groceries as well.

Wally's Milk Pail, 3320 W. Devon,
Lincolnwood, 60645   (773) 673-3459
Supervision: Chicago Rabbinical Council.
Sells groceries as well.

Groceries

Kol Tuv
2938 W. Devon, 60659   (773) 764-1800
Supervision: Chicago Rabbinical Council.

Museums

Spertus Museum of Judaica, 618 S. Michigan
Avenue, 60605   (312) 922-9012
Fax: (312) 922-6406

Booksellers

Chicago Hebrew Book Store
2942 W. Devon, 60645

Rosenblum, 2906 W. Devon, 60659

Spertus College Museum Store
618 S. Michigan Avenue, 60605

North and Northwest

Area telephone code (847) unless shown

Synagogues

Orthodox

Young Israel of Northbrook
3545 West Walters Road, Northbrook, 60062
(708) 480-946;

Young Israel of Skokie, 3708 North
Dempster, Skokie, 60076   329-0990
Shul is located in the Timber Ridge School,
Samoset and Davis.

Media

Newspapers
Chicago Jewish Star
PO Box 268, Skokie, 60076

Restaurants

Meat
Bugsy's Charhouse
3353 Dempster, Skokie, 60076   679-4030
Supervision: Chicago Rabbinical Council.

Falafel King
4507 W. Oakton, Skokie, 60076   677-6020
Supervision: Chicago Rabbinical Council.

Hy Life Bistro
4120 W. Dempster, Skokie, 60076   674-2021
Supervision: Chicago Rabbinical Council.

Ken's Diner
3353 Dempster, Skokie, 60076   679-4030
Supervision: Chicago Rabbinical Council.

Dairy
Bagel Country
9306 Skokie Blvd, Skokie, 60077   673-3030
Supervision: Chicago Rabbinical Council.

Da'Nali's
4032 Oakton, Skokie, 60076   677-2782
Supervision: Chicago Rabbinical Council.

Dunkin Donuts
1169 Old McHenry Road, Buffalo Grove,
60089   821-0044
Supervision: Chicago Rabbinical Council.

Slice of Life
4120 W. Dempster, Skokie, 60076   674-2021
Supervision: Chicago Rabbinical Council.

Bakeries

King David's Bakery
1731 Howard, Evanston, 60202   475-0270
Supervision: Chicago Rabbinical Council.

The Glenview Breadsmith
2771 Pfingsten, Glenview, 60025   509-9955
Supervision: Chicago Rabbinical Council.

Delicatessens

Chaim's Kosher Deli & Supermarket
4956 Dempster, Skokie, 60077   675-1005
Supervision: Chicago Rabbinical Council.
Bakery and grocery shop as well.

Hungarian Kosher Foods
4020 Oakton, Skokie, 60076   674-8008
Supervision: Chicago Rabbinical Council.
Butcher shop and sells groceries as well.

Selig's Kosher Deli, 209 Skokie Valley Road,
Highland Park, 60035   831-5560
Supervision: Chicago Rabbinical Council.
Sells groceries as well.

Booksellers

Hamakor Judaica
4150 Dempster, Skokie, 60076

Peoria

Area telephone code (309)

Community Organisations

Jewish Federation, Town Hall Bldg., 5901 N.
Prospect Road, 61604   689-0063

Synagogues

Orthodox
Agudas Achim
5614 N. University, 61604   692-4848

Reform
Anshai Emeth   691-3323

Rock Island

Community Organisations

Jewish Federation of the Quad Cities
209 18th Street, Rock Island, 61201

Rockford

Area telephone code (815)

Community Organisations

Jewish Federation, 1500 Parkview Avenue,
61107   399-5497

Synagogues

Conservative
Ohave Sholom
3730 Guildford Road, 61107

Reform
Temple Beth El
1203 Comanche Drive, 61107   398-5020

Indiana

Community Organisations

Jewish Federation of North West Indiana
2939 Jewett Street, Highland,
46322   (219) 972-2251
Serving Gary, Hammond, Michigan City,
Valparaiso and Whiting.

Bloomington

Area telephone code (812)

Synagogues

Orthodox
Chabad House
516 E. 17th Street, 47408   332-6784

Reform
Congregation Beth Shalom
3750 E. Third, 47401   334-2440

East Chicago

Synagogues

Orthodox
B'nai Israel, 3517 Hemlock Street, 46312

Conservative
Beth Sholom, 4508 Baring Avenue, 46312

Evansville

Synagogues

Adath Israel
3600 E. Washington Avenue, 47715

Reform
Washington Avenue Temple, 100
Washington Avenue, 47714

Fort Wayne

Area telephone code (219)

Synagogues

Conservative
B'nai Jacob, 7227 Bittersweet Moors Drive,
46804   672-8459

Reform
Achduth Vesholom
5200 Old Mill Road, 46807   744-4245

Gary

Synagogues

Temple Israel, 601 N. Montgomery Street,
46403   (219) 938-5232

Hammond

Synagogues

Conservative
Beth Israel, 7105 Hohman Avenue, 46324

Reform
Temple Beth-El, 6947 Hohman Ave, 46324

Indianapolis

Area telephone code (317)

Community Organisations

Bureau of Jewish Education
6711 Hoover Road, 46260   255-3124
Anglo-Jewish visitors are invited to get in
touch with the Executive Vice President.

Jewish Federation of Greater Indianapolis
6705 Hoover Road, 46260

Synagogues

Orthodox
B'nai Torah
6510 Hoover Road, 46260   253-5253

Etz Chaim (Sephardi)
826 64th Street, 46260   251-6220

Conservative

Beth-El Zedeck
600 W. 70th Street, 46260   253-3441

Shaarey Tefilla Congregation
5879 Central Avenue, 46220   253-4591

Reform

Indianapolis Hebrew Congregation
6501 N. Meridian Street, 46260   255-6647

Lafayette

Synagogues

Orthodox
Sons of Abraham, 661 N. 7th Street, 47906

Reform
Temple Israel, 620 Cumberland Street, 47901

Groceries

Jewel Food Store

Michigan City

Synagogues *(Reform)*

Sinai Temple
2800 S. Franklin Street, 46360 (219) 874-4477

Muncie

Area telephone code (317)

Synagogues

Temple Beth El
525 W. Jackson Street, cnr. Council Street,
47305   288-4662

South Bend

Area telephone code (219)

Community Organisations

Jewish Federation of St. Joseph Valley, 105
Jefferson Center, Suite 804, 46601   233-1164
    Fax: 288-4103

Synagogues

Orthodox
Hebrew Orthodox Congregation
3207 S. High Street, 46614

Conservative
Sinai, 1102 E. Laselle Street, 46617

Reform
Beth-El
305 W. Madison Street, 46601   234-4402

Mikvaot
    291-6240

Kashrut Information

Hebrew Orthodox Congregation
3207 S. High Street, 46614   291-4239
    Fax: 291-6100

Contact Information

Rabbi Y. Gettinger
Hebrew Orthodox Congregation, 3207 S. High
Street, 46614   291-4239; 291-6100
Visitors requiring information about kashrut,
temporary accommodation, etc., should
contact Rabbi Gettinger. Or contact Michael
Lerman, 1-800-348-2529.

Terre Haute

Delicatessens

Kosher Meat & Sandwiches
410 W. Western Avenue, 47807

Valparaiso

Synagogues

Conservative
Temple Israel, PO Box 2051, 46383

Whiting

Synagogues

Orthodox
B'nai Judah, 116th Street & Davis Ave, 46394

Iowa

Cedar Rapids

Synagogues
Temple Judah
3221 Lindsay Lane S.E., 52403 (319) 362-1261

Davenport

Synagogues *(Reform)*
Temple Emanuel
12th Street & Mississippi Avenue, 52803
Davenport is part of the Rock Island, Illinois area, which is divided by the Mississippi River. See the Rock Island entry.

Des Moines

Area telephone code (515)

Community Organisations
Jewish Federation of Greater Des Moines
910 Polk Blvd, 50312   277-6321

Synagogues

Orthodox
Beth El Jacob, 954 Cummins Parkway, 50312

Conservative
Tifereth Israel, 924 Polk Blvd., 50312

Reform
B'nai Jerusalem
51st & Grand, 50312   277-1718

Delicatessens
Pickle Barrel, 1241 6th Avenue, 50314
The Nosh, 800 First Street, 50265

Dubuque

Synagogues
Beth El
475 W. Locust Street, 52001

Fort Dodge

Synagogues *(Conservative)*
Beth El, 501 N. 12th St, 50501
                            (515) 572-8925

Iowa City

Synagogues

Conservative & Reform
Agudas Achim
602 E. Washington St, 52240   (319) 337-3813

Sioux City

Community Organisations
Jewish Federation
525 14th Street, 51105   (712) 258-0618

Synagogues

Orthodox
United Orthodox, 14th & Nebraska St, 51105

Conservative
Beth Sholom, 815 38th Street, 51105

Groceries
Sam's Food Market, 1911 Grandview, 51104

Kansas

Overland Park

Synagogues *(Orthodox)*
Young Israel of Overland Park
8716 Woodward, 66212   (913) 341-1597

Media

Newspapers
Kansas City Jewish Chronicle
7375 W. 107th Street, 66204
Weekly publication.

Prairie Village

Synagogues *(Conservative)*
Ohev Shalom, 5311 W. 75th Street, 66208
Orthodox rite but mixed seating.

Butchers
Jacobsons Strictly Kosher Foods
5200 W95th Street, 66207

Topeka

Community Organisations
Topeka Lawrence Jewish Federation
4200 Munson Street, 66604

Synagogues

Reform
Beth Sholom, 4200 Munson Street, 66604

Wichita

Synagogues

Orthodox
Hebrew Cong., 1850 N. Woodlawn, 6/∠08

Reform
Temple Emanu-El, 7011 E. Central St, 67206

Groceries
Dillon's
13th Street & Woodlawn Street, 67208
Dillon's, 21st Street & Rock Road, 67208
The Bread Lady, 20205 Rock Road, #80

Kentucky

Lexington
Area telephone code (606)

Organisations
Central Kentucky Jewish Federation
340 Romany Road, 40502   268-0775

Synagogues
Conservative
Lexington Havurah, PO Box 54958, 40551
Ohavay Zion, 2048 Edgewater Ct., 40502

Reform
Adath Israel, 124 N. Ashland Avenue, 40502

Louisville

Community Organisations
Jewish Community Federation
3630 Dutchman's Lane, 40205

Synagogues

Orthodox
Anshei Sfard, 3700 Dutchman's Lane, 40205
Mikvah attached.

Conservative
Adath Jeshurun
2401 Woodbourne Avenue, 40205

Traditional
Keneseth Israel
2531 Taylorsville Road, 40205

Reform
Temple Shalom, 4615 Lowe Road, 40205
The Temple, 5101 Brownsboro Road, 40241

Paducah

Synagogues
Temple Israel, 330 Joe Clifton Drive, 42001

Louisiana

Alexandria

Synagogues

Conservative
B'nai Israel, 1907 Vance Street, 71301

Reform
Gemiluth Chassodim, 2021 Turner St, 71301

Groceries

100 Park Place, 71301   445-9367
Kosher food by arrangement.

Libraries

Meyer Kaplan Memorial Library (Judiaca)
c/o B'nai Israel, 1908 Vance Street, 71301

Baton Rouge

Area telephone code (504)

Community Organisations

Jewish Federation of Greater Baton Rouge
P.O.B. 80827, 70898   291-5895

Synagogues

Reform

B'nai Israel, 3354 Kleinert Avenue, 70806
Beth Shalom, 9111 Jefferson Highway, 70809

Lafayette

Synagogues

Temple Rodef Sholom
603 Lee Avenue, 70501
There is a very fine Judaica library at the
University of Southwestern Louisiana.

New Orleans

Area telephone code (504)

Community Organisations

Jewish Federation of Greater New Orleans
3500 N. Causeway Blvd., #1240, Metairie,
70002   828-2125
                                    Fax: 828-2827

Synagogues

Orthodox

Anshe Sfard
2230 Carondelet Street, 70130   422-4714

Mikvaot

Beth Israel, 7000 Canal Blvd, 70124

Delicatessens

Kosher Cajun Deli & Grocery, 3250 N. Hullen
Street, Metrairie, 70002   888-2010
                                    Fax: 888-2014
Under strict rabbinical supervision. Hours:
Monday to Thursday, 10 am to 7 pm; Friday
and Sunday, to 3 pm.

Groceries

Casablanca, 3030 Seven Avenue, Metrairie,
70002-4826   888-2209
Touro Infirmary
1401 Foucher Street, 70115   897-8246
Glatt kosher meals available.

Hotels

The Pontchartrain Grand Heritage Hotel,
2031 St Charles Ave, 70140   524-0581
                                    800-777-6193
                                    Fax: 529-1165
Kosher food available on request.

Home Hospitality

Dr & Mrs Saul Kahn, 4000 Clifford Drive,
Metrairie, 70002   831-2230
                                    Fax: 522-8981
Glatt kosher. 'Having guests from all over the
world enriches our lives.'

Media

Newspapers

The Jewish News, 3500 N. Causeway Blvd,
#1240, Metairie, 70002

Shreveport

Area telephone code (318)

Community Organisations

Jewish Federation
2032 Line Avenue, 71104   221-4129

Synagogues

Conservative

Agudath Achim, 401 Village Green Drive,
71115   797-6401

Reform

B'nai Zion, 245 Southfield Road, 71105

Maine

Auburn

Synagogues

Conservative
Congregation Beth Abraham, Main Street & Laurel Avenue, 04210   (207) 783-1302
Temple Shalom, 74 Bradman Street, 04210

Bangor

Area telephone code (207)

Synagogues

Orthodox
Beth Abraham, 145 York Street, 04401

Conservative
Congregation Beth Israel, 144 York Street, 04401

Bakeries
The Bagel Shop, 1 Main St, 04451   947-1654

Lewiston

Area telephone code (207)

Community Organisations
Lewiston-Auburn Jewish Federation
74 Bradman Street, 04210   786-4201

Old Orchard Beach

Area telephone code (207)

Synagogues

Orthodox
Beth Israel
49 E. Grand Avenue, 04064   934-2973
Daily minyan, May 28 to Yom Kippur, Shabbat & Yom Tov minyan all year round.

Kashrut Information
Eber Weinstein
187 E. Grand Avenue, 04064   934-7522
Eddie Hakim   934-7223
Harold Goodkovski   934-4210

Portland

Area telephone code (207)

Community Organisations
Jewish Fed.-Com. Council of Southern Maine, 57 Ashmont Street, 04103   773-7254

Synagogues
Etz Chaim, 267 Congress Street, 04101
Shaarey Tphiloh, 76 Noyes Street, 04103

Conservative
Beth El, 400 Deering Ave, 04103   774-2649

Mikvaot
Beth El, 400 Deering Ave, 04103   774-2649
Etz Chaim, 267 Congress Street, 04101
Shaarey Tphiloh, 76 Noyes Street, 04103

Butchers
Penny Wise Super Market
182 Ocean Avenue, 04130
Take-out counter at a local supermarket.

Maryland

Bethesda, Bowie, Chevy Chase, Gaithersburg, Greenbelt, Hyattsville, Kensington, Laurel, Lexington Park, Olney, Potomac, Rockville, Silver Spring & Wheaton and Temple Hills are all part of Greater Washington, DC.

Annapolis

Synagogues

Conservative
Congregation Kol Ami, 1909 Hidden Meadow Lane, 21401

Reform
Temple Beth Shalom
1461 Baltimore-Annapolis Blvd., 21012

Baltimore

Area telephone code (410)

Community Organisations

Associated Jewish Community Federation of Baltimore, 101 W. Mount Royal Avenue, 21201   727-4828

The Baltimore Jewish Council, 5750 Park Heights Ave., 21215

The Jewish Historical Society of Maryland 15 Lloyd Street, 21202   732-6400

Synagogues

There are more than 50 synagogues in the Baltimore metropolitan area. Visitors are advised to contact one of the community organisations in the area to find the synagogue nearest them.

Mikvaot

Mikva of Baltimore Inc., 3207 Clarks Lane, 21225   664-5834

Kashrut Information

Jewish Information Service
5750 Park Heights Avenue, 21215   466-4636
Open daily from 10am to 2pm for help on almost anything.

Orthodox Jewish Council Vaad Hakashrut
11 Warren Road, 21208   484-4110

Restaurants

Chapps Kosher Chinese, Pomona Square Shopping Center, 1700 Reistertown Rd, 21208

Kosher Bite, 6309 Reistertown Road, 21215

Royal Restaurant
7006 Reistertown Road, 21208

Tov Pizza
6313 Reistertown Road, 21215   358-5238
Supervision: Kof-K.

Bakeries

Brooklyn Bakery
222 Riesterstown Road, 21208
Supervision: Kof-K.

Goldman's Kosher Bakery
6848 Reistertown Road, 21215

Pariser's Kosher Bakery
6711 Reistertown Road, 21215

Schmell & Azman Kosher Bakery, 21215

Delicatessens

Danielle's, 401 Reistertown Road, 21208

Knish Shop, 508 Reistertown Road, 21208

Liebes Kosher Deli Carry Out
607 Reistertown Road, 21208   653-1977
Only glatt kosher meats. Hours: Sunday to Wednesday, 8:30 am to 6 pm; Thursday, late nite; Friday, to 1 hour before sundown.

Groceries

Mirakle Market
6836 Reistertown Road, 21215   358-3443

Seven Mile Market, 4000 Seven Mile Lane, Pikesville, 21208   653-2000

Shlomo Meat & Fish
4030 Falstaff Road, 21215   358-9633

Wasseman & Lemberger
610 Reistertown Road   486-4191
Will deliver to DC on Monday.

Wasserman & Lemberger
70006-D Reistertown Road, 21208   486-4191

Museums

The Jewish Heritage Center
15 Lloyd Street, 21202   732-6400
This building is the only one of its kind in Baltimore, holding two synagogues (Lloyd St., built 1845, & B'nai Israel, built 1876, which is the oldest synagogue in continuous use in Baltimore), a museum and a research center.

Monument

Holocaust Memorial, Gay & Water Sts.

Bethesda

Community Organisations

United Jewish Appeal Federation of Greater Washington, 7900 Wisconsin Avenue, 20814   (301) 652-6480

Bowie

Synagogues

Conservative
Nevey Shalom
12218 Torah Lane, 20715   262-4020

Reform
Temple Solel
2901 Mitchelville Road, 20716   249-2424

Chevy Chase

Synagogues

Conservative
Ohr Kodesh
8402 Freyman Drive, 20815   589-3880

Reform
Temple Shalom
8401 Grubb Road, 20815   587-2273

Cumberland

Synagogues

Conservative
Beth Jacob, 1 Columbia Street, 21502

Reform
B'Er Chayim, 107 Union Street, 21502

Restaurants

The Bagel Shop
1 Main St, 04401   (207) 947-1654
Restaurant, deli, bakery and take-out.

Gaithersburg

Area telephone code (301)

Synagogues

Conservative
Kehilat Shalom
9915 Apple Ridge Road, 20879   869-7699
                                       Fax: 977-7870

Greenbelt

Synagogues *(Conservative)*
Mishkan Torah, Westway and Ridge Road,
20770   474-4223

Hagerstown

Area telephone code (301)

Synagogues *(Reform)*
B'nai Abraham
53 E. Baltimore Street, 21740   733-5039

Delicatessens
Celebrity Deli
6700 Adelphi Road, 20782   927-5525

Kensington

Synagogues *(Reform)*
Temple Emanuel, 10101 Connecticut Avenue,
20895   (301) 942-2000
               Fax: (301) 942-9488

Laurel

Synagogues *(Reconstructionist)*
Oseh Shalom
8604 Briarwood Drive, 20708   498-5151

Lexington Park

Synagogues *(Conservative)*
Beth Israel
Bunker Hill Drive, 20650   862-2021

Olney

Synagogues
B'nai Shalom
18401 Burtfield Drive, 20832   774-0879

Pocomoke

Synagogues
Temple Israel, 3rd Street, 21851

Potomac

Area telephone code (301)

Synagogues

Orthodox
Beth Sholom of Potomac
11825 Seven Locks Road, 20854   279-7010
Young Israel of Ezras Israel of Potomac
11618 Seven Locks Road, 20854   299-2827

Conservative
Har Shalom
11510 Falls Road, 20854   299-7087

Restaurants
Hunan Gourmet
350 Fortune Terrace (7 Locks Plaza)   424-0192

Rockville

Area telephone code (301)

Synagogues

Orthodox
Mogen David Sephardic Cong., 11418 Old
Georgetown Road, 20852   770-6818

Conservative
B'nai Israel, 6301 Montrose Road, 20852
Beth Tikvah, 2200 Baltimore Road, 20853

Reform
Temple Beth Ami
800 Hurley Avenue, 20850   340-6818

Restaurants
Kat'z Kafe
4860 Boiling Brook Parkway   468-0400
Sells groceries as well.
Royal Dragon
4840 Boiling Brook, Parkway   468-1922

Salisbury

Synagogues

Conservative
Beth Israel
Camden Avenue & Wicomico Street, 21801

Silver Spring & Wheaton

Area telephone code (301)

Synagogues

Orthodox
Silver Spring Jewish Center, 1401 Arcola
Avenue, 20902   649-4425
South-East Hebrew Cong., 10900 Lockwood
Drive, 20902
Woodside Syn. Ahavas Torah, 9001 Georgia
Avenue, 20910
Young Israel Shomrei Emunah, 1132 Arcola
Avenue, 20902

Conservative
Har Tzeon-Agudath Achim, 1840 University
Blvd. W., 20902
Shaare Tefila, 11120 Lockwood Drive, 20901
Temple Israel
420 University Blvd. E., 20901   439-3600

Mikvaot
Mikva, 8901 Georgia Avenue, 20907

Restaurants
The Nut House
11419 Georgia Avenue, 20902   942-5900

Bakeries
The Wooden Shoe Pastry Shop
11301 Georgia Avenue, 20902   942-9330
Virtuoso
11230a Lockwood Avenue, 50901   593-6034

Groceries
Shalom Meat Market
2307 University Blvd West   946-6500
Shaul & Hersehl Meat Market   949-8477
Delivers to G. W. Hillel every Wednesday.

Guest House
Hebrew Sheltering Society, 11524 Daffodil
Lane, 20902   649-3141; 649-4425; 649-2799
For people unable to afford accommodation,
will get 3 free nights' stay at the shelter.

Booksellers
Lisbon's Hebrew Book Store & Giftshop
2305 University Blvd, 20902
The Jewish Bookstore
11250 Georgia Avenue, 20902

Temple Hills

Synagogues *(Conservative)*
Shaare Tikva, 5405 Old Temple Hills Road,
20748   894-4303

Massachusetts

Acton

Synagogues *(Independent)*
Beth Elohim
10 Hennessy Drive, 07120   (508) 263-3061

Amherst

Synagogues
Jewish Community
724 Main Street, 01002   (413) 256-0160

Andover

Synagogues *(Reform)*
Temple Emanuel, 7 Haggett's Pond Road,
01810   (508) 470-1356

Arlington

Bakeries
Dough-C-Donuts, 1460 Massachusetts
Avenue, 02174   (617) 643-4550
Supervision: Vaad Harabonim of
Massachusetts.

Athol

Synagogues *(Independent)*
Temple Israel
107 Walnut Street, 01331   (508) 249-9481

Attleboro

Synagogues *(Reform)*
Agudas Achim Congregation
Kelly & Toner Blvds., 02703   (508) 222-2243

Ayer

Synagogues *(Independent)*
Congregation Anshey Sholom
Cambridge Street, 01432   (508) 772-0896

Belmont

Synagogues *(Reform)*
Beth El Temple Center
2 Concord Avenue, 02178   (617) 484-6668

Beverly

Area telephone code (508)

Synagogues *(Conservative)*
B'nai Abraham
200 E. Lothrop Street, 01915   (508) 927-3211

Boston *(Greater Boston)*

Area telephone code (617)

Community Organisations
Jewish Community Relations Council of
Greater Boston
1 Lincoln Plaza, Suite 308, 02111   330-9600
Represents 34 community organisations in the
area.

Religious Organisations
Rabbinical Council of New England
177 Tremont Street, 02111   426-2139

Synagogues

Orthodox
Chabad House, 491 Commonwealth Avenue,
02215   523-0453

United States of America / Massachusetts

The Boston Synagogue at Charles River Park
55 Martha Road, 02114   523-0453

Cong. Kadimah-Toras Moshe, 113
Washington Street, Brighton, 02135 254-1333

Lubavitch Shul of Brighton, 239 Chestnut
Hill Avenue, Brighton, 02135   782-8340

Zvhiller Beis Medrash, 15 School Street,
02108   227-8200

Conservative

Hillel B'nai Torah, 120 Corey St., W. Roxbury,
02132   323-0486

Temple B'nai Moshe, 1845 Commonwealth
Avenue, Brighton, 02135   254-3620

Reform

Temple Israel, Plymouth Street & Longwood
Avenue, 02115   566-3960

Mikvaot

Daughters of Israel
101 Washington Street, Brighton, 02135

Kashrut Information

Kashruth Commission
177 Tremont Street, 02111   426-2139

Synagogue Council of Massachusetts, 1320
Center St, Newton Center, 02159   244-6506
Fax: 964-7055
Email: syncouncil@aol.com.

Vaad Harabonim of Massachusetts
177 Tremont Street, 02111   426-2139

Embassy

Consulate General
1020 Statler Office Blvd, 02116

Restaurants

B.U. Hillel
233 Bay State Road, 02215   353-3663
Supervision: Vaad Harabonim of MA.

Hillel Foundation, Boston University 353-7200
Fax: 353-7660
Supervision: Rabbi Joseph Polak and Vaad
HaRabanim of Massachusetts.
Hours: 11:30 am to 1:15 pm; 5 to 7 pm.
Shabbat meals need to be pre-paid. For
information: 353-2947.

Milk Street Cafe, The Park at Post Office
Square, Zero Post Office Square   350-PARK
Supervision: Orthodox Rabbinic Council of
Greater Boston.

Milk Street Cafe, 50 Milk Street   542-FOOD
Fax: 451-5FAX
Supervision: Orthodox Rabbinic Council of
Greater Boston.
Hours: Monday to Friday, 7 am to 3 pm.

Media

Guides

Jewish Guide to Boston and New England
15 School Street, 02108   367-9100
Fax: 367-9310

Synagogue Council of Massachusetts, 1320
Center St, Newton Center, 02159   244-6506
Fax: 964-7055
Email: syncouncil@aol.com.

Newspapers
Boston Jewish Times
The Jewish Advocate

Tours

**BostonWalks and The Jewish Friendship
Trail**   489-5020
Email: rossocp@gis.net

Braintree

Area telephone code (617)

Synagogues (Conservative)

Temple Bnai Shalom
41 Storrs Avenue, 02184   843-3687

Bakeries

Sara's Kitchen
South Shore Plaza, 01501   843-8803
Supervision: Vaad Harabonim of
Massachusetts.

Bridgewater

Bakeries

J & E Baking Company, 10 Bedford Park, Unit
#5, 02324   (508) 279-0990
Supervision: Vaad Harabonim of
Massachusetts. Shomer Shabbat.

Brighton

Area telephone code (617)

Restaurants

B-B-N J.C.C. Dining Hall
50 Sutherland Road, 02146   278-2950
Supervision: Vaad Harabonim of MA.

J.C.H.E. Dining Hall
30 Wallingford Road, 02146   254-9001
Supervision: Vaad Harabonim of MA.

Brockton

Area telephone code (508)

Synagogues

Orthodox

Agudath Achim
144 Belmont Avenue, 02401   583-0717

Conservative

Beth Emunah
Pearl & Torrey Streets, 02401   583-5810

Reform

Temple Israel
184 W. Elm Street, 02401   587-4130

Brookline

Area telephone code (617)

Synagogues

Orthodox

Beth David, 64 Corey Rd., 02146   232-2349

Beth Pinchas (Bostoner Rebbe), 1710 Beacon Street, 02146   734-5100

Chai Odom, 77 Englewood Av., 02146   734-5359

Young Israel of Brookline
62 Green Street, 02146   734-0276

Conservative

Beth Zion, 1566 Beacon St., 02146   566-8171

Kehillath Israel
384 Harvard St., 02146   277-9155

Reform

Ohabei Shalom
1187 Beacon St., 02146   277-6610

Temple Sinai, Charles St. & Sewall Av., Coolidge Cnr., 02146   277-5888

Sephardic

Sfardic Cong. of New England, 151 Salisbury Road   964-1526

Kashrut Information

Jewish Commercial Center, Harvard Street
Harvard Street is the Jewish commercial Center, with art & bookshops, as well as many kosher butcher's shops and bakeries.

Restaurants

Cafe Shiraz, 1030 Commonwealth Avenue, 02215   566-8888
Glatt kosher Persian and Middle Eastern cuisine. Alcohol served. Catering available. Wheelchair accessible. Hours: Monday to Thursday, 5 pm to 10 pm; Saturday, 45 minutes after sundown to midnight; Sunday, 4 pm to 10 pm.

Rami's, 324 Harvard Street, 02146   738-3577
Supervision: Vaad Harabonim of Massachusetts. Glatt kosher.

Rubin's, 500 Harvard Street, 02146   566-8761
Supervision: Vaad Harabonim of Massachusetts. Glatt kosher.

Ruth's Kitchen, 401 Harvard Street   734-9810

Shalom Hunan
92 Harvard Street, 02146   731-9760
Supervision: Vaad Harabonim of Massachusetts. Glatt kosher.

Victor's Pizza
1364 Beacon Street, 02146   730-9903

Bakeries

Catering by Andrew
404A Harvard Street, 02148   731-6585
Supervision: Vaad Harabonim of Massachusetts. Shomer Shabbat.

Taam Tov Bakery
305A Harvard Street, 02146   566-8136
Supervision: Vaad Harabonim of Massachusetts. Shomer Shabbat. Pareve.

Burlington

Synagogues *(Reform)*
Temple Shalom Emeth
14-16 Lexington St, 01803   (617) 272-2351

Cambridge

Synagogues *(Conservative)*
Temple Beth Shalom of Cambridge
8 Tremont Street, 02139   (617) 864-6388

Restaurants
Harvard Hillel Dining Hall, 52 Mt. Auburn
Street, 02138   495-4695; 495-4696
Supervision: Vaad Harabonim of
Massachusetts.   876-3535
M.I.T. Hillel
40 Massachusetts Ave, 02138   253-2982
Supervision: Vaad Harabonim of MA.

Canton

Area telephone code (617)

Synagogues

Conservative
Beth Abraham
1301 Washington Street, 02021   828-5250

Reform
Temple Beth David of the South Shore
256 Randolph Street, 02021   828-2275

Chelmsford

Synagogues
Congregation Shalom
Richardson Road, 01824   (508) 251-8091

Chestnut Hill

Bakeries
Cheryl Ann's Bakery, 1010 West Roxbury
Parkway, 02167   (617) 469-9241
Supervision: Vaad Harabonim of MA.

Clinton

Synagogues *(Independent)*
Shaarei Zedeck
Water Street, 01510   (508) 365-3320

East Dedham

Bakeries
Cookies Express
252 Bussey Street, 02026   (617) 461-0044
Supervision: Vaad Harabonim of
Massachusetts. Shomer Shabbat.

East Falmouth

Synagogues *(Reform)*
Falmouth Jewish Congregation
7 Hatchville Road, 02536   (508) 540-0602

Easton

Synagogues *(Traditional)*
Temple Chayai Shalom
9 Mechanic Street, 02356   (508) 238-4896

Everett

Synagogues
Tifereth Israel
34 Malden Street, 02149   (617) 387-0200

Fall River

Community Organisations
Fall River Jewish Council
Room 327, 56 N. Main St, 02720

Synagogues

Orthodox
Adas Israel
1647 Robeson Street, 02720   (508) 674-9761

Conservative
Beth El, 385 High St, 02720   (508) 674-3529

Fitchburg

Synagogues *(Independent)*

Agudas Achim
40 Boutelle Street, 01420   (508) 342-7704

Framingham

Area telephone code (508)

Synagogues

Orthodox
Chabad House
74 Joseph Road, 01701   877-8888

Conservative
Beth Sholom, Pamela Road, 01701   877-2540

Reform
Beth Am, 300 Pleasant St, 01701   872-8300

Bakeries

Boston Cookie, Framingham Mall, Route 30,
01701   872-1052
Supervision: Vaad Harabonim of MA.
Bread Basket Bakery
151 Cochituate Road, 01701   875-9441
Supervision: Vaad Harabonim of MA.

Gloucester

Synagogues *(Conservative)*
Ahavath Achim
86 Middle Street, 01930   (508) 281-0739

Greenfield

Synagogues
Temple Israel
27 Pierce Street, 01301   (413) 773-5884

Haverhill

Area telephone code (508)

Synagogues

Orthodox
Anshe Sholom, 427 Main St, 01830 372-2276

Reform
Temple Emanu-El
514 Main Street, 01830   373-3861

Hingham

Synagogues
Congregation Sha'aray Shalom
1112 Main Street, 02043   (617) 749-4922

Holbrook

Synagogues *(Conservative)*
Temple Beth Shalom
95 Plymouth Street, 02343   (617) 767-4922

Holliston

Synagogues
Temple Beth Torah
2162 Washington St, 01746   (508) 429-6268

Holyoke

Area telephone code (413)

Synagogues

Orthodox
Rodphey Sholom
1800 Northampton Street, 01040   534-5262

Conservative
Sons of Zion, 378 Maple St, 01040   534-3369

Hull

Area telephone code (617)

Synagogues
Temple Beth Sholom
600 Nantasket Avenue, 02045   925-0091
Temple Israel of Nantasket
3 Hadassah Way, 02045   925-0289
Summer only.

Hyannis

Synagogues *(Reform)*

Cape Cod Synagogue
145 Winter Street, 02601   (508) 775-2988

Hyde Park

Synagogues *(Conservative)*

Temple Adas Hadrath Israel
28 Arlington Street, 02136   (617) 364-2661

Lawrence

Community Organisations

Jewish Com. Council of Greater Lawrence
580 Haverhill Street, 01841   (617) 686-4157

Synagogues

Orthodox
Anshai Sholum
411 Hampshire Street, 01843   (508) 683-4544

Leominster

Synagogues *(Conservative)*

Congregation Agudat Achim
268 Washington St, 01453   (508) 534-6121

Lexington

Area telephone code (617)

Synagogues

Orthodox
Chabad Center
9 Burlington Street, 02173   863-8656

Conservative
Temple Emunah, 9 Piper Rd, 02173 861-0300

Reform
Temple Isaiah
55 Lincoln Street, 02173   862-7160

Lowell

Area telephone code (508)

Synagogues

Orthodox
Montefiore Synagogue
460 Westford Street, 01851   459-9400

Conservative
Temple Beth El
105 Princeton Blvd., 01851   453-7744

Reform
Temple Emanuel of Merrimack Valley
101 W. Forest Street, 01851   454-1372

Mikvaot

Mikvah, 48 Academy Drive   970-2008

Bakeries

Donut Shak, 487 Westford Street   937-0178
Supervision: Vaad Harabonim of MA.

Bed & Breakfast

The Very Victorian Sherman-Berry House
c/o Montefiore Synagogue
48 Academy Drive   970-2008

Lynn

Area telephone code (617)

Synagogues *(Orthodox)*

Ahabat Shalom
151 Ocean Street, 01902   593-9255
Houses the Eliot Feuerstein Library.
Anshai Sfard
150 S. Common Street, 01905   599-7131
Chevra Tehilim, 12 Breed St, 01902 598-2964

Malden

Area telephone code (617)

Synagogues

Orthodox
Beth Israel, 10 Dexter St, 02148   322-5686
Young Israel, 45 Holyoke St, 02148 961-9817

Conservative

Ezrath Israel, 245 Bryant St, 02148   322-7205

Traditional

Agudas Achim
160 Harvard Street, 02148   322-9380

Reform

Tifereth Israel, 539 Salem St, 02148 322-2794

Bakeries

Brick Oven Bakery
237 Ferry Street, 02148   322-3269
Supervision: Vaad Harabonim of MA.

Marblehead

Area telephone code (617)

Community Organisations

Jewish Federation of the North Shore
4 Community Road, 01945   598-1810

Synagogues

Orthodox
Orthodox Congregation of the North Shore
4 Community Road, 01945   598-1810

Conservative
Temple Sinai
1 Community Road, 01945   631-2244

Reform
Temple Emanu-El
393 Atlantic Avenue, 01945   631-9300

Marlboro

Synagogues (Conservative)

Temple Emanuel   (508) 485-7565
150 Berlin Road, 01752   (508) 562-5105

Medford

Area telephone code (617)

Synagogues

Temple Shalom
475 Winthrop Street, 02155   396-3262

Restaurants

Tufts Hillel
474 Boston Avenue, 02155   627-3242
Supervision: Vaad Harabonim of MA.

Bakeries

Donuts with a Difference
35 Riverside Avenue, 02155   396-1021
Supervision: Vaad Harabonim of MA.

Melrose

Synagogues (Reform)

Temple Beth Shalom
21 E. Foster Street, 02176   (617) 665-4520

Milford

Synagogues (Conservative)

Beth Shalom
49 Pine St, 01757   (508) 473-1590

Millis

Synagogues

Ael Chunon
334 Village Street, 02054   (508) 376-5984

Milton

Area telephone code (617)

Synagogues

Orthodox
B'nai Jacob
100 Blue Hill Parkway, 02187   698-0698

Conservative
Temple Shalom
180 Blue Hill Avenue, 02186   698-3394

Natick

Synagogues

Orthodox
Chabad Lubavitch Center
2 East Mill Street, 01760   (508) 650-1499

Conservative
Temple Israel, 145 Hartford Street, 01760

Needham

Area telephone code (617)

Synagogues

Conservative
Temple Aliyah
1664 Central Avenue, 02192   444-8522
                                    Fax: 449-7066

Reform
Temple Beth Shalom, Highland & Webster
Needham Heights, 02194   777-0077

New Bedford

Area telephone code (508)

Community Organisations
Jewish Federation of Greater New Bedford
467 Hawthorn Street,
N. Dartmouth, 02747   997-7471

Synagogues

Orthodox
Ahavath Achim
385 County Street, 02740   994-1760

Conservative
Tifereth Israel
145 Brownell Avenue, 02740   997-3171

Newburyport

Synagogues
Congregation Ahavas Achim, Washington &
Olive Streets, 09150   (508) 462-2461

Newton

Area telephone code (617)

Community Organisations
**Jewish Community Center of Greater
Boston,** 333 Nahanton St, 02159   558-6522
Kosher snack bar provided. See below.
Synagogue Council of Massachusetts, 1320
Center St, Newton Center, 02159   244-6506

Restaurants
Golda Meir House, 160 Stanton Avenue,
Dining Hall, 02166   969-1764
Supervision: Vaad Harabonim of MA.
Kitchen   965-0770.
J.C.C. Campus Snack Bar
333 Nahanton Street, 02159   965-7410
Supervision: Vaad Harabonim of MA.

Bakeries
Lederman's Bakery
1223 Centre Street, 02159   527-7896
Supervision: Vaad Harabonim of MA.
Tuler's Bakery
551 Commonwealth Avenue, 02159 964-5653
Supervision: Vaad Harabonim of MA. Pareve.
Shomer Shabbat.

Cafeterias
**Orthodox Rabbinical Council of
Massachusetts**   558-6475
Provides snack bar for Jewish Community
Center of Greater Boston.

North Adams

Synagogues (Conservative)
Congregation Beth Israel
265 Church Street, 01247   (413) 663-5830

Northampton

Synagogues
B'nai Israel
253 Prospect Road, 01060   (413) 584-3593

Norwood

Synagogues

Temple Shaare Tefilah
556 Nichols Street, 02062   (617) 762-8670

Onset

Area telephone code (508)

Synagogues (Orthodox)

Beth Israel, cnr. of Onset Avenue & Locust
Stree, PO Box 24, 02558   295-9184
Services 3 times daily from last Sat. in June to
Labour Day. Services are also held on the Holy
days. Efficiency apartments available near
synagogue. Further information from Burt
Parker.

Hotels

Bridge View Hotel
12 S. Water Street, 02558   295-9820
Welcomes Jewish guests. Self-catering flatlets
available. Kosher meat and other products
available.

Onset Pointe Inn
9 Eagle Way, 02558   295-8442
Breakfast included.

Peabody

Area telephone code (508)

Synagogues

Conservative
Temple Ner Tamid
368 Lowell Street, 01960   532-1293

Traditional
Congregation Sons of Israel
Park & Spring Streets, 01960   531-7576

Reform
Beth Shalom
489 Lowell Street, 01960   535-2100

Independent
Congregation Tifereth Israel
Pierpont Street, 01960   531-8135

Bakeries

Anthony's Bakery, 4 Lake St, 01906 535-5335
Supervision: Vaad Harabonim of MA.

Pittsfield (Berkshires)

Community Organisations

Jewish Federation of the Berkshires
235 East Street, 01201   (413) 442-4360

Plymouth

Synagogues (Reform)

Congregation Beth Jabob
8 Pleasant Street, 02361   (508) 746-1575

Quincy

Area telephone code (617)

Synagogues

Orthodox
Beth Israel, 33 Grafton St, 02169   472-6796

Conservative
Adas Shalom
435 Adams Street, 02169   471-1818
Temple Beth El
1001 Hancock Street, 02169   479-4309

Randolph

Area telephone code (617)

Synagogues

Orthodox
**Young Israel - Kehillath Jacob of Mattapan
& Randolph,** 374 N. Main St, 02368 986-6461

Conservative
Temple Beth Am
871 N. Main Street, 02368   963-0440

Bakeries

Zeppy's Bakery
937 North Main Street, 02368   963-9837
Supervision: Vaad Harabonim of MA.

Booksellers

Davidson's Hebrew Book Store
1106 Main Street, 02368

Revere

Area telephone code (617)

Synagogues

Orthodox
Ahavas Achim Anshei Sfard
89 Walnut Way, 02151   289-1026
Tifereth Israel
43 Nahant Avenue, 02151   284-9255

Independent
B'nai Israel, 1 Wave Ave, 02151   284-8388

Restaurants

Chelsea-Revere J.C.C.
65 Nahant Avenue, 02151   584-8395
Supervision: Vaad Harabonim of MA.

Delicatessens

Myer's Kosher Kitchen
168 Shirley Avenue, 02151

Salem

Synagogues *(Conservative)*
Temple Shalom
287 Lafayette Street, 01970   (508) 741-4880

Sharon

Area telephone code (614)

Religious Organisations
Eruv Society   784-6112
Eruv maintained by Sharon County Eruv
Society.

Synagogues

Orthodox
Chabad Center
101 Worcester Road, 02067   784-8167
Young Israel of Sharon
9 Dunbar Street, 02067   784-6112/5391

Conservative
Adath Sharon
18 Harding Street, 02067   784-2517
Temple Israel
125 Pond Street, 02067   784-3986

Reform
Temple Sinai, 100 Ames St, 02067   784-6081

Mikvaot

Young Israel of Sharon
9 Dunbar Street, 02067   784-6112
Operated by the Mikvah Organisation of the
South Shore, Chevrat Nashim.

Somerville

Area telephone code (617)

Synagogues *(Independent)*
B'nai B'rith of Somerville
201 Central Street, 02145   625-0333

Bakeries

La Ronga
599 Somerville Avenue, 02143   625-8600
Supervision: Vaad Harabonim of MA. Pareve.
Bread and rolls with KVH emblem only.

Springfield & Longmeadow

Area telephone code (413)

Community Organisations

Jewish Federation of Greater Springfield
1160 Dickinson Street, 01108   737-4313

Synagogues

Orthodox
Beth Israel, 1280 Williams St., Longmeadow,
01106   567-3210
Cong. Kodimoh, 124 Sumner Avenue, 01108
781-0171
The largest Orthodox cong. in New England.
Kesser Israel
19 Oakland Street, 01108   732-8492
Lubavitcher Yeshiva Syn., 1148 Converse St.,
Longmeadow, 01106   567-8665

Conservative

B'nai Jacob, 2 Eunice Dr., Longmeadow,
01106   567-3163

Temple Beth El
979 Dickinson Street, 01108   733-4149

Reform

Temple Sinai
1100 Dickinson Street, 01108   736-3619

Mikvaot

Mikveh Association
1138 Converse Street, 01106

Groceries

Waldbaum's Food Mart
355 Belmont Avenue, 01108   732-3866

Stoughton

Area telephone code (617)

Synagogues

**Striar Jewish Community Center on the
Fireman Campus**
445 Central Street, 02072   341-2016

Congregation Ahavath Torah
1179 Central Street, 03083   344-8733

Restaurants

Café Choopar Striar J.C.C.
445 Central Street, 02072   341-2016
Supervision: Vaad Harabonim of MA.

Bakeries

Green Manor
31 Tosca Drive, 02072   828-3018
Supervision: Vaad Harabonim of MA. Shomer
Shabbat.

Ruth's Bake Shop
987 Central Street, 02021   344-8993
Supervision: Vaad Harabonim of MA.

Sudbury

Area telephone code (508)

Synagogues

Reform

Cong. Beth El, Hudson Rd., 01776   443-9622

Independent

Congregation B'nai Torah
Woodside Road, 01776   443-2082

Swampscott

Area telephone code (617)

Synagogues

Conservative

Beth El, 55 Atlantic Ave, 01907   599-8005

Temple Israel
837 Humphrey Street, 01907   595-6635

Bakeries

Newman's
252 Humphrey Street, 01901   592-1550
Supervision: Vaad Harabonim of MA.

Vineyard Haven

Synagogues

Martha's Vineyard Hebrew Center
Center Street, 02568   (508) 693-0745

Wakefield

Synagogues (Conservative)

Temple Emmanuel
120 Chestnut Street, 01880   (617) 245-1886

Waltham

Area telephone code (617)

Cultural Organisations

**American Jewish Historical Society
(Brandeis University campus)**   891-8110
2 Thornton Road, 02154   Fax: 899-9208

Synagogues

Conservative

Beth Israel
25 Harvard Street, 02154   894-5146

Watertown

Bakeries
Tabrizi Bakery
56A Mt. Auburn St, 02172   (617) 926-0880
Supervision: Vaad Harabonim of MA.

Wayland

Synagogues *(Reform)*
Temple Shir Tikva
141 Boston Post Road, 01778   (508) 358-5312

Wellesley Hills

Synagogues
Beth Elohim
10 Bethel Road, 02181   (617) 235-8419

Westboro

Synagogues
B'nai Shalom, 117 E. Main Street, PO Box
1019, 01581-6019   (508) 366-7191

Westwood

Synagogues
Beth David
40 Pond Street, 02090   (617) 769-5270

Winchester

Synagogues *(Reform)*
Temple Shir Tikvah   (617) 792-1188

Winthrop

Area telephone code (617)

Synagogues *(Orthodox)*
Tifereth Abraham
283 Shirley St, 02152   846-5063

Tifereth Israel
93 Veteran's Road, 02152   846-1390

Bakeries
Fabiano Bakery
7 Somerset Avenue, 02152   846-5946
Supervision: Vaad Harabonim of MA.

Worcester

Area telephone code (508)

Community Organisations
Jewish Federation
633 Salisbury Street, 01609   756-1543

Synagogues

Orthodox
Young Israel of Worcester
889 Pleasant Street, 01602   754-3681

Mikvaot
Mikva, Huntley Street, 01602   755-1257

Contact Information
**Agudath Israel of America Hachnosas
Orchim Committee,** 69 S. Flagg Street, 01602
Contact Rabbi Reuven Fischer.
Rabbi Hershel Fogelman
22 Newton Avenue   752-5791
Visitors requiring information about kashrut,
temporary accommodation, etc., should
contact Rabbi Fogelman.

Michigan

Ann Arbor

Organisations
Jewish Federation/UJA
2939 Birch Hollow Drive, 48108

Mikvaot
Chabad House Mikva, 715 Hill Street, 48104

Benton Harbour (St Joseph)

Synagogues (Conservative)

Temple B'nai Shalom, 2050 Broadway, 49022

Detroit

Community Organisations

B'nai B'rith Hillel Foundations
Wayne State University, 667 Charles Grosberg
Religious Ctr., 48202
Hot lunch, sandwiches, salads, soups served
during academic year (Sept. - April).

**Council of Orthodox Rabbis of Detroit
(Vaad Harabonim),** 17071 W. Ten Mile Road,
Southfield, 48075   (313) 559-5005/06

Jewish Community Center of Metr. Detroit
6600 W. Maple Road,
W. Bloomfield, 48322   (810) 661-1000
Fax: (810) 661-3680

Jewish Federation of Metr. Detroit
Telegraph Road, Bloomfield Hills, 48303

**Machon L'Torah (The Jewish Network of
Michigan),** W. 10 Mile Road, 48237

Synagogues

With tens of synagogues in the Bloomfield,
Oak Park and Southfield areas, visitors are
recommmended to contact one of the local
religious organisations listed for the nearest
synagogue.

Kashrut Information

Council of Orthodox Rabbis, 17071 W. Ten
Mile Road, Southfield, 48075   (313) 559-5005
(313) 559-5006

Restaurants

Center Branch
Jimmy Prentis Morris Building, 15110 W. Ten
Mile Road, Oak Park, 48237   (810) 967-4030

Mertz's Cafe Katon, 23055 Coolidge Road,
Oak Park, 48237   (313) 547-3581

Delicatessens

Sarah's Glatt Kosher Deli, 15600 W. Ten Mile
Road, Southfield, 48075   (313) 443-2425

Groceries

Sperber's Kosher Karry-Out, 25250 W. Ten
Mile Road, Oak Park, 48237   (313) 443-2425

Museums

Holocaust Memorial Center, 6602 W. Maple
Road, W. Bloomfield, 48322-3005
(810) 661-0840
Fax: (810) 661-4240
First institution of its kind in USA.

Media

Newspapers

Jewish News, Franklin Rd, Southfield, 48034

East Lansing

Area telephone code (517)

Organisations

B'nai B'rith Hillel Foundation, Michigan State
University, 402 Linden St, 48823   332-1916
Fax: 332-4142
Kosher meals available during academic year.

Synagogues

Conservative & Reform

Shaarey Zedek, 1924 Coolidge Road, 48823

Flint

Area telephone code (810)

Community Organisations

Flint Jewish Federation
619 Wallenberg Street, 48502   767-5922

Synagogues

Orthodox

Chabad House
5385 Calkins, 48532   230-0770

Conservative

Congregation Beth Israel
5240 Calkins Road, 48532   732-6310

Reform

Temple Beth El
501 S. Ballenger Highway, 48532   232-3138

Grand Rapids

Synagogues

Orthodox
Chabad House of Western Michigan
2615 Michigan Street N.E., 49506

Conservative
Congregation Ahavas Israel
2727 Michigian Street N.E., 49506

Reform
Temple Emanuel
1715 E. Fulton Street, 49503

Jackson

Synagogues
Temple Beth Israel
801 W. Michigan Avenue, 49202

Kalamazoo

Synagogues (Conservative)
Sons of Moses, 2501 Stadium Drive, 49008

Lansing

Synagogues (Reconstructionist)
Kehillat Israel
2014 Forest Rd, 48910   (517) 882-0049

Saginaw

Synagogues

Conservative
Temple B'nai Israel
1424 S. Washington Avenue, 48601

Reform
Congregation Beth El
100 S. Washington Avenue, 48607

South Haven

Synagogues (Orthodox)
First Hebrew Congregation
249 Broadway, 49090   (616) 637-1603

Minnesota

Duluth

Area telephone code (218)

Community Organisations
Jewish Federation & Com. Council
1602 E. 2nd Street, 55812   724-8857

Synagogues

Orthodox
Adas Israel, 302 E. Third Street, 55802

Conservative & Reform
Temple Israel, 1602 E. 2nd Street, 55812

Minneapolis

Community Organisations
Jewish Com. Center of Greater Minneapolis
4330 Cedar Lake Rd. S, 55416

Synagogues

Orthodox
Congregation Bais Yisroel
4221 Sunset Blvd, 55416   926-7867
Knesseth Israel
4330 W. 28th Street, 55416   920-2183

Mikvaot
Knesseth Israel
4330 W. 28th Street, 55416   926-3829

Contact Information
Rabbi Perez   926-3185
Contact for kosher establishments in the area
and for eruv information.

Butchers
Fishman's Kosher
4000 Minnetonka Blvd, 55416   926-5611
Glatt butcher and take-out certified by the
local Orthodox vaad.

Rochester

Hospitality

Lubavitch Bais Chaya Moussia Hospitality Center
730 2nd St S.W., 55902   (507) 288-7500
Also provides Shabbat dinners and hospital visitations. Mikva on premises.

St Paul

Area telephone code (612)

Restaurants

Dairy
Old City Cafe
1571 Grand Avenue   699-5347
Supervision: Upper Midwest Kashrus.
Dairy/vegetarian. Hours: Sun, 10 am to 9 pm; Mon to Thurs, 11 am to 9 pm; Fri, to 2 pm.

Groceries
L'chaim, 655 Snelling Avenue, 55116

Mississippi

Greenville

Synagogues (Reform)
Hebrew Union Cong., 504 Main St, 38701

Greenwood

Synagogues (Orthodox)
Ahavath Rayim, Market & George Streets, PO Box 1235, 38935-1235   453-7537

Natchez

Synagogues (Reform)
B'nai Israel, Washington & S. Commerce Streets, PO Box 2081, 39120
Oldest synagogue in Mississippi.

Tupelo

Synagogues (Conservative)
B'nai Israel, Marshall & Hamlin Streets, 38801

Missouri

Kansas City

Note: Please consult under Kansas, Overland Park and Prairie Village, since Kansas City spans both Missouri and Kansas.

Community Organisations
Jewish Federation of Greater Kansas City
5801 W. 115th Street, Suite 201, Overland Park, 66211

Restaurants
Sensations, 1148 W. 103 Street, 64114

Media

Newspapers
Kansas City Jewish Chronicle
7375 W. 107th Street, Overland Park, 66204

St Louis

Area telephone code (314)

Community Organisations
Jewish Federation
12 Millstone Campus Drive, 63146   432-0020
                                    Fax: 432-1277

The Vaad Hoeir (United Orthodox Jewish Community of St. Louis)
4 Millstone Campus, 63141   569-2770
Recognised Orthodox religious authority for the city.

Synagogues

Orthodox
Young Israel of St Louis
8101 Delmar Blvd, 63130   727-1880

Mikvaot

Mikva, 4 Millstone Campus, 63146   569-2770

Kashrut Information

The Vaad Hoeir, 4 Millstone Campus, 63141

Restaurants

Diamant's, 618 North & South Rd.   712-9624
NoBull Cafe, 10477 Old Olive   991-9533
Simon Kohn's, 10424 Old Olive   569-0727

Bakeries

Schnuck's Nancy Ann Bakery
Olive & Mason   434-7323

Butchers

Diamant's Kosher Meat Market
618 North & South Road   721-9624
S. Kohn's, 10424 Old Olive   569-0727
Sol's, 8627 Olive   993-9977

Groceries

Lazy Suzan Imaginative Cartering
110 Millwell Drive   291-6050
Simon Kohn's Kosher Meat & Deli
10424 Old Olive   569-0727
Sol's Kosher Meat Market
8627 Olive   993-9977

Libraries

The Brodsky Jewish Community Library
12 Millstone Campus Drive, 63146

Monument

Jewish Tercentenary, Forest Park
Home to the Monument & Flagpole.

Montana

Billings

Synagogues

Congregation Beth Aaron
1148 N. Broadway, 59101   (406) 248-6412

Great Falls

Synagogues *(Reform)*

Aitz Chayim
PO Box 6192, 59406   (406) 542-9521

Missoula

Synagogues

Har Shalom
PO Box 7581, 59807   (406) 523-5671

Nebraska

Lincoln

Synagogues

Conservative
Tifereth Israel, 3219 Sheridan Blvd., 68502

Reform
South Street Temple B'nai Jeshurun
20th & South Streets, 68502

Omaha

Area telephone code (402)

Community Organisations

Jewish Federation of Omaha
333 S. 132nd Street   334-8200

Synagogues

Orthodox
Beth Israel, 1502 N. 52nd Street, 68104

Conservative
Beth El, 14506 California Street, 68154

Reform
Temple Israel, 7023 Cass Street, 68132

Mikvaot

Com. Mikva, 323 S. 132nd Street, 68154

Nevada
Area telephone code (702)

Las Vegas

Synagogues *(Orthodox)*
Young Israel of Las Vegas
1724 Winners Cup, 89117   360-8909

Kashrut Information
Community Relations   732-0556

Delicatessens
Casba Glatt Kosher
2845 Las Vegas Blvd   791-3344
Jerusalem Kosher Restaurant & Deli
1305 Vegas Valley, 89109   791-3668
Rafi's Place
6135 West Sahara, 89102   253-0033
Sara's Place, 4972 S. Maryland

Reno

Synagogues

Conservative
Temple Emanu-El, 1031 Manzanita Lane at Lakeside Dr., 89509   825-5600
This is the oldest active congregation in Nevada.

Reform
Temple Sinai
3405 Gulling Road, 89503   747-5508

New Hampshire
Area telephone code (603)

Bethlehem

Synagogues

Orthodox
Machzikei Hadas, Lewis Hill Road, 03574
Summer only.

Conservative
Bethlehem Hebrew Congregation
Strawberry Hill, 03574

Manchester

Community Organisations
Jewish Federation of Greater Manchester
698 Beech Street, 03104   627-7679

Synagogues

Orthodox
Lubavitch, 7 Camelot Place, 03104   647-0204

Conservative
Temple Israel, 66 Salmon St, 03104   622-6171

Reform
Adath Yeshurun
152 Prospect Street, 03104   669-5650

Media

Newspapers
The Reporter, 698 Beech St, 03104   627-7679
                                  Fax: 627-7963
Lists further communities in Amherst, Concord, Derry, Dover, Durham, Hanover, Keene, Laconia and Nashua.

Portsmouth

Synagogues
Temple Israel
200 State Street, 03801   436-5301

Community Information
The Curator of the Historic Waterfront Neighbourhood reports the creation of a Jewish (Russian immigrants) home at
Strawberry Banke   433-1100
                          Fax: 433-1115

New Jersey

Note: RCBC stands for the Rabbinical Council of Bergen County.

Aberdeen

Synagogues *(Orthodox)*

Bet Tefilah
479 Lloyd Rd, 07747   (908) 583-6262

Atlantic City

Synagogues

Orthodox
Rodef Shalom, 3833 Atlantic Av., 08401

Conservative
Beth El, 500 N. Jerome Ave, Margate, 08402
Beth Judah, 6725 Ventnor Av., Ventnor, 08406
Chelsea Hebrew Cong., 4001 Atlantic Av., 08401
Community Syn., Maryland & Pacific Avs., 08401

Reform
Beth Israel, 2501 Shore Rd., Northfield, 08225
Temple Emeth Shalom, 8501 Ventnor Av., Margate, 08402

Bayonne

Community Organisations

Jewish Community Center, 1050 Kennedy Blvd, 07002   (201) 436-6900

Synagogues

Orthodox
Ohab Sholom, 1016-1022 Ave. C, 07002
Ohav Zedek, 912 Ave. C, 07002
Uptown Synagogue, 49th St. & Ave C, 07002

Conservative
Temple Emanuel, 735 Kennedy Blvd, 07002

Reform
Temple Beth Am, 111 Avenue B, 07002

Belmar

Synagogues *(Orthodox)*

Sons of Israel Cong., PO Box 298, 07719

Hotels

New Irvington, 112 12th Avenue, 07719

Bergenfield

Butchers

Glatt World, 89 Newbridge Rd (201) 439-9675
Supervision: RCBC. Sells food provisions too.

Bordentown

Synagogues *(Non-affiliated)*

Congregation B'nai Abraham
59 Crosswicks Street, 08505

Bradley Beach

Synagogues *(Orthodox)*

Congregation Agudath Achim
301 McCabe Avenue, 07720

Bridgeton

Community Organisations

Jewish Federation of Cumberland County.
See entry for Vineland, NJ.

Synagogues *(Conservative)*

Congregation Beth Abraham
330 Fayette Street, 08302

Burlington

Synagogues

B'nai Israel, 212 High Street, 08332

Carmel

Synagogues

Temple Beth Hillel, 08332

Cherry Hill

Area telephone code (609)

Community Organisations

Jewish Federation of Southern New Jersey
2393 W. Marlton Pike, 08002   665-6100

Synagogues

Conservative

Beth El, 2901 W. Chapel Avenue, 08002
Beth Shalom, 1901 Kresson Road, 08003
Congregation Beth Tikva
115 Evesboro-Medford Road, Marlton

Reform

Congregation M'kor Shalom
850 Evesham Road
Temple Emmanuel, 1101 Springdale Road

Mikvaot

Sons of Israel
720 Cooper Landing Road, 08002   667-9700

Restaurants

Maxim's
404 Route 70 East, 08034   428-5045
Supervision: Tri-County Vaad.
Glatt kosher middle eastern cuisine.

Bakeries

Pastry Palace Kosher Bakery
State Highway 70, 08034   429-3606

Butchers

Cherry Hill Kosher Meat Market
907 W. Marlton Pike, 08002

Media

Newspapers
The Jewish Community Voice
2393 W. Marlton Pike, 08002

Cinnaminson

Synagogues *(Conservative)*

Temple Sinai
New Albany Road, & Route 130, 08077

Clark

Synagogues

Temple Beth O'r
111 Valley Road, 07066   (908) 381-8403

Clifton

Area telephone code (201)

Community Organisations

Jewish Federation of Greater Clifton-Passaic
199 Scoles Avenue, 07012   777-7031
                                  Fax: 777-6701

Synagogues

Conservative

Clifton Jewish Center
18 Delaware Street, 07011

Reform

Beth Shalom, 733 Passaic Avenue, 07012

Media

Newspapers
Jewish Community News
199 Scoles Avenue, 07012

Colonia

Synagogues *(Conservative)*

Ohev Shalom
220 Temple Way, 07067   (908) 388-7222

Cranbury

Synagogues

Jewish Congregation of Concordia
c/o Club House, 08512   (609) 655-8136

Cranford

Synagogues *(Conservative)*

Temple Beth El, 338 Walnut Avenue, 07016

Contact Information

Rabbi Hoffberg   276-9231
Contact for kosher hospitality.

Deal

Area telephone code (908)

Synagogues

Orthodox
128 Norwood Avenue, 07723   531-3200

Ohel Yaacob
6 Ocean Avenue, 07723   531-0217

Restaurants
Deal Gardens   531-4887
Lhangmao, 214 Roosevelt Avenue, Oakhurst, 07755

Pizzerias
J II Pizza
106 Norwood Avenue, 07723   531-7936

Booksellers
Nathan's Judaica Bookstore
256 Norwood Avenue, 07723   531-8657

East Brunswick

Synagogues

Orthodox
Young Israel of E. Brunswick
193 Dunham Corner Road, 08816   254-1860

Conservative
E. Brunswick Jewish Center
511 Ryders Lane, 08816   257-7070

Reform
Temple B'nai Shalom, Old Stage Road & Fern Road, 08816   251-4300

Butchers
East Brunswick Kosher Meats
1020 State Highway 18, 08816   257-0007

Edison

Community Organisations
Jewish Community Center of Middlesex County, 1775 Oak Tree Road, 08820

Jewish Federation of Greater Middlesex County
230 Old Bridge Turnpike, 08882   432-7711
                        Fax: 432-0292

Synagogues (Conservative)
Beth El, 91 Jefferson Blvd, 08817

Butchers
Edison Kosher Meats, State Highway 27, and Evergreen Rd   549-3707

Elizabeth

Area telephone code (908)

Synagogues

Orthodox
Adath Israel, 1391 North Av., 07208

Adath Jeshurun
200 Murray St., 07202   355-6723

Bais Yitzchok Chevrah Thilim, 153 Bellevue St., 07202   354-4789

Elmora Hebrew Center, 420 West End Avenue, 07202   353-1740

Jewish Educational Center, 330 Elmora Avenue, 07208

Jewish Education Center (Adath Israel), 1391 North Avenue, 07208

Reform
Temple Beth El of Elizabeth, 737 N. Broad Street, 07208   354-3021

Mikvaot
Mikva, 35 North Avenue, 07208

Contact Information
Rabbi Elazar Teitz
35 North Avenue, 07208
Contact for information about kosher rooms, temporary accommodation, etc.

Restaurants
Dunkin' Donuts, 186 Elmora Avenue, 07202
Jerusalem Restaurant
150 Elmora Avenue, 07202
New Kosher Special
163 Elmora Avenue, 07202   353-1818

Delicatessens

Superior Deli & Restaurant
150 Elmora Avenue, 07202

Groceries

Kosher Express, 155 Elmora Avenue, 07202

Englewood

Area telephone code (201)

Synagogues

Orthodox

Ahavath Torah   568-1315
240 Broad Avenue, 07631   Fax: 568-2991

Shomrei Emunah, 89 Huguenot Ave, 07631

Conservative

Temple Emanu-El
147 Tenafly Road, 07631   567-1300

Mikvaot

Mikva, 89 Huguenot Avenue   567-1143

Restaurants

J.C. Pizza at Jerusalem V
24 W. Palisade Avenue, 07631   569-5546
Supervision: RCBC.

Groceries

Kosher By the Case & Less
255 Van Nostrand Avenue, 07631   568-2281
Supervision: RCBC.

The Menageries
41 East Palisade Avenue, 07631   569-2704
Supervision: RCBC. Dairy and meat.

Fair Lawn

Area telephone code (201)

Restaurants

J.C. Pizza of Fairlawn
14-20 Plaza Road, 07410   703-0801
Supervision: RCBC.

Bakeries

New Royal Bakery
19-09 Fair Lawn Avenue, 07410   796-6565
Supervision: RCBC. Pat Yisrael.

Bagels

Hot Bagels
6-07 Saddle River Road, 07410   796-9625
13-38 River Road, 07410   791-5646
Supervision: RCBC.
Dairy. Only the bagels are under supervision.

Butchers

Food Showcase
24-28 Fair Lawn Avenue, 07410   475-0077
Supervision: RCBC.
Sells food provisions as well.

Groceries

Kosher Express
22-16 Morlot Avenue, 07410   791-8818
Supervision: RCBC.

Petak's Glatt Kosher Fine Foods
19-03 Fair Lawn Avenue, 07410   797-5010
Supervision: RCBC. Glatt kosher caterers.

Fort Lee

Synagogues (Orthodox)

Young Israel of Fort Lee
1610 Parker Avenue, 07024   592-1110

Freehold

Synagogues

Agudath Achim, Broad & Stokes Sts, 07728

Congregation Agudath Achim, Freehold
Jewish Center, Broad & Stokes Streets, 07728

Restaurants

Fred and Murry's, Pond Road Shopping
Center, Route 9, 07728   462-3343
Not glatt kosher or shomer Shabbat, but has
Conservative supervision.

Hackensack

Community Organisations

**Jewish Federation of Community Services
of Bergen County,** 170 State Street, 07601

Synagogues (Conservative)

Temple Beth El, 280 Summit Avenue, 07601

Haddonfield

Butchers

Sarah's Kosher Kitchen, 63 Ellis Road

Highland Park

Area telephone code (908)

Synagogues

Orthodox

Cong. Ahavas Achim	247-0532

Cong. Etz Ahaim (Sephardi), 230 Dennison
St., 08904   247-3839
Cong. Ohav Emeth
415 Raritan Avenue, 08904   247-3038

Conservative

**Highland Park Conservative Temple &
Center,** 201 S. 3rd Av. 08904   545-6482

Mikvaot

Park Mikva, 112 S. 1st Avenue, 08904

Groceries

B&E Kosher Meat Market
76 Raritan Avenue   846-3444
Berkley Bakery, 405 Raritan Avenue, 08904
Dan's Deli & Meat Market
515 Raritan Avenue, 08904
Kosher Catch, 239 Raritan Avenue   572-9052
Mystic Gourmet, 229 Raritan Avenue, 08904

Booksellers

Highland Park Sefarim & Judaica
227 Raritan Avenue

Hillside

Area telephone code (908)

Synagogues

Orthodox

Congregation Sinai Torath Chaim
1531 Maple Avenue, 07205   923-9500

Conservative

Shomrei Torah Ohel Yosef Yitzchok
910 Salem Avenue, 07205   289-0770

Hoboken

Area telephone code (201)

Synagogues

United Synagogue of Hoboken, 830 Hudson
Street & 115 Park Avenue, 07030   659-2614
                                        Fax: 659-7944

James Burg

Synagogues

**Rossmoor Jewish Congregation Meeting
Room,** 08831   (609) 655-0439

Lakewood

Area telephone code (201)

Community Organisations

Ocean County Jewish Federation
301 Madison Avenue, 08701   363-0530

Synagogues

Orthodox

Lakewood Yeshiva
Private Way & 6th Street, 08701
Sons of Israel
Madison Avenue & 6th Street, 08701

Conservative

Ahavat Shalom, Forest Ave & 11th St, 08701

Reform

Beth Am, Madison Ave & Carey St, 08701

Restaurants

Kosher Experience, Kennedy Blvd, 08701
Supervision: Rabbi Chumsky. Closed on
Shabbat and all holidays and festivals.
R. & S. Kosher Restaurant and Deli
416 Clifton Avenue, 08701   363-668
Glatt kosher meat only. Hours: Sun to Thurs,
12:30pm to 9pm; Fri, 8am to 2:30pm.

Linden

Synagogues
Congregation Anshe Chesed, 100 Orchard
Terrace at St George Av, 07036   486-8616

Conservative
Mekor Chayim Suburban Jewish Center
Deerfield Road & Academy Terrace,
07036   925-2283

Livingston
Area telephone code (201)

Synagogues

Orthodox
Etz Chaim Synagogue, Mt Pleasant Avenue
Suburban Torah Center, 85 W. Mount
Pleasant Avenue, 07039   994-0122; 994-2620

Restaurants
Moshavi
515 S. Livingston Avenue, 07039   740-8777
Supervision: Vaad Hakashrus of the Council of
Orthodox Rabbis Metrowest.

Pizzerias
Jerusalem Pizza, 16 East Mt. Pleasant Avenue,
07039   533-1424
Supervision: Vaad Hakashrus of the Council of
Orthodox Rabbis Metrowest.

Delicatessens
Super Duper Bagels
498 S. Livingston Avenue, 07052   533-1703
Supervision: Vaad Hakashrus of the Council of
Orthodox Rabbis Metrowest.

Manalapan
Area telephone code (908)

Restaurants
Kosher Chinese Express   866-1677
335 Route 9 South, 07726   Fax: 866-1621
Glatt kosher and Shomer Shabbat.

Metuchen

Synagogues *(Conservative)*
Neve Shalom
250 Grove Avenue, 08840   548-2238

Millville

Community Organisations
Jewish Federation of Cumberland County

Synagogues *(Conservative)*
Beth Hillel, 3rd Avenue & Oak Street, 08332

Morristown
Area telephone code (201)

Synagogues
Morristown Jewish Center
177 Speedwell Avenue, 07960   538-9292

Congregation of Ahavath Yisrael
9 Cutler Street, 07960   267-4184

Reform
Temple B'nai Or, Overlook Road, 07960

Kashrut Information
Baila Mandel   267-4184
Ahavath Yisrael operates a kosher food buying
service for the community, dealing only in
strictly kosher products.
Rabbinical College of America
226 Sussex Avenue, 07960   267-9404

New Brunswick
Area telephone code (908)

Synagogues

Orthodox
Chabad Hse. Friends of Lubavitch, 8 Sicard
St., 08901   828-9191

Reform
Anshe Emeth Memorial Temple, 222
Livingston Av., 08901   545-6484

Unaffiliated
Cong. Poile Zedek
145 Neilson St., 08901   545-6123

Bakeries
Sam's Club, 290 State Highway 18   613-9323
Supervision: Kof-K. This store only.

Newark

Area telephone code (201)

Community Organisations
United Jewish Federation of Metrowest
901 Route 10, Whippany, 07981   884-4800
Fax: 884-7361

Synagogues
With dozens of synagogues in the district, visitors are advised to contact a local or national religious organisation to locate the most convenient synagogue.

Mikvaot
Mikvah of Essex County
717 Pleasant Valley Way, West Orange, 07052
Sarah Esther Rosenhaus Mikvah Institutue
93 Lake Road, 07960

Restaurants
Jerusalem West
16 E. Mt. Pleasant Avenue, 07039   533-1424
Metro Glatt/Delancy Street
515 Livingston Avenue, 07039   992-9189
Fax: 992-6430
Fax number for take-out orders.
Pleasantdale Kosher Meat, 470 Pleasant Valley Way, West Orange, 07052   731-3216

Delicatessens
Arlington Kosher Deli, Restaurant & Caterers, Arlington Shopping Center, 744 Route 46W, Parsippany, 07054   335-9400
David's Deco-Tessen, 555 Passaic Avenue, West Caldwell, 07006   808-3354
Fax: 808-5806
Kosher Inn, Newark Airport - International Building, Terminal B   961-3300...ext 237
Supervision: Rabbi Eliezer Lipa Weingarten, Cong. Beth Eliyahu of Shomrei Emunah.

Located after ticket check-point between gates 55 and 58.
Reuben's Deli Delite, 500 Pleasant Valley Way, West Orange, 07052   731-6351

Groceries
Zayda's Super Value Meat Market & Deli
309 Irvington Avenue,
South Orange, 07079   762-1812

Media
Newspapers
The Metrowest Jewish News
901 Route 10, Whippany, 07981   887-3900
Weekly publication owned by Jewish Fed. of Metrowest.

Booksellers
Hebrew Bookstore, 1923 Springfield Avenue, Maplewood, 07040   763-4244/5

North Brunswick
Area telephone code (908)

Synagogues (Conservative)
Congregation B'nai tikvah
1001 Finnegans Lane, 08902   297-0696

Parlin

Synagogues
Ohav Shalom, 3018 Bordertown Avenue, 08859   (201) 727-4334

Passaic
Area telephone code (201)

Community Organisations
Jewish Federation of Greater Clifton-Passaic

Synagogues
Orthodox
Young Israel of Passaic-Clifton
200 Brook Avenue, 07055   778-7117

Restaurants

Beth Israel Hospital
70 Parker Avenue, 07055   365-5000

Brook Kosher, 222 Brook Avenue, 07055

China Pagoda, 227 Main Avenue   777-4900

Pizzerias

Jerusalem II Pizza of Passaic
224 Brook Avenue, 07055

Delicatessens

B&Y Kosher Korner Inc.,
200 Main Avenue, 07055   777-1120

Paterson

Synagogues (Conservative)

Temple Emanuel, 151 E. 33rd Street, 07514

Perth Amboy

Synagogues

Orthodox

Shaarey Teflioh
15 Market Street, 08861   826-2977

Conservative

Beth Mordechai
224 High Street, 08861   442-2431

Piscataway

Area telephone code (908)

Synagogues (Reform)

B'nai Shalom
25 Netherwood Ave, 08854   (908) 885-9444

Plainfield

Synagogues

Orthodox

United Orthodox Synagogue
526 W. 7th Street, 07060

Conservative

Beth El
225 E. 7th Street, 07060   (201) 755-0043

Reform

Temple Sholom
815 W. 7th Street, 07063   (201) 756-6447

Princeton

Area telephone code (609)

Synagogues (Traditional)

Jewish Center   921-0100
435 Nassau Street, 08540   Fax: 921-7531

Rahway

Synagogues (Conservative)

Temple Beth Torah
1389 Bryant Street, 07065   576-8432

Randolph

Synagogues (Orthodox)

Mount Freedom Jewish Center
1209 Sussex Turnpike, 07970

River Edge

Synagogues (Reform)

Temple Sholom, 385 Howland Avenue, 07661

Roselle

Area telephone code (908)

Community Organisations

Jewish Federation of Central New Jersey
843 St Georges Avenue, 07203   298-8200
       Fax: 298-8220

Media

Guides

Shalom Book   298-8200
843 St Georges Avenue, 07203   Fax: 298-8220

Rumson

Synagogues *(Conservative)*
Congregation B'nai Israel
Hance & Ridge Roads, 07760 (908) 842-1800

Scotch Plains

Community Organisations
Jewish Community Center of Central New Jersey
1391 Martine Avenue, 07076 (908) 889-1830

Synagogues

Conservative
Temple Israel Fanwood
1920 Cliffwood Street, 07076 (908) 889-1830

Somerset

Synagogues
Temple Beth El
1945 Amwell Road, 08873 (201) 873-2325

South River

Synagogues *(Traditional)*
Congregation Anshe Emeth
88 Main Street, 08882 257-4190
See also Edison

Spotswood

Synagogues *(Reform)*
Monroe Township Jewish Center
11 Cornell Avenue, 08884 251-1119

Teaneck

Area telephone code (201)

Synagogues

Orthodox
Bnai Yeshurun, 641 W. Englewood Avenue, 07666 836-8916
Cong. Beth Aaron, 950 Queen Anne Rd, 07666
Rinat Yisrael, 389 W. Englewood Av., 07666
Roemer Syn., Whittier School, W. Englewood Av., 07666
Young Israel of Teaneck
868 Perry Lane, 07666 833-4419

Conservative
Beth Sholom, Rugby Rd. & Rutland Av., 07666
Jewish Center of Teaneck, 70 Sterling Place, 07666 833-0515

Reform
Beth Am, 510 Claremont Av., 07666
Temple Emeth, 1666 Windsor Rd., 07666

Mikvaot
1726 Windsor Road, 07666 837-8220

Restaurants

Meat
Fliegels, 456 Cedar Lane, 07666 692-8060
Supervision: RCBC.
Hunan Teaneck 692-0099
515 Cedar Lane, 07666 Fax: 692-1907
Supervision: RCBC.
Glatt kosher Chinese and American cuisine. Eat in or take out. Mashgiach temidi. Hours: Sunday to Thursday, 11:30 am to 9:45 pm; Friday, to 4 pm; Saturday night, after Shabbat until midnight.
Mabat Steak House
540 Cedar Lane, 07666 836-4115
Supervision: RCBC. Glatt kosher.
Noah's Ark 692-1200
493 Cedar Lane, 07666 Fax: 692-1890
Supervision: RCBC.
Chassidishe shechita meats. Hours: Monday to Thursday, 10:30 am to 10:30 pm; Friday, 8 am to 4 pm; Sunday, 9:30 am to 10:30 pm; Saturday during winter, after Shabbat to midnight. Ten minutes from GW Bridge.

Dairy

Jerusalem Pizza
496 Cedar Lane, 07666   836-2120
Supervision: RCBC.

Plaza Pizza & Restaurant
1431 Queen Anne Road, 07666   837-9500
Supervision: RCBC.

Shelly's, 482 Cedar Lane, 07666   692-0001
Supervision: RCBC. Chalav Yisrael. Hours:
Monday to Thursday, 10:30 am to 10 pm;
Sunday, 9 am to 10 pm. Ten minutes from the
George Washington Bridge.

Bakeries

Butterflake Bake Shop
448 Cedar Lane, 07666   836-3516
Supervision: RCBC. Pat Yisrael.

Gruenbaum Bakeries
477B Cedar Lane, 07666   836-3128
Supervision: RCBC. Pat Yisrael.

Royal Too Bakery, 172 West Englewood
Avenue, 07666   833-0114
Supervision: RCBC. Pat Yisrael.

Sammy's New York Bagels
1443 Queen Anne Road, 07666   837-0515
Supervision: Kof-K. Pat Yisrael.

Bagels

Hot Bagels
976 Teaneck Road, 07666   833-0410
Supervision: RCBC.
Dairy. Only the bagels are under supervision.

Butchers

Glatt Express
1400 Queen Anne Road, 07666   837-8110
Supervision: RCBC. Sells food provisions too.

Marketplace at Teaneck
647 Cedar Lane, 07666   692-1290
Supervision: RCBC. Sells food provisions too.

Delicatessens

Chopstix, 172 West Englewood Avenue,
07666   833-0200
Fax: 833-8326
Supervision: RCBC. Glatt kosher Chinese take-
out. Hours: Sunday to Thursday, 11:30 am to
10 pm; Friday, closing times vary – please call.
Ma'adan, 446 Cedar Lane, 07666   692-0192
Supervision: RCBC. Take-out.

Groceries

Dovid's Fresh Fish Market
736 Chestnut Avenue, 07666   928-0888
Supervision: RCBC.

Booksellers

Zoldan's Judaica Center
406 Cedar Lane, 07666   907-0034

Tenafly

Restaurants

P.K. Café & Pizza at the JCC
411 East Clinton Avenue   894-0801
Supervision: RCBC.

Trenton

Community Organisations

**Jewish Federation of Mercer & Bucks
Counties**
999 Lower Ferry Road, 08628   (609) 883-5000

Union

Area telephone code (201)

Community Organisations

Jewish Federation of Central New Jersey
Green Lane, 07083   351-5060

Synagogues

Conservative
Beth Shalom, 2046 Vauxhall Road, 07083
Temple Israel
2372 Morris Avenue, 07083   686-2120

Vineland

Area telephone code (609)

Community Organisations

Jewish Federation of Cumberland County
629 Wood St, Suite 202-204, 08360   696-4445
Also serves the Bridgeton & Cumberland
County areas.

Synagogues

Orthodox
Ahavas Achim, 618 Plum Street, 08360
Sons of Jacob, 321 Grape Street, 08360

Conservative
Beth Israel, 1015 E. Park Avenue, 08630

Warren
Area telephone code (908)

Community Organisations
Jewish Federation of Central New Jersey
Suburban Services Office, 150 Mt. Bethel Rd.,
07059   647-0232
                                         Fax: 647-3115

Synagogues *(Reform)*
Mountain Jewish Community Center
104 Mount Horeb Road, 07060   356-8777

Wayne
Area telephone code (201)

Community Organisations
Jewish Federation of New Jersey
1 Pike Drive, 07470   595-0555

Synagogues

Conservative
Shomrei Torah, 30 Hinchman Avenue, 07470

Reform
Temple Beth Tikvah
950 Preakness Avenue, 07470

West New York

Synagogues

Orthodox
Congregation Shaare Zedek
5308 Palisade Avenue, 07093

West Orange
Area telephone code (201)

Synagogues
**Congregation Ahawas Achim B'nai Jacob
and David**
700 Pleasant Valley Way, 07052   736-1407

Mikvaot
Essex County Ritualarim   731-1427
717 Pleasant Valley Way, 07052   669-0462

Restaurants
Eden Wok
478 Pleasant Valley Way, 07052   243-0115
Supervision: Vaad Hakashrus of the Council of
Orthodox Rabbis Metrowest. Chinese food.

Gourmet Galaxy
659 Eagle Rock Avenue, 07052   736-0060
Supervision: Vaad Hakashrus of the Council of
Orthodox Rabbis Metrowest. Dairy and meat
available.

Booksellers
Lubavitch Center of Essex County
456 Pleasant Valley Way, 07052   731-0770

Westfield

Synagogues *(Reform)*
Temple Emanu-El
756 E. Broad Street, 07090   (908) 232-6770
                            Fax: (908) 233-3959

Willingboro

Synagogues
Adath Emanu-El
299 John F. Kennedy Way, 08046

Woodbridge

Synagogues *(Conservative)*
Adath Israel
424 Amboy, 07095   (908) 634-9601

New Mexico

Alberquerque
Area telephone code (505)

Community Organisations
Jewish Federation of Greater Alberquerque
5520 Wyoming Blvd N.E., 87109   821-3214
                                     Fax: 821-3351

Kashrut Information
JFGA   821-3214

Media
Newspapers
The Link   821-3214
5520 Wyoming Blvd, 87109   Fax: 821-3351

Las Cruces

Synagogues
Temple Beth El, Parker Road, at Melendres

Los Alamos
Area telephone code (505)

Synagogues
Jewish Center
2400 Canyon Road, 87544   662-2440

Rio Rancho

Synagogues
Rio Rancho Jewish Center
2009 Grande Blvd., 87124   892-8511

Santa Fe

Synagogues
Conservative & Reform
Temple Beth Shalom
205 E. Barcelona Road, 87501   982-1376
Rabbi Bentley   983-7446

Mikvaot
Pardes Yisroel
205 E. Barcelona Road, 98501

Contact Information
For information about home hospitality,
Shabbat, Mikva, Kosher catering   986-2091

Groceries
Kosher Food Town, Wild Oats, Market Place

New York State

New York City encompasses so much territory and so much activity that it can sometimes be easy to forget that there is also a whole state named New York. The Empire State stretches from New York City in the south to the Canadian border at Quebec and Ontario provinces in the north; from the New England border with Connecticut, Massachusetts and Vermont in the east to Pennsylvania and the Great Lakes of Erie and Ontario in the southwest and west.

Within this 50,000 square mile expanse lie metropolis, suburb, small town, large city, village, vast state parks and preserves, seashores, islands, high mountains and rolling foothills, and abundant natural wilderness.

To New York City residents, anything outside the five boroughs (Manhattan, Queens, Brooklyn, the Bronx, and Staten Island) is either upstate or Long Island. But within those areas are numerous large and thriving Jewish communities. The cities of Buffalo, Rochester, Binghamton, Syracuse, and Schenectady, the suburban counties of Westchester and Rockland, and the Long Island counties of Nassau and Suffolk count hundreds of thousands of Jews among their residents.

Jewish settlement began in New York in early September, 1654 when twenty-three Sephardic and Ashkenazi Jews disembarked at the harbor of New Amsterdam from the French ship St. Catherine. They had escaped the Spanish Inquisition in Recife, Brazil to settle in the Dutch colony. Though Governor Peter Stuyvesant forbade their admission to his jurisdiction, the travellers' protests to his bosses at the Dutch West India Company were accepted and the Jews were allowed to settle. Ten years later, in 1664, four British men-of-war appropriated New Amsterdam in the name of King Charles II of England who in turn made a gift of it to his brother, James, Duke of York. Hence the name, New York.

Jewish immigration was sparse for the next 150 years, but it increased dramatically, especially in New York City between 1880 and 1924 as more than two million Jews made their way to 'der goldene medinah' (the golden door) from eastern and central Europe.

From that original group of 23 Jews in 1654 some made their way up the Hudson river as far as Albany (now the state capital). Two of them, Asser Levy and Jacob de Lucena, became Hudson river traders and also dealt in real estate in the Albany and Kingston areas. South of Albany, in nearby Newburgh, Jewish merchants established a trading post in 1777, but no Jewish community existed there until 1848.

New York's first Jewish community outside of New York City was the town of Sholom in the Catskill mountains in Ulster county. Founded by twelve families, it no longer exists. The oldest existing community is Congregation Beth El, founded in 1838 in Albany and later merged with Congregation Beth Emeth.

Westchester (just north of New York City) county's present Jewish population of close to 150,000 dates to 1860.

Rockland

Southeast of the Catskills, in Rockland county just north of New York City are a number of communities with large Hasidic and orthodox populations. New Square, a corruption of the name Skvir was founded by the Skvirer Hasidim and is incorporated as separate village within the town of Ramapo. With such an administrative and legal designation, New Square has its own zoning rules, its own village council, its own mayor, etc. and is run along strictly orthodox precepts. Monroe, Monsey and Spring Valley have very large orthodox and Hasidic communities. Though observant Jews are predominant, these communities are also home to non-Jews and less observant Jews. There are a number of villages in the area which have been incorporated with the express purpose of keeping orthodox and Hasidim out through such regulations as zoning to prevent synagogues from being built too close to residences and through the prohibition of having a synagogue in one's house.

New York City

Nowhere in the United States is there a city richer in Jewish heritage than New York. From the city's beginnings as a Dutch trading post in the seventeenth century up to the present day, Jews have flocked to New York, made it their home, and left an indelible mark on the city's heritage, language, culture, physical structure, and day to day life. There are more Jews in the New York metropolitan area than in any other city in the world, and more than in any country except Israel. So without a great deal of effort just being in this largest urban Jewish community in history affords you the opportunity to be a tourist without concern about the ease of observing kashrut and Shabbat.

New York City is the largest Jewish community in the world outside Israel. The estimated Jewish population of New York City proper is just over 1 million. Another million or so live in the immediate suburbs which include not only New York, but New Jersey and Connecticut as well. Roughly one third of American Jews live in and around New York City and virtually every national Jewish organization has its headquarters here.

New York City neighborhoods with large Jewish populations are the upper west and upper east sides of Manhattan (modern orthodox and secular Jewish), Borough Park, Williamsburg (orthodox and Hasidic) and Brighton Beach (Russian) in Brooklyn, Forest Hills (Israelis and Russians), Kew Gardens, Kew Garden Hills (orthodox) in Queens, Riverdale in the Bronx, and Staten Island.

In this largest urban Jewish community in history, the Jewish traveller is overwhelmed with choices of where to eat, where to find a minyan, what to see of Jewish interest and so on. And the variety of kosher restaurants makes choosing a pleasure: Chinese, Moroccan, Italian (both meat and dairy), traditional European, Indian, Japanese and seafood.

Though Jews from numerous countries of origin live together throughout New York's Jewish communities, many groups tend to congregate in their own neighborhoods or sections of neighborhoods.

Ever since the fateful year of 1654 Jews have been coming to New York City. Sometimes a few, sometimes more, and sometimes by the boat load as was the case between 1880 and 1924 when some two million Jews entered the United States. Today, nearly one-third of all American Jews live in and around New York City. And though one might argue cause and effect, New York City is still the commercial, intellectual and financial center of the country.

Synagogues

Hundreds if not thousands of synagogues, chavurot, shtiblech lie within the city representing the myriad expressions of Judaism: Orthodox, Hasidic, Conservative, Reform and Reconstructionist.

Complete lists of synagogues in all five boroughs can be obtained from the various umbrella organizations listed in the beginning of the section on the USA (see page 267, General Information).

The 1,300 seat Moorish-style Central Synagogue (Reform) at 652 Lexington Avenue in Manhattan is the city's oldest synagogue on an original site and is an official New York City landmark; the oldest Ahskenazi congregation, founded in 1825, is B'nai Jeshrun (Conservative) at 270 West 89th Street; Shearith Israel, the Spanish and Portuguese synagogue on Central Park West at 70th Street, is one of the oldest congregations in the United States and originated with those 23 refugees from the Spanish Inquisition in Brazil back in 1654. The present building still has religious items from the earliest days of the congregation and its small chapel is representative of the American colonial period; Temple Emanu-El (Reform) at Fifth Avenue and 65th Street is not only the city's largest, but the world's largest synagogue. The congregation was founded in 1848 and the building, built in 1929, can seat over 2,000 people; the Fifth Avenue synagogue at 5 East 62nd Street was, until early 1967, presided over by Rabbi Dr. Immanuel Jakobovits, who went on to become the Chief Rabbi of Great Britain and the Commonwealth; the Park East synagogue at 163 East 67th Street on the very fashionable upper east side was founded in 1890 and is an historic landmark. Kehilath Jeshurun (Orthodox), 125 E. 85th Street, is a popular option if you are on the Upper East Side. On the Upper West Side, Lincoln Square Synagogue (Orthodox), 200 Amsterdam Avenue at 69th Street, and Ohab Zedek (Orthodox), 118 West 95th Street, are both very popular options.

Libraries, Museums, and Institutes of Learning
One of New York's living museums is the Eldridge Street Synagogue (14 Eldridge Street, 212-219-0888). At 108 years old the Eldridge Street synagogue is a ghost of its former splendor. But in its heyday at the turn of the century, it was among the busiest synagogues on the lower east side, and the first built for that purpose by New York's eastern European Jews. An official New York City landmark, and listed on the National Register of Historic Places, the synagogue is an ongoing restoration project. The synagogue functions as a museum and has a whole host of programs.

In the same neighborhood and sociologically related is the Lower East Side Tenement Museum (97 Orchard Street, 212-431-0233). Contrary to popular opinion, the word tenement does not mean slum housing, but a particular building design devised to house the masses of immigrants who came to New York in the latter part of the nineteenth century. Tenements are five or six storey walk up buildings distinguished by narrow entry halls and a central air shaft. Each floor contained four apartments. Toilet facilities, located in the hallway, were shared by all the residents. Baths were taken at numerous local public bath houses.

The museum, located in a restored tenement built in 1863, shows visitors what tenement life was like via a model apartment. In addition, actors in period dress present 90-minute shows in a small theater. This is how the vast majority of Jews lived when they first came to New York City.

Ellis Island National Monument (212-269-5755) was once the point of entry for Jews and other immigrants. Some five million Jews came to the United States between 1850 and 1948 and most were processed through immigration at Castle Garden (the present ferry ticket office) or, after 1890, Ellis Island.

The Jewish Museum (Fifth Avenue and 92nd Street, 212-423-3200) has been in existence since 1904. Under the auspices of the Conservative Jewish Theological Seminary, the museum has permanent and changing exhibits and programs and an excellent collection of Jewish ritual and ceremonial objects.

The library at the Jewish Theological Seminary (3080 Broadway at 122nd Street, 212-678-8000), houses one of the greatest collections of Judaica and Hebraica in the world. Its holdings include a rare manuscript by Maimonides (the Rambam).

The YIVO Institute for Jewish Research (555 West 57th Street, 212-246-6080) houses a large collection of books, documents, photographs and recordings pertaining to Jewish life in Europe before the Holocaust.

Other libraries with large Judaica collections are at Yeshiva University (212-960-5400), the Judaica Collection at the New York Public Library (212-340-0849), New York University (212-998-1212), Columbia University (212-854-1754), the House of Living Judaism at Temple Emanu-El (212-744-1400) and the Leo Baeck Institute (212-744-6400). Inquire at each one individually as to availability of the collections. Note that the New York Public Library is, during 1998, undergoing renovation and access to the Judaica collection may be limited.

The main Jewish universities and seminaries are Yeshiva University which offers undergraduate and graduate degrees in the arts, sciences and humanities, rabbinical study and professional degrees such as medicine and social work, including the renowned Albert Einstein College of Medicine in the Bronx; Hebrew Union College; Touro College and the Jewish Theological Seminary.

Neighborhoods and areas of historical interest

Manhattan

The Lower East Side has physically changed very little in over a century. Cramped tenements and crowded, dirty streets have always characterized the area. But for the absence of vendors calling out 'I cash clothes' one can get a pretty good idea of what life looked like for Jews newly arrived to New York City from eastern European countries. Though it is tough to imagine the strangeness of a new language or being away from home for the first time.

Though the Lower East Side is not as Jewish as it once was and many Jewish shops have closed, it is appropriate that historical jaunts in New York begin in its tangle of streets and alleys. For the ancestors of some 80 per cent of American Jews, this was the first piece of America they saw. Now other immigrant groups call the Lower East Side home. Settlement houses such as the Henry Street Settlement and the Educational Alliance on East Broadway once served the Jewish immigrant population in their need to learn English and become Americanized. Still in existence, they provide services to current residents Jewish and non-Jewish alike.

Many Jews still do business in the neighborhood and the area is filled with historic buildings, Jewish shops, foodstores and stores selling all manner of ritual items (kipot, taliltot, tefilin, siddurim, etc). Look along Essex, Orchard, Grand, Rivington, Hester and Canal streets.

One of the best guidebooks for this area (as well as the rest of New York City) is the 'AIA (American Institute of Architects) Guide to New York City' by Elliot Willensky and Norval White. An organization called Big Onion Walking Tours gives Lower East Side tours and they are worth a telephone call (212-439-1090).

You may notice that a number of churches on the Lower East Side used to be synagogues. They were re-consecrated as churches when the Jewish community dwindled. But in many cases you still can tell which were synagogues. Look for things like Stars of David on building cornerstones, darkened mezuzah shaped areas on doorposts, and shadows of Stars of David on building facades. They are quite evident if you look.

Synagogues of note in the area are the Bialystoker synagogue (7 Wilet Street); Beth Midrash HaGadol (60 Norfolk Street); First Roumanian American Congregation (89 Rivington Street); and the Eldridge Street Synagogue (14 Eldridge Street).

The only kosher winery in Manhattan is Schapiro's Kosher Winery, (126 Rivington Street, 674-4404), founded in 1899. Call for tour information.

And no visit to the Lower East Side would be complete without a dairy meal at Ratner's (Delancy Street). It is the one remaining dairy restaurant in an area that used to support several. For Jewish New Yorkers it is a tie with the past, for visitors it is an experience not to be missed.

Along Second Avenue below 14th Street you can still see the remnants of the scores of Yiddish theaters that once lined the street. Note particularly the movie theater on Second Avenue at 12th Street, currently the City Cinemas Village East. In the upper level auditorium you can get an idea of what the place looked like when stars like Molly Picon and Boris Tomeshevsky held forth on the stage.

Forty-seventh Street between Fifth Avenue and Avenue of the Americas is the diamond center. Some 75 per cent of all the diamonds which enter the United States pass through here. As this is overwhelmingly a Jewish and Hasidic business, the street is bustling with diamond dealers concluding deals in the open market atmosphere that is pervasive. Most deals are made with a handshake. There are a number of small kosher restaurants up and down block and on the mezzanines of office buildings.

Historical Cemeteries

Manhattan

Shearith Israel Cemeteries

Vestiges of early Jewish settlement in New York can be gleaned from the remnants of the community's first cemeteries. The following three are owned by New York's oldest congregation, Shearith Israel, the Spanish Portuguese Synagogue.

First Shearith Israel Graveyard: 55 St. James Place (between Oliver and James St): The first Jewish cemetery in New Amsterdam was consecrated in 1656 and was located near the present Chatham Square. Its remains were moved to this location. It contains the remains of Sephardic Jews who emigrated from Brazil.

Second Cemetery of the Spanish and Portuguese Synagogue (1805–1829): 72-76 West 11th Street, just east of Sixth Avenue on the south side of the street.

Third Cemetery of the Spanish and Portuguese Synagogue (1829-1851): 98-110 west 21st Street, just west of Sixth avenue on the south side of the street.

Brooklyn

Green-Wood Cemetery (Fifth Avenue and Fort Hamilton Parkway, Brooklyn) contains the graves of many prominent Jewish figures.

Queens

Fourth Cemetery of the Spanish and Portuguese Synagogue: Cypress Hills street and Cypress avenue, Queens. The beautiful chapel and gate were built in 1885.

Arts and Entertainment

As American entertainment is largely a secular Jewish enterprise, one need not look very far for Jewish references in plays and musicals. However, there are some dedicated Jewish theatrical companies and venues: the Jewish Repertory Company (212-831-2000); the American Jewish Theater (212-633-1588); the YM & YWHA (212-427-6000) has several outstanding lecture series' some with specific Jewish themes. For other events of Jewish interest consult one of the weekly listings magazines such as *Time Out New York* or *New York Magazine,* or the Sunday Arts & Leisure section of the *New York Times.* Jewish newspapers with events listings are the *Jewish Week,* the *Forward,* and the *Jewish Press,* all available at most newsstands.

Jewish Neighborhoods of Interest outside Manhattan

Brooklyn
Williamsburg was for many years the center of Hasidic life in New York City. But in the last decade many rebbes and their followers have moved to the suburbs, particularly Rockland county. However, a trip to Williamsburg is still worthwhile.

Boro Park is almost completely orthodox and is almost a world apart from the rest of the city.

Crown Heights is populated by Hasidim of many sects, but particularly the Lubavitch whose world headquarters is at 770 Eastern Parkway. The neighborhood is not totally Jewish and there are often clashes (sometimes violent) between the Caribbean residents and Jewish residents.

New Jersey
Many towns in northern and central New Jersey are less than 40 minutes travel time by either car or public transit from Manhattan and as such are part of metropolitan New York. They are: Bayonne, Clifton, Elizabeth, Englewood, Fairlawn, Hackensack, Hoboken, Jersey City, Newark, Passaic, Teaneck, Union and West New York.

Restaurants
By law in New York State the selling of non-kosher food as kosher is a punishable fraud. Administered by the Kosher Law Enforcement Section of the New York State Department of Agriculture, it imposes heavy penalties on violaters. An orthodox rabbi oversees the operation. Business selling kosher food must display proper signage indicating under whose hashgacha they operate and establishments which sell both kosher and non-kosher food must display that as well with a sign in block letters no smaller than four inches high.

The Kosher Directory, issued by the Union of Orthodox Jewish Congregations, lists foods and services which bear the symbol. It is available for a charge by calling 212-563-4000. Other reliable kashruth insignias are Circle K, and the Hebrew letter KOF-K.

Note that kosher packaged foods including bread, meat, fish, cake, biscuits and virtually anything you can think of are widely available in supermarkets throughout the New York metropolitan area. Many foodstores, especially on the upper west side of Manhattan and in Jewish neighborhoods in Brooklyn and Queens sell fresh, kosher prepared meals as well.

Albany

Area telephone code (518)

Synagogues

Orthodox

Beth Abraham-Jacob, 380 Whitehall Rd.,
12208   489-5819; 489-5179

Shomray Torah, 463 New Scotland Av.,
12208

**Chabad-Lubavitch Center of the Capital
District**, 122 S. Main Av., 12208   482-5781

Conservative

Ohav Shalom
New Krumkill Rd., 12208   489-4706

Temple Israel
600 New Scotland Av., 12208   438-7858

Reform

Daughters of Sarah Nursing Home,
Washington Av. Extension, 12208   456-7831
Traditional service, Sat. 9:15 am. Reform
service, Fri. 3 pm

Beth Emeth
100 Academy Rd., 12208   436-9761
At this 160-year-old congregation, Rabbi Isaac
Mayer Wise, founder of American Reform
Judaism, served when he first arrived in the
United States.

B'nai Sholom
420 Whitehall Rd., 12208   482-5283

Mikvaot

Bnos Israel of the Capital District
190 Elm Street, 12202

Restaurants

Dahlia Vegetarian & Dairy Restaurant
858 Madison Avenue, Between Ontario &
Partridge Streets, 12203   482-0931
Supervision: Vaad Kashrut.

Groceries

Price Chopper Market
1892 Central Avenue, 12205   456-2970
Supervision: Vaad Hakashruth.

Home Hospitality

Shabbos House, State University of New York,
67 Fuller Road   438-4227

Amsterdam

Synagogues (Conservative)

Congregation of Sons of Israel
355 Guy Park Avenue, 12010   (518) 842-8691

Beacon

Synagogues

Hebrew Alliance
55 Fishkill Avenue, 12508   (914) 831-2012

Binghamton

Area telephone code (607)

Community Organisations

Jewish Federation of Broom County
500 Clubhouse Road, Vestal, 13850 724-2332
Fax: 724-2311
Email: JCC13850@AOL.com

Synagogues

Orthodox

Beth David
39 Riverside Drive, 13905   722-1793

Conservative

Temple Israel
Deerfield Place, Vestal, 13850   723-7461

Reform

Temple Concord
9 Riverside Drive, 13905   723-7355

Mikvaot

Beth David
39 Riverside Drive, 13905   722-1793

Media

Newspapers

Reporter
500 Clubhouse Road, Vestal, 13850 724-2360
Fax: 724-2311
Email: TReporter@AOL.com

Buffalo

Area telephone code (716)

Community Organisations

Jewish Federation of Greater Buffalo
787 Delaware Avenue, 14209   886-7750
                                 Fax: 886-1367

Synagogues

Orthodox

B'nai Shalom
1675 N. Forest Rd., 14221   689-8203

Beth Abraham
1073 Elmwood Av., 14222   874-4786

Chabad House, 3292 Main St., 14214 & 2501
N. Forest Rd., 14068   688-1642

Saranac Synagogue, 85 Saranac Avenue,
14216   837-0989

Young Israel of Greater Buffalo, 105 Maple
Rd., Williamsville, 14221   634-0212

Traditional

Kehilat Shalom
700 Sweet Home Rd., 14226   885-6650

Conservative

Beth El, 2360 Eggert Road, Tonawanda,
14223   836-3762

Hillel Foundation
40 Capen Blvd., 14214   838-3232

Shaarey Zedek
621 Getzville Rd., 14226   838-3232

Reform

Beth Am, 4660 Sheridan Dr., 14221 633-8877

Beth Shalom, Union & Center Sts., Hamburg

Beth Zion, 805 Delaware Av., 14209 886-7150

Cong. Havurah
6320 Main St., 14221   874-3517

Reconstructionist

Temple Sinai, 50 Alberta Dr., 14226 834-0708

Mikvaot

Mikva, 1248 Kenmore Ave, 14216 875-8451

Media

Guides

Shalom Buffalo

787 Delaware Avenue, 14209   886-7750
                                 Fax: 886-1367

Newspapers

Buffalo Jewish Review
15 Mohawk Street, 14203   854-2192

Catskills

The famous Catskills region, northwest of New York City covers parts of Sullivan and Ulster counties. From the 1920s through the late 1960s, the large resort hotels formed the so-called Borscht Belt or Circuit of the entertainment industry. The term circuit, in this sense, comes from vaudeville wherein performers would go from theater to theater in various towns all over the United States within an ownership chain. Stars like Jerry Lewis, Milton Berle, Danny Kaye, Eddie Fisher, Sammy Davis Jr and others played to packed houses during the summer season and on holiday weekends during the rest of the year. Many of American show business's biggest names got their start singing, acting or telling jokes on stage on summer evenings in the Catskills. On Shabbat and holidays, the finest cantors could be heard. When a Jew said he or she was going to the mountains, it meant just one thing: the Catskills.

It was in the early part of the twentieth century that Jews from the slums of New York City's lower east side began to visit other Jews who lived and farmed in the Catskills in order to escape the scourge of tuberculosis and other diseases of poverty and crowded living conditions. The fresh air, space and fresh food was a restorative even if other living conditions were pretty rustic. Those Jewish farmers, seldom very successful at working the land, usually took in boarders to make ends meet and out of that grew boarding houses. Whole families would flee to the mountains to get a respite, however brief, from the city.

Boarding houses evolved into kuchaleins...a yiddish word which means to cook alone. To go to a kuchalein meant you shared living space with other families but did your own cooking. Those evolved into bungalow colonies. Most bungalows were small and simple places, cheaply constructed and meant for very rudimentary living. It was an inexpensive vacation for what was becoming a burgeoning Jewish middle class barely a generation removed from their immigrant roots and the shtetls of Europe. Hundreds of colonies dotted the Catskills, and entire neighborhoods would transplant themselves from city to country year after year. It bred another level of cameraderie and Jews who experienced it are wont to wax poetic when reminiscing.

But those boarding houses cum kuchaleins also evolved in another direction: the world renowned Catskills resort hotels. From their humble beginnings at the start of the twentieth century to their bittersweet nadir at the end dozens of hotels became summer playgrounds for hundreds of thousands of Jews. There were vast opulent resorts like Grossingers, the Nevele, the Concord and Brown's to smaller, but no less ornate establishments like Stevensville, Brickman's, the Raleigh, to more haimische hotels like the Pioneer Country Club, Kutsher's, the Pines, the Pineview and several dozen others. Included in the price of a room were huge, multi-course meals served three times a day. And to work that all off one merely had to avail oneself of every conceivable sport available on premises.

A few hotels still remain though they are but shadows of their former selves. Maintenance tends to be lax and the facilities are frayed and worn. Some are no longer kosher and reflect the need to attract non-Jewish guests in order to remain viable.

The current generation, the baby-boomers, is more affluent and more cosmopolitan than the previous generation and so tends to go farther afield for vacation. The Catskills have for the most part become the vacation place for Hasidic Jews who have larger families and lower incomes than their modern orthodox counterparts. They populate the bungalow colonies that generations ago represented the admixture of the Jewish community.

Note that the level of observance varies from hotel to hotel and travellers may want to inquire about this before booking.

Ellenville

Mikvaot
Ezrath Israel   (914) 647-4450/72

Fallsburg/South Fallsburg

Hotels
The Pines Resort Hotel

Kiamesha Lake

Hotels
Concord   (914) 794-4000
                            Fax: (914) 794-7471

Loch Sheldrake

Synagogues (Orthodox)
Young Israel of Vacation Village
PO Box 650, 12759   436-8359

Hotels
Brown's

Monticello

Synagogues

Orthodox
Tifereth Israel
18 Landfield Avenue, 12701   794-8470
Daily services.

Reform
Temple Sholom
Port Jervis & Dillon Roads, 12701
Daily services.

Mikvaot
Mikva, 16 North Street, 12701   794-6757

Hotels
Kutsher's Country Club

Woodbourne

Hotels
Chalet Vim, 12788
Glatt kosher.

Clifton Park

Synagogues *(Conservative)*
Beth Shalom, Center Road, 12065   371-0608

Delmar

Synagogues

Orthodox
Delmar Chabad Center
109 Elsmere Avenue, 12054   439-8280

Reconstructionist
Reconstructionist Havurah of the Capital District, 98 Meadowland St, 12054 439-5870

Dewitt

Synagogues *(Orthodox)*
Young Israel Shaarei Torah of Syracuse
4313 E Genesee St, 13214   (315) 446-6194

Elmira

Synagogues

Shomray Hadath, Cobbles Park, 14905
B'nai Israel, Water & Guinnip Streets, 14905

Fleischmanns

Hotels

Kosher
Oppenheimer's Regis, 12430 (914) 254-5080
Supervision: Rabbinate of K'hal Adas Jeshurun, NYC.

Geneva

Synagogues *(Reform)*
Temple Beth El
755 South Main St, 14456   (315) 789-2945

Gilboa

Tours

Catskill Mountain "Dude Ranch Vacations", Near Howe Caverns, Cooperstown, Catskill Game Farm.
Golden Acres Farm & Ranch (800) 847-2251
    (800) 252-7787
Under Rabbinical Supervision, Services.

Glens Falls

Synagogues

Conservative
Shaarey Tefila, 68 Bay St, 12801   792-4945

Reform
Temple Beth El
3 Marion Avenue, 12801   792-4364

Gloversville

Synagogues *(Conservative)*
Knesseth Israel
34 E. Fulton Street, 12078   725-0649

Harrison

Synagogues *(Orthodox)*
Young Israel of Harrison
207 Union Avenue, 10528   (914) 835-1893

Haverstraw

Synagogues

Congregation Sons of Jacob
37 Clove Avenue, 10927

Hudson

Synagogues *(Conservative)*
Anshe Emeth
240 Jolsen Blvd., 12534   828-9040

Ithaca
Area telephone code (607)

Synagogues
Orthodox
Young Israel of Cornell
106 West Avenue, 14850   272-5810

Conservative
Temple Beth El, 402 N. Tioga Street, 14850

Lake Placid
Synagogues
Traditional
20 Saranac Avenue
PO Box 521, 12946-0521   (518) 523-3876
                                Fax: 891-3458

Latham
Community Organisations
United Jewish Federation of Northeastern New York
800 New Loudon Road, 12110   783-7800
Covers Albany, Colens Falls, Saratoga, Schenectady and Troy.

Long Island
Area telephone code (516) unless stated otherwise

By 1760 Jews had settled on Long Island, whose present day Jewish population is around 500,000 with some 150 synagogues. Though two of New York City's five boroughs, Brooklyn and Queens, are geographically part of Long Island, when New Yorkers say Long Island they mean the counties of Nassau and Suffolk. Large concentrations of Jews are in the communities of West Hempstead, Plainview, Great Neck, Long Beach, Cedarhurst, Lawrence, Hewlett, and Woodmere. The latter four are part of what is known as the Five Towns.

Baldwin
Restaurants
Ben's, 933 Atlantic Avenue   868-2072

Commack
Community Organisations
Suffolk Jewish Communal Planning Council
74 Hauppage Road, 11725   462-5826
Publishes "Suffolk Jewish Directory".

Restaurants
Pastrami 'N Friends
110a Commack Road, 11725   499-9537

Dix Hills
Tourist Information
Jewish Geneaology Society of Long Island
37 Westcliff Drive, 11746-5627   549-9532
                   Email: rsteinig@suffolk.lib.ny.us
Offers assistance to Jewish travellers about their New York or US roots.

Elmont
Bakeries
Sapienza
1376 Hempstead Turnpike, 11003   352-5232
Supervision: Kof-K.

Five Towns
Incorporates the towns of Cedarhurst, Hewlett, Inwood, Lawrence and Woodmere.

Synagogues
Orthodox
Shaarey Tefila
25 Central Avenue, Lawrence, 11559
Young Israel of North Woodmere
785 Golf Drive, 11581   791-5099

Mikvaot
Peninsula Blvd., Hewlett, 11557   569-5514

Kashrut Information

Vaad HaKashrus of the Five Towns, 859
Peninsula Blvd., Woodmere, 11598   569-4536

Restaurants

Meat

Cedar Club
564 Central Avenue, Cedarhurst   374-1714
Supervision: Vaad HaKashrus of Five Towns.

Cho-Sen Island, 367 Central Avenue,
Lawrence, 11559   374-1199
Supervision: Vaad HaKashrus of Five Towns.

Dave's Glatt Kosher Deli Restaurant
1508 Broadway, Hewlett   374-3296
Supervision: Vaad HaKashrus of Five Towns.

King David Delicatessen and Caterers
550 Central Avenue, Cedarhurst   569-2920
Supervision: Vaad HaKashrus of Five Towns.
Glatt kosher, shomer shabbat. 20 minutes
from JFK International Airport.

La-Pina
600 Central Avenue, Cedarhurst   569-2922
Supervision: Vaad HaKashrus of Five Towns.

Traditions, 302 Central Avenue, Lawrence,
11559   295-3630
Supervision: Vaad HaKashrus of Five Towns.

Wok Tov
594 Central Avenue, Cedarhurst   295-3843
Supervision: Vaad HaKashrus of Five Towns.

Dairy

Bagel Delight
598 Central Avenue, Cedarhurst   374-7644
Supervision: Vaad HaKashrus of Five Towns.

Delicious Kosher Dairy
698 Central Avenue, Cedarhurst   569-6725
Supervision: Vaad HaKashrus of Five Towns.

Jerusalem Pizza Plus, 344 Central Avenue,
Lawrence, 11559   569-0074
Supervision: Vaad HaKashrus of Five Towns.

Pizza Pious
1063 Broadway, Woodmere, 11598 295-2050
Supervision: Vaad HaKashrus of Five Towns.

Sabra Kosher Pizza
560 Central Avenue, Cedarhurst   569-1563
Supervision: Vaad HaKashrus of Five Towns.

Ultimate Yogurt Shop
602 Central Avenue, Cedarhurst   569-7821
Supervision: Vaad HaKashrus of Five Towns.

Take-Outs

Chap-A-Nosh
410 Central Avenue, Cedarhurst   374-5100
Supervision: Vaad HaKashrus of Five Towns.

Mauzone, 341 Central Avenue, Lawrence,
11559   569-6411
Supervision: Vaad HaKashrus of Five Towns.

Bakeries

Gotta Getta Bagel
1033 Broadway, Woodmere, 11598 374-5245
Supervision: Vaad HaKashrus of Five Towns.

Hungry Harbor Bakery, 311 Central Avenue,
Lawrence, 11559   374-1131
Supervision: Vaad HaKashrus of Five Towns.

Moish's Bake Shop
536 Central Avenue, Cedarhurst   374-2525
Supervision: Vaad HaKashrus of Five Towns.

Zomick's Bake Shop
444 Central Avenue, Cedarhurst   569-5520
Supervision: Vaad HaKashrus of Five Towns.

Donuts

Donut Delite
125 Cedarhurst Avenue, Cedarhurst 295-5005
Supervision: Vaad HaKashrus of Five Towns.

Dunkin' Donuts, 299 Burnside Avenue,
Lawrence, 11559   239-2052
Supervision: Vaad HaKashrus of Five Towns.

Groceries

Gourmet Glatt Emporium
137 Spruce Street, Cedarhurst   569-2662
Supervision: Vaad HaKashrus of Five Towns.

Supersol, 330 Central Avenue, Lawrence,
11559   295-3300
Supervision: Vaad HaKashrus of Five Towns.

Great Neck

Mikvaot

26 Old Mill Road, 11023   487-2726

Restaurants

Colbeh, 75 N. Station Plaza, 11021 466-8181
Supervision: Kof-K. Glatt kosher.

Hunan Restaurant
505/07 Middle Neck Road, 11023   482-7912
Supervision: Vaad Harabonim of Queens.
Chinese food.

United States of America / New York

Shish Kabob Palace
90 Middle Neck Road, 11021   487-2228
Supervision: Vaad Harabonim of Queens.

Pizzerias

Great Neck Kosher Pizza
770 Middle Neck Road, 11024   829-2660
Supervision: Kof-K.

La Pizzeria
114 Middle Neck Road, 11021   466-5114
Supervision: Vaad Harabonim of Queens.

Bakeries

Strauss Bake Shop
607 Middle Neck Road, 11023   487-6853
Supervision: Vaad Harabonim of Queens.

Butchers

Great Neck Glatt
501 Middle Neck Road, 11023   773-6328
Supervision: Vaad Harabonim of Queens.

Media

Newspapers

Long Island Jewish Week
98 Cutter Mill Road, 11020   773-3679

Long Island Jewish World
115 Middle Neck Road, 11021   829-4000

Greenvale

Restaurants

Ben's, 140 Wheatley Plaza   621-3340

Huntington Station

Booksellers

Zion Lion
444 West Jericho Turnpike, 11746   549-5155

Lake Grove

Restaurants

Ben's, 135 Alexander Avenue   979-8770
    Fax: 979-8774
Supervision: Rabbi Buchler, Conservative.
Hours: 9 am to 10 pm.

Long Beach

Mikvaot

Sharf Manor
274 W. Broadway, 11561   431-7758

Oceanside

Mikvaot

3397 Park Avenue, 11572   766-3242

Plainview

Restaurants

Te'Avone
64 Manetto Hall Road, 11803   822-4545

Syosset

Representative Organisations

Conference of Jewish Organisations of Nassau County, North Shore Atrium, 6900 Jericho Turnpike, 11791   364-4477

UJA Federation
6900 Jericho Turnpike, 11791   677-1800

Wantagh

Bakeries

B & B Bakery Bagels
2845 Jerusalem Avenue, 11793
Supervision: Kof-K. Pat Yisrael.

West Hempstead

Mikvaot

775 Hempstead Avenue, 11552   489-9358

Restaurants

Pizzerias

Hunki's Kosher Pizza & Felafel
338 Hempstead Avenue, 11552   538-6655
Supervision: Vaad Harabonim of Queens.

Bakeries
The Bagel Gallery
540 Hempstead Turnpike, 11552   483-7311
Supervision: Vaad Harabonim of Queens.

Butchers
J & M Glatt
177 Hempstead Avenue, 11552   489-6926
Supervision: Vaad Harabonim of Queens.

Monroe
Area telephone code (914)

Synagogues
Monroe Temple of Liberal Judaism
314 N. Main Street, 10950

Congregation Eitz Chaim
County Route 105, 10950   783-7424

Monsey

Synagogues
Orthodox
Young Israel of Monsey and Wesley Hills Inc
58 Parker Blvd, 10952   362-1838

Mount Vernon

Synagogues
Brothers of Israel, 116 Crary Avenue, 10550
Fleetwood, 11 E. Broad Street, 10552

Nassau
Area telephone code (914)

Community Organisations
Jewish Federation of Greater Orange County
360 Powell Avenue, 12550   562-7860

Synagogues
Route 20, Albany Street   477-6691

Newburgh
Area telephone code (914)

Kashrut Information
Agudas Israel
290 North Street, 12550   562-5604

Museums
Gomez Mill House
Millhouse Road, Marlboro, 12542   236-3126
Oldest Jewish residence maintained as a museum.

New City
Area telephone code (914)

Synagogues
Conservative
New City Jewish Center
47 Old Schoolhouse Road, 10956   634-3619

Reform
Temple Beth Sholom
228 New Hampstead Road, 10956

Delicatessens
Steve's Deli-Bake
179 South Main Street, 10956   634-8749

Groceries
M&S Kosher Meats
191a South Main Street, 10956   638-9494

New Hyde Park
Area telephone code (718)

Kashrut Information
Long Island Commission of Rabbis
1300 Jericho Turnpike, 11040   343-5993

New Rochelle
Area telephone code (914)

Synagogues
Orthodox
Anshe Shalom
50 North Avenue, 10805   632-2426
Young Israel of New Rochelle
1228 North Avenue, 10804   636-2215

Conservative
Bethel, Northfield Road

Reform
Temple Israel, 1000 Pine Brook Blvd., 10804

New York City

Bronx
Area telephone code (718)

Restaurants
Second Helpings, 3532 Johnson Avenue,
Bronx, 10463   548-1818
Supervision: Rabbi Jonathan Rosenblatt,
Riverdale Jewish Center.
Yeshiva University: Bronx Center
Eastchester Rd. & Morris Park Avenue, Bronx,
10461   430-2131

Bakeries
Gruenebaum Bakery, 3530 Johnson Avenue,
Bronx, 10463   884-5656
Supervision: Rabbi Jonathan Rosenblatt,
Riverdale Jewish Center.

Butchers
Glatt Shop, 3540 Johnson Avenue, Bronx,
10463   548-4855
Supervision: Rabbi Jonathan Rosenblatt,
Riverdale Jewish Center. Stock groceries too.

Booksellers
Judaica Book Store, 3706 Riverdale Avenue,
Bronx, 10463   601-7563

Restaurants
Meat
Szechuan Garden Chinese Restaurant
3717 Riverdale Avenue,
Riverdale, 10463   884-4242
Supervision: Rabbi Jonathan Rosenblatt,
Riverdale Jewish Center.

Dairy
Corner Café and Bakery, 3552 Johnson
Avenue, Riverdale, 10463   601-2861
Supervision: Rabbi Jonathan Rosenblatt,
Riverdale Jewish Center.

Main Event, 3708 Riverdale Avenue, Riverdale,
10463   601-6246
Supervision: Rabbi Jonathan Rosenblatt,
Riverdale Jewish Center.

Bakeries
Heisler's Pastry Shop
3601 Riverdale Avenue, at 236th Street,
Riverdale, 10463   549-0770
Supervision: Westchester Vaad.
Mr Bagel of Broadway
5672 Broadway, Riverdale, 10463   549-0408
Supervision: Rabbi Jonathan Rosenblatt,
Riverdale Jewish Center.

Butchers
Glatt Emporium, 3711 Riverdale Avenue,
Riverdale, 10463   884-1200
Supervision: Rabbi Jonathan Rosenblatt,
Riverdale Jewish Center.

Delicatessens
The Riverdelight, 3534 Johnson Avenue,
Riverdale, 10463   543-4270
Supervision: Rabbi Jonathan Rosenblatt,
Riverdale Jewish Center.

Brooklyn

Restaurants
Adelman's, 1906 Kings Highway,   336-4915
La Casa Verde
811 Kings Highway, 11223   339-9733
Lelot Tel Aviv
1910 Coney Island Avenue, 11223   934-6786

Meat

Cachet Restaurant, 815 Kings Highway,
Midwood, 11223   336-8600
                            Fax: 615-2185
Supervision: OU. Continental cuisine.

Cafeteria, Crown Palace Hotel, 570-600
Crown Street, 11213   604-1777

Chaap-a-Nosh, 1426 Elm Avenue   627-0072
Supervision: ARK. Glatt kosher.

Edna's Restaurant & Deli
125 Church Avenue, 11202   438-8207

Gottlieb's Glatt Kosher
352 Roebling Street   384-9037

Jay & Lloyd's Kosher Deli
2718 Avenue U   891-5298

Jerusalem Steak House
533 Kings Highway, 11223   336-5115

Kosher Delight Glatt Kosher, 1223 Avenue J
(E. 13th Street), Flatbush, 11230   377-6873
                            Fax: 253-6189
Supervision: Rav S.D. Beck and Vaad Rabonim
of Flatbush. Hours: Sun. to Thurs., 11 am to
11 pm; Fri., to 3 pm; after Shabbat to 1 am.

Mama's Restaurant
906 Kings Highway, 11223   382-7200
Supervision: Kehilah (Flatbush).

Shalom Hunan, 1619 Avenue M   382-6000

Shang-Chai Glatt Kosher
2189 Flatbush Avenue, 11234   377-6100

Sushi Kosher
1626 Coney Island Avenue, 11230   338-6363
                            Fax: 338-2922
Supervision: Kehilah (Flatbush).

Wok Mavin
97-20A 64th Avenue, Rego Park   897-2888

Yun-Kee Glatt Kosher, 1424 Elm Avenue, cnr.
E.15th Street & Avenue M   627-0072
Supervision: ARK.

Dairy

Garden of Eat-In
1416 Avenue J, 11230   252-5289
                            Fax: 252-1856
Supervision: Kehilah (Flatbush).

Ossie's Table, 1314 50th Street   435-0635

Pizzerias

Chadash Pizza
1919 Avenue M, 11230   253-4793
Supervision: Kehilah (Flatbush).

Kosher Hut
709 Kings Highway, 11223   376-8996

Supervision: Kehilah (Flatbush).

Bakeries

Donuts

Dunkin' Donuts, 1410 Avenue J, 11230
1611 Avenue M, 11230   336-2641
2630 86th Street, 11223   372-0650
All three locations: Kof-K. Pat Yisrael.

Delicatessens

Eden Delicatessen and Steak House
5928 Glenwood Road, 11236   209-4244
                            Fax: 209-3268
Supervision: Kehilah (Flatbush).

Essex on Coney
1359 Coney Island Avenue, 11230   253-1002
                            Fax: 253-8322
Supervision: Kehilah (Flatbush).

Gourmet on J
1412 Avenue J, 11230   338-9181
Supervision: Kehilah (Flatbush). Take out only.

Kenereth
1920 Avenue U, 11229   743-2473
Supervision: Kehilah (Flatbush). Take out only.

Kings Glatt Deli
924 Kings Highway, 11223   336-7500
Supervision: Kehilah (Flatbush). Take out only.

Groceries

Mountain Fruit
1520 Avenue M, 11230   998-3333
                            Fax: 998-0726
Supervision: Kehilah (Flatbush). Hashgacha is
limited to appetising, bakery, store packaged
dry fruits and nuts, and candies.

Shop Smart   377-4166
2640 Nostrand Avenue, 11210   Fax: 252-2363
Supervision: Kehilah (Flatbush).

Hotels

The Crown Palace Hotel
570-600 Crown Street   604-1777
Glatt kosher.

The Park House Hotel, 1206 48th Street,
11219   871-8100

Museums

The Chasidic Art Institute, 375 Kingston Ave

Libraries

Levi Yitzhak Library, 305 Kingston Ave 11213

Manhattan

Area telephone code (212)

Community Organisations

UJA-Federation Resource Line
130 E. 59th Street, 10022

Embassy

Consulate General, 800 Second Ave, 10017
Permanent Mission of Israel to the United Nations, 800 Second Avenue, 10017

Restaurants

Meat

Abigael's Grill and Caterers
9 East 37th Street   725-0130
Supervision: Kof-K. Glatt kosher.

Alexi on 56
25 West 56th Street, 10019   767-1234
                                     Fax: 767-8254
Supervision: OU. Continental cuisine.

Cafe Classico, 35 West 57th Street   355-5411
Glatt kosher.

Cafe Masada, 1239 First Avenue   988-0950

Chick Chack Chicken
121 University Place   228-3100
Supervision: OU.

China Shalom II, 686 Columbus Avenue,
10025   662-9676
Supervision: Kof-K. Glatt kosher.

Colbeh, 43 West 39th Street, 10018 354-8181
Supervision: Kof-K. Glatt kosher.

Deli Glatt, 152 Fulton Street   349-3622

Deli Kasbah, 251 W. 85th Street   496-1500
Supervision: Circle K.
Hours: Sunday to Thursday, 12 pm to 11 pm.

Deli Kasbah II
2553 Amsterdam Avenue   568-4600

Dougie's BBQ
222 West 72nd Street, 10023   724-2222
Supervision: OU. Glatt kosher.

Galil, 1252 Lexington Ave, 10028   439-9886
Supervision: Kof-K.

Glatt Dynasty
1049 Second Avenue, 10022   888-9119
Supervision: Kof-K. Glatt kosher.

Grand Deli, 399-401 Grand Street   477-5200
Supervision: OU.

Haikara (First Class Restaurant)

1016 2nd Avenue   355-7000
Supervision: OU.

Jasmine, 11 East 30 Street, between Madison and 5th Avenues   251-8884
Supervision: Vaad l'Kashrut Badatz Sepharadic. Glatt kosher Persian and Middle Eastern cuisine. Open Sunday to Friday, for lunch and dinner.

Jerusalem Pita Glatt Kosher
212 E. 45th Street   922-0009

Kosher Delight Glatt Kosher
1359 Broadway (37th Street)   563-3366

Kosher Tea Room
193 Second Avenue   677-2947
Glatt kosher.

La Fontana
309 East 83rd Street, 10028   734-6343
Supervision: Kof-K. Glatt kosher.

La Marais, 150 W. 46th Street   869-0900
Supervision: Circle K. Glatt kosher. Hours: Sunday to Thursday, 12 pm to 12 am; Friday, to 3 pm; Saturday, October to May, one hour after sundown to 1 am.

Levana
141 West 69th Street, 10023   877-8457
Supervision: Kof-K. Glatt kosher.

Mendy's Restaurant
61 East 34th Street, 10016   576-1010
Supervision: OU.

Mendy's West
210 West 70th Street, 10023   877-6787
Supervision: OU.

Mr. Broadway, 1372 Broadway   921-2152
Supervision: OU.

Pita Express
1470 2nd Avenue (77th Street)   249-1300
261 1st Avenue (15th Street)   533-1956
Glatt kosher.

Siegel's Kosher Deli & Restaurant
1646 2nd Avenue   288-3632

Tevere '84'
155 E. 84th Street, 10028   744-0210
Supervision: OU.
Glatt kosher Italian restaurant. Private party available. Open for lunch, brunch and dinner.

Village Crown
96 Third Avenue, 10003   674-2061
Supervision: Kof-K. Glatt kosher.

Yeshiva University: Main Center
500 W. 185th Street, 10033   960-5248
Mid-town Center, 245 Lexington Avenue at 35th Street, 10016   340-7712

Dairy

All-American Health Bar
24 E. 42nd Street   370-4525
American Cafe Health Bar and Pizza
160 Broadway, 10038   732-1426
Supervision: Kof-K. Chalav Yisrael.
Cafe I II III, 2 Park Avenue   685-7117
Diamond Dairy Kosher Lunchonette
2-4 W. 47th Street, 10036   719-2694
On the gallery overlooking the diamond & jewelry exchange. Hours: Monday to Thursday, 7:30 am to 5 pm; Friday, to 2 pm.
Gourmet Garden
175 Madison Avenue, 10016   545-7666
    Fax: 545-7445
Supervision: Kof-K.
Great American Health Bar
821 Third Avenue   758-0883
Great American Health Bar
35 W. 57th Street   355-5177
Jerusalem II
1375 Broadway   398-1475
Supervision: OU. Chalav Yisrael.
Joseph's Cafe, 50 West 72 St   721-1943
My Most Favorite Café
120 West 45th Street   997-5130
Supervision: OU. Chalav Yisrael.
Ratner's Restaurant and Soup Carts
138 Delancey Street, 10002   677-5588
Supervision: Kof-K. Call for location of soup carts.
Va Bene
1589 Second Avenue, 10028   517-4448
Supervision: OU. Chalav Yisrael Italian restaurant.
Vege-Vege II, 544 3rd Avenue   679-4710
Vegetable Garden
15 East 40th Street, 10016   545-7444
Supervision: Kof-K.
Vegetarian Heaven, 364 W. 58th St 956-4678
Village Crown Italian Dairy Cuisine
96 Third Avenue, 10003   777-8816; 388-9639
Supervision: Kof-K.

Bakeries

H & H / The Excellent Bagel
2239 Broadway, New York, 10024   692-2435
Supervision: Kof-K.
Mom's Bagels of NY, 15 West 45th Street,
New York, 10036   764-1566
Supervision: Kof-K. Pat Yisrael.

Delicatessens

Essen West
226 West 72nd Street, 10023   362-1234
Supervision: OU. Meat take out and caterers.
L'Chaim Caterers
4464 Broadway, 10040   304-4852
Supervision: Kof-K. Take out food store.
Lou G. Siegel, 240 West 14th St   921-4433
Supervision: OU. Meat, take out only.
Second Avenue Delicatessan-Restaurant
156 2nd Avenue cnr. 10th Street   677-0606

Winery

Shapiro's Wine Company
124 Rivington Street   475-7383
In business since 1899. Providing free tours.

Museums

Jewish Museum, 1109 Fifth Avenue, 10028
Jewish Theological Seminary of America
3080 Broadway at 122nd Street, 10027
Housing rare manuscripts, including a work in the hand of Maimonides, as well as Cairo Geniza fragments (on application to the librarian only). Has what is believed to be the greatest collection of Judaica and Hebraica in the world.
Leo Baeck Institute, 129 E. 73rd St, 10021
Has a vast collection of books, manuscripts, letters and photographs of German Jewish authors, scientists, rabbis and communal leaders, as well as an art collection of the Jews of Germany.
The House of Living Judaism
5th Avenue and 65th Street
Frequently shows paintings and ritual objects.
Theological Seminary of America
Fifth Avenue & 92nd Street, 10028
An outstanding museum, with permanent displays of Jewish ritual and ceremonial art, along with notable paintings and sculptures.
Yeshiva University, Amsterdam Avenue, 185th Street, New York, 10033
The museum's salient feature is a permanent display of scale-model synagogues.
Yivo Institute for Jewish Research
555 West 57th Street   246-6080
Has a large collection of original documents on Jewish life, along with some 300,000 volumes, and thousands of photographs, music sheets, gramophone records, etc.

PARK AVENUE SYNAGOGUE

Rabbi Emeritus **Judah Nadich**
Senior Rabbi **David H. Lincoln**
Rabbi **Elana Zaiman**
Rabbi **Kenneth A. Stern**
Senior Cantor **David Lefkowitz**
Cantor **Nancy Abramson**
Executive Director **Barrie Modlin**

50 East 87 Street, New York, NY 10128
Tel. (212) 369 2600   Fax (212) 410 7879

SERVICES
Mornings
Daily: 7.15am
Sundays & Holidays: 9.00am
Sabbath & Festivals: 9.15am

Evenings
Daily: 5.45pm
Fridays: 6.15pm

Libraries

Butler Library of Colombia University
Broadway at 116th Street, New York, 10027
Has some 6,000 Hebrew books and
pamphlets, plus 1,000 manuscripts and a
Hebrew psalter printed at Cambridge
University in 1685 and used by Samuel
Johnson at the graduation of the first
candidates for bachelor's degrees.

**New York University of Judaica and
Hebraica**
Housing a stunning collection of priceless
items.

**The Jewish Division of the New York Public
Library,** Fifth Avenue at 42nd Street, 10017
Has 125,000 volumes of Judaica and Hebraica,
along with extensive microfilm and bound files
of Jewish publications, one of the finest
collections in existence.

Theatre

Jewish Repertory Theatre, c/o Midtown
YMHA, 344 E. 14th Street 505-2667; 674-7200

Queens

Area telephone code (718)

Restaurants

Meat

Annie's Kitchen
72-24 Main Street, Flushing, 11367   268-0960
Supervision: Vaad Harabonim of Queens.
Chinese food.

Burger Nosh
69-48 Main Street, Flushing, 11367   520-1933
Supervision: Vaad Harabonim of Queens.

Chosen Garden, 64-43 108th Street, Forest
Hills, 11375   275-130
Supervision: Vaad Harabonim of Queens.
Chinese food.

Empire Kosher Roasters #1, 100-19 Queens
Blvd, Forest Hills, 11375   997-731
Supervision: Vaad Harabonim of Queens.

Empire Kosher Roasters #2, 180-30 Union
Turnpike, Flushing, 11365   591-422
Supervision: Vaad Harabonim of Queens.

Glatt Wok Express, 190-11 Union Turnpike,
Flushing, 11366   740-167
Supervision: Vaad Harabonim of Queens.
Chinese food. Take away service available.

Hapina
69-54 Main Street, Flushing, 11367   544-626
Supervision: Vaad Harabonim of Queens.

Hapisgah, 147-25 Union Turnpike, Flushing,
11367   380-444
Supervision: Vaad Harabonim of Queens.

Kosher Haven, 65-30 Kissena Blvd, Flushing,
11367   261-014
Supervision: Vaad Harabonim of Queens.
Located at Queens College.

Kosher International Restaurant
JFK Airport, Arrivals Bldg, Queens   656-175

Kosher King
72-30 Main Street, Flushing, 11367   793-546
Supervision: Vaad Harabonim of Queens.

Pastrami King
124-24 Queens Blvd, Kew Gardens   263-171

Pninat Hamizrach, 178-07 Union Turnpike,
Fresh Meadows, 11365   591-336
Supervision: Vaad Harabonim of Queens.

Stargate
73-27 Main Street, Flushing, 11367   793-11
Supervision: Vaad Harabonim of Queens.

Steakiat Mabat, 68-36 Main Street, Flushing, 11367   793-2926
Supervision: Vaad Harabonim of Queens.

Surf Deli, 101-05 Queens Blvd, Forest Hills, 11375   459-7875
Supervision: Vaad Harabonim of Queens.

Tashkent Glatt Kosher Restaurant, 149-15 Union Turnpike, Flushing, 11367   969-9810
Supervision: Vaad Harabonim of Queens.

Dairy

Chef's Market, 30-00 47th Avenue, Long Island City, 11101   706-8070
Supervision: Vaad Harabonim of Queens.

Jerusalem Café, 72-02 Main Street, Flushing, 11367   520-8940
Supervision: Vaad Harabonim of Queens.

Main Street Kosher Corner
73-01 Main Street, Flushing, 11367 263-1177
Supervision: Vaad Harabonim of Queens.

Pizzerias

Benjy Kosher Pizza and Falafel
72-72 Main Street, Flushing, 11367 268-0791
Supervision: Vaad Harabonim of Queens.

Dan Carmel Ice Cream and Pizza, 98-98 Queens Blvd, Forest Hills, 11375   544-8530
Supervision: Vaad Harabonim of Queens.

Hamakom Pizza, 101-11 Queens Blvd, Forest Hills, 11375   275-3992
Supervision: Vaad Harabonim of Queens.

King Solomon Pizza, 75-43 Main Street, Flushing, 11367   793-0710
Supervision: Vaad Harabonim of Queens.

Manna Kosher Pizza, 68-28 Main Street, Flushing, 11367   520-8754
Supervision: Vaad Harabonim of Queens.

Moshe's Kosher Pizza, 181-30 Union Turnpike, Flushing, 11366   969-1928
Supervision: Vaad Harabonim of Queens.

Shimon's Kosher Pizza, 71-24 Main Street, Flushing, 11367   793-1491
Supervision: Vaad Harabonim of Queens.

Spencer's Pizza, 248-06 Union Turnpike, Bellerose, 11426   347-5862
Supervision: Vaad Harabonim of Queens.

Bakeries

Aron's Bake Shop, 71-71 Yellowstone Blvd, Forest Hills, 11375   263-5045
Supervision: Vaad Harabonim of Queens.

Bagel King, 116-26 Metropolitan Avenue, Kew Gardens, 11418   847-3623
Supervision: Vaad Harabonim of Queens.

Beigel's Bakery, 189-09 Union Turnpike, Flushing, 11366   468-1243
Supervision: Vaad Harabonim of Queens.

G & I Bakeries, 69-49 Main Street, Flushing, 11367   261-1155
Supervision: Vaad Harabonim of Queens.

G & I Bakeries, 72-22 Main Street, Flushing, 11367   544-8736
Supervision: Vaad Harabonim of Queens.

Hot Bagels and Bialys, 67-11 Main Street, Flushing, 11367   575-1071
Supervision: Vaad Harabonim of Queens.

King David Bakery, 77-51 Vleigh Place, Flushing, 11367   969-6165
Supervision: Vaad Harabonim of Queens.

L & L Bakery, 64-17 108th Street, Forest Hills, 11375   997-1088
Supervision: Vaad Harabonim of Queens.

Queens Kosher Pita, 68-36 Main Street, Flushing, 11367   263-8000
Supervision: Vaad Harabonim of Queens.

Donuts

Dunkin' Donuts, 83-47 Parsons Blvd, Jamaica, 11432   738-0465
Supervision: Vaad Harabonim of Queens.

Butchers

Abe's Glatt Kosher Meats, 98-106 Queens Blvd, Forest Hills, 11375   459-5820
Supervision: Vaad Harabonim of Queens.

Herman Glick's Sons, 101-15 Queens Blvd, Forest Hills, 11375   896-7736
Supervision: Vaad Harabonim of Queens.

Herskowitz Glatt Meat Market, 164-08 69th Avenue, Hillcrest, 11365   591-0750
Supervision: Vaad Harabonim of Queens.

S & L Glatt Kosher Meats, 75-37 Main Street, Flushing, 11367   459-4888
Supervision: Vaad Harabonim of Queens.

Super Glatt Meat, 189-23 Union Turnpike, Flushing, 11367   776-7727
Supervision: Vaad Harabonim of Queens.

Tov Hamativ, 69-38 Main Street, Flushing, 11367   263-7009
Supervision: Vaad Harabonim of Queens.

Delicatessens

Asian Glatt, 67-21 Main Street, Flushing,
11367 793-3061
Supervision: Vaad Harabonim of Queens.
Take out only.

Berso Foods, 64-20 108th Street, Forest Hills,
11375 275-9793
Supervision: Vaad Harabonim of Queens.
Take out only.

Mauzone Home Foods of Queens
69-60 Main Street, Flushing, 11367   261-7723
Supervision: Vaad Harabonim of Queens.
Take out only.

Mauzone Take Home Foods, 61-36
Springfield Blvd, Bayside, 11364   225-1188
Supervision: Vaad Harabonim of Queens.
Take out only.

Maven Kosher Foods, 188-09 Union
Turnpike, Fresh Meadows, 11366   479-5504
Supervision: Vaad Harabonim of Queens.
Take out only.

Meal Mart, 72-10 Main Street, Flushing,
11367 261-3300
Supervision: Vaad Harabonim of Queens.
Take out only.

The Wok, 100-19 Queens Blvd, Forest Hills,
11375 896-0310
Supervision: Vaad Harabonim of Queens.
Chinese. Take out only.

Tov Caterers
97-22 63 Road, Rego Park, 11374   896-7788
Supervision: Vaad Harabonim of Queens.
Take out only.

Groceries

Supersol, 68-18 Main Street, Flushing, 11367
268-6469
Supervision: Vaad Harabonim of Queens.

Wasserman Supermarket, 72-68 Main Street,
Flushing, 11367 544-7413
Supervision: Vaad Harabonim of Queens.

Ice Cream Parlors

Yogurt Planet, 71-26 Main Street, Flushing,
11367 793-8629
Supervision: Vaad Harabonim of Queens.

Hotels

Washington Hotel, 124-19 Rockaway Beach
Blvd, Rockaway Park, 11694   474-9671
Supervision: OU.

Staten Island

Kashrut Information

Directories

Organised Kashrus Laboratories   851-6428
Including the Circle K trademark.
The Dining Guide of the Jewish Press
330-1100
Providing information on where to get kosher
Won-Ton soup, couscous, hot pastrami and
corned (salt) beef sandwiches, gefilte fish,
hummus, tehina and much, much more.

Niagara Falls

Area telephone code (716)

Organisations

Jewish Federation of Niagra Falls
c/o Beth Israel 284-4575

Synagogues

Conservative
Beth Israel
College & Madison Avenues, 14305   285-9894

Reform
Beth El
720 Ashland Avenue, 14301 282-2717

Orangeburg

Synagogues (Conservative)
Orangetown Jewish Center
Independence Avenue, 10962

Peekskil

Synagogues
First Hebrew Congregation
1821 E. Main Street, 10566   (914) 739-050●

Port Chester

Synagogues (Conservative)
Kneses Tifereth Israel
575 King Street, 10573   (914) 939-1004

Poughkeepsie

Community Organisations
Jewish Community Center of Dutchess
County, 110 Grand Avenue, 12603
                        (914) 471-0430

Synagogues

Orthodox
Shomre Israel, 18 Park Avenue, 12603

Conservative
Temple Beth El, 118 Grand Avenue, 12603

Reform
Vassar Temple, 140 Hooker Avenue, 12601

Rochester

Area telephone code (716)

Community Organisations
Jewish Community Federation
441 E. Avenue, 14607   461-0490

Restaurants
Jewish Home of Rochester Cafeteria
2021 S. Winton Road, 14618

Bakeries
Brighton Donuts, Monroe Avenue   271-6940

Delicatessens
Brownstein's Deli and Bakery
1862 Monroe Avenue, 14618
Fox's Kosher Restaurant and Deli
3450 Winton Place, 14623

Media

Newspapers
Jewish Ledger
2525 Brighton-Henrietta Town Line R, 14623

Saratoga Springs

Area telephone code (518)

Synagogues

Orthodox
Congregation Mikveh Israel
26 Lafayette Street, 12866   584-6338
Services in July & August.
Orthodox Minyan
510 1/2 Broadway, 12866   587-8980

Conservative
Shaare Tfille
260 Broadway, 12866   584-2370

Reform
Temple Sinai
509 Broadway, 12866   584-8730

Scarsdale

Area telephone code (914)

Synagogues
Magen David Sephardie Congregation
1225 Weaver Street, 10583   633-3728
Young Israel of Scarsdale
1313 Weaver Street, 10583   636-8686

Schenectady

Area telephone code (518)

Synagogues
Beth Israel
2195 Eastern Parkway, 12309   377-3700

Conservative
Agudat Achim
2117 Union Street, 12309   393-9211

Reform
Gates of Heaven
852 Ashmore Avenue, 12309   374-8173

Sharon Springs

Hotels

Yarkony's Adler Hotel
PO Box 428, 13459   284-2285
Supervision: OU.

Spring Glen

Area telephone code (914)

Hotels

Homowack Hotel
PO Box 369, 12483   647-6800; 800-243-4567
                                    Fax: 647-4908
Supervision: OU. Glatt kosher.

Spring Valley

Area telephone code (914)

Synagogues (Orthodox)

Young Israel of Spring Valley
23 Union Road, 10977   356-3363

Restaurants

Mehadrin Restaurant
82 Route 59, Monsey, 10952

Pizzerias

Hershey's Kosher Pizza
33.5 Maple Avenue, 10977

Delicatessens

Crest Hill Deli, 279 Main Street, 10977
GPG Deli, Main Street, 10977
K&G Deli, 31 S. Central Avenue, 10977

Hotels

Gartner's Inn
Hungry Hollow Road, 10977   356-0875

Home Hospitality

Mendel & Margalit Zuber
32 Blauvelt Road, Monsey, 10952   425-6213
The hospitable Zuber's write 'Anyone wishing
to spend a Shabbat or Yom Tov with us is
more than welcome. We are Lubavitch
Chasidim, glatt kosher.'

Troy

Area telephone code (315)

Synagogues

Conservative
Temple Beth El
411 Hoosick Street, 12180   272-6113

Reform
Berith Shalom
167 3rd Street, 12180   272-8872

Mikvaot
Troy Chabad Center
2306 15th Street, 12180   274-5572

Utica

Area telephone code (315)

Community Organisations
Jewish Community Federation of the
Mohawk Valley
2310 Oneida Street, 13501   733-2343
                                    Fax: 733-2346

Synagogues

Orthodox
Congregation Zvi Jacob
112 Memorial Parkway, 13501

Conservative
Temple Beth El, 1607 Genesee Street, 13501
Temple Emanu-El, 2710 Genesee St, 13502

White Plains

Area telephone code (914)

Synagogues

Orthodox
Hebrew Institute of White Plains
20 Greenridge Avenue, 10605
Young Israel of White Plains
2 Gedney Way, 10605   683-YIWP

Conservative
Temple Israel, Old Mamaroneck Road, at
Miles Avenue, 10605

Reform
Jewish Community Center
252 Soundview Avenue, 10606

Reconstructionist
Bet Am Shalom
295 Soundview Avenue, 10606

Restaurants

Lexington Glatt Kosher Restaurant
166 Mamaroneck Avenue, 10601   682-7400
Glatt kosher.

Woodridge

Area telephone code (914)

Hotels

The Lake House Hotel, 12789   434-7800
Glatt kosher. Chalav Yisrael products only.
Open Pesach to Succot.

Yonkers

Synagogues

Orthodox
Rosh Pinah, Riverdale Avenue, 10705
Sons of Israel, 105 Radford Avenue, 10705

Conservative
Agudas Achim, 21 Hudson Street, 10701
Lincoln Park Center
323 Central Park Avenue, 10704

Reform
Temple Emanu-El
306 Rumsey Road, 10705

North Carolina

Asheville

Synagogues

Conservative
Congregation Beth Israel
229 Murdoch Avenue, 28804

Reform
Beth Ha-Tephila
43 N. Liberty Street, 28801

Charlotte

Area telephone code (704)

Community Organisations
Jewish Federation
5007 Providence Road, 28226   366-5007

Synagogues

Orthodox
Chabad House
6619 Sardir Road, 28270   366-3984

Conservative
Temple Israel
4901 Providence Road   362-2796

Reform
Temple Beth El
5101 Providence Road, 28207   366-1948

Mikvaot
Chabad House   366-3984

Delicatessens
Shalom Park Sandwich Shoppe
5007 Providence Rd,   366-5007

The Kosher Mart & Delicatessen
Amity Gardens Shopping Center, 3840 E.
Independence Blvd, 28205   563-8288
                                Fax: 532-9111
Sandwiches and deli department are glatt
kosher. Groceries also sold here. Hours:
Monday to Wednesday, 10 am to 6 pm;
Thursday, to 7 pm; Friday to 3 pm; Sunday, to
3:30 pm; Shabbat, closed.

Libraries
Speizman Jewish Library
5007 Providence Road, 28226

Media
Newspapers
Charlotte Jewish News   366-5007

Durham
Area telephone code (919)

Community Organisations
Durham-Chapel Hill Jewish Federation and
Community Council, 205 Mt. Bolus Road,
Chapel Hill, 27514   967-6916

Synagogues
Conservative
Beth El, Watts Street, 27701

Reform
Judea, 2115 Cornwallis Road, 27705

Kashrut Information
Leon Dworsky, 1100 Leon St, Apt. 28, 27705

Fayetteville

Synagogues *(Conservative)*
Beth Israel Congregation
2204 Morganton Road, 28303 (919) 484-6462

Greensboro
Area telephone code (910)

Community Organisations
Jewish Federation
713a N. Greene Street, 27401   272-3189

Synagogues
Conservative
Beth David
804 Winview Drive, 27410   294-0006

Hendersonville

Synagogues
Agudas Israel Congregation
328 N. King Street, PO Box 668, 28793

Raleigh
Area telephone code (919)

Community Organisations
Wake County Jewish Federation
3900 Merton Drive, 27609   751-5459

Synagogues
Conservative
Beth Meyer, 504 Newton Rd, 27615 848-1420

Reform
Temple Beth Or
5315 Creedmoor Road, 27612   781-4895

Mikvaot
Congregation of Sha'arei Israel, 7400 Falls of
the Neuse Road, 27615   847-8986

Groceries
Congregation of Sha'arei Israel, 7400 Falls of
the Neuse Road, 27615   847-8986

Wilmington

Synagogues
Conservative
Beth Jacob, 1833 Academy Street, 27101

Reform
Temple Emanuel
201 Oakwood Drive, 27103   722-6640

North Dakota

Fargo

Synagogues

Orthodox
Fargo Hebrew Cong., 901 S. 9th St, 58103

Reform
Temple Beth El, 809 11th Avenue S., 58103

Ohio

Akron

Community Organisations
Jewish Community Federation
750 White Pond Drive, 44320   (216) 869-2424

Synagogues

Orthodox
Ansbe Sfard, Revere Road, Revere Avenue, & Smith Road, 44320

Conservative
Beth El, 464 S. Hawkins Avenue, 44320

Reform
Temple Israel, 133 Merriman Road, 44303

Beachwood

Synagogues *(Orthodox)*
Young Israel of Beachwood
2463 South Green Rd, 44122   (216) 691-9007

Canton

Area telephone code (216)

Community Organisations
Jewish Community Federation
2631 Harvard Avenue, 44709   452-6444

Synagogues

Orthodox
Agudas Achim
2508 Market Street N., 44704

Conservative
Shaaray Torah
423 30th Street N.W., 44709

Reform
Temple Israel
333 25th Street N.W., 44709

Cincinnati

Area telephone code (513)

Community Organisations
Community Center
1580 Summit Road, 45237   761-7500
Jewish Federation, 1811 Losantiville, Suite 320, 45237   351-3800

Mikvaot
Kehelath B'nai Israel
1546 Beaverton Avenue, 45237   761-5260

Bakeries
Golf Manor, 2200 Losantiville Avenue
All pareve. Closed Shabbat.
Hot Bagels Factory
7617 Reading Road, 45237
Supervision: Vaad Ho-ir of Cincinnati. DBA Marx Hot Bagels also at 316 Northland Blvd, 9701 Kenwood Road, 2327 Buttermilk Crossings and I-75 Cres. Spgs, Kentucky. Open daily, 6 am to 9 pm.
Hot Bagels Factory
477 E. Kemper Road, 45246

Delicatessens
Bilkers, 7648 Reading Road, 45237

Groceries
Pilder's Kosher Foods
7601 Reading Road, 45237
Toron's Meat
1436 Section Road, 45237

Libraries

The Hebrew Union College-Jewish Institute of Religion, 3101 Clifton Avenue, 45220
One of the largest Jewish libraries in the world. It is also has an art gallery of artefacts, houses a collection Jewish 'objets d'art' and religious and ceremonial appurtenances as well as rare books and manuscripts.

Media

Newspapers

American Israelite, 906 Main Street, 45202
Oldest Anglo-Jewish weekly in the US.

Cleveland

Area telephone code (216)

Community Organisations

Jewish Community Federation of Cleveland
1750 Euclid Avenue, 44115   566-9200

Synagogues

With literally dozens of synagogues of each denomination, it is advisable to contact the local religious organisation for specific details.

Mikvaot

1774 Lee Road, 44118

Restaurants

Academy Party Center, Cellar, Hillel Building, CWRU, 11291 Euclid Av., 44106
Academy Party Center
4182 Mayfield Road, 44121
Kinneret Kosher Restaurant
1869 S. Taylor Road, 44118
Yacov's Restaurant
13969 Cedar Road, 44118

Meat

Empire Kosher Kitchen
2234 Warrensville Center Road   691-0006
Peking Kosher Chinese Restaurant
1841 S. Taylor Road, 44118

Museums

Park Synagogue, 3300 Mayfield Road, 44118
Holding a collection of Jewish art and sculpture.

Libraries

The Temple Museum of Religious Art Library, University Circle, Silver Park, 44106
Housing Abba Hillel Silver Archives (Jewish art objects, religious & ceremonial treasures, rare books and manuscripts).

Media

Newspapers

Cleveland Jewish News, 3645 Warrensville Center Road, Suite 230, 44122

Columbus

Area telephone code (614)

Representative Organisations

Jewish Federation
1175 College Avenue, 43209   237-7686

Synagogues

Orthodox

Agudas Achim Synagogue
2568 E. Broad Street, 43209   237-2747
Beth Jacob Congregation
1223 College Avenue, 43209   237-8641
Congregation Ahavas Shalom
2568 E. Broad Street, 43209   252-4815

Mikvaot

Beth Jacob
1223 College Avenue, 43209   237-8641

Restaurants

Meat

Yitzi's Kosher Dogs
207 E. 15th Avenue, 43214   294-3296
Supervision: Vaad Ho-ir of Columbus.

Dairy

Sammy's New York Bagels
40 N. James Road, 43213   237-2444
Supervision: Vaad Ho-ir of Columbus.
Deli as well.

Bakeries

Block's Hot Bagels
2847 Festival Lane   798-1550
Supervision: Vaad Ho-ir of Columbus.

Baked goods only are kosher. Also, all 5 Block's Hot Bagels located inside the Kroger grocery stores at the Chambers, Gahanna, Pickerington, Reynoldsburg and Bethel Roads have supervised baked goods.

Block's Hot Bagels
6115 McNaughten Center   863-0470
Supervision: Vaad Ho-ir of Columbus.
Baked goods only are kosher.

Block's Hot Bagels
3415 E. Broad Street   235-2551
Supervision: Vaad Ho-ir of Columbus.
Baked goods only are kosher.

Block's Hot Bagels
6800 E. Broad Street, 43068   575-9690
Supervision: Vaad Ho-ir of Columbus.
Baked goods only are kosher.

Delicatessens

Kosher Buckeye
2942 E. Broad Street, 43209   235-8070
Supervision: Vaad Ho-ir of Columbus.

Groceries

Bexley Kosher Market
3012 E. Broad Street, 43209   231-3653
Supervision: Vaad Ho-ir of Columbus.
Butcher as well.

Ice Cream Parlors

Graeters Ice Cream
6255 Franz Road   799-2663
2282 E. Main Street   236-2663
1534 Lane Avenue   488-3222
Supervision: Vaad Ho-ir of Columbus.

Dayton

Area telephone code (513)

Community Organisations

Jewish Federation of Greater Dayton
Jesse Phillips Building, 4501 Denlinger Rd.,
45426   854-4150
          Fax: 854-2850

Synagogues

Orthodox
Young Israel of Dayton
1706 Salem Avenue, 45406   274-6941

Mikvaot
556 Kenwood Avenue, 45406

Bakeries

Rinaldo's Bake Shoppe
910 W. Fairview Avenue   274-1311

Media

Newspapers
Dayton Jewish Advocate
4501 Denlinger Road, 45426

Lorain

Synagogues *(Conservative)*

Agudath B'nai Israel
1715 Meister Road, 44053

Toledo

Synagogues

The Temple-Congregation Shomer Emunium, 6453 Sylvania Avenue, 43560

Orthodox
Congregation Etz Chayim
3852 Woodley Road, 43606

Conservative
B'nai Israel, 2727 Kenwood Blvd., 43606

Westerville

Ice Cream Parlors

Graeters Ice Cream
1 State St   (614) 895-0553
Supervision: Vaad Ho-ir of Columbus.

Worthington

Ice Cream Parlors

Graeters Ice Cream
654 High St   (614) 848-5151
Supervision: Vaad Ho-ir of Columbus.

Youngstown

Area telephone code (216)

Organisations

Youngstown Area Jewish Federation
505 Gypsy Lane, 44501   746-3251

Synagogues

Conservative

Beth Israel Temple Center
2138 E. Market Street, Warren, 44482

Ohev Tzedek-Shaarei Torah
5245 Glenwood Avenue, 44512

Temple El Emeth
3970 Logan Way, 44505

Reform

Rodef Sholom
Elm Street & Woodbine Avenue, 44505

Temple Beth Israel
840 Highland Road, Sharon, 16146

Mikvaot

Children of Israel
3970 1/3 Logan Way, 44505

Oklahoma

Oklahoma City

Area telephone code (405)

Community Organisations

Jewish Federation of Greater Oklahoma City
3022 N.W. Expressway,
Suite 116, 73112   949-0111

Synagogues

Conservative

Emanuel Synagogue
900 N.W. 47th Street, 73106

Reform

Temple B'nai Israel
4901 N. Pennsylvania Avenue, 73112

Bakeries

Ingrid's Kitchen
2309 N.W. 36th Street, 73112

Tulsa

Area telephone code (918)

Community Organisations

Jewish Federation
2021 E. 71st Street, 74136   495-1100

Synagogues

Conservative

B'nai Emunah
1719 S. Owasso Avenue, 74120

Reform

Temple Israel
2004 E. 22nd Place, 74114

Kashrut Information

Lubavitch of Oklahoma
6622 S. Utica Avenue   492-4499; 493-7006
Hospitality for travellers.

Museums

The Gershon & Rebecca Fenster Museum of Jewish Art, 1223 E. 17th Place, 74120
Only Jewish Museum in the South-West. Well worth a visit.

Media

Newspapers

Tulsa Jewish Review
2021 E. 71st Street, 74136   495-1100

Oregon

Ashland

Synagogues (Reform)

Temple Emek Shalom-Rogue Valley Jewish Community Center
PO Box 1092, 97520   (541) 488-2909

Eugene

Area telephone code (503)

Synagogues *(Conservative)*

Beth Israel
42 W. 25th Avenue, 97405   485-7218

Portland

Area telephone code (503)

Community Organisations

Jewish Federation of Portland
6651 S.W. Capitol Highway, 97219   245-6219

Mikvaot

Ritualarium
1425 S.W. Harrison Street, 97219   224-3409

Restaurants

**Mittleman Jewish Community Center
(Kosher restaurant)**
6651 S. W. Capitol Highway, 97219 244-0111

Groceries

Albertson's, 5415 SW Beaverton Hillsdale
Highway, 97221   246-1713

Salem

Synagogues *(Reconstructionist)*

Beth Shalom
1795 Broadway NE, 97303   (503) 362-5004

Pennsylvania

Allentown

Area telephone code (610)

Community Organisations

Jewish Federation
702 22nd Street, 18104   821-5500

Mikvaot

1834 Whitehall Street, 18104   776-7948

Restaurants

Meat

Abe's Place, 1741 Allen St, 18104   435-1735
Supervision: Lehigh Valley Kashrut
Commission. Closed Shabbat. Call for hours.

Glatt Kosher Community Center
702 N. 22nd Street, 18104   435-3571
Since opening hours vary according to season,
it is advisable to call before visiting.

Altoona

Synagogues

Conservative
Agudath Achim
1306 17th Street, 16601

Reform
Temple Beth Israel
3004 Union Avenue, 16602

Bethlehem

Synagogues

Agudath Achim
1555 Linwood Street, 18017

Conservative
Congregation Brith Sholom
Macada & Jacksonville Roads, 18017

Blue Bell

Synagogues

Tiferet Bet Israel
1920 Skippack Pike, 19422   (610) 275-8797

Easton

Synagogues

B'nai Abraham, 16th & Bushkill Streets, 18042
Established 1888.

Reform
Covenant of Peace
15th & Northampton Streets, 18042
Established 1839.

Elkins Park

Synagogues *(Orthodox)*
Young Israel of Elkins Park
7715 Montgomery Avenue, 19027

Erie

Area telephone code (814)

Community Organisations
Jewish Community Council
Suite 405, Professional Building, 161 Peach St,
16501   455-4474
                                    Fax: 455-4475

Synagogues

Conservative
Brith Sholom Jewish Center
3207 State Street, 16508

Reform
Anshe Hesed, 10th & Liberty Streets, 16502

Harrisburg

Area telephone code (717)

Community Organisations
**United Jewish Community of Greater
Harrisburg**
100 Vaughn Street, 17110   236-9555

Synagogues

Orthodox
Kesher Israel, 2945 N. Front Street, 17110

Conservative
Beth El, 2637 N. Front Street, 17110
Chisuk Emuna, 5th & Division Streets, 17110

Reform
Ohev Sholom, 2345 N. Front Street, 17110

Caterers
Norman Gras
3000 Green Street, 17110-1234   234-2196
Supervision: Rabbi Chaim Schertz.
Stocks kosher vending machines at the JCC,
3301 N. Front Street, Tel: 236-9555. Offers
catering for groups as well.

Groceries
Bakeries Giant Food Store and Weis Market
Linglestown Road
Quality Kosher, 7th Division Street, 17110

Hazleton

Synagogues

Conservative
Agudas Israel, 77 N. Pine Street, 18201

Reform
Beth Israel, 98 N. Church Street, 18201

Johnstown

Community Organisations
United Jewish Federation
700 Indiana Street, 15905   (814) 536-0647

Synagogues *(Conservative)*
Beth Sholom Congregation
700 Indiana Street, 15905

Lancaster

Community Organisations
Jewish Federation
2120 Oregon Pike, 17601   (717) 597-7354

Synagogues

Orthodox
Degel Israel, 1120 Columbia Avenue, 17603

Conservative
Beth El, 25 N. Lime Street, 17602

Reform
Temple Shaarei Shomayim
N. Duke & James Streets, 17602

Levittown

Area telephone code (215)

Synagogues

Conservative
Congregation Beth El, 21 Penn Valley Road,
Fallsington, 19054   945-9500

Reform
Temple Shalom, Edgley Road, off Mill Creek
Pkwy., 19057   945-4154

McKeesport

Area telephone code (412)

Synagogues

Orthodox
Gemilas Chesed, 1400 Summit Street, White
Oak, 15131   678-9859

Conservative
Tree of Life-Sfard, Cypress Avenue, 15131

Reform
B'nai Israel, 536 Shaw Avenue, 15132

Philadelphia

Area telephone code (215)

Cultural Organisations
Annenberg Research Institute
420 Walnut Street, 19106   238-1290
Approximately 180,000 books and thousands
of periodicals with emphasis on Judaic and
Near Eastern studies. Rare book collection
Archives of American Judaica particularly that
of Philadelphia

Synagogues
With dozens of synagogues of the various
denominations in the area, travellers are
advised to contact a local religious
organisation for specific details.

Mikvaot
Allentown Mikveh, 1834 Whitehall Street,
Allentown, 18104   776-7948

**Mikveh Association of Philadelphia
(Ardmore)**
Torah Academy, Wynnewood and Argyle
Roads, Ardmore, 19003   642-8679

**Mikveh Association of Philadelphia
(Northern)**
7525 Loretto Avenue, 19111   745-3334

Sons of Israel, 720 Cooper Landing Road,
Cherry Hill, 08002   667-9700

Kashrut Information
Board of Rabbis of Greater Philadelphia
1616 Walnut Street, 19103   985-1818

Ko Kosher Service
5871 Drexel Road, 19131   879-1100

Orthodox Vaad of Philadelphia
7505 Brookhaven Road, 19123
Rabbi Shlomo Caplan   473-0951
Rabbi Aaron Felder   745-2968
Rabbi Yehoshua Kaganoff   742-8421

Rabbinical Assembly, United Synagogue of
Conservative, Judaism, 1510 Chestnut Street,
19102   563-8814

Rabbinical Council of Greater Philadelphia
44 North 4th Street, 19106   922-5446

**Vaad Hakashruth and Beth Din of
Philadelphia**
1147 Gilham Street, 19111   725-5181

Contact Information
Jewish Information and Referral Service
226 South 16th Street, 19102   893-5821
A free confidential service that provides
answers to questions about Jewish
organisations, institutions, community services
and various subjects of Jewish interest in the
five-county Greater Philadelphia area. JIRS is
your connection to the Jewish community. It is
open to callers weekdays from 9 am to 5 p.m.

Embassy
Consulate General, 230 South 15th St, 19102

Restaurants
Cherry Street Chinese vegeterian
1010 Cherry Street, 19107   923-3663
Supervision: Rabbinical Assembly.

Dragon Inn
7628 Castor Avenue, 19152   742-2575
Supervision: Rabbi Dov Brisman.

Gratz College Cafeteria, Mandell Education
Campus, Old York Road and Melrose Avenue,
Melrose Park, 19027   635-7300
Supervision: Rabbinical Council.

Hillel Dining Room
University of Pennsylvania, 202 South 36th
Street, 19104   725-7444
Supervision: Orthodox Vaad of Philadelphia.

Jonathan's
130 South 11th Street, 19152   829-8101
Supervision: Rabbi Dov Brisman.

Maccabeam
128 South 12th Street, 19107   922-5922
Supervision: Rabbinical Council.

Oasis Falafel, 17th and Market Streets
(vendor), 19103   879-6956
                        Fax: 879-0575
Supervision: Orthodox Vaad of Philadelphia.

Tiberias Cafeteria
8010 Castor Avenue, 19152   898-7391
Supervision: Orthodox Vaad of Philadelphia.

Traditions Restaurant
9550 Bustleton Avenue, 19115   677-2221
Supervision: Orthodox Vaad of Philadelphia.

Zenya Snack Bar, Jewish Community Centers
of Greater, Philadelphia, Red lion Road and
Jamison Avenue, 19116   677-0280
Supervision: Ko Kosher Service.

Dairy

Shalom Pizza
7598A Haverford Avenue, 19151   878-1500
Supervision: Orthodox Vaad of Philadelphia.
Chalav Yisrael pizza and Middle Eastern
cuisine. Around the corner from the Bestcake
Bakery. Take out or eat in. Hours: Sunday to
Thursday, 11 am to 9 pm; Friday, to 4 pm.

Bakeries

Arthur's Bakery
Academy Plaza, Red Lion and Academy Roads,
19114   637-9146
Supervision: Rabbinical Assembly.
An additional location in the Northeast.

Bestcake Bakery
7594 Haverford Avenue, 19151   878-1127
Supervision: Orthodox Vaad of Philadelphia.
Pat Yisrael. Hours: 7 am to 7 pm; closed
Shabbat and holidays.

Buy the Dozen
219 Haverford Avenue, 19072   667-9440
Supervision: Orthodox Vaad of Philadelphia.
Wholesale bakery open to the public.

Dante's Bakery
Richboro Centre, Bustleton and Second Street
Pikes, Richboro, 18954   357-9599
Supervision: Rabbinical Assembly.

Hesh's Eclair Bake Shoppe
7721 Castor Avenue, 19152   742-8575
Supervision: Vaad Hakashruth.
Closed on Shabbat.

Hutchinson's Classic Bakery
13023 Bustleton Pike, 19116   676-8612
Supervision: Rabbinical Assembly.

Kaplan's New Model Bakery
901 Norht 3rd Street, 19123   627-5288
Supervision: Rabbi Solomon Isaacson.

Lipkin an Sons Bakery
8013 Castor Avenue, 19152   342-3005
Supervision: Rabbi Abraham Novitsky.

Masi-Schaber Wedding Cakes
1848 South 15th Street, 19145   336-4557
Supervision: Rabbinical Council.

Michael's
6635 Castor Avenue, 19149   745-1423
Supervision: Rabbi Dov Brisman.

Moish's Addison Bakery
10865 Bustleton Avenue, 19116   469-8054
Supervision: Rabbinical Assembly.

Rilling's Bakery
2990 Southampton Road, 19154   698-6171
Supervision: Rabbinical Assembly.

The Village Baker, 2801 South Eagle Road,
Newton, 18940   579-1235
Supervision: Rabbinical Assembly.

Viking Bakery, 39 Cricket Avenue, Ardmore,
19003   642-9227
Supervision: Rabbi Joshua Toledano.

Weiss Bakery
6635 Castor Avenue, 19149   722-4506
Supervision: Rabbi Dov Brisman.

Zach's Bakery
6419 Rising Sun Avenue, 19111   722-1688
Supervision: Rabbinical Assembly.

Butchers

Aries Kosher Meats
6530 Castor Avenue, 19149   533-3222
Supervision: Vaad Hakashruth.

Best Value Kosher Meat Center
8564 Bustleton Avenue, 19152   342-1902
Supervision: Rabbi Dov Brisman.

Bustleton Kosher Meat Market
6834 Bustlton Avenue, 19149   332-0100
Supervision: Rabbi Shalom Novoseller.

Glendale Meats
7730 Bustleton Avenue, 19152   725-4100
Supervision: Vaad Hakashruth.

Main Line Kosher Meats
75621 Haverford Avenue, 19151   877-3222
Supervision: Vaad Hakashruth.

Modern Kosher Meat Market
5948 Otgontz Avenue, 19141   924-8259
Supervision: Vaad Hakashruth.

Rhawnhurst Kosher Meat Market
8261 Bustleton Avenue, 19152   742-5287
Supervision: Vaad Hakashruth.

Simons Kosher Meats and Poultry
6926 Bustleton Avenue, 19149   624-5695
Supervision: Vaad Hakashruth.

Wallace's Krewstown Kosher Meat Market
8919 Krewstown Road, 19115   464-7800
Supervision: Vaad Hakashruth.

Groceries

Best Value Losher Meat Center
8564 Bustleton Avenue, 19152   342-1902
Supervision: Rabbi Dov Brisman.

Kosher Plus
7534 Haverford Avenue, 19151   871-0774
                                Fax: 871-0779
Supervision: Orthodox Vaad of Philadelphia.

Milk and Honey
7618, Castor Avenue, 19152   342-3224
Supervision: Vaad Hakashruth.

R & R Produce and Fish
7551 Haverford Avenue, 19151   878-6264
Supervision: Orthodox Vaad of Philadelphia.

Museums

Balch Institute for Ethnic Studies
18 South 7th Street, 19106   925-8090
Documents and interprets American multi-culturalism Research library has an Yiddish collection. Houses the Jewish Archives Center.

Borowsky Gallery, Jewish Community Centers of Greater Philadelphia, 401 South Broad Street, 19147   545-4400
Continuing exhibits of special interest to the Jewish community.

Fred Wolf Jr Gallery, Jewish Community Centers of Greater Philadelphia, 10100 Jamison Avenue, 19116   698-7300
Continuing exhibits of special interest to the Jewish community.

Holocaust Awareness Museum, Gratz College, Mandell Education Campus, 7601 Old York Road, Melrose Park, 19027   635-6480

Previously known as the Jewish Identity Center it contains donations from Holocaust survivors and concentration camp liberators. The collection documents and teaches the facts of genocide and dangers of ethnic hatred and bigotry.

National Museum of American Jewish History, 55 North 5th Street, Independence Mall East, 19106   923-3811
                                Fax: 923-0763
Dedicated to documenting the American Jewish experience. With a gift shop.

Congregation Rodeph Shalom, 615 North Broad Street, 19123   627-6747
Nationally recognised for exhibits of contemporary Jewish art and history. Permanent collection of 20th-century Jewish art and photographs.

Rosenbach Museum and Library
2010 Delancey Place, 19103   732-1600
The collection includes the first Haggadah printed in America and letters of the Gratz family of Philadelphia. Access to books is by appointment only.

Temple Judea/Museum of Keneseth Israel
Old York and Rownship Line Roads, Elkins Park, 19027   887-8700
This synagogue museum has four changing exhibits of Judaica and Jewish art each year.

Landmarks

Beth Sholom Congregation, 8231 Old York Road, Elkins Park, 19027   887-1342
Conservative synagogue whose building is the only synagogue ever designed by renowned architect Frank Lloyd Wright.

Congregation Beth T'fillah of Overbrook Park
7630 Woodbine Avenue, 19151   477-2415
Conservative synagogue with a 10-foot high replica of the Western Wall in its lobby.

Congregation Mikveh Israel
44 North 4th Street, 19106   922-5446
Spanish-Portuguese synagogue founded in 1748. Located on Independence Mall. Entrance is through the National Museum of American Jewish History.

Mikveh Israel Cemetery
8th and Spruce Streets, 19107   922-5446
One of the oldest Jewish cemeteries in the United States, with graves dating from 1740. Interred here are Haym Solomon, Rebecca Gratz and 21 veterans of the American Revolution.

Monument to the Six Million Jewish Martyrs, 16th Street and the Benjamin, Franklin Parkway, 19103
This memorial sculpture was the first public Holocaust monument in the United States.

The Frank Synagogue
Albert Einstein Medical Center, Old York and Tabor Roads, 19141   456-7890
Modelled after first- and second-century synagogues discovered in the Galilee region of Israel, this small, historically certified synagogue was originally dedicated in 1901.

Tours

Jewish Historic Tours
1304 Andover Road, 19151   649-4383
Tours may be arranged to suit personal or group interests or needs.

Walking Tour of Jewish Historic Society Hill
934-7184
Sunday mornings April through Thanksgiving.

Libraries

Philadelphia Jewish Archives Center
Balch Institute for Ethnic Studies, 18 South 7th Street, 19106   925-8090
Jewish community archives containing records of agencies, synagogues and community organisations, personal and family papers, autobiographies and memoirs and a photograph collection. Open to the public.

Reconstructionist Rabbinical College Library
Church Road and Greenwood Avenue, Wyncote, 19095   576-0800
The Kaplan Library serves rabbinical students and the general public. 33,000 books and periodicals in English, Hebrew and other languages. Houses documents of the Reconstructionist movement.

Talmudical Yeshivah Library
6063 Dexel Road, 19131   477-1000

Temple University
Paley Library, 13th Street and Berks Mall, 19122   787-8231
Large collection of Judaica, Hebraica and Talmudic studies and literature in Hebrew and in translation. Main stacks are open.

The Free Library of Philadelphia, Central Library, Logan Square, 19103   686-5392
3,000-volume Moses Marx Collection of Judaica central collection.

Tuttlemann Library, Gratz College, Mandell Education Campus, 7601 Old York Road,

Melrose Park, 19027   635-7304
Specialised library of Judaic and Hebraic studies. Multilingual collection of approximately 100,000 books, periodicals, music and audio-visual materials. Special collections include a rare book room, a music library and a Holocaust oral history archive. Open to the public.

University of Pennsylvania, Van Pelt Library, 3420 Walnut Street, 19104   898-7556
Large collection of biblical studies, rabbinics, Jewish history and medieval and modern Hebrew language and literature. Stacks and seminar rooms open to the public.

Media

Magazines

Inside Magazine, Jewish Publihing Group, 226 South 16th Street, 19102   893-5759
Quarterly magazine of Jewish life and style. Sold at news-stands.

Jewish Quarterly Review
420 Walnut Street, 19106   238-1290
Scholarly quarterly journal of the Annenberg Research Institute.

Shofar Magazine
P.O. Box 51591, 19115   676-8304
Russian-language monthly magazine.

Newspapers

Jewish Exponent
Jewish Publishing Group, 226 South 16th Street, Philadelphia, 19102   893-5700
Weekly newspaper.

Jewish Post
P.O.Box 442, Yardley, 19067   321-3443
Monthly newspaper serving Bucks County, PA and Mercer County, NJ.

Jewish Times
Jewish Publishing Group, 103A Tomlinson Road, Huntingdon Valley, 19006   938-1177
Weekly newspaper.

Mir
P.O. Box 6162, Philadelphia, 19115   934-5512
Local weekly Russian-language newspaper.

Radio & TV

Barry Reisman Show   365-5600
WSSJ (1310AM). Jewish music in Yiddish, Hebrew and English and Jewish news.
Mondays through Fridays 3.30 to 5.30pm
Sundays 9.30 am to 1 pm.

Bucks County Jewish Life 949-1490
WBCB (1490AM). Rabbi Allan Tuffs hosts this weekly Sun. morning radio program at 10 am.

Comcast Cablevisiion of Philadelphia
4400 Wayne Avenue, 19140 673-6600
Channel 66 (Cable Television). Half-hour program on Jewish culture shown twice a week.

Dialogue 878-9700
WPVI - TV (channel 6). Discussion program on religious issues sponsored by Delaware Valley Media Ministry, Sundays 6.30 to 7.30am.

Pulse, WSSJ, Camden 365-5600
WSSJ (1310AM). Russian-language news and music program, Sundays 9.30 to 10.30am

Meridian 962-8000
Russian language program, Sat. 10-10.30 am.

Theatre

Theatre Ariel/Habima Ariel, P.O. Box 0334, Merion Station, 19066 567-0670
Theatre productions, readings workshops, mini-performances and speakers all dedicated to exploring the Jewish theatrical experience.

Booksellers

Bala Judaica Center 664-1303
222 Bala Avenue, 19004 Fax: 664-4319

Because We Care, Mandell Education Campus, 7603 Old York Rd, 19027 635-4774

Gratz College
Mandell Education Campus, 7601 Old York Road, Melrose Park, 19027 635-7300

Jerusalem Israeli Gift Shop
7818 Castor Avenue, 19152 342-1452

Mazel Stuff
44 Antler Drive, Holland, 18966 860-7744

Neo Judaica Gifts 922-1161

Raanan Enterprises, 1096 Sparrow Road, Jenkintown, 19046 886-1297

Rosen's Hebrew Books and Gifts
6743 Castor Avenue, 19149 742-2397

Rosenberg Hebrew Book Store, 409 Old York Road, 19046 884-1728
800-301-8608
Fax: 884-6648

Rosenberg Hebrew Book Store (Northeast)
6408 Castor Avenue, 19149 744-5205
Fax: 533-9248

Pittsburgh

Area telephone code (610)

There are about 45,000 Jews in Pittsburgh, a significant number in the Squirrel Hill area (where an Eruv is in operation), which also houses the majority of Jewish institutions. There are smaller communities in East Liberty, Stanton Heights, Oakland and the South Hills and East and North Hills areas around Pittsburgh.

Community Organisations

Jewish Federation
1700 City Line St,., 19604 921-2766

Jewish Federation of Greater Wilkes-Barre & Community Center 822-4146
60 S. River Street Fax: 824-5966

Scranton-Lackawanna Jewish Federation
601 Jefferson Avenue, 18510 961-2300
Fax: 346-6147

United Jewish Federation of Greater Pittsburgh, 234 McKee Pl, 15213 681-8000
Fax: 681-8804
Houses all administrative office of the Federal and Community Relations Committee.

Synagogues

Orthodox

Adath Israel, 3257 Ward St., 15213

Adath Jeshurun, 5643 E. Liberty Blvd., 15224

Beth Hamedrash Hagodol, 1230 Colwell St., 15219

B'nai Emunoh, 4315 Murray Av., 15217

B'nai Zion, 6404 Forbes Av., 15217

Bohnei Yisroel, 6401 Forbes Av., 15217

Kether Torah, 5706 Bartlett St., 15217

Kneseth Israel, 1112 N. Negley Av., 15206

Machsikei Hadas, 814 N. Negley Av., 15206

Poale Zedeck, Phillips & Shady Avs., 15217

Shaare Tefillah, 5741 Bartlett St., 15217

Shaare Torah, 2319 Murray Av., 15217

Shaare Zedeck, 5751 Bartlett St., 15217

Torath Chaim, 728 N. Negley Av., 15206

Young Israel of Greater Pittsburgh
5831 Bartlett Street, 15217-1636 421-7224

Conservative

Ahavath Achim, Lydia & Chestnut Sts., Carnegie, 15106

Beth El of South Hills, 1900 Cochran Rd., 15220

Beth Shalom, Beacon & Shady Avs., 15217

B'nai Israel, 327 N. Negley Av., 15206

New Light, 1700 Beechwood Blvd., 15217

Parkway Jewish Center, 300 Princeton Dr., 15235

Tree of Life , Wilkins & Shady Avs., 15217

Reform

Rodef Shalom, 4905 5th Av., 15213

Temple David, 4415 Northern Pike, Monroeville, 15146

Temple Emanuel, 1250 Bower Hill Rd., South Hills, 15243

Temple Sinai, 5505 Forbes Av., 15217

Reconstructionist

Dor Hadash, 6401 Forbes Av., 15217

Mikvaot

2326 Shady Avenue, 15217   422-8010

Restaurants

Brauner's Emporium
2023 Murray Avenue, 15217

Greenberg's Kosher Poultry
2223 Murray Avenue, 15217

King David's
2020 Murray Avenue, 15217   422-3370

Prime Kosher, 1916 Murray Avenue, 15217

Yaacov's
2109 Murray Avenue, 15217   421-7208

Bakeries

Pastries Unlimited
2119 Murray Avenue, 15217

Pastries Unlimited, 4743 Liberty Avenue

Groceries

Koshermart, 2121 Murray Avenue, 15217

Museums

Holocaust Center of the United Jewish Federation
242 McKee Place, 15213   682-7111
Serves as a living memorial by providing educational resources, sponsoring community activities, housing archives and cultural materials related to the Holocaust.

Media

Newspapers

Pittsburgh Jewish Chronicle
5600 Baum Blvd   687-1000

Booksellers

Pinskers Judaica Center, 2028 Murray Avenue, 15217   421-5175; 800-JUDAISM
Fax: 421-6103
Email: info@judaism.com

Pottstown

Synagogues *(Conservative)*

Congregation Mercy & Truth
575 N. Keim Street, 19464

Reading

Synagogues

Orthodox

Shomrei Habrith
2320 Hampden Blvd., 19604

Conservative

Kesher Zion
Eckert & Perkiomen Sts, 19602

Reform

Oheb Shalom
13th & Perkiomen Sts, 19604

Scranton

Synagogues

Orthodox

Beth Shalom, Clay Avenue at Vine St, 18510

Congregation Machzikeh Hadas
cnr. Monroe & Olive, 18510

Ohev Zedek, 1432 Mulberry Street, 18510

Conservative

Temple Israel
Gibson Street & Monroe Avenue, 18510

Reform
Temple Hesed, Lake Scranton, 18505

Butchers
Blatt's Butcher Block, 420 Prescott Avenue,
18510   342-3886; 800-221-4528
                              Fax: 342-9711
Supervision: Rabbi Fine and Rabbi Herman of
Scranton. Glatt kosher meat, poultry,
delicatessen and groceries.

Sharon

Synagogues *(Reform)*
Temple Beth Israel
840 Highland Avenue, 16146

Wallingford

Synagogues *(Conservative)*
Ohev Shalom, 2 Chester Road, 19086
The synagogue vestibule contains 12 stained
glass panes (designed & executed by Rose
Isaacson) each depicting a Jewish holiday.

Wilkes-Barre

Synagogues

Orthodox
Ohav Zedek, 242 S. Franklin Street, 18702
United Orthodox Synagogue
13 S. Welles Street, 18702

Conservative
Temple Israel, 236 S. River Street, 18702

Reform
B'nai B'rith
408 Wyoming Street, Kingston, 18704

Williamsport

Synagogues
Ohev Sholom, Cherry & Belmont Sts, 17701

Reform
Beth Ha-Sholom, 425 Center Street, 17701

Yardley
Area telephone code (215)

Contact Information
Rabbi Budow   493-1800

Bakeries
Cramer Bakery
18 E. Afton Avenue, 19067   493-2760

Rhode Island

Barrington

Synagogues *(Reform)*
Temple Habonim
165 New Meadow Road, 02806

Bristol

Synagogues *(Conservative)*
United Brothers, 215 High Street, 02809

Cranston

Synagogues
Temple Torat Yisrael, 330 Park Ave, 02905
Temple Sinai, 30 Hagan Avenue, 02920

Middletown

Synagogues *(Conservative)*
Temple Shalom, 223 Valley Road, 02842

Narragansett

Synagogues

Congregation Beth David
Kingstown Road, 02882   (401) 846-9002

Newport

Tourist Sites

Sephardi, 85 Touro Street, 02840   847-4794
The synagogue, designed by Peter Harrison
and dedicated in 1763, is one of the finest
examples of 18th-century Colonial
architecture. It has been declared a national
site by the US government. The Jewish
cemetery, the 2nd oldest in the US, dates back
to 1677 and was immortalised in Longfellow's
poem 'The Jewish Cemetery of Newport'.
Judah Touro is buried here.

Pawtucket

Synagogues

Ohawe Shalom, East Avenue, 02860

Orthodox
Young Israel of Pawtucket
671 East Avenue, 02862   722-3146

Providence

Area telephone code (401)

Community Organisations

Jewish Federation of Rhode Island
130 Sessions Street, 02906   421-4111

Synagogues

Orthodox

Beth Shalom, 275 Camp Avenue, 02906
Congregation Sons of Jacob
24 Douglas Avenue, 02908
Mishkon Tfiloh
203 Summit Avenue, 02906
Shaare Zedek, 688 Broad Street, 02907

Conservative
Temple Emanu-El, 99 Taft Avenue, 02906

Reform
Beth El, 70 Orchard Avenue, 02906

Mikvaot

401 Elmgrove Avenue, 02906

Kashrut Information

Brown University Hillel
80 Brown Street, 02912
Vaad Hakashrut   331-9393

Bakeries

Kaplan's Bakery   621-8107
Supervision: Rabbi Ephraim Berlinski, Vaad of
Rhode Island.

Butchers

Marty Weissman's Butcher Shop   467-8903
Supervision: Rabbi Ephraim Berlinski, Vaad of
Rhode Island.
Butcher shop only; 'Deli Counter' meat and hot
dogs not under supervision.

Museums

Rhode Island Holocaust Memorial Museum
401 Elmgrove Avenue, 02906   861-8800
The state memorial to the victims of the
Holocaust. Many survivors now living in Rhode
Island have donated memorabilia and personal
mementoes. There is also a garden of
remembrance.

Documentation Centres

Rhode Island Jewish Historical Association
                              863-2805
Has a vast amount of material regarding
Colonial Jewry.

Media

Magazines
L'Chaim
130 Sessions Street, 02906   421-4111

Warwick

Synagogues *(Conservative)*
Temple Am David, 40 Gardiner Street, 02888

Westerly

Synagogues *(Orthodox)*
Cong. Shaare Zedek, Union Street, 02891

Woonsocket

Synagogues *(Conservative)*
B'nai Israel, 224 Prospect Street, 02895

South Carolina

Charleston

Area telephone code (803)

Community Organisations
Jewish Federation and Community Center
1645 Raoul Wallenberg Blvd, PO Box 31298,
29416   571-6565
                                            Fax: 556-6206

Synagogues *(Reform)*
Beth Elohim
86 Hasell Street, 29401   723-1090

Bakeries
Ashley Bakery
1662 Savannah Highway, 29407   763-4125
Great Harvest Bread Company
975 Savannah Highway, 29407   763-2055

Delicatessens
Nathan's Deli
1836 Ashley River Road, 29407   556-3354
West Side Market and Deli
1300 Savannah Highway, 29407   763-9988
                                            Fax: 763-4476
Kosher market, restaurant and catering. Open
Sunday to Friday.

Tourist Sites
Beth Elohim
86 Hasell Street, 29401   723-1090
Dating from 1749, it is the birthplace of
Reform Judaism in the United States, the
Second oldest synagogue building in the
country, and the oldest surviving Reform
synagogue in the world. It has been
designated a national historic landmark. A
museum is housed in the administration
building next door.

Columbia

Community Organisations
Columbia Jewish Federation
4540 Trenholm Road, Cola, 29206   787-2023

Synagogues
Conservative
Beth Shalom
5827 N. Trenholm Road, 29206

Reform
Tree of Life
6719 Trenholm Road, Cola, 29206   787-0580

Delicatessens
Groucho's, Five Points, 29205

Georgetown

Although there are now very few Jews in
Georgetown, and there is no synagogue, there
is a very old Jewish cemetery, which is
maintained by the city.

Myrtle Beach

Area telephone code (803)

Synagogues
Orthodox
Beth El, 401 Highway 17 N., 56th Avenue,
29577   449-3140
Chabad Lubavitch, 2803 N. Oak St   626-6403

South Dakota

Aberdeen

Synagogues *(Conservative)*
B'nai Isaac
202 N. Kline Street, 57401   225-3404/7360

Rapid City

Synagogues *(Reform)*
Synagogue of the Hills
PO Box 2320, 57709   (605) 394-3310

Tennessee

Chattanooga

Area telephone code (423)

Community Organisations
Jewish Community Federation
5326 Lynnland Terrace, 47311   894-1317
                                  Fax: 894-1319

Synagogues

Orthodox
Beth Sholom
20 Pisgah Avenue, 37411   894-0801

Conservative
B'nai Zion
114 McBrien Road, 37411   894-8900

Reform
Mizpah Congregation
923 McCallie Avenue, 37403   264-9771

Museums
Siskin Museum of Religious Artefacts
1 Siskin Plaza, 37403   634-1700

Memphis

Area telephone code (901)

Community Organisations
Jewish Federation and Community Center
6560 Poplar Avenue, 38138   767-7100

Synagogues

Orthodox
Anshei Sephard-Beth El Emeth
120 E. Yates Road N., 38117
Baron Hirsch Congregation
369 Winter Oak Lane, 38119
Mikva on premises.

Conservative
Beth Sholom, 482 S. Mendenhall Ave, 38117

Reform
Temple Israel, 1376 E. Massey Road

Kashrut Information
Vaad Hakehilloth of Memphis
Memphis Orthodox Jewish Community
Council, PO Box 41133, 38104   767-0810

Restaurants

Meat
M.I. Gottlieb's
5062 Park Avenue, 38120   763-3663
Supervision: Vaad Hakehilloth of Memphis.
Hours: Sunday to Thursday, 9 am to 7 pm;
Friday, 7 am to 2:30 pm.

Dairy
Jon's Place
764 Mt. Moriah Road, 38117   374-0600
Supervision: Vaad Hakehilloth of Memphis.
Open daily except Shabbat for dairy and fish
lunch and dinner.

Bakeries
Carl's Bakery
1688 Jackson Avenue, 38107   276-2304
Supervision: Vaad Hakehilloth of Memphis.
Open daily except Shabbat and Monday.

Delicatessens
Rubenstein's, 4965 Summer Avenue, 38122
Closed Shabbat.

Nashville

Area telephone code (615)

Community Organisations

Jewish Federation of Nashville and Middle Tennessee
801 Percy Warner Blvd., 37205   356-3242
                                        Fax: 352-0056

Synagogues

Orthodox
Sherith Israel
3600 West End Avenue, 37205   292-6614
Mikva on premises.

Conservative
West End Synagogue
3814 West End Avenue, 37205   269-4592

Reform
The Temple
5015 Harding Road, 37205   352-7620

Texas

Amarillo

Synagogues *(Reform)*
Temple B'nai Israel
4316 Albert Street, 79106   (806) 352-7191

Austin

Area telephone code (512)

Community Organisations

Jewish Federation and Community Center of Austin   331-1144
11713 Jollyville Road, 78759   Fax: 331-7059

Synagogues

Orthodox
Chabad House
2101 Neuces Street, 78705   499-8202
Mikvah on premises.

Conservative
Agudas Achim, 4300 Bull Creek Road, 78731
Congregation Beth El
8902 Mesa Drive, 78759   346-1776

Reform
Temple Beth Israel
3901 Shoal Creek Blvd., 78756   454-6806

Beaumont

Synagogues
Temple Emanuel
1120 Broadway, 7740   (409) 832-6131

Bellaire

Bakeries
Ashcraft, 1301 N. First, 77401

Corpus Christi

Synagogues

Conservative
B'nai Israel, 3434 Fort Worth Avenue, 78411

Reform
Temple Beth El, 4402 Saratoga Street, 78413

Dallas

Area telephone codes (972) unless shown

Dallas stands at the western edge of the American South both regionally and culturally. The Dallas Jewish community was founded in the decade following the Civil War by predominantly German Jews. The founders left their imprint in numerous institutions and a style of worship that reflects the German Reform Jewish culture of the mid-19th century. The social importance of German Jewish ancestry can still be seen in the Temple Emanu-El cemetery which is home to scores of 19th-century headstones bearing German regional names for eastern European birth-places. Proud descendants of eastern European Jews founded many important institutions as well, including vibrant Conservative Jewish congregations and Jewish day schools. In the post World War II community, openness to Jewish ethnicity and community building largely replaced assimilationist ideologies.

Newer generations of traditional Jewish immigrants from South Africa, Great Britain, Mexico, Central and South America, the Middle East and central Asia have joined and strengthened those institutions, creating an influential and privileged traditional community very different from that envisioned by the community's founders.

The JCC sponsors a prestigious Jewish Arts Festival each August along with concerts and gallery exhibitions. Another highlight of the Jewish calendar is the Kosher Chile Cookoff, with participation from virtually all synagogues and other community organizations. A Holocaust Museum has served as a regional focal point for preserving the memory of the Shoah and teaching the lessons of hatred to a larger public. The present Jewish population in the Dallas area stands at approximately 35,000. For more information, see the Dallas Virtual Jewish Community website at www.dvjc.org.

Community Organisations

Jewish Federation of Greater Dallas and Community Center, 7800 Northaven Road, Suite A, 75230 (214) 369-3313
Fax: (214) 369-8943
The Center houses the Dallas Memorial Center for Holocaust studies and the Dallas Jewish Historical Society. There is a kosher kids café only on Sundays, under the supervision of the Vaad Hakashrus of Greater Dallas.

Religious Organisations

Dallas Area Torah Association (Kollel)
5840 Forest Lane, 75230 (214) 987-3282
Web site: www.datanet.org

Mikvah Association
5640 McShann, 75230 776-0037
Beeper: (972) 397-3428

Rabbinic Association of Greater Dallas
6930 Alpha Road 661-1810

Vaad Hakashrus of Greater Dallas, 7900 Northaven Road, 75230 (214) 739-OKDK
Also known as 'Dallas Kosher', they can be contacted for all kashrut information.

Synagogues

Orthodox
Chabad of Plano, 75230 596-8270
Congregation Ohev Shalom
6821 McCallum Blvd, 75230 380-1292
Forest Lane Shul
7008 Forest Lane, 75230 (214) 361-8600
Shaare Tefilla, 6131 Churchill Way, off Preston Road, 75230 661-0127
Young Israel of Dallas
6504 Dykes Way, 75230 386-7162

Conservative
Congregation Anshai Emet
5220 Village Creek Drive 735-9818
Cong. Beth Emunah, 75230 416-8016
Congregation Beth Torah
720 Lookout 234-1542
Congregation Shearith Israel
9401 Douglas, 75230 (214) 361-6606

Traditional
Tiferet Israel Congregation
10909 Hillcrest Road, 75230 (214) 691-3611

Reform
Cong. Beth-El Binah, Gay and Lesbian Center, 2701 Regan, 75219 (214) 497-1591
Congregation Kol Ami
1887 Timbercreek 539-1938
Congregation Ner Tamid, 2312 Trinity Mills Road, Suites 160A and B 416-9738
Temple Emanu-El
8500 Hillcrest Road, 75230 (214) 706-0000
Temple Shalom
6930 Alpha Road, 75230 661-1810

Mikvaot
Congregation Tiferet Israel (214) 397-3428
Call for appointment.

Media

Newspapers
Texas Jewish Post
11333 N. Central Expressway, 75230
Weekly publication. Includes weekly listing of synagogue services and times in the Greater Dallas area. Includes addresses and phone numbers.

Bakeries

Cakes of Elegance
9205 Skillman, 75243   (214) 343-2253
Supervision: Vaad Hakashrus of Greater Dallas.

Minyards Kosher Bakery & Deli
714 Preston Forest Shopping Center, 75230
Supervision: Vaad Hakashrus of Greater Dallas.

Neiman-Marcus Bakery
North Park   (214) 363-8311
Supervision: Vaad Hakashrus of Greater Dallas.
Location only. Closed Sats.

Strictly Cheesecake
8139 Forest Lane, Suite 117, Forest Central
Village, 75243   783-6545
Supervision: Vaad Hakashrus of Greater Dallas.

Tom Thumb Bakery & Kosher Deli
11920 Preston Road, 75230   392-2501
Supervision: Vaad Hakashrus of Greater Dallas.
Forest Lane only open 24 hours. Most Tom
Thumb and Albertson grocery stores in North
Dallas have a small kosher section for dried
goods.

Delicatessens

Kosher Link
7517 Campbell Road, 75230   248-3773
Fax: 248-3931
Supervision: Vaad Hakashrus of Greater Dallas.
Prepare fresh meals to be sent to your hotel.
Call if you need a menu faxed. Orders should
be placed 24 hours in advance. Meals are glatt
kosher. Hours: Sunday and Friday, 9 am to 3
pm; Monday to Thursday, to 6:30 pm.

Caterers

Simcha Kosher Caterers, 75230   620-7293
Supervision: Vaad Hakashrus of Greater Dallas.
Prepares and delivers meals to order.

Hotels

Grand Kempinski Hotel
15201 Dallas Parkway, 75248   386-6000
Fax: 404-1848

Sheraton Park Central
12720 Merit Drive, 75240   385-3000

Westin Hotel, 13340 Dallas Pkwy   934-9494

Lock-up kosher kitchens under the supervision
of the Vaad Hakashrus of Dallas in all three
hotels. There is some banquet service going
on almost every weekend and it might be
possible to arrange a kosher meal at the
above three hotels.

Sites

Zaide Reuven's Esrog Farm   931-5596
Fax: 931-5476
Email: ZRsEsrog@aol.com
Web site: members.aol.com/ARsEsrog
Dallas' only Esrog tree farm is open by appt.

El Paso

Area telephone code (915)

Community Organisations

Chabad House
6515 Westwind, 79912   584-8218
Have a mikva as well.

Jewish Federation
405 Wallenberg Drive, 79912   584-4437

Synagogues

Conservative
B'nai Zion, 805 Cherry Hill Lane, 79912
Have a mikva as well.

Reform
Sinai, 4408 N. Stanton Street, 79902

Bakeries

Kahn's Bakery and Sweet Shop
918 N. Oregon Street, 79901
Under rabbinical supervision.

Museums

**El Paso Holocaust Museum and Study
Center**
401 Wallenberg Drive, 79912   833-5656

Fort Worth/Arlington

Area telephone code (817)

Synagogues

Orthodox
Chabad-Lubavitch, 6804 Del Prado 346-7700

Conservative
Ahavath Shalom
4050 South Hulen, 76109   731-4721

Beth Shalom
1211 Thannisch Drive   860-5448

Reform
Beth-El Congregation
207 W. Broadway, 76104   332-7141
Fax: 332-7157
Just south of downtown Fort Worth, offers a
full range of Shabbat and holiday worship
services and other programs for children and
adults. Call for service times and other
information.

Houston
Area telephone code (713) or (281)

Community Organisations
Jewish Federation of Greater Houston
5603 S. Braeswood Blvd., 77096   729-7000

Synagogues
Orthodox
Beth Rambam, 11333 Braesridge Blvd., 77071
Chabad Lubavitch Center, 10900 Fondren
Rd., 77096
United Orthodox Syns., 4221 S. Braeswood
Blvd., 77096
Young Israel of Houston
7823 Ludington Drive, 77071   729-0719

Conservative
Beth Am, 1431 Brittmore Rd., 77043
Beth Yeshurun, 4525 Beechnut St., 77096
B'rith Shalom, 4610 Bellaire Blvd., 77401
Cong. Shaar Hashalom, 16020 El Camino
Real, 77062

Reform
Beth Israel, 5600 N. Braeswood Blvd., 77096
Emanu-El, 1500 Sunset Blvd., 77005
Jewish Community North, 18519 Klein
Church Rd., Spring, 77039
Cong. for Reform Judaism, 801 Bering Dr.,
77057
Temple Sinai, 783 Country Pl., 77079

Unaffiliated
K'nesseth Israel
cnr. Sterling & Commerce Sts., Baytown

Mikvaot
Chabad Lubavitch Center
10900 Fondren Road, 77096
United Orthodox Synagogues
4221 S. Braeswood Blvd., 77096

Kashrut Information
Houston Kashrut Association
9001 Greenwillow, 77096   723-3850

Embassy
Consulate General
Suite 1500, 24 Greenway Plaza, 77046

Restaurants
Drumsticks, 10200 S. Main Street, 77025
Supervision: Houston Kashruth Association.
Madras Pavilion, 3910 Kirby, 77098
Supervision: Houston Kashruth Association.
Nosher at the Jewish Community Center
5601 S. Braeswood, 77096
Supervision: Houston Kashruth Association.
Simon's Gourmet Kosher Foods
5411 Braeswood, 77096
Supervision: Houston Kashruth Association.
Butcher shop as well.
Wonderful Vegetarian
7549 Westheimer, 77063
Supervision: Houston Kashruth Association.

Bakeries
Kroger Store 313, 10306 S. Post Oak, 77096
Supervision: Houston Kashruth Association.
LeMoulin, 5645 Beechnut, 77096
Supervision: Houston Kashruth Association.
New York Bagels, 9724 Hillcroft, 77096
Supervision: Houston Kashruth Association.
Randall's Bakery
Supervision: Houston Kashruth Association.
Can be found at seven locations: Clear Lake,
Sugar Land, Highway 6 & Memorial, Fondren
& Bissonnet, W. Bellfort & S. Post Oak,
Gesner & W. Bellfort, and Holcombe & Kirby.
Three Brothers
4036 S. Braeswood, 77025
Supervision: Houston Kashruth Association.

Lubbock

Area telephone code (806)

Synagogues
Congregation Shaareth Israel
6928 3rd Street, 79424   794-7517
Mailing address: PO Box 93594, 79493-3594

Caterers
Souper Salad, 6703 Slide Road   794-0997

Groceries
Albertson's   794-6761
Good selection for Passover.
Lowe's Supermarket, 82nd & Slide Rd
Good selection for Passover. Stocks matzot and white fish.
United   791-0220
Good selection for Passover.

San Antonio

Area telephone code (512)

Community Organisations
Jewish Federation
8434 Ahern Drive, 78216   341-8234

Synagogues
Orthodox
Rodfei Sholom
3003 Sholom Drive, 78230   492-4277
Mikvah on premises.

Conservative
Agudas Achim
1201 Donaldson Avenue, 78228

Reform
Beth El, 211 Belknap Place, 78212

Delicatessens
Delicious Food
7460 Callaghan Road, 78229   366-1844

Museums
Holocaust Museum, 8434 Ahern Drive, 78216
Institute of Texan Cultures
Hemisphere Plaza, Downtown Riverfront.

Waco

Synagogues
Conservative
Agudath Jacob, 4925 Hillcrest Drive, 76710

Reform
Rodef Sholom, 1717 N. New Road, 76707

Utah

Salt Lake City

Area telephone code (801)

Community Organisations
United Jewish Federation of Utah
2416 E. 1700 Street S., 84108   581-0102

Synagogues
Kol Ami
2425 E. Heritage Way, 84109   484-1501

Reconstructionist
Chavurah B'yachad
509 E. Northmont Way, 84103   364-7060

Vermont

Burlington

Synagogues
Orthodox
Ahavath Gerim
cnr. Archibald & Hyde Streets, 05401

Conservative
Ohavi Zedek, 188 N. Prospect Street, 05401

Reform
Temple Sinai, 500 Swift Street, 05401

Virginia

Alexandria

Synagogues

Conservative
Agudas Achim, 2908 Valley Drive, 22302

Reform
Beth El Hebrew Congregation
3830 Seminary Road, 22304

Arlington

Area telephone code (703)

Synagogues

Conservative
Arlington-Fairfax Jewish Congregation
2920 Arlington Blvd., 22204   979-4466
Daily Minyan and Shabbat services. Includes
areas Crystal City, Rosslyn and Skyline.

Charlottesville

Area telephone code (804)

Synagogues

The Hillel Jewish Center
The University of Virginia, 1824 University
Circle, 22903   295-4963

Reform
Temple Beth Israel
301 E. Jefferson Street, 22902   295-6382

Danville

Synagogues

Temple Beth Sholom, Sutherlin Avenue
This building is 95 years old, one of oldest
synagogues in the South. Friday evening and
holiday services.

Fairfax

Synagogues *(Conservative)*
Congregation Olam Tikvah
3800 Glenbrook Road, 22031   (703) 425-1880
2 miles from Beltway Exit 6W.

Falls Church

Synagogues *(Reform)*
Temple Rodef Shalom, 2100 Westmoreland
Street, 22043   (703) 532-2217

Norfolk

Area telephone code (804)

Community Organisations
United Jewish Federation of Tidewater
7300 Newport Avenue, 23505   489-8040
                                Fax: 489-8230

Synagogues

Orthodox
B'nai Israel Cong., 420 Spotswood Avenue,
23517   627-7358

Conservative
Beth El, 422 Shirley Av., 23517   625-7821
Temple Israel
7255 Granby St., 23505   489-4550

Reform
Ohef Sholom, Stockley Gdns. at Raleigh Av.,
23507   625-4295

The Commodore Levy Chapel, Frazier Hall,
Bldg. C-7 (inside Gate 2), Norfolk US Navy
Station is the US. Navy's oldest synagogue.
Services are open to civilians. Inq. to the
Jewish Chaplain.

Mikvaot
B'nai Israel   444-7361
                                     627-7358

Kashrut Information
Va'ad Hakashrut, c/o B'nai Israel

Groceries

The Kosher Place
738 W. 22nd Street   623-1770
Supervision: Vaad Hakashrus of Tidewater.
Meats, deli, prepared foods. Hours: Monday to
Thursday, 9 am to 6 pm; Friday, to 3 pm;
Sunday, 10 am to 4 pm. Close to colonial
Williamsburg and Virginia Beach.

Hotels

Omni International
Waterside Drive, 23510   622-6664
Supervision: Va'ad.

Media

Magazines

Renewal Magazine
7300 Newport Avenue, 23505
Quarterly publication

Newspapers

UJF Virginia News, 7300 Newport Ave, 23505
Bi-weekly publication

Richmond

Area telephone code (804)

Community Organisations

Jewish Community Federation
5403 Monument Avenue, 23226   288-0045

Synagogues

Orthodox

Keneseth Beth Israel
6300 Patterson Avenue, 23226   288-7953

Young Israel of Richmond
4811 Patterson Avenue, 23226   353-5831

Conservative

Or Atid, 501 Parham Road, 23229

Reform

Or Ami, 9400 N. Huguenot Road, 23235

Mikvaot

Young Israel, 4811 Patterson Avenue, 23226

Bakeries

Chesapeake Bagel Bakery, Willow Lawn

Shopping Center, 5100 Monument Ave, 23226
Supervision: Vaad of Richmond.
Kosher bagels, challah and rolls.

Fishmongers

Andersons Fish, Willow Lawn Shopping
Center, 5100 Monument Avenue, 23226
Supervision: Vaad of Richmond. Fresh fish.

Groceries

Hannafords, Willow Lawn Shopping Center,
5100 Monument Avenue, 23226
Supervision: Vaad of Richmond.
Newly opened supermarket with a kosher deli.

Museums

Beth Ahabah, 1117 W. Franklin Street, 23220
Also housing Jewish archives which are of
great historical interest.

Chabad-Lubavitch of the Virginias
212 Gaskins Road, 23233   740-2000
Holding the cemetery for the Jewish soldiers
of the Civil War. Kosher facilities and rooms
for Shabbat and holidays available.

Virginia Beach

Synagogues

Orthodox

Chabad Lubavitch
533 Gleneagle Drive, 23462   499-0507

Conservative

Kehillat Bet Hamidrash
952 Indian Lakes Blvd., 23464   495-8510

Temple Emanuel, 25th Street, 23451

Reform

Beth Chaverim, 3820 Stoneshore Road,
23452-7965   463-3226

Virginia Peninsula

Area telephone code (804)

Community Organisations

**United Jewish Community of the Virginia
Peninsula,** 2700 Spring Road, Newport News,
23606   930-1422

Synagogues

Conservative
Rodef Shalom
318 Whealton Road, Hampton, 23666

Traditional
B'nai Israel
3116 Kecoughtan Road, Hampton, 23661

Reform
Temple Sinai
11620 Warwick Blvd., Newport News, 23601

Mikvaot

Adath Jeshurun
12646 Nettles Drive, Newport News, 23606

Bakeries

Brenner's Warwick Bakery
240 31st Street, Newport News, 23607
Supervision: Va'ad Hakashrut.

Washington

Aberdeen

Synagogues (Conservative)
Temple Beth Israel
1219 Spur Street, 98520   (360) 533-3784

Seattle

Area telephone code (206)

Community Organisations

Jewish Federation of Greater Seattle
2031 3rd Avenue, 98121   443-5400

Northend Community Center
8606 35th Ave NE   526-8073

Kashrut Information

Va'ad HaRabanim   760-0805
6500 52nd Avenue S., 98118   Fax: 725-0347
                    Email: seavaad@aol.com
The Va'ad HaRabanim was organised in 1993
to replace the former Seattle Kashruth Board
which had been organised in the early 1900s
to provide kosher meat for the community. In
addition to providing kosher meat, the new
board provides kosher supervision for many
restaurants, bakeries, retail outlets and
catering facilities. For further information,
contact David Grashin at the number above.

Restaurants

Bamboo Garden, 364 Roy Street, near Seattle
Center   282-6616
Supervision: Va'ad HaRabanim of Greater
Seattle.

Bakeries

Bagel Deli, 340 15th Avenue E.   322-2471
Supervision: Va'ad HaRabanim of Greater
Seattle.
All bagels, bialys and fragels are pareve;
brownies are dairy. Pat Yisrael. No other food
products are under kosher supervision. Hours:
Monday to Friday, 6:30 am to 6 pm; Saturday,
to 5 pm; Sunday, 7 am to 4 pm.
Bagel Oasis, 2112 NE 65th Street   526-0525
Supervision: Va'ad HaRabanim of Greater
Seattle. Bagels, bialys are pareve. Pat Yisrael.
International Biscuit
5028 Wilson Avenue   722-5595
Supervision: Va'ad HaRabanim of Greater
Seattle. All bakery goods on site are under
supervision and Pat Yisrael. Available at
various grocery stores.

Delicatessens

Bagel Deli, 1309 N.E. 43rd Street   634-3770
Betay Avone
113 Blanchard Avenue, 98121   448-5597
Supervision: Va'ad HaRabanim of Greater
Seattle.
Kosher Delight, 1509 First Avenue, Pike Place
Market, 98101   682-8140
Supervision: Va'ad HaRabanim of Greater
Seattle.
Park Deli, 5011 South Dawson Street, Seward
Park, 98118   722-6674
Supervision: Va'ad HaRabanim of Greater
Seattle.
Park Deli, 5011 S. Dawson Street, Seward
Park, 98118   722-NOSH

Museums

Community Center, 3801 E. Mercer Way,
Mercer Island, 98040   232-7115
A Holocaust memorial with a bronze sculpture
by Gizel Berman has been dedicated here.

Libraries

B'nai B'rith Hillel Foundation, University of Washington
4745 17th Av. N.E., 98105   527-1997
The University Library has a Jewish archives section dealing with the Seattle community.

Media

The Jewish Transcript, 2031 3rd Ave, 98121

Spokane

Area telephone code (509)

Community Organisations

Jewish Community Council, North 221 Wall, Suite 500, 99201   838-4261

Synagogues *(Conservative)*

Temple Beth Shalom
11322 E. 30th Street, 99203   747-3304

West Virginia

Huntingdon

Synagogues

B'nai Sholom
949 10th Avenue, 25701   (304) 522-2980

Wisconsin

Madison

Area telephone code (608)

Community Organisations

Madison Jewish Community Council
6434 Enterprise Lane, 53179   278-1808

Synagogues

Orthodox
Chabad House, 1722 Regent Street, 53705

Conservative
Beth Israel Center, 1406 Mound St, 53711

Reform
Beth El, 2702 Arbor Drive, 53711

Milwaukee

Area telephone code (414)

Community Organisations

Milkwaukee Jewish Federation
1360 N. Prospect Avenue, 53202   271-8338
                                        Fax: 271-7081
Publish directory   271-2992

Synagogues

With more than a dozen synagogues in the area, travellers are advised to contact a local religious organisation for specific details.

Media

Newspapers
Wisconsin Jewish Chronicle
1360 N. Prospect Avenue, 53202   271-2992

Sheboygan

Synagogues *(Traditional)*

Temple Beth El, 1007 North Avenue, 53083

Wyoming

Casper

Synagogues

Temple Beth El, 4105 S. Poplar, PO Box 3534, 82602   (307) 237-2330

Cheyenne

Synagogues

Mount Sinai
2610 Pioneer Avenue, 82001   634-3052

Green River

Synagogues
Congregation of Beth Israel, PO Box 648
Green River Way, 82935   875-4194

Laramie

Synagogues
Laramie JCC
PO Box 202, 82070   745-8813

Uruguay

GMT – 3 hours
Country calling code (598)

Montevideo
Area telephone code (442)

Community Organisations
Centro Lubavitch
Av. Brasil 2704, CP 11300   793-444; 785-169
Fax: 713-696

Comite Central Israelita
Rio Negro 1308, Piso 5, Esc. 9   916-057;
906-562; 982-833

Synagogues
Adat Israel
Democracia 2370

Anshei Jeshurun
Durazno 972

Bet Aharon, Harishona, Inca 2287

Comunidad Israelita Hungara
Durazno 972   908-456

Nueva Congregacion Israelita (Central European)
Wilson F Aldunete 1168   926-620

Social Isralite Adat Yeshurun
Alarcon 1396

Vaad Ha'ir, Canelones 828

Ashkenazi
Comunidad Israelita de Uruguay
Canelones 1084, Piso 1   925-750

Sephardi
Comunidad Israelita Sefardi
Buenos Aires 234, 21 de Setiembre 3111
710-179

Templo Sefardi
de Pocitos L. Franzini 888

Embassy
Israel Embassy
Bulevar Artigas 1585-89   404-164/5/6
Fax: 494-821

Media
Newspapers
Semanario Hebreo
Soriano 875/201   925-311
Spanish-language weekly. Editor also directs daily Yiddish radio programme.

Restaurants
Kasherissimo
Camacua 623   950-128
Supervision: Chief Rabbi Eliahu Birnbaum. The restaurant is situated in the Hebraica Macabi building.

Vegetarian
La Vegetariana
Avda. Brasil 3086
La Vegetariana
San Jose 1056

Museums
Museo del Holocausto
Canelones 1084, Planta Baja

Tourist Sites
Memorial a Golda Meir
Reconquista y Ciudadela
Memorial al Holocausto del Pueblo Judio
Rambla Wilson, opposite campo de Golf

Uzbekistan

GMT + 5 to 6 hours
Country calling code (7)

Andizhan

Synagogues
7 Sovetskaya Street

Bukhara

Synagogues
20 Tsentralnaya Street

Katta-Kurgan

Synagogues
1 Karl Marx Alley

Kermine

Synagogues
36 Narimanov Street

Kokand

Synagogues
Dekabristov Street, Fergan Oblast

Margelan

Synagogues
Turtkilskaya Street, Fergan Oblast

Navoy

Synagogues
36 Narimanov Street

Samarkand

Synagogues
5 Denauskaya Street
34 Khudzumskaya Street
45 Respublikanskaya Street

Tashkent

Area telephone code (3712)

Synagogues
9 Chkalov Street
62 Gorbunova Street   53-5447

Ashkenazi
77 Chempianov Street

Sephardi
3 Sagban Street   40-0768

Embassy
Embassy of Israel
16A Lachuti Street, 5th floor

Venezuela

The Jewish community of Venezuela now numbers between 20,000 and 23,000, about 90 per cent of whom live in Caracas, the capital, with the rest mainly in the oil centre of Maracaibo. The earliest important Jewish settlement in Venezuela was in the coastal town of Coro, where probably the oldest Jewish cemetery still in use in South America is situated. While the Coro community was made up of Sephardim from nearby Curaçao, the community in Venezuela today is about equally divided between Sephardim and Ashkenazim.

GMT – 4 hours
Country calling code (58)

Caracas
Area telephone code (2)

Synagogues

Ashkenazi
Great Synagogue of Caracas
Av Francisco Javier Ustariz, San Bernardino
511-869

Shomrei Shabbat Assoc. Synagogue
Av Anauco, San Bernardino   517-197

Union Israelita de Caracas Synagogue & Community Centre, Av Marques del Toro 9, San Bernardino   528-222
If notified in advance, they can arrange kosher lunches. There is also a meat snack bar open in the evening. Contact 526-280.

Sephardi
Keter Tora, Av Lopez Mendez, San Bernardino
Bet El, Av Cajigal, San Bernardino   522-008
Shaare Shalom
Av Bogota, Quinta Julieta, Los Caobos
Tiferet Yisrael
Av Mariperez, Los Caobos   781-1942

Mikvaot
Shomrei Shabbat Association Synagogue
Av Anauco, San Bernardino   517-197
Tiferet Yisrael
Av Mariperez, Los Caobos   781-1942

Union Israelita de Caracas Synagogue & Community Centre, Av Marques del Toro 9, San Bernardino   528-222

Contact Information
Chabad-Lubavitch Centre
Apartado 5454, 1010A   523-887

Embassy
Embassy of Israel
Avenida Francisco de Miranda, Centro Empresarial Miranda, 4 Piso Oficina 4-D, Apartado Postal Los Ruices 70081
239-4511; 239-4921
Fax: 239-4320

Media
Newspaper
Nuevo Mundo Israelita
Av Marques del Toro 9, Los Caobos

Restaurants
Dairy
Caffé Pizzería La Finestra, Av. Principal de Las Palmas, Quinta Silvania, La Florida   793-6012
Supervision: Asociación Israelita de Venezuela. Italian dairy.

Papparazi, Calle Los Chaguaramos con Av. Mohedano, Centro Gerencial Mehedano, 1070, La Castellana   266-4316

Supervision: Asociación Israelita de Venezuela. Italian dairy.

Bakeries

Le Notre, Avenida Andres Bello   782-4448

Pasteleria Kasher
Avenida Los Proceres   515-086

Delicatessens

La Belle Delicatesses, Av. Bogotá, Edif Santa María, Local 2, Los Caobos   781-7204
                                          Fax: 781-7182
Kosher delicatessen and mini-market, restaurant and take-out.

Groceries

Mini Market, Avenida Los Caobas   781-7204
Take away.

Hotels

Hotel Aventura
A short walk away from the Union Synagogue, convenient for Shabbat observers.

Hotel Avila
Next door to the Union Synagogue, convenient for Shabbat observers.

Booksellers

Libreria Cultural Maimonides
Av Altamira Edif. Carlitos PB, San Bernardino
                                          516-356
                                          Fax: 524-242

Maracaibo

Area telephone code (61)

Community Organisations

Associación Israelita de Maracaibo
Calle 74 No 13-26   70333

Porlamar

Synagogues

Or Meir, Margarita Island
Mikva on premises.

Virgin Islands

There have been Jews in the Virgin Islands since the eighteenth century, and they played an important part in the life of the islands under Danish rule. The Virgin Islands have been American territory since 1917. Today the community numbers about 450, of whom some 125 families are affiliated to the Hebrew congregation of St Thomas.

GMT – 4 hours
Country calling code (1 809)

St Thomas

Synagogues

St Thomas Synagogue
PO Box 266, Charlotte Amalie, 00804
                                          774-4312
This synagogue was built in 1833.

Orthodox

Khal Hakodesh   779-2000
There is a conservative synagogue on the island of St Croix.

Yugoslavia

GMT + 1 hour
Country calling code (381)

Belgrade (Beograd)
Area telephone code (11)

Representative Organisations
Federation of Jewish Communities
7 Kralja Petra Street 71a/111, PO Box 841,
11001   624-359/621-837
                                    Fax: 626-674

Community Organisations
Local Community
7 Kralja Petra Street 71a/11, 11001   624-289

Synagogues
Birjuzova Street 19
Services are held Friday evenings and Jewish holidays.

Museums
Jewish Museum
7 Kralja Petra Street 71a/1, 11001   622-634
It is open daily from 10 am to 12 pm except Mondays.

Cemeteries
Jewish Cemetery
There are monuments to fallen fighters and martyrs of fascism, fallen Jewish soldiers in the Serbian army in the First World War here. In 1990 a new monument to Jews killed in Serbia was erected by the Danube, in the pre-war Jewish quarter Dorcol.

Novi Sad
Area telephone code (21)

Community Organisations
Community Offices
Jevrejska 11   613-882

Cemeteries
Jewish Cemetery
There is a monument to the Jews who fell in the war and the victims of fascism. The synagogue here is no longer open. It is reported to be extremely beautiful, but is currently being converted into a concert hall.

Subotica

Community Organisations
Community Offices
Dimitrija Tucovica Street 13   28483

Zambia

GMT + 2 hours
Country calling code (260)

Lusaka
Area telephone code (1)

Synagogues
Lusaka Hebrew Congregation
Chachacha Road, POB 30020   229-190
                                  Fax: 221-428

Zimbabwe

GMT + 2 hours
Country calling code (263)

Bulawayo
Area telephone code (9)

Synagogues
Bulawayo Hebrew Congregation
Jason Moyo Street, PO Box 337   60829

Harare
Area telephone code (4)

Representative Organisations
Zimbabwe Jewish Board of Deputies
POB 342   723-647

Synagogues
Harare Hebrew Congregation
Milton Park Jewish Centre, Lezard Avenue,
POB 342   727-576

Sephardi Congregation, 54 Josiah
Chinamano Avenue, POB 1051   722-899

Kosher Fish Around the World

Courtesy of Kashrut Division, London Beth Din,
and United Synagogue Publications Ltd

UK	France	Holland	Italy	Spain
Anchovy	Anchois	Anchovis	Acciugia	Boqueron
Barbel	Barbue	Barbeel	-	-
Bass	Bar Commun	Baars	Persico, Branzino	Lubina
Bream	Breme	Brasum	-	-
Brill	Barbue	Griet	Rombo, Liscio	-
Brisling	-	-	-	-
Carp	Carpe	Karper	Carpa	-
Coalfish	-	Koolvis	-	-
Cod	Morue, Cabillaud	Kabeljauw	Merluzzo	Bacalao
Dab	Limbaude	Schar	-	-
Dace	-	-	-	-
Flounder	Flet	-	-	-
Grayling	Ombre	Vlagzalm	-	-
Gurnard	Grondin	Poon	Pesce Capone	-
Haddock	Aiglefin	Schelvis	-	-
Hake	Merluche	Kabeljauw	Nasello	Merluza
Halibut	Fletan	Helibot	-	-
Herring	Hareng	Hareng	Aringa	-
John Dory	-	-	-	-
Ling	-	Leng	-	-
Mackerel	Maquereau	Makreel	Sgombro	Caballa
Mullet	Mulet	Baars	-	-
Perch	Perche	Baars	Pesce Persico	-
Pike	Brochet	Snoek	Luccio	-
Pilchard	Pilchard	-	Sardina	Sardina
Plaice	Carrelet, Plie	Schol	-	-
Polack	Lieu Jaune	Pollak	-	-
Roach	Gardon	Blankvoorn	-	-
Saithe	-	-	-	-
Salmon	Saumon	Zalm	Salmone	Salmon
Sardine	Sardine	Sardine	Sardina	Sardina
Shad	Alose	Elft	-	-
Sild	-	-	-	-
Smelt	Eperlan	Spiering	-	-
Snoek	Snoek	Snoek	-	-
Sole	Sole	Tong	Sogliola	Lenguado
Sprat	Sprat	Sprot	Spratto	-
Tench	Tanche	Zeelt	Tinca	-
Trout	Truite	Forel	Trota	Trucha
Tuna	Thon	Tonijin	Tonno	Atun
Whitebait	Blanchaille	-	Bianchetti	-
Whiting	Merlan	Wijting	Bianchetti	-

Kosher Fish Around the World

Australia

Anchovy
Baramundi
Barracouta
Barracuda
Blue Eye
Blue Grenadier
Bluefin
Bream
Carp
Cod
Coral Perch
Duckfish
Flathead
Flounder
Garfish
Groper
Haddock
Hake
Harpuka
Herring
Jewfish
John Dory
Lemon Sole
Mackerel

Morwong
Mullet
Murray Cod
Murray Perch
Murray Perth Tuna
Northern Blue Fin
Orange Roughy
Perch
Pike
Pilchard
Redfin
Salmon
Sardine
Shad
Sild
Skipjack (Striped)
Snapper
Southern Blue Fin
Tailor
Terakiji
Trevally
Trout
Yellowfin
Yellowtail
Whiting

Hong Kong

Anchovy
Bigeye
Carp
Crevalle
Croaker
Giant Perch
Grey Mullet
Grouper
Japanese Sea Perch
Leopard Coral Trout
Pampano
Pilchard
Red Sea Bream
Round Herring
Sardine
Scad
Whitefish

Japan

Maguro = Tuna

Index

A

Aachen 101
Aargau see Bremgarten
Aberdeen 265
Aberdeen (NJ) 330
Aberdeen (SD) 384
Aberdeen (WA) 392
Acre see Akko
Acton (MA) 313
Addis Ababa 63
Adelaide 10–11
Afghanistan 1
Afula 133
Agadir 168
Agen 65
Ahmedabad 123
Aix-en-Provence 65
Aix-le-Bains 65–66
Ajaccio 99
Akhaltsikhe 100
Akko 133
Akron (OH) 369
Alabama 268
Alameda (CA) 271
Alaska 268
Albania 1
Albany (NY) 350
Alberta 37–38
Albuquerque (NM) 341
Alderney (C.I.) 264
Aldershot 248
Alexandria 61
Alexandria (LA) 307–308
Alexandria (VA) 390
Alfortville 86
Algarve 188
Algeria 2
Algiers 2
Alicante 209
Allentown (PA) 373
Almati (formerly Alma-Ata) 160
Alsenz 101
Altoona (PA) 373
Amarillo (TX) 385
Amazonas 29
Amberg 101
Amersfoort 172
Amherst (MA) 313
Amiens 66

Amstelveen see Amsterdam
Amsterdam 172–175
Amsterdam (NY) 350
Anaheim (CA) 271
Anchorage (AK) 268
Ancona 151
Andernach 101
Andizhan 396
Andover (MA) 313
Angers 66
Ankara 227
Ann Arbor (MI) 324
Annapolis (MD) 309
Annecy 66
Annemasse 66
Annweiler 102
Antibes 66
Antony 86
Antwerp 22–23
Arad (Israel) 133
Arad (Romania) 190
Arcachon 66
Arcadia (CA) 271
Argentina 3–6
Argyll and Bute 265
Arica 50
Arizona 269–270
Arkansas 270–271
Arleta (CA) 271
Arlington (MA) 313
Arlington (TX) see Fort Worth (TX)
Arlington (VA) 390
Arlon 23
Arnhem 175
Arosa 219
Aruba 178
Ashdod 134
Asheville (NC) 367
Ashkelon 134
Ashland (OR) 372
Asmara 63
Asnières 86
Asti 151
Astrakhan 195
Asunción (Paraguay) 183
Athens 115
Athens (GA) 299
Athis-Mons 86
Athol (MA) 313
Atlanta (GA) 299

Index

Index

Index

Index

Index

Index

Index

Moghilev	21	Navoy	396
Mogi das Cruzes	32	Nebraska	328
Moldova	167	Needham (MA)	320
Monaco	167	Negev	145–146
Mönchengladbach-Rheydt	110	Netanya	146
Moncton (N.B.)	41	Netherlands	172–177
Monroe (NY)	357	Netherlands Antilles	178
Mons	25	Neuilly	90–91
Monsey (NY)	357	Neustadt/Rheinpfalz	110
Montana	328	Nevada	329
Montauban	75	Neve Zohar	146
Montbéliard	75	New Bedford (MA)	320
Montblanc	212	New Britain (CT)	289
Monte Carlo	167	New Brunswick (Canada)	41
Monterrey (Mexico)	166	New Brunswick (NJ)	335–336
Montevideo	395	New City (NY)	357
Montgomery (AL)	268	New Delhi	124
Monticello (NY)	352	New Hampshire	329
Montpellier	76	New Haven (CT)	289–290
Montreal (Que.)	47–48	New Hyde Park (NY)	357
Montreuil	90	New Jersey	330–340
Montreux	222	New London (CT)	290
Montrouge	90	New Mexico	341
Moose Jaw (Sask.)	48	New Orleans (LA)	308
Morocco	168–170	New Rochelle (NY)	358
Morristown (NJ)	335	New South Wales	7–10
Moscow	196	New York City (NY)	358–364
Moshav Shoresh	145	Bronx	358
Mount Vernon (NY)	357	Brooklyn	358–359
Mozambique	171	Manhattan	360–362
Mülheim	110	Queens	362–364
Mulhouse	76	Staten Island	364
Muncie (IN)	305	New York State	342–367
Munich	110	New Zealand	179–180
Münster	110	Newark	259
Myanmar	171	Newark (DE)	291
Myrtle Beach (SC)	383	Newark (NJ)	336
		Newburgh (NY)	357
N		Newburyport (MA)	320
		Newcastle (N.S.W.)	7
Nagasaki	159	Newcastle upon Tyne	259–260
Naharia	145	Newfoundland	41
Nairobi	160	Newport (Gwent)	266
Nalchik	196	Newport (RI)	382
Namibia	171	Newport News (VA) see	
Nancy	76	Virginia Peninsula	
Nantes	76	Newton (MA)	320
Naples	154	Niagara Falls (NY)	364
Napoli see Naples		Niagara Falls (Ont.)	44
Narragansett (RI)	382	Nice	76
Nashville (TN)	385	Nicosia	55
Nassau (NY)	357	Nikolsburg see Mikulov	
Natal	203–204	Nîmes	76–77
Natchez (MS)	327	Niteroi	31
Natick (MA)	320	Nogent-sur-Marne	91

Index

Index

Peoria (IL)	303	Pueblo (CO)	287–288
Périgueux	94	Puerto Rico	189
Perm	196	Pune	125
Pernambuco	30		
Perpignan	94	**Q**	
Perth (Australia)	14		
Perth Amboy (NJ)	337	Quebec	47–48
Peru	184–185	Quebec City (Que.)	48
Perugia	154	Queens (NYC)	362–364
Petach Tikva	146	Queensland	10
Peterborough (Ont.)	45	Quincy (MA)	321
Petropolis	31	Quito	61
Phalsbourg	95		
Philadelphia (PA)	375–379	**R**	
Philippines Republic	185		
Phoenix (AZ)	269	Ra'anana	147
Piatra Neamt	192–193	Rabat	170
Piestany	199	Radauti	193
Pilsen see Plzen		Rahway (NJ)	337
Pisa	154	Raleigh (NC)	368
Piscataway (NJ)	337	Ramat Gan	147
Pittsburgh (PA)	379–380	Ramat Hanegev	147
Pittsfield (MA)	321	Ramat Yohanan	147
Plainfield (NJ)	337	Ramsgate	261
Plainview (NY)	356	Rancagua	50
Plovdiv	35	Randolph (MA)	321–322
Plymouth	261	Randolph (NJ)	337
Plymouth (MA)	321	Rangoon	171
Plzen	58	Rapid City (SD)	384
Pocomoke (MD)	311	Reading	261
Poitiers	95	Reading (PA)	380
Poland	186–187	Rechitsa	21
Ponta Delgada	188	Recife	30
Porlamar	398	Regensburg	111
Port au Prince	118	Regina (Sask.)	48
Port Chester (NY)	365	Rehovot	147
Port Elizabeth (C.P.)	203	Reichenberg see Liberec	
Portland (ME)	309	Reims	95
Portland (OR)	373	Rennes	95
Porto Alegre	31–32	Reno (NV)	329
Portsmouth & Southsea	261	Réunion	99
Portsmouth (NH)	329	Revere (MA)	322
Portugal	188–189	Rezhitsa	161
Poti	100	Rhode Island	381–383
Potomac (MD)	312	Rhodes (Greece)	116
Potsdam	111	Riccione	154
Pottstown (PA)	380	Richmond (B.C.)	38
Poughkeepsie (NY)	365	Richmond (VA)	391
Prague	58	Richmond Hill (Ont.)	45
Prairie Village (KS)	307	Riga	161
Presov	200	Rijeka	54
Pressburg see Bratislava		Rio de Janeiro (City)	30–31
Pretoria (Transvaal)	207	Rio de Janeiro (State)	30–31
Princeton (NJ)	337	Rio Grande do Sul	31–32
Providence (RI)	382	Rio Rancho (NM)	341

Index

Index

Index

Index

Index

Index to Advertisers

ADVERTISEMENT ORDER FORM 1999

Please complete and return Jewish Travel Guide form to us by 1 September 1998

Please reserve the following advertising space in
Jewish Travel Guide 1999:

☐ Full Page   £475   190 x 102 mm

☐ Half Page   £245   93 x 102 mm

☐ Quarter Page   £145   44 x 102 mm

(UK advertisers please note that the above rates are subject to VAT)
Special positions by arrangement

☐ **Please insert the attached copy (If setting is required a 10% setting charge will be made.)**

☐ **Copy will be forwarded from our Advertising Agents (*see below*)**

Contact Name: _____

Advertisers Name:_____

Address for invoicing: _____

_____

Tel: _____ Fax: _____

Signed: _____ Title: _____

VAT No:_____

Date:_____

Agency Name (if applicable): _____

Address: _____

_____

Tel: _____ Fax: _____

All advertisements set by the publisher will only be included if they have been signed and approved by the advertiser.

To the Advertising Department
Jewish Travel Guide
Vallentine Mitchell & Co. Ltd.
Newbury House, 890–900 Eastern Avenue, Newbury Park, Ilford, Essex IG2 7HH
Tel: +44(0)181-599 8866 Fax: + 44(0)181-599 0984. E-mail: jtg@vmbooks.com

Update for Jewish Travel Guide 1999

PUBLISHER'S REQUEST

Readers are asked kindly to draw attention to any errors or omissions. If errors are discovered, it would be appreciated if you could give up-to-date information, referring to page, place/institution, etc., and return this form to the Editor at the address given below.

With reference to the following entry:

Page:

Country:

Entry should read:

Kindly list on separate sheet if preferred.

Signed:_____ Date: _____

Name (BLOCK CAPITALS) _____

Address: _____

_____

Telephone: _____

SEND TO:

The Editor
Jewish Travel Guide
Vallentine Mitchell & Co. Ltd.
Newbury House, 890–900 Eastern Avenue,
Newbury Park, Ilford, Essex IG2 7HH
Fax: + 44(0)181-599 0984. E-mail: jtg@vmbooks.com

JEWISH TRAVEL GUIDE

Formerly Published by
*Jewish Chronicle
Publications*

New Entry Form

Name of Establishment:_____

_____

Category (circle one):

HOTEL	BUTCHER	MIKVAH
RESTAURANT	BOOKSELLER	KASHRUT INFORMATION
DELICATESSEN	MUSEUM	CONTACT INFORMATION
GROCERY	TOURIST SITE	JEWISH MEDIA
BAKERY	SYNAGOGUE	

Address of Establishment: _____

(Include Metropolitan area) _____

_____

_____

_____

City/ Town: _____

State: _____

Postcode:_____

Country: _____

Telephone, Fax and E-mail Numbers: _____

_____

(Please indicate country and city code) _____

_____

Supervision Details (who gives *Hashgacha*?): _____

_____

Contact Person: _____

Hours: _____

Price Range ($ = inexpensive, $$ = moderate, $$$ =
expensive): _____

May we contact you to verify information?

Your Name and Address (if different to above):_____

_____

_____

_____

**Vallentine Mitchell
& Co. Ltd**

**Newbury House,
900 Eastern Avenue,
Newbury Park, Ilford,
Essex IG2 7HH, UK**
Tel: +44 (0)181 599 8866
Fax: +44 (0)181 599 0984
E-mail: jtg@vmbooks.com

Registered Office:
Newbury House,
890–900 Eastern Avenue,
Newbury Park, Ilford,
Essex IG2 7HH

Registered No. 472549
(England)

Directors:
Frank Cass (Managing),
Stewart Cass, BSC, ACA,
A.E. Cass, H.J. Osen
M.P. Zaidner, FCMA, ACIS.

Building Jerusalem

Jewish Architecture in Britain

Edited and introduced by SHARMAN KADISH

The subject of synagogue art and architecture has for too long stood outside the mainstream of architectural history. In the 1990s a series of important conferences in the United States and England has drawn attention to this fact and secured recognition of the Jewish-built heritage by the major conservation agencies. Only now is the 'heritage industry' beginning to open up to the reality of a multi-cultural society. In Britain, where Jews have enjoyed 300 years of continuous settlement, the definitive history of Jewish monuments, both sacred and secular, has yet to be written. A comprehensive survey of extant Jewish sites likewise awaits completion. This book aims to fill that gap.

Building Jerusalem is richly illustrated, featuring in particular, original artwork by Beverley-Jane Stewart and photographs by Anthony Harris.

illus 250 pages 90 black & white photographs
ISBN 0 85303 283 1 cloth £45.00/$59.50 ❖ ISBN 0 85303 309 9 paper £19.50/$25.00

A World Apart

The Story of the Chasidim in Britain

With a foreword by HARRY RABINOWICZ and
CHIEF RABBI DR JONATHAN SACKS

Chasidism, the greatest revivalist and mystical movement in Judaism, was established in Eastern Europe in the mid-eighteenth century. It gained immediate and widespread recognition there: almost half of the Jews in the region followed its precepts prior to the Second World War.

The destruction of the great centres of European Chasidism during the Second World War was an unprecedented catastrophe. Nevertheless, the Chasidi community has been revived and is expanding. Surrounded by a pluralistic society, the present day British Chasidism maintain an insular existence, living in accordance with Chasidic beliefs and ideals.

This work is the first detailed and comprehensive study of the Chasidim in Britain. It describes the early Chasidic pioneers in Victorian England, the shtieblech in the East End of London in the first half of the twentieth century, the Chasidic Rebbes in London in the inter-war years the present non-homogenous structure of Chasidism in Stamford Hill, the proliferation of educational institutions, pattern of life, culture and customs, and the views of Anglo-Jewish writers and historians on this community.

March 1997 310 pages
ISBN 0 85303 261 0 cloth £37.50/$49.50 ❖ ISBN 0 85303 278 5 paper £19.50/$27.50

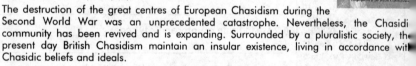

Vallentine Mitchell

UK AND OVERSEAS ORDERS TO:

Vallentine Mitchell, Newbury House, 900 Eastern Avenue, London IG2 7HH, England
Tel: +44(0)181 599 8866 Fax: +44(0)181 599 0984 E-Mail: info@vmbooks.com

US AND NORTH AMERICA ORDERS:

c/o ISBS, 5804 NE Hassalo Street, Portland, OR 97213-3644, USA
Tel: (503) 287-3093, (800) 944 6190 Fax: (503) 280-8832 E-mail: orders@isbs.com